NATIVE ADMINISTRATION IN THE UNION OF SOUTH AFRICA

BEING

A BRIEF SURVEY OF THE ORGANISATION, FUNCTIONS AND ACTIVITIES OF THE DEPARTMENT OF NATIVE AFFAIRS OF THE UNION OF SOUTH AFRICA

BY

HOWARD ROGERS, B.A., LL.B.,
OF THE NATIVE AFFAIRS DEPARTMENT

WITH A PREFACE
BY
THE SECRETARY FOR NATIVE AFFAIRS
(J. F. HERBST, ESQ., C.B.E.)

NEGRO UNIVERSITIES PRESS
NEW YORK

Originally published in 1933
by University of The Witwatersrand Press

Reprinted in 1970 by
Negro Universities Press
A Division of Greenwood Press, Inc.
Westport, Connecticut

SBN 8371-3637-7

Printed in United States of America

SPECIAL NUMBER

OF

"BANTU STUDIES"

Journal devoted to the Scientific Study of
BANTU, HOTTENTOT, and BUSHMAN

SUPPLEMENT No 6.

MAY 1933

FOREWORD

The general public have only a very limited knowledge of the wide range of the functions of the Department of Native Affairs. Even those who might be expected to know something of the laws the Department is called upon to administer and the principles of policy observed in relation thereto, often criticise in ignorance.

Visitors from overseas interested in the subject frequently approach the Department for information and literature. Of such as we have we give freely, but the method is unsatisfactory and literature of any real value is sadly lacking.

Impressed with the material benefits to be derived from a publication which would not only supply the public with authoritative information upon so interesting a subject, but which would form also a valuable *vade mecum* for officers of the Department in the country districts, I instructed Mr. Howard Rogers, B.A., LL.B., one of our able young men in the Department and by experience exceptionally qualified for the task, to prepare the necessary material on the lines followed in this compilation.

It had been my intention to present the volume as a departmental publication, but the depression which followed and the consequent restriction of funds prevented the realisation of this purpose and it was pigeonholed.

It is with unfeigned pleasure and satisfaction that I now comply with the suggestion of the Editors of the journal *Bantu Studies* that the work be published by them as a further volume in the excellent series of works on Bantu Linguistics, History, etc., which they have issued as special supplements of *Bantu Studies*.

The time is opportune, the author exceptionally qualified and the information authentic, circumstances which I feel sure will give Mr. Rogers' work a welcome, not only by the general public but by officials and those students who with ever-increasing numbers desire to qualify in the subject of Native administration for the University examinations.

J. F. HERBST
Secretary for Native Affairs

Department of Native Affairs,
Pretoria.
9th May, 1933.

PRELIMINARY NOTE

This monograph was in the first instance prepared for official purposes in 1930 and, consequently, departmental reports and memoranda were freely utilised in compiling it. It has since been revised and brought up to date.

I wish to place on record my grateful thanks to various officers of the Department for their generous assistance in furnishing statistical and other information.

I also desire to express my gratitude to the Editors of *Bantu Studies*, who have undertaken not only to publish this work but to shoulder the entire financial responsibility in connection therewith.

It is trusted that the volume will prove of interest and assistance to officers of the Department, students of Native Administration and others interested in Native Affairs.

HOWARD ROGERS

Native Affairs Department,
Pretoria.
31st March, 1933.

CONTENTS

CHAPTER VI.

CHAPTER IX (*continued*)

CHAPTER X.

NATIVE EDUCATION

APPENDICES

APPENDIX

APPENDIX (*continued*)

NATIVE ADMINISTRATION
IN THE
UNION OF SOUTH AFRICA

I

INTRODUCTORY REMARKS AND DEPARTMENTAL ORGANISATION

A

BASIC LAW

The Union of South Africa was constituted under the South Africa Act, 1909, (9 Edward VII), which provided for the union of the four pre-existing Colonies on terms and conditions to which they had agreed by resolutions of their respective Parliaments. The Act, after having been passed by the Imperial Parliament, was by proclamation of His Majesty the King dated the 2nd December, 1909, brought into operation on the 31st May, 1910.

Section *one hundred and thirty-five* of the South Africa Act provided that all laws in force in the several Colonies at the establishment of the Union should continue to be in force until repealed or amended by Parliament, and section *one hundred and forty-seven* specifically laid down that the control and administration of Native affairs throughout the Union should vest in the Governor-General-in-Council, i.e. the Governor-General acting by and with the advice of the Executive Council, who should exercise all special powers in regard to Native administration previously vested in the Governors of the several Colonies or exercised by them as Supreme Chiefs. Section *one hundred and forty-seven* provided also that any land vested in the Governor or Governor and Executive Council in any of the Colonies for the purpose of reserves for Native locations should vest in the Governor-General-in-Council, who should exercise all special powers in relation to such reserves as might previously have been exercisable by any such Governor or Governor and Executive

A

Council. It provided further that no lands set aside for the occupation of Natives, which could not at the establishment of the Union be alienated except by an Act of the Colonial Legislature concerned, should be alienated or in any way diverted from the purposes for which they were set apart except under the authority of an Act of Parliament.

In explanation of the provisions of section *one hundred and forty-seven*, it should perhaps be pointed out that the experience of the pre-existing Governments of the various Colonies had clearly shown that some special executive authority conferred by Parliament was required for the adequate administration and control of large masses of Native population. Though this special authority assumed different forms in the various Colonies, the broad principle was uniformly adopted of vesting certain extraordinary powers in respect of the administration of Native affairs in the Governor or the Governor and Executive Council.

Thus, as the different Native territories beyond the Kei River were annexed to the Cape Colony, the various Annexation Acts conferred upon the Governor of the Colony an absolute and unrestricted power of edictal legislation in respect of such territories and even went so far as to lay down that no Act of Parliament of the Colonial Legislature should apply thereto unless extended either by express words contained in the Act itself or in some other Act of Parliament or by proclamation of the Governor. This unfettered power of edictal legislation was re-affirmed in respect of all the Transkeian Native territories by Cape Act No. 29 of 1897.

In Natal, the Governor had been constituted Supreme Chief of the Native population with certain extraordinary powers expressly defined in the Natal Code of Native Law. Under that Code, the Governor as Supreme Chief exercised all political power over Natives in Natal ; he appointed and removed chiefs ; he decided questions of heirship to deceased chiefs ; he could divide and amalgamate tribes ; he might remove tribes or portions of tribes or individual Natives ; he might call out armed men or levies and had power to call upon Natives to supply labour for public works ; he was the upper guardian of Native orphans and minors ; he could punish political offenders and impose penalties for disobedience to his orders ; he might impose a fine upon a Native community as a whole for suppressing evidence of crime ; and, finally, his actions as Supreme Chief were not cognisable by the courts.

Transvaal Law No. 4 of 1885 provided that " the laws, habits and customs hitherto observed among the Natives " should continue in force " as long as they have not appeared to be inconsistent with the general principles of civilisation recognised in the civilised world " and constituted the State President as Paramount Chief of the Native population with power to exercise over all Natives in the Republic all authority vesting according to Native laws, usages and customs in any paramount chief. He was further empowered with the advice and consent of the Executive Council to make and frame regulations and orders for the better working and maintenance of that law.

After annexation, these special powers of the State President vested in the Governor of the Colony and the Letters Patent issued upon the grant of responsible government in 1907 contained the following specific provisions as regards Native administration :—

" LI.—(1) The Governor shall continue to exercise over all Chiefs and Natives in the Colony all power and authority now vested in him as Paramount Chief.

(2) The Governor in Council may at any time summon an assembly of Native Chiefs, and also, if it shall seem expedient, of other persons having special knowledge and experience in Native affairs, to discuss with the Governor, or such representative as the Governor in Council may appoint, any matters concerning the administration of Native affairs or the interests of Natives, and the Governor in Council shall consider any reports or representations submitted to him by any such assembly, and shall take such action thereupon as may seem necessary or proper.

(3) No lands which have been, or may hereafter be, set aside for the occupation of Natives shall be alienated or in any way diverted from the purposes for which they are set apart otherwise than in accordance with a law passed by the Legislature."

Article LII. of the Letters Patent issued upon the grant of responsible government to the Orange River Colony in 1907 constituted the Governor Paramount Chief of the Native population and was couched in language practically identical with that of Article LI. of the Transvaal Letters Patent quoted above.

The Native Affairs Department of the Union of South Africa was established *pari passu* with the constitution of the Union itself. Section *fourteen* of the South Africa Act empowered the Governor-General to appoint officers not exceeding ten (subsequently increased to eleven under Act No. 34 of 1925) to administer such Departments of State of the Union as the Governor-General-in-Council might establish ; and under Government Notice No. 1 of 1910 dated the 31st May, 1910, the establishment of certain thirteen Departments of State, included among which was the Department of Native Affairs, was notified. The Government Notice intimated further that the administration of Native Affairs had been entrusted to the Honourable Henry Burton, K.C., with the title of Minister of Native Affairs.

Government Notice No. 8 of 1910, likewise published on the 31st May, 1910, which purported to define the functions of the various Departments of State, discharged its onerous duty in so far as the Department of Native Affairs was concerned in the following laconic fashion :—

" The Department of Native Affairs will administer matters heretofore vested in the Native Affairs Departments of the four Colonies."

In such fashion were transferred to the Governor-General, the Executive Government and the Department of Native Affairs of the Union of South Africa the difficulties, complexities and intricacies of Native administration in its different aspects throughout the several Provinces, each of which, it must be borne in mind, had previously possessed its own form of government, each of which presented its own peculiar problems, each of which had its own separate laws specially affecting the Native population and each of which had developed its own system, policy and traditions of Native administration.

B

DEPARTMENTAL ORGANISATION

1. Prior to Union

Three of the four constituent Provinces, namely the Cape of Good Hope, the Transvaal, and Natal, had prior to Union possessed each its own Department of Native Affairs with its permanent head, the Secretary for Native Affairs, subordinate to a responsible Minister of the Crown.   As regards the Orange Free State, it may be mentioned that it had likewise previously possessed its own Department of Native Affairs, which, however, had been abolished in 1908, when the administration of Native Affairs was transferred to the Colonial Secretary's Department.

Upon Union, therefore, three separate Departments of Native Affairs, each with its own staff and specific organisation were merged into one. Each of the pre-existing Departments had its Head Office and special system of District Administration, while, in so far as the Transvaal was concerned, there was in addition a Government Native Labour Bureau, with headquarters in Johannesburg, which had been established for the protection, supervision and control of Natives employed on mines and works and in industries.

Prior to Union district Native administration in each Colony was carried out under the general direction of the Head Office of the Department concerned but the administrative system differed in the various Colonies.

As regards the Cape Colony, a Chief Magistrate, with headquarters at Umtata, was primarily responsible for the administration of the twenty-nine districts then comprising the Transkeian Territories. The Chief Magistrate in addition was chairman of the Transkeian Territories General Council and President of the Native Appeal Court, and exercised jurisdiction as a Divorce Court throughout the Territories in European as well as Native cases. Immediate district administration in the Transkeian Territories was entrusted to the District Magistrates, who were officers of the Native Affairs Department as were also the Magistrates of the districts of Herschel and Glen Grey in the Cape Province proper. In the remaining districts of the Cape Province proper, the administration of Native affairs was entrusted to Magistrates belonging to the Department of Justice, assisted in areas densely populated by Natives by " Superintendents of Natives " who were officers of the Native Affairs Department.

In the Transvaal, district administration of Native affairs was in the hands of the Magistrates of the various districts, all of whom belonged to the Department of Justice. They were, however, also " ex officio " Native Commissioners and in this capacity functioned to all intents and purposes as officers of the Native Affairs Department. In many of the districts one member of the Magistrate's staff was specially assigned for the performance of work in connection with Native affairs. Further, in areas more densely populated by Natives, special Native Affairs Department officials, viz. Sub-Native Commissioners and detached clerks, were appointed for the administration of Native affairs under the Native Commissioners.

Natal Act No. 1 of 1909 provided for the division of the Colony for Native administration purposes into four districts, each comprising several magisterial divisions. Each such district was placed under the control of a District Native Commissioner who was charged with certain specific administrative powers and duties laid down in the Act. The Act provided further for the establishment of a Council for Native Affairs, which was a deliberative, consultative and advisory body consisting of the Secretary for Native Affairs, the four District Native Commissioners and four non-official members. This Council, it may be stated, functioned actively during the year which elapsed between the passing of the Act and the consummation of Union, but after Union it became moribund and ceased to operate. This body may possibly be regarded as the precursor of the Union Native Affairs Commission.

In addition to the District Native Commissioners, Magistrates, all of whom belonged to the Department of Justice, were charged with the administration of Native affairs within their respective areas.

It may be added that the Natal Native Affairs Department had an agent at Johannesburg to watch over the interests of Natal Natives employed upon the Witwatersrand Mines.

In the Orange Free State prior to Union district Native administration was carried out entirely by the Magistrates of the various districts, except as regards the Witzieshoek Native Reserve, to administer the affairs of which a " Commandant " had been appointed by the Republican Government. This appointment was perpetuated by the Crown Colony Administration after annexation.

In all of the four Colonies the respective Governments had utilised in a greater or less degree the services of Native chiefs and headmen in the administration of local Native affairs. But in this regard too there were wide divergencies of policy, ranging from that adopted in Natal, where the principle of codifying and recognising Native law, of maintaining and perpetuating the tribal system and the authority of the chiefs and of governing the Natives in so far as possible according to their own institutions and ideas had been applied, to that followed in the Cape Province (exclusive of Bechuanaland), where the fundamental idea was to break down the power of the chiefs and to institute a system of paid headmen entirely subordinate to the Magistrate of the District, who would carry out certain specific administrative duties but exercise no civil or criminal jurisdiction whatsoever.

2. Subsequent to Union

Head Office

Upon Union, it was recognised that the ultimate objective must be to co-ordinate and harmonise the divergent and disparate systems of Native administration previously operative in the various Provinces into a flexible and homogeneous system for the Union as a whole ; but it was realised that immediately to introduce revolutionary changes would be to court disaster and that a matter of such magnitude, importance and intricacy could successfully be achieved only by a gradual process in the light of experience and careful consideration of the cardinal principles and features of each particular system. Immediate necessities, however, postulated organisation of the head office of and, in the first place, the appointment of a permanent head for the newly constituted Department. The appointment of Mr. E. E. Dower, who was previously Secretary to the Cape Native Affairs Department, as acting Secretary for Native Affairs for the Union was gazetted under Government Notice No. 53 of 1910, an appointment which was subsequently confirmed. The Transvaal Secretary for Native Affairs (Mr. W. Windham), the Natal Secretary for Native Affairs (Mr. A. J. Shepstone, C.M.G.), and the Chief Clerk of the Cape Native Affairs Department (Mr. E. Barrett) were appointed as acting Under Secretaries for Native Affairs in the Transvaal, Natal and Cape Provinces respectively.

Mr. Windham retired on pension in December, 1910, and in 1912 the first important change in district organisation was effected, when, under the provisions of section *three* of Act No. 1 of 1912, the post of Chief Native Commissioner, Natal, was created and the four posts of District Native Commissioners in Natal were abolished.

Mr. A. J. Shepstone was appointed to the newly created post of Chief Native Commissioner and the way was then clear for the appointment of one permanent Under Secretary for the Department as a whole, which appointment was in due course conferred upon Mr. E. Barrett.

The head office establishment of the Department was then organised upon the following basis :

> Permanent Head and Accounting Officer—The Secretary for Native Affairs.
> Permanent Under Secretary for Native Affairs.
> *Chief Clerk* responsible for the general administration and control of the office and dealing more particularly with staff matters.
> *Accountant* and staff.
> *Lands Branch*, consisting of a principal clerk and three assistants.
> *Local Government* and General Branch, consisting of a principal clerk and three assistants.
> *Staff Clerk* and two assistants.
> *Record Clerk* and staff.
> Personal Clerk to the Secretary for Native Affairs.
> Typing Section.
> One European and four Native messengers.
> Native interpreter and translator.

The essential features of the head office organisation indicated above remain in existence to-day. There have from time to time been alterations and adjustments as regards the number and grading of posts, which, however, have been of no great consequence save to the officers immediately affected.

There have, however, been the following very significant and important additions to the head office establishment, which are specified in the chronological order of the appointments as made :—

Firstly, the passing of the Natives (Urban Areas) Act, No. 21 of 1923, threw a large volume of additional work upon the head office necessitating the creation of additional posts. Two officials—a senior and a second grade clerk—are now fully occupied with the work involved in the administration of this Act.

Secondly, a long felt want was supplied by the appointment to the head office staff in 1926 of an ethnologist—a specially qualified officer whose full time is devoted to studying, investigating and conducting original research into anthropology and Bantu ethnology, sociology and philology.

A most important and far-reaching development was the appointment in the beginning of 1929 to the head office staff of a Director of Native Agriculture and the establishment of a School of Agriculture for Natives at Fort Cox in the Middledrift District of the Cape Province, primarily for the training of demonstrators for work in Native areas. Since 1929, Assistant Directors of Native Agriculture have been appointed for the Cape and Natal Provinces and, in addition to a number of European agricultural supervisors in Native areas in different parts of the Union, approximately one hundred trained Native demonstrators are at present employed in Native areas other than the Transkeian Territories. All these demonstrators hold diplomas in agriculture from one or other of the recognised Native schools of agriculture. They are paid from the Native Development Account established under Act No. 41 of 1925.

In July, 1929, a senior officer was appointed to the head office staff, known as the Native Welfare Officer, to whom was assigned the duty of investigating the conditions under which Natives are employed in rural areas, of enquiring into complaints, disputes, etc., and of endeavouring where necessary to secure more favourable treatment for Natives employed in such areas. This post became vacant in December, 1931, and owing to the general financial stringency has not yet been filled.

In September, 1931, a further addition to the head office establishment was made by the appointment on the staff of the Director of Native

Agriculture of an engineer for the Transvaal and Bechuanaland for the purpose of developing the water supply and irrigation possibilities of the locations, supervising the sinking of boreholes, the erection of windmills, the construction of reservoirs, stock dams and dipping tanks and generally carrying out engineering works in the Native areas. The salary of the engineer is paid from the Native Development Account.

Native Affairs Commission

Before leaving the question of the organisation of the head office of the Department and proceeding to deal with the district administrative machinery, mention must be made of the Native Affairs Commission, which, though not actually portion of the head office establishment, is closely associated therewith and has its headquarters in Pretoria.

The Native Affairs Commission was constituted under the Native Affairs Act, No. 23 of 1920. The Act provided that the Commission should be an advisory body consisting of the Minister of Native Affairs (as chairman) and of not less than three nor more than five other members.

Three members were appointed in 1920 immediately after the passing of the Act and up to the present the minimum number of three appointed members has not been exceeded.

District Organisation

Turning now to the question of the district administrative machinery of the Department, it has already been indicated that there were cardinal differences of organisation in the systems operative in the various Colonies prior to Union and that the first important change was introduced when, under the provisions of section *three* of Act No. 1 of 1912, a Chief Native Commissioner was appointed for the Natal Province and the four Natal District Native Commissionerships were abolished. In lieu of these four District Native Commissioners, there were appointed a senior inspector of Native reserves for Zululand and six supervisors of locations and mission reserves for Natal proper.

The next important change was that effected under Act No. 12 of 1913, which provided for the excision from the Transkeian Territories and the inclusion within the Cape Province proper, as from the 1st January, 1914, of the districts of Maclear and Elliot, which were preponderatingly European. The excision took the form of removing the districts in question from the purview of the special system of edictal legislation operative in the Transkeian Territories, while the administrative changes involved were firstly, that the districts ceased to fall under the jurisdiction of the Chief Magistrate and secondly, that the respective Magistrates, with their staffs, were transferred from the Native Affairs Department to the Department of Justice.

During the next decade there were no momentous changes, the most important being the appointment of nine superintendents of Natives in certain districts of the Cape Province proper.

In 1923, the Department was reorganised and, having regard to the serious depression which the country was then experiencing, certain drastic changes were made with a view to economy. The departmental establishment was reduced from 528 Europeans and (including police constables assigned to the Department for administrative and clerical duties) 929 Natives—a total of 1457—to 419 Europeans and 792 Natives —a total of 1211. The reduction was principally due to the transfer of a number of Native Affairs officers in the Transvaal, with their staffs, to the Department of Justice. The wisdom of these changes was seriously questioned by the Department at the time and exigencies of Native administration have since necessitated the restoration of a large number, if not the majority, of these posts.

In 1923, too, an important development took place in the appointment of a Chief Native Commissioner for the Ciskeian districts with headquarters at King William's Town. It had long been felt that Native affairs in the Ciskeian districts had received insufficient attention and in this connection it should be emphasised that the old Cape Government, which had developed an enlightened and progressive policy in the Transkeian Territories, had for the rest apparently been content to adopt an attitude of *laisser faire*, in consequence of which a chaotic state of affairs had arisen as regards many aspects of Native administration in the Ciskei, more particularly in reference to the ownership and occupation of land in the Native locations. The Chief Native Commissioner's appointment was made with a view to bringing the Ciskeian districts more or less into line with the Transkeian system of administration and to simplifying and unifying control of Native Affairs in those districts. Instructions were issued that Ciskeian Magistrates and local officers of the Native Affairs Department should in all matters pertaining to the administration of Native affairs communicate with and take their instructions from the Chief Native Commissioner, who, subject, of course, to control from the head office of the Department in matters of general policy, was made primarily responsible for the administration and supervision of the Native population within his area of jurisdiction.

A considerable advance too was made in or about this period when an understanding was achieved with the Department of Justice that appointments of Magistrates in districts carrying a large Native population would be made by that Department only after reference to, and consultation with the Department of Native Affairs.

The Native Administration Act

In 1927, the Native Administration Act (No. 38 of 1927) was passed " to provide for the better control and management of Native affairs." The primary object of the measure was to co-ordinate Native administration throughout the four Provinces, and it embraced within its purview practically every phase of (if one may be permitted to use the term) " internal " Native administration. It was said of the Bill when introduced into Parliament that there was little in its ambit which was more than a general application of principles which had been found to work satisfactorily in one or other of the Provinces and that it might be described as " selective synthesis of existing conditions " designed to facilitate and harmonise Native administration throughout the Union It represented the result of lengthy experience and careful consideration and comparison of the different administrative systems previously operative in the various Provinces and the selection from each of its most useful features and soundest principles with a view to evolving in so far as practicable a uniform and homogeneous system for the Union as a whole.

For the moment, however, we are concerned only with the question of district administrative organisation, a matter which was dealt with in section *two* of the Act. This section (as amended by section *three* of Act No. 9 of 1929) reads as follows :—

"2. (1) The Governor-General may, subject to the law relating to the public service, appoint for any area an officer, to be styled Chief Native Commissioner, who shall exercise such powers and perform such duties as the Minister may from time to time prescribe.

(2) The Governor-General may, subject to the law relating to the public service, appoint for any area in which large numbers of Natives reside a Native Commissioner and so many additional Native Commissioners and Assistant Native Commissioners as he may deem necessary. Such officers shall perform such duties as may be required by any law or assigned to them by the Minister and shall, within the area for which they are appointed, have the powers of Justices of the Peace.

(3) Any person who at the commencement of this Act holds the position of Native Commissioner or Sub-Commissioner shall be eligible for appointment under sub-section (2). No person other than an officer in the public service who has since the 31st day of May, 1910, been on the fixed establishment of either the Department of Native Affairs or the Department of Justice shall thereafter be appointed to be a Native Commissioner or Assistant Native Commissioner unless he has passed the civil service lower law examination or an examination determined by the Public Service Commission for the purposes of this section to be equivalent thereto.

(4) Every Native Commissioner and every Assistant Native Commissioner in the Transvaal Province shall, within the area for which he is appointed, have the power to solemnize marriages under Law No. 3 of 1897 (Transvaal).

(5) Notwithstanding the provisions of sub-section (3), the Minister may, when circumstances require, appoint any person to act temporarily as a Native Commissioner, Additional Native Commissioner or Assistant Native Commissioner in the place of or in addition to the ordinary incumbent of the post.

(6) The Minister may appoint Superintendents to assist in the control and supervision of locations, and may prescribe their duties.

(7) The Governor-General may recognise or appoint any person as a chief or headman in charge of a tribe or of a location, and is hereby authorised to make regulations prescribing the duties, powers and privileges of such chiefs or headmen. The Governor-General may depose any chief or headman so recognized or appointed.

(8) The Minister may appoint any person to act temporarily as a chief or headman in the place of or in addition to the ordinary incumbent of the post.

(9) Any person obstructing any officer, chief or headman in this section mentioned in the lawful execution of his duty shall be guilty of an offence."

The Native Administration Act in providing for appointments of Chief Native Commissioners, Native Commissioners, Additional Native Commissioners, Assistant Native Commissioners, Location Superintendents, Chiefs and Headmen, not only aimed at establishing coherently the administrative framework of the Native Affairs Department, which previously existed in unrelated and disparate systems operative in the several Provinces, but may be regarded as having accorded statutory recognition to the very important principle that in areas, which are densely populated by Natives and in which the Native population preponderates over Europeans, administrative and executive functions should, where separate appointments are not possible, be carried out by officers belonging to the Department of Native Affairs, who are specially trained for Native administration, look to the Department for their future advancement and are not liable to be transferred at any moment to purely European areas as are officials of the Department of Justice.

Thus, in purely Native districts such as those of the Transkeian Territories, the local chief executive officer (formerly the Magistrate) belongs to the Native Affairs Department and is primarily a *Native Commissioner* though he may be, and uniformly is, appointed by the Department of Justice to exercise magisterial functions as well.

In districts carrying a large population both European and Native, e.g. the Districts of Umgeni, Pietersburg and King William's Town, the chief local executive officer still remains the Magistrate, an official of the Department of Justice. He is, however, also appointed as a Native Commissioner under the Native Administration Act, while in addition special provision to subserve the interests of the Natives is made by the appointment of a senior Native Affairs Department official as Additional Native Commissioner.

That since the passing of the Native Administration Act practical recognition has been accorded by the Government to this very important principle will be gathered from the fact that within the last few years the Department of Native Affairs has taken over from the Department of Justice the Magistrates (with their staffs) of no less than fifteen districts and sub-districts, viz., Ingwavuma, Ubombo, Nongoma, Hlabisa, Mahlabatini, Entonjaneni, Nkandhla and Nqutu in Zululand, Msinga, Mapumulo and Ndwedwe in Natal proper, and Victoria East, Peddie, Keiskama Hoek and Middledrift in the Cape Province proper. These Magistrates now function primarily as Native Commissioners.

In districts where the European population preponderates but which at the same time carry a fair Native population living under tribal conditions or employed in industries, the position is met by appointing the Magistrate as a Native Commissioner under the Act and a Native Affairs officer as an Assistant Native Commissioner.

In preponderatingly European districts where there are but few Natives, no appointment of Native Commissioner, Additional Native Commissioner or Assistant Native Commissioner is made and the administration of Native affairs is entrusted to the Magistrate.

Five appointments of Chief Native Commissioners have been effected in terms of section *two* of Act No. 38 of 1927, viz., one for the Transkeian Territories with headquarters at Umtata ; one for the Natal Province with headquarters at Pietermaritzburg ; one for what may conveniently but not quite accurately be styled the Ciskeian districts*, with headquarters at King William's Town ; one for the Transvaal magisterial districts of Springs, Benoni, Boksburg, Germiston, Johannesburg and Krugersdorp, with headquarters at Johannesburg, and the Under Secretary for Native Affairs *ex officio* in respect of the magisterial districts of Kuruman, Mafeking, Taung and Vryburg in the Cape Province and the whole of the Transvaal Province excluding the magisterial districts of Springs, Benoni, Boksburg, Germiston, Johannesburg and Krugersdorp.

One hundred and forty-nine Native Commissioners have been appointed under the Act. Of these, forty-seven belong to the Native Affairs Department their districts being predominantly Native, while the remainder are officers of the Department of Justice.

In addition, nine additional and fifty-eight Assistant Native Commissioners have been appointed, of whom eight and forty-six respectively are officials of the Native Affairs Department.

A statement of the duties assigned to Chief Native Commissioners by the Minister under sub-section (1) of section *two* of the Native Administration Act figures as Appendix " A."

The duties of (*a*) Native Commissioners and Assistant Native Commissioners, (*b*) Superintendents of Locations and (*c*) Chiefs and Headmen, were likewise prescribed by the Minister under section *two* of the Act and were published for general information under Government Notices Nos. 2250, 2251 and 2252 of 1928 respectively. Copies of these Government Notices appear in Appendices " B," " C " and " D."

---

*The area of jurisdiction of the Chief Native Commissioner at King Williams's Town is defined under Government Notice No. 1864 of 1928, as amended by Government Notice No. 410 of 1929, as follows :—
The area in the Province of the Cape of Good Hope comprising the following magisterial districts : Adelaide, Albany, Albert, Alexandria, Aliwal, Barkly East, Barkly West, Bathurst, Bedford, Cathcart, East London, Elliot, Fort Beaufort, Glen Grey, Hay, Herbert, Herschel, Humansdorp, King William's Town, Komgha, Maclear, Molteno, Peddie, Port Elizabeth, Queenstown, Stockenstroom, Stutterheim, Tarka, Uitenhage, Victoria East, Wodehouse.

Director of Native Labour

Reference has already been made to the fact that there existed a sub-department of the old Transvaal Native Affairs Department known as the Government Native Labour Bureau with headquarters in Johannesburg. This Bureau was established by the Transvaal Administration in May, 1907, primarily with a view to securing the replacement by African labour of the Chinese labour which was then in process of repatriation. The exertions of the Bureau were such as to facilitate the successful recruiting of more than sufficient Natives to replace the 50,000 Chinese labourers who were finally repatriated before the middle of the year 1910.

Shortly after Union it was decided, with the object of securing uniformity of policy and control, to delegate to the Director of the Bureau the administration of the various laws regulating the issue of labour agents' licences and the recruiting and employment of Native labour throughout the Union.

In 1911, the Native Labour Regulation Act (Act No. 15 of 1911) was passed to consolidate and co-ordinate these diverse Provincial laws, its expressed intention being " to regulate the recruiting and employment of Native labour and to provide for compensation to Native labourers in certain cases."

Under the provisions of this Act, a Director of Native Labour for the Union was appointed and his establishment, into which was merged the old Transvaal Native Labour Bureau, virtually constituted a sub-department of the Native Affairs Department. The Act imposed very wide executive powers and duties upon the Director, e.g. the issue of employers' and agents' labour recruiting licences, the assessment of compensation and the power of cancelling contracts and repatriating sick Natives, necessitating the employment of a considerable " head office " staff.

The Act provided further for the appointment of Inspectors to enquire into and, if possible, redress the grievances of Native labourers. These Inspectors may be regarded as the field officers of the Native labour sub-department.

The Director of Native Labour was appointed Chief Native Commissioner for the Witwatersrand districts (vide page 14 *supra*) and has under his control a number of Native Commissioners and pass officers.

Particulars of the Director's establishment and organisation are furnished in a subsequent chapter of this volume—vide page 208 *infra*.

Native Appeal Courts

Special mention must be made of the constitution, under the provisions of section *thirteen* of the Native Administration Act, No. 38 of 1927, of two Native Appeal Courts, one for the Provinces of the Cape of Good Hope and the Orange Free State with headquarters at King William's Town, and one for the Transvaal and Natal with headquarters at Pretoria.

The nature, jurisdiction and activities of these Courts will be fully dealt with when the judicial functions of the Department are under consideration, and in the meantime it is sufficient to mention that each Court consists of three persons, viz., a permanent President appointed by the Governor-General and two other members who are selected by the Minister, from time to time as required, from Magistrates, Native Commissioners or other qualified persons.

To each court is attached a permanent registrar with the rank of senior clerk, and the presidents, sitting alone, exercise jurisdiction as Native divorce courts within their respective areas.

Local Government, etc.

Before leaving the question of departmental organisation, mention must be made of the fact that certain Native trusts and local government bodies, e.g. the Natal and Zululand Native Trusts, the United Transkeian Territories General Council and the Glen Grey District Council, administer their own finances and employ their own special officials, whose salaries are met not from the vote of the Department but from the funds of the particular organisation concerned. The activities and functions of these bodies are considered in detail in a subsequent portion of this work.

Certain special officers too are employed by the Minister of Native Affairs in his administration of the Native Development Account established under the provisions of the Natives Taxation and Development Act, No. 41 of 1925. A brief account of this special fund is likewise furnished in a subsequent portion of this work.

II

FUNCTIONS AND POWERS OF THE ADMINISTRATION

A

FUNCTIONS

Having briefly reviewed the establishment of the Department and the development of its administrative machinery, it is desirable to afford some indication of the general nature and scope of its functions and activities.

The essential function of the Native Affairs Department is to assist, guide, protect and generally to subserve the interests of a large, undeveloped and, for the most part, inarticulate Native population, which is rapidly emerging from barbarism and is in the process faced with the necessity of accommodating itself to a novel and highly complex environment, while at the same time its own tribal organisation, control, discipline, customs and traditions are rapidly and inevitably breaking down with the ever increasing impact of European ways and standards of life.

The Department's primary endeavour is to guide Native thought and progress aright in the laborious and difficult process of the absorption by the people of the ideas and methods of Western civilization.

It is concerned to safeguard large masses of ignorant and untutored Natives, who are rapidly developing a sense of race consciousness, against the extravagances of fanatical agitators on the one hand and to protect them from exploitation for personal profit and gain by unscrupulous persons—whether white or black—on the other.

It must in the widest sense govern the Native population in their own areas ; it must provide special tribunals for the determination of disputes according to their own laws and customs in so far as such are recognised by the law of the land ; it must regulate the ownership and occupation of land in Native locations and reserves and must inculcate among the people improved methods of agriculture and stock raising so

B

as to ensure beneficial occupation of Native areas ; it must provide facilities for the dipping and cleansing of stock ; it is concerned to secure for the people such educational facilities as are best suited to their present stage of development ; it must in so far as practicable foster and promote the establishment of local councils or boards with limited powers of self-government so as to afford a suitable substitute for the rapidly disappearing tribal system, to the disruption of which reference has already been made.

The Department must endeavour with sympathy and discretion to adjust difficult and delicate points of contact between Natives and non-Natives and to provide a just and equitable balance where the interests of the one race impinge upon those of the other.

It falls to the Department to administer a wide variety of statutes specially affecting the Native in his life in areas other than his own reserves and locations ; statutes which govern the acquisition and tenure by him of land in such areas and his contractual relationships with the European farmer ; statutes which control his movements in such areas, e.g. the pass laws ; statutes which regulate his residence and employment in urban and industrial areas, e.g. the Native Labour Regulation Act, No. 15 of 1911, and the Natives Urban Areas Act, No. 21 of 1923.

The Department too is in a very large measure responsible for the administration and winding up of Native estates. It, no less than the Treasury, is concerned with the fiscal relations of the Native population and in particular with the administration of the Natives Taxation and Development Act, No. 41 of 1925.

Recourse to the Department of Native Affairs is invariably had by all other Departments of State in reference to matters falling within their purview, in which questions regarding Native policy, administration or interest are involved.

It is the business of the Department to subserve individual, no less than general, Native interests and to ensure that the all-important personal factor, which tends more than anything else to secure the loyalty, confidence and good-will of the Natives, is not lacking in its administration.

Embraced within the purview of the Native Affairs Department are those activities in relation to the Native population, which in so far as Europeans are concerned, absorb the energies of separate and specific departments.

In a word, in its relationship to the Native population, the Department of Native Affairs must as nearly as possible be " all things to all men."

It is obvious from what has been said above that for the efficient performance of the multiplicity of its duties and the satisfactory discharge of its enormous responsibility to the Native people, the responsible Minister in charge of the Department must not only be able to set in motion, from time to time as required, extraordinary legislative and executive powers far wider than those usually conceded by Parliament to State departments, but, in the complicated matters with which he is called upon to deal, he must be in a position to consult, in addition to the permanent head of the Department, an independent body of experts who, while being well versed and experienced in Native affairs, making a close study of Native problems and able to furnish authoritative advice, would not necessarily represent the official point of view and would give calm and dispassionate consideration to any complex and difficult question which might arise.

These two essential requirements have been met, the former by special executive and legislative powers conferred by the Native Administration Act, No. 38 of 1927, and the latter by the establishment under the provisions of the Native Affairs Act, 1920 (Act No. 23 of 1920), of a standing Native Affairs Commission.

B

SPECIAL EXECUTIVE AND LEGISLATIVE POWERS CONFERRED BY THE NATIVE ADMINISTRATION ACT, NO. 38 OF 1927

1. POWERS OF " SUPREME CHIEF "

Reference has already been made, in discussing the provisions of section *one hundred and forty-seven* of the South Africa Act, to the special executive authority which had prior to Union been conferred upon the Governors of Natal, the Transvaal and the Orange Free State by virtue of the fact that they were constituted Supreme or Paramount Chiefs of the respective Native populations. As has already been pointed out, the Governor's considerable powers as Supreme Chief in Natal were expressly defined in the Natal Code of Native Law (contained in the Schedule to Natal Law No. 19 of 1891 as amended from time to time). In the Trans-

vaal and Orange Free State, however, the powers of the Paramount Chief
had never been clearly defined but depended on Native law and custom,
with the result that with the breaking down of tribal organisation, control
and discipline, it became with the effluxion of time increasingly unsatisfactory and difficult for the Paramount Chief to exercise powers and rely
upon customs which undoubtedly previously existed. On occasions
when such powers were exercised in the Transvaal, the Administration
was not infrequently faced with the necessity of establishing them in the
courts, and, in more than one such case, judges strongly expressed the
view that the Legislature should take steps to resolve the uncertainty
existing as to the Native usages and customs referred to in Law No. 4 of
1885.

The matter was placed beyond doubt by section *one* of the Native
Administration Act, which (as amended by Act No. 9 of 1929) reads as
follows :—

> " The Governor-General shall be the Supreme Chief of all
> Natives in the Provinces of Natal, Transvaal and Orange Free
> State, and shall in any part of the said Provinces be vested with
> all such rights, immunities, powers and authorities in respect of
> all Natives as are or may be from time to time vested in him in
> respect of Natives in the Province of Natal."

Some indication of the Supreme Chief's special powers in Natal
prior to Union has already been furnished (vide page 2 *supra*). The
reference in the section to such powers as " may be from time to time
vested in him in respect of Natives in the Province of Natal " must be
read in conjunction with section *twenty-four* of the Act, which empowers
the Governor-General from time to time by proclamation in the Gazette
to amend the provisions of the Natal Code of Native Law.

It will be observed that the Governor-General's powers as Supreme
Chief of the Native population have not been extended to the Cape Province. This is to be ascribed to the fact that the policy of the Cape
Government was, except as regards British Bechuanaland, to break down
rather than to perpetuate the tribal system and, consequently, Native
chiefs were never officially recognised as possessing any special administrative, or for that matter judicial, powers over their tribesmen. In these
circumstances, it was considered that it would serve no useful purpose,
but merely give rise to difficulties and complications, to extend to the
Cape Province the executive powers enjoyed by the Governor-General as
Supreme Chief in Natal.

2. POWERS OF GENERAL-GOVERNOR AND MINISTER OF NATIVE AFFAIRS

Secondly, Chapter II (comprising sections *three, four* and *five*) of the Native Administration Act, relating to tribal organization and control, conferred certain special administrative powers upon the Governor-General and the Minister of Native Affairs respectively.

Section *three* limited the contractual powers of Native chiefs acting in the name and on behalf of their tribes. It enunciated the very sound principles, which previously had been expressly laid down by law only in the Transvaal, that a Native tribe shall not be responsible for the personal obligations of its chiefs and that no tribe or tribal land shall be bound by any contract entered into or liability incurred by a chief unless it has been approved by the Minister after having been adopted by a majority of the adult male members of the tribe present at a public meeting convened for the purpose of considering such contract or liability.

This is a most beneficial provision in that it ensures reference to and careful consideration by the Department of all tribal contracts, some of which are of very considerable importance, such as prospecting and mineral agreements, trading concessions and the like, in which issues involving thousands of pounds are not infrequently involved.

Section *four* confers upon the Governor-General the power of vetoing the institution by malcontent tribesmen against their tribes or chiefs of frivolous legal proceedings in respect of the ownership or occupation of tribal land.

Natives are notorious for their love of litigation and, in the past, more particularly in the Transvaal, thousands of pounds have been dissipated in, and tribes have been financially ruined by, the institution by dissatisfied sections against their chiefs or tribes of legal proceedings of a frivolous or merely vexatious nature. The salutary provision contained in the section under consideration will ensure that no action falling within the restrictions imposed will be brought before the courts unless there is, at any rate, a *bona fide* or *prima facie* case.

Section *five* confers upon the Governor-General, *qua* Governor-General and not in his capacity as Supreme Chief, in respect of the Union as a whole special powers, regarding the definition of tribal and location boundaries, the fusion and fission of tribes and the removal of tribes or individual Natives.

3. Legislation by Proclamation

The most striking feature of the Native Administration Act is the wide power conferred upon the Governor-General (and it is important to bear in mind that the expression " Governor-General " is defined in section *three* of the Interpretation of Laws Act, No. 5 of 1910, as meaning " the officer for the time being administering the government of the Union acting by and with the advice of the Executive Council thereof ") to legislate by *proclamation*.

This principle of edictal legislation had, as previously pointed out, been operative in the Transkeian Territories ever since annexation, i.e. for some fifty years, and had been attended with conspicuous success.

The key-note of the system is its flexibility and elasticity, attributes which rendered it possible for the Transkeian Administration to adapt its organisation to the ever changing needs of a primitive people rapidly emerging from barbarism and to keep pace with advancing conditions.

The advantages of the system were clearly manifested in the Transkeian Territories as regards the control and regulation of land tenure in Native locations, the recognition and modification of Native law and custom, the establishment and development of the Council system of local government, and, in short, as regards practically every phase of Native administration in those Territories.

Legislation by proclamation allows too of emergencies being dealt with as they arise, when prompt official action may be imperative, and in this connection it must be borne in mind that large Native areas are peculiarly liable to circumstances and conditions requiring immediate action.

The system has the supreme advantage of removing to a great degree questions of Native administration from the arena of party politics ; and it is particularly suitable for application in the Native areas of the Union to-day having regard to the varied and diverse conditions obtaining in those areas in different parts of the country.

The different Native tribes have not reached the same stage of civilisation and development. In some parts, e.g. the Transkei, the people are comparatively advanced and progressive ; in others, e.g. the Northern Transvaal, they remain steeped in barbarism. Under the stress and strain of parliamentary life to-day, it is not possible for a Legislature, whose attention is, and must of necessity be, occupied mainly with European affairs, to devote the time and consideration necessary for investigating the diverse conditions existing in Native areas in different parts of the Union with a view to deciding what modification of any law should be introduced to meet the requirements of any particular area or community. Parliament cannot do more than legislate on broad lines for the Native population as a whole and under the edictal system alone is it possible to legislate for the Natives according to their varying needs in their own areas in different parts of the country.

The main objections which have been advanced against the Proclamation system of legislation are, firstly, that it does not afford the general public any opportunity for consideration and discussion of any measure before it becomes law; secondly, that it invests the Executive Government with autocratic powers which should be exercised by the supreme legislative authority, and, thirdly, that it is liable to abuse.

It seems clear that the considerations advanced above both for and against the system were carefully weighed by Parliament in the enactment of sections *twenty-five* and *twenty-six* of the Native Administration Act, which read as follows :—

" 25 (1)   From and after the commencement of this Act, any law then in force or subsequently coming into force within the areas included in the Schedule to the Natives Land Act, 1913 (Act No. 27 of 1913), or any amendment thereof, or such areas as may by resolution of both Houses of Parliament be designated as Native areas for the purpose of this section, may be repealed or amended, and new laws applicable to the said areas may be made, amended and repealed by the Governor-General by proclamation in the Gazette.

(2)   Save where delay would, in the opinion of the Governor-General, be prejudicial to the public interest, no such proclamation shall be issued unless a draft of its provisions or of its principal provisions shall have been published in the Gazette at least one month previously; but the omission of such publication shall not invalidate any such proclamation.

(3)   Nothing in this Act contained shall affect the powers vested in the Governor-General under the Transkeian Annexation Act, 1877 (Act No. 38 of 1877), the Walfish Bay and St. John's River Territories Annexation Act, 1884 (Act No. 35 of 1884) so far as it relates to the St. John's River Territory; the Tembuland Annexation Act, 1885 (Act No. 3 of 1885), and the Transkeian

Territories, Tembuland and Pondoland Laws Act, 1897 (Act No. 29 of 1897) of the Cape of Good Hope.

26 (1) Every proclamation issued by the Governor-General under the authority of this Act shall be laid upon the Tables of both Houses of Parliament within fourteen days after its promulgation if Parliament is then in ordinary session, or if Parliament is not then in ordinary session within fourteen days after the commencement of its next ensuing ordinary session, and every such proclamation shall be in operation unless and until both Houses of Parliament have, by resolutions passed in the same session, requested the Governor-General to repeal such proclamation or to modify its operation, in which case such proclamation shall forthwith be repealed or modified, as the case may be, by a further proclamation in the Gazette.

(2) If the Native Affairs Commission established in terms of section *one* of the Native Affairs Act, 1920 (Act No. 23 of 1920), has dissented from any provision contained in a proclamation issued under section *twenty-five*, the record of, and the reasons for, such dissent shall, when the proclamation is laid upon the Tables of both Houses of Parliament as aforesaid, simultaneously be so presented to Parliament."

These sections, it will be observed, not only conserve the power which previously vested in the Governor-General to legislate by Proclamation for the Transkeian Territories but gave him almost unfettered power and authority so to legislate for purely Native areas throughout the Union.

The necessary safeguards have been provided by :—

(a) the stipulation that proclamations must be published in the Gazette in draft form for general information at least one month prior to promulgation ;

(b) the necessity for bringing proclamations to the notice of Parliament in the manner prescribed and the provision for the repeal or modification of any proclamation at the instance of Parliament signified by resolution of both Houses ;

(c) the power vested in the Native Affairs Commission of recording its dissent from any provision contained in a proclamation and the fact that the record of any such dissent must be brought to the notice of Parliament.

The Act not only vested in the Executive Government a practically unrestricted power of edictal legislation in respect of Native areas throughout the Union but, as already pointed out, made the Natal Native Code susceptible of revision by Proclamation, and further, in reference to certain specified topics, made provision for legislation by proclamation or regulation, the application of which should be general, or, at any rate, not confined to Native areas.

Thus, section *twenty-seven* lays down that the Governor-General may make regulations with reference to all or any of the following matters :—

" (a) the exhibition of pictures of an undesirable character in any location or Native compound or in any urban location or Native village constituted under the Natives (Urban Areas) Act, 1923 (Act No. 21 of 1923) ;

(b) the carrying of assegais, knives, kerries, sticks or other weapons or instruments by Natives ;

(c) the prohibition, control or regulation of gatherings or assemblies of Natives ;

(d) the observance by Natives of decency ; and

(e) generally for such other purposes as he may consider necessary for the protection, control, improvement, and welfare of the Natives, and in furtherance of peace, order and good government."

The section further provides that any such regulations may be made applicable only in any particular areas or in respect only of particular classes of persons, and that different regulations may be made for different areas or in respect of different classes.

Section *twenty-eight*, again, dealing with pass areas and the control of movements of Natives, reads as follows :—

" 28 (1) The Governor-General may, by proclamation in the Gazette—

(a) create and define pass areas within which Natives may be required to carry passes ;

(b) prescribe regulations for the control and prohibition of the movement of Natives into, within or from any such areas ; and

(c) repeal all or any of the laws relating to the carrying of passes by Natives ;

Provided that no area included in the Schedule to the Natives Land Act, 1913 (Act No. 27 of 1913), or any amendment thereof shall be included within a pass area.

(2) Such regulations may provide penalties for any breach thereof not exceeding a fine of five pounds or imprisonment with or without hard labour for a period not exceeding three months."

Further section *thirty* of the Act lays down that the Governor-General may make regulations—

" (a) for the control and management of any village or township not falling under the operation of the Natives (Urban Areas) Act, 1923 (Act No. 21 of 1923), if not less than two-thirds of its inhabitants are Natives ; and

(b) for the imposition of rates or charges upon the owners of land or residents in any such village or township ;   Provided that such rates or charges which may be imposed upon the owners of any such land shall not exceed one and one-quarter per cent. of the value of such land in any one year."

Certain important proclamations have already been promulgated under the special powers vested in the Governor-General by the Native Administration Act as indicated above.   Such are :—

Proclamation No. 252 of 1928, which prohibited the holding in any Native location, reserve or mission reserve in Natal, the Transvaal or the Orange Free State of gatherings or assemblies of Natives in excess of ten in number for purposes, other than religious services or the regulation of the domestic affairs of any particular kraal or official administrative purposes, without the permission of the chief or headman of the location or reserve and the approval of the magistrate of the district.

Proclamation No. 257 of 1928, which prescribed regulations for the control of the cutting of wood in Native reserves in British Bechuanaland.

Proclamation No. 302 of 1928 (as amended by Proclamation No. 398 of 1931), which promulgated regulations for the administration of communally occupied Native locations in the Cape Province proper exclusive of British Bechuanaland.

Proclamation No. 10 of 1929, which applied the special procedure prescribed for the collection of outstanding taxes, under the Natives Taxation and Development Act, No. 41 of 1925, to the recovery from

Natives of arrear rentals and fees due to the Natal and Zululand Native Trusts in respect of the occupation of land in Native areas.

Proclamation No. 58 of 1929, which provided for the imposition of penalties upon Natives, who, in consideration of cash advances, enter into agreements, in a prescribed form and attested in a prescribed manner, undertaking upon a date or within a period specified to present themselves for attestation and service in accordance with the terms of their agreements, and fail, without reasonable cause or excuse, to do so.

Proclamation No. 116 of 1929, which prescribed regulations for the eradication and destruction of noxious weeds in Native areas exclusive of the Transkeian Territories. This proclamation was amended by Proclamation No. 43 of 1931.

Proclamation No. 165 of 1929, which provided for the appointment of a special Commissioner to investigate and determine certain land claims in the Umtwalumi Mission Reserve in the Province of Natal.

Proclamation No. 179 of 1929, which prescribed special regulations for the filling of cattle and sheep dipping tanks in Native areas in the Province of Natal where such filling requires to be done by manual labour.

Proclamation No. 275 of 1929, which provides for the amendment in certain respects of the Mission Reserves Act, No. 49 of 1903 (Natal) and for the establishment of local councils and general councils for mission reserves and groups of mission reserves in Natal.

Proclamation No. 1 of 1930, which implemented the Liquor Act, No. 30 of 1928, by prescribing regulations for the brewing, possession and consumption of kafir beer in Native areas other than those in the Transkeian Territories and British Bechuanaland.

Proclamation No. 42 of 1931, which was designed to foster and encourage the production of sugar cane by Natives in the Natal locations and reserves.

Proclamation No. 101 of 1931, under which regulations for the checking and prevention of soil erosion in Native locations, reserves and trust lands were promulgated.

Proclamation No. 102 of 1931, under which special regulations for the checking and prevention of soil erosion in the locations in the Glen Grey district were promulgated.

Proclamation No. 117 of 1931 (as amended by Proclamations Nos. 411 of 1931, 150 of 1932 and 12 of 1933), which prescribed regulations for the administration of surveyed locations in the Ciskeian districts.

Proclamation No. 123 of 1931 (as amended by Proclamation No. 160 of 1932), which promulgated general regulations for the administration of Native locations and reserves in the Natal Province.

Proclamation No. 142 of 1931, which made provision for the prohibition of the grazing of inferior stallions, bulls and sheep or goat rams and Persian or cross-bred Persian sheep on Native location commonages.

Proclamation No. 283 of 1931, which applied to the district of Glen Grey (at the request of the people and of the Glen Grey District Council) the principle of collective responsibility in respect of stock theft, damage to dipping tanks and fences and assaults upon travellers.

Proclamation No. 30 of 1932, under which were promulgated regulations for the control of tourists and the holding of mock war-dances and other Native ceremonies in Native areas in Natal.

Proclamation No. 123 of 1932, by virtue of which the provisions of the Natal Pound Act, No. 42 of 1898, were applied to the Native locations and reserves in that Province.

Proclamation No. 195 of 1932, prescribing regulations for the administration and control of irrigation works on Native Trust land in the Natal Province.

Proclamation No. 196 of 1932, under which regulations were promulgated for controlling and limiting the number of donkeys in Native areas.

Proclamation No. 232 of 1932, which applied to Native areas in Natal the principle of collective responsibility in respect of damage to dipping tanks, fences, dams, water furrows, irrigation works and soil reclamation works or arising out of any affray, riot, faction fight, hut-burning, cattle raid or disturbance of a similiar nature or occasioned by unlawful interference with travellers.

Proclamation No. 13 of 1933, prohibiting the occupation for residential purposes of arable allotments in Ciskeian surveyed locations save with the written approval of the Native Commissioner.

Proclamation No. 29 of 1933, under which the Native Reserves Management Ordinance, No. 6 of 1907 (O.F.S.), was applied in modified form to the northern portion of the farm " Bofulo," No. 1031, in the District of Thaba 'Nchu.

All of the foregoing proclamations were promulgated by virtue of the general powers of edictal legislation vested in the Governor-General under section *twenty-five* of the Native Administration Act and their diversity, scope and importance sufficiently illustrate the usefulness, and in fact indispensability, of the system in its application to Native areas.

Special regulations framed under section *twenty-seven* of the Act for the financial protection of Natives were promulgated under Proclamation No. 272 of 1930, while this section was also invoked for the issue under Government Notice No. 962 of 1931 of curfew regulations in respect of the Premier Mine area, and under Government Notice No. 1498 of 1932 of regulations governing the financial liabilities of chiefs in the Transvaal and Natal Provinces.

Regulations for the control and management of the Vryheid East township were framed under the provisions of section *thirty* of the Act and published under Government Notice No. 902 of 1932, as amended by Government Notice No. 324 of 1933.

III

THE NATIVE AFFAIRS COMMISSION

In discussing the question of the organisation of the Department, a passing reference has already been made to the Native Affairs Commission.

The Commission was established under the provisions of the Native Affairs Act, No. 23 of 1920, the relevant sections of which are as follows :—

" 1.   The Governor-General may establish a commission which shall be known as the Native Affairs Commission and is hereinafter referred to as the Commission.   The Commission shall consist of the Minister of Native Affairs (who shall be chairman), or alternatively to him some fit and proper person designated by the Minister to be deputy chairman in his absence from any meeting of the Commission, and of not less than three nor more than five other members.   Notwithstanding anything to the contrary in the South Africa Act, 1909, a member of either House of Parliament may be appointed a member of the Commission and though he receive remuneration as such he shall not thereby be deemed to hold an office of profit under the Crown within the Union.   The chairman and the deputy chairman when presiding shall have a deliberative as well as a casting vote.   The names of the members of the Commission shall be published in the Gazette.

2.   The functions and duties of the Commission shall include the consideration of any matter relating to the general conduct of the administration of Native affairs, or to legislation in so far as it may affect the Native population (other than matters of departmental administration), and the submission to the Minister of Native Affairs of its recommendations on any such matter. The Commission shall also consider, and make recommendations with regard to, any matter of administrative routine submitted to it by direction of the Minister.

3. (1) If in regard to any matter the Minister does not accept the recommendation of the Commission or takes any action contrary thereto the Commission may require that such matter, together with a memorandum of its views thereon, be submitted to the Governor-General ; and thereupon if the Governor-General does not accept the Commission's recommendation the Commission may require that all papers relative to the matter be laid before both Houses of Parliament, and the Minister, if such request is made, shall lay such papers before both Houses.

(2) Where a question has been decided by the casting vote of the chairman or the deputy chairman at any meeting of the Commission, any member who dissented from the decision of the Commission may request that his views, as stated by him in writing, shall be recorded and laid before both Houses of Parliament, and the Minister, if such request is made, shall lay the record of such member's views before such Houses.

4. The Governor-General may make regulations prescribing the procedure at meetings of the Commission, the conduct of its business, the qualifications of members, their remuneration, the period for which they shall hold office, and the appointment of alternative members, and generally for giving effect to the purposes of the preceding sections."

While section *two* of Act No. 23 of 1920 prescribes general consultative and advisory functions for the Commission, subsequent sections of that Act and certain provisions of later Acts lay down specific matters in regard to which the Commission's advice and recommendations must be sought.

Thus, local and general Native Councils can under the provisions of sections *five* and *fourteen* of the 1920 Act be established by the Governor-General only upon the recommendation of the Native Affairs Commission.

Secondly, under section *fourteen*, the advice of the Commission must be sought regarding the constitution of and allocation of powers to any general council it may be proposed to establish under the Act.

Thirdly, the holding of representative Native conferences from time to time, for the purpose of discussing any contemplated legislation in so far as it affects the interests of the Native population, is by section *sixteen* of the Act, made contingent upon the Commission submitting a recommendation to the Governor-General.

Further, section *thirteen* of the Natives Taxation and Development Act makes it incumbent upon the Minister of Native Affairs to consult the Native Affairs Commission in reference to the appropriation of monies accruing to the special fund established under that Act and known as " the Native Development Account." The furnishing of advice in reference to the administration of this fund has, as will be more fully pointed out in dealing in detail with the Development Account, become a special feature of the Commission's activities.

Again, section *twenty-five* of the Native Administration Act, which has already been fully considered in discussing the system of edictal legislation, by implication places upon the Administration the duty of consulting the Native Affairs Commission regarding such legislation and, failing such consultation, the Commission must *suo motu* take cognisance of all proclamations issued.

Lastly, mention should be made of the fact that the Select Committee on Native Affairs, 1925, put forward the recommendation that mission sites in Native locations and other privileges depending upon Government recognition should, as a general rule, be granted only to Churches long established and enjoying universal public recognition, and that in all other cases, before any application is considered by the Native Affairs Department, a report should be submitted by the Native Affairs Commission regarding the applicant body, the demand for its existence, its stability, its capacity both financially and educationally and its general fitness for religious work amongst Natives.

This recommendation was accepted by the Government and has been consistently carried out.

The following regulations, framed for the Native Affairs Commission under section *four* of the Native Affairs Act, No. 23 of 1920, were published under Government Notice No. 2004 of 1920 :—

" 1. The members of the Native Affairs Commission appointed by the Governor-General shall hold office for a period of five years, and shall be eligible for re-appointment for successive terms of the same duration.

2. In the event of the absence or incapacity of any member, the Governor-General may appoint some fit and proper person to act in his place during such absence or incapacity.

3. Members may resign with the approval of the Governor-General but any member may be removed from the Commission (otherwise than at his own instance) by the Governor-General, and in

such case a full statement of the reasons for such removal shall be laid before both Houses of Parliament.

4. The members of the Commission shall each be entitled to a fixed salary at the rate of £1000 (one thousand pounds) per annum, in addition to the travelling and subsistence allowance prescribed by the Civil Service Regulations for the time being.

5. The Commission shall be a standing commission, and the members shall be in permanent attendance subject to the discretion of the chairman.

6. The Commission shall meet in Council at such intervals or at such times as it may determine, and also whenever the Minister or two of its members may require.

7. The Minister as chairman or the deputy-chairman designated, in terms of section *one* of the Act, shall, together with any two other members of the Commission, form a quorum.

8. It shall be competent for the Minister on the advice of the Commission to nominate and summon Native assessors to attend and assist the deliberations of the Commission. Such Natives shall be entitled to fees and allowances as approved by the Minister for the period of such attendance.

9. The venue of the Commission shall be determined by the Minister, by whom it may be varied as convenience shall direct.

10. The Commission shall have access to all official records concerning any subject brought before it for consideration. Minutes shall be kept of the proceedings at every meeting of the Commission.

11. The Commission may resolve itself into committees of one or more members for purposes of enquiry, investigation, or report.

12. Any recommendations submitted by the Commission, pursuant to sections *five, fourteen* or *sixteen* of the Act, shall be accompanied by a summary of the reasons *pro et contra*, discussed by the Commission.

13. The Commission may receive representations from Natives, whether individual or delegate, in regard to any matter of concern to such Natives.

14. The Commission shall prepare an annual report of its work for submission to the Governor-General."

In the initial stages of its activities, which commenced in April 1921, the Commission accepted for the governance of its general policy the following guiding principles :—

    (a) that the Native Affairs Commission is primarily and essentially the friend of the Native people, and as such the needs, aspirations and progress of the Natives should be considered sympathetically by it ;

    (b) that the Commission is the adviser of the Government where the interests of the Natives are concerned ;

    (c) that the Commission should endeavour to win the confidence of the Natives ;

    (d) that the Commission should endeavour to educate public opinion, both Native and non-Native, so as to bring about the most harmonious relations possible between White and Black in South Africa.

Since the establishment of the Commission, the appointed members have travelled widely throughout the Union for the purposes of the closer study of Native problems and of coming into contact personally with the Natives so as to ascertain first-hand their points of view. They have dealt with a large number of specific matters of Native administration and have investigated certain general questions of Native policy, such as Native taxation and education, marriage under Native law and custom, the pass laws, the control of Natives in urban areas, the land question, the extension of the council system, Native franchise rights, etc. They have in addition conducted enquiries into special matters of Native interest referred to them by the Government for investigation and report, e.g. the Bulhoek imbroglio ; the prevalence of typhus amongst Natives ; the problem of Native separatist churches ; economic conditions in Namaqualand ; the question of Dunn's Reserve in Natal, and the administration of the Richtersveld. In addition it should be mentioned that two members of the Native Affairs Commission, Dr. Roberts and Senator the Hon. P. W. le Roux van Niekerk, served from May, 1930, to February, 1932, as members of the Native Economic Commission.

Further information as regards the activities of the Commission is to be found in the periodical reports of the Commission itself.

IV

SYSTEMS OF LOCAL GOVERNMENT IN NATIVE AREAS

The Native Affairs Act, No. 23 of 1920, provided for the constitution not only of the Native Affairs Commission but of Native councils as well, and, having dealt with the Commission, we may now consider the various systems of local government operative amongst the Natives within the Union,

The " District Council " system for the local administration of Native areas had its origin under the Glen Grey Act, No. 25 of 1894 (Cape of Good Hope).

A

GLEN GREY COUNCIL SYSTEM

The system of local government instituted under the Glen Grey Act contemplates the establishment of two separate types of local authority, viz. subsidiary bodies known as location boards for the control of individual locations and a higher body termed " the District Council," constituted on the lines of the Cape Divisional Councils, for the administration of local affairs in the Glen Grey District as a whole.

1. LOCATION BOARDS UNDER THE GLEN GREY ACT

Section *seven* of the Glen Grey Act provides that each location in the district shall be under the control of a board of three persons who shall be appointed by the Governor after consideration of the wishes and recommendations of the resident holders of land in the location determined and expressed in such manner as may be prescribed by regulation.

The regulations under the section provide for the holding of a public meeting by the magistrate annually in each location. The magistrate must give the headman of each location at least seven days written notice of the time and place fixed for the meeting and the headman must notify all landholders within the location. The wishes and recommendations of the people must then be expressed openly at the meeting.

Members of location boards must be holders of land in the location concerned and they hold office, during pleasure, for one year but are eligible for re-appointment. A member of the location board automatically loses his seat if he ceases to hold land in the location, is convicted of any offence punishable by imprisonment without the option of a fine, leaves the limits of the community for the space of three calendar months, fails to attend three consecutive meetings of the board, resigns, or through death, illness or other cause becomes incapable of further service. In the event of any vacancy occurring on a location board, the Governor-General appoints a substitute to hold office for the unexpired period during which the member whose seat has been vacated would have held office.

It is provided by regulation that each location board must meet for the despatch of business on the second Saturday in each month and that at the first meeting in each year the members of each board must elect one of their number to act as chairman.

Special meetings of boards may be convened at any time, on three days' notice, by the chairman at the instance of any member or upon the request of five or more registered holders of land within the location.

The Act empowered the Governor to promulgate regulations from time to time conferring upon location boards such of the powers vested in Village Boards of Management under the Villages Management Act, 1881, and subsequent enactments, as might be deemed to be desirable and applicable.

Regulations framed under this provision were published under Government Notice No. 936 of 1919, and briefly it may be stated that the powers and functions of the boards are the following :—

The construction and control of all watercourses in locations ; the regulation of the supply of water to irrigable agricultural lots ; the control of grass burning and of the cutting of fire-wood, brush-wood and thatching grass upon location commonages ; general supervision as regards the eradication of burr-weed in locations ; regulation of the grazing of stock upon the commonages and the impounding of stock trespassing thereon.

Section *six* of the Glen Grey Amendment Act, No. 14 of 1905, definitely made location boards subordinate to the Glen Grey District Council in that it empowered the Council to review, refer back for reconsideration, modify or rescind any resolution adopted or any decision arrived at by any board.

In practice the boards, with a few exceptions, do not function precisely as contemplated by the regulations. Many of the members are uneducated and on this account the holding of regular meetings and the keeping of minutes are often disregarded. Nevertheless the boards perform a useful service. They act as commonage rangers and water bailiffs ; they serve as the mouthpiece of the people and frequently advise the Magistrate in land administration. Service on a location board is a good apprenticeship for the District Council, for which the boards function as a college of electors.

2. THE GLEN GREY DISTRICT COUNCIL

Section *thirty-eight* of the Glen Grey Act empowered the Governor by proclamation to establish a Council styled " The District Council " for the administration of local affairs in the Glen Grey District, and by virtue of this provision the Council was actually established by Proclamation No. 32 dated the 22nd January, 1895.

The Council consists of twelve members, called councillors, with the magistrate of the district as an additional member and as chairman. Of the twelve councillors six are nominated and appointed by the Governor-General. The remaining six are nominated by the location boards (which are divided into two groups for the purpose, each group nominating three) for appointment by the Governor-General, who has the right to refer back or veto any such nomination.

The councillors hold office, during pleasure, for a period of three years, at the expiration of which they are eligible for re-appointment.

In the event of any vacancy occurring in the Council, a substitute is nominated and appointed by the Governor-General, or nominated by the location boards and appointed by the Governor-General, as the case may be, for the unexpired period during which the councillor whose seat has been vacated would have held office, and in this connection it may be remarked that district councillors become disqualified and lose their seats under the same circumstances as members of location boards.

The magistrate, as chairman, exercises at meetings a deliberative as well as a casting vote and four members of the council, with or without the magistrate, constitute a quorum.

Meetings of the Council are ordinarily held once a month (on the second Thursday in each month) and the procedure thereat is governed by regulations framed in terms of section *forty-three* of the Act and published (with other regulations under the Act) under Government Notice No. 936 of 1919.

The Act empowered the Governor to frame a tariff of fees and allowances to be paid to councillors for attendance at meetings and for the performance of such other duties as might be authorised by the Minister. Councillors are prohibited, on pain of forfeiture of their seats, from accepting any remuneration whatsoever for any duty or service performed by them as councillors otherwise than in accordance with the tariff and it is expressly provided that no councillor shall become a contractor with the Council or be interested directly or indirectly in any contract entered into with the Council.

The tariff of fees and allowances prescribed for councillors figures as Schedule I to the regulations published under Government Notice No. 936 of 1919 referred to above.

The Act empowered the District Council, for the due performance of its functions and obligations, to levy

(a) upon all persons owning immovable property in the district, other than land granted under the provisions of the Act or land owned by Europeans under title issued prior to the commencement of the Act, an immovable property rate, not exceeding twopence in the pound per annum upon the value of the rateable property ; and

(b) a rate of not less than five shillings per annum to be paid by every registered holder of quitrent title issued under the Act and by every other male adult Native resident in the district, who is fit for and capable of labour, but excluding Natives in possession of lands under ordinary quitrent title or in freehold. This rate, it may be remarked, was uniformly assessed at 10/- per annum.

The Natives Taxation and Development Act, No. 41 of 1925, which had as its object the consolidation and co-ordination of Native taxation throughout the Union, while increasing the tax payable by the ordinary Native in the Cape Province, made special provision for the allocation of funds to various councils and local authorities, so as to obviate the necessity for the imposition by such bodies of local rates upon the people save under exceptional circumstances.

Under the provisions of this Act, which came into force on the 1st January, 1926, the Glen Grey District Council receives the Native quit-rents collected in the district which were previously paid to the Government (and here it must be borne in mind that the Glen Grey Act applied the quitrent individual tenure system throughout the locations) as also any local tax collected in the district. In consideration thereof, the Council is precluded from levying the rate referred to under paragraph (b) above without the special approval of the Minister of Native Affairs.

The Council still, however, retains the right at its own instance to levy the immovable property rate mentioned in paragraph (a) above.

Section *fifty-three* of the Glen Grey Act enumerates the purposes for which the revenues of the Council are to be appropriated and this enumeration sufficiently indicates the various functions and activities which it was intended by the Legislature that the Council should exercise. The most important of these functions are the following :—

The dipping and cleansing of stock ; the construction and maintenance of roads ; the encouragement of Native agriculture ; the eradication of noxious weeds ; afforestation ; irrigation ; public health ; the construction and maintenance of bridges.

For many years the Council was called upon to contribute largely to the cost of Native education within the district. In 1920, however, by Ordinance No. 26 of that year, afterwards embodied in the Consolidated Education Ordinance of 1921, the Cape Provincial Administration assumed responsibility for the payment of all teachers' salaries and thus relieved the Council of this very heavy drain upon its resources.

The following are brief notes on certain activities and enterprises of the Council :—

(a) *Dipping :* The Council has constructed and maintains 26 cattle dipping tanks and 60 sheep tanks which have all been paid for in full. Cattle dipping is free to quitrent and local tax payers within the district but the Natives pay for the dip used for their sheep.

(b) *Roads :* The Council is responsible for the maintenance of all roads within the district except the main road from Queenstown, and from the date of Union to the 31st December, 1930, it expended £48,137 in the construction and maintenance of roads. Six road parties comprising about seventy-five labourers are constantly at work and, speaking generally, the roads are in good order.

(c) *Glen Grey District Council Farm.* At the time of the general survey of the Glen Grey district, the Government reserved two pieces of land, now known as the " Council Farm," to be used ultimately for the purposes of an agricultural school and for afforestation. The farm is well suited for these purposes, its area being 1,432 morgen of which an extent of 800 morgen is arable while the remainder affords good grazing.

For some years the property was worked under the general surveillance of the District Council, with the sanction of the Department, by Natives who cultivated portions of it on the half share system—an arrangement from which small monetary profits accrued to the Council but which was otherwise not satisfactory.

On the 22nd December, 1909, formal permission to occupy the land was granted by the Government to the District Council, for the express purpose of carrying on stock-breeding and general farming operations leading up to the establishment of an Agricultural School, subject to the following conditions :—

(1) that an annual rental of one shilling should be paid in advance for each piece of land ;

(2) that the permission might be withdrawn by the Government by giving twelve months' notice at any time ;

(3) that in the event of the land being no longer required for the purpose mentioned, the permission should *ipso facto* terminate ;

(4) that the permission should convey no claim to a grant of the land or *to compensation for improvements effected thereon.*

On obtaining the lease of the property, the Council placed a European official, who had qualified in agriculture at Elsenburg, in immediate charge of the farm, while one of the Government location inspectors was made responsible for the general superintendence of farming operations.

Since then the farm has been conducted at a financial loss by the Council for the benefit of the Natives of the district, stud stock being kept on the property and seed grain produced there in order to afford the Natives facilities for the grading up of their crops and herds.

The staff employed at the farm is as follows :—

A European farm manager.
A European overseer.
12 Adult Native labourers.
9 Native juveniles.

In addition casual labourers are employed from time to time as occasion demands for special seasonal requirements, e.g., reaping, shearing, etc.

Four hundred morgen are under cultivation, the principal crops being mealies, kafir-corn, wheat, oats, barley and lucerne.

At present there are 901 sheep, 133 cattle, 13 horses and 300 fowls upon the property—all good well-bred stock. The fees charged to the Natives for the services of pedigree animals for stud purposes are as follows :—

Stallions   10/- and 5/-.
Bulls   3/-

Well-bred three year old bulls are sold to the Natives at £3 per head, and selected young flock rams at 20/- each.

(d) *Staff*. The Council employs a permanent staff, excluding road parties, of thirteen, including three Europeans, namely the farm manager, the farm overseer and the Council inspector. The Native staff consists of a Council clerk, a dipping supervisor and eight dipping assistants.

(e) *Financial*. The revenue of the Council during the first twelve months after Union amounted to £5,946. For the twelve months ending the 31st December, 1925, it was £9,177.

For the twelve months ending the 31st December, 1926, that is for the first completed financial year under the new basis introduced by the Natives Taxation and Development Act, 1925, to which reference has already been made, the revenue of the Council was £9,752, while for the twelve months ending the 31st December, 1930, it amounted to £9,785.

The general financial position of the Council is sound.

In conclusion it should be recorded that the councillors have uniformly manifested a keen and intelligent interest in local affairs and that the Council has consequently functioned satisfactorily, while, as providing an avenue for the expression of Native public opinion, it has proved of the greatest assistance in the administration of the district.

B

TRANSKEIAN TERRITORIES COUNCIL SYSTEM

1. IN THE TRANSKEI PROPER, TEMBULAND AND EAST GRIQUALAND

Immediately after the promulgation of the Glen Grey Act on the 31st August, 1894, the Cape Administration, by virtue of the system of edictal legislation operative in the Transkei, took steps to establish councils for the administration of local affairs there, adopting in this connection the broad lines of policy which had been laid down by Parliament in respect of Glen Grey.

Under Proclamation No. 352 dated the 4th October, 1894, the Governor established four District Councils, for the districts of Butterworth, Idutywa, Nqamakwe and Tsomo respectively.

Thus arose the somewhat curious position that, though the Transkeian Council system had its origin in the Glen Grey Act, councils were actually established in the Transkei earlier than in Glen Grey, where, as has already been stated, the Council was brought into being only in January, 1895.

The Transkeian proclamation differed from the Glen Grey Act in two important respects, in that

(a) it eliminated the factor of location boards ; and

(b) it provided not only for the establishment of district councils but for the creation of a combined body representative of the various district councils and known as " The Transkei General Council." This represented a development which was logical and practical in dealing with a purely Native territory such as the Transkei but which could not be applied in so far as a more or less isolated Native district such as Glen Grey was concerned.

The Proclamation laid down that each District Council should consist of six members, of whom two should be nominated and appointed by the Governor, while the remaining four should be headmen nominated by the district headmen, at a meeting convened by the Magistrate for the purpose, for appointment by the Governor, the right being reserved to the Governor to refer back or veto any such nomination. It was further provided that the Magistrate of the District should *ex officio* be an additional member of the District Council and should preside at all meetings thereof ; that four councillors, with the Magistrate, should constitute a quorum ; that ordinary Council meetings should take place quarterly, in February, May, August, and November of each year ; that special meetings might be convened by the Magistrate at any time on his being satisfied as to the necessity for so doing ; that at each meeting the Chairman should advise the members of the subjects to be discussed ; that after discussion of each subject the members should by voting record their opinions thereon, and that the Chairman should then decide upon the action to be taken and should, if necessary, apply to the General Council for authority to carry out the proposal, or take such other steps as might be required.

The tenure of office and disqualifications prescribed in respect of councillors under the Proclamation were the same as those laid down under the Glen Grey Act.

The proclamation provided further that at its first meeting, and thereafter at the November meeting in each year, the members of the District Council of each district should nominate two of their number for appointment by the Governor to represent such district upon a " General Council " for the ensuing twelve months ; and that the said Council, which should be styled " The Transkei General Council," should consist of the Chief Magistrate of Tembuland and the Transkei, the Magistrates of Butterworth, Idutywa, Nqamakwe and Tsomo and of such other districts as might thereafter be placed under the administration of the said Council, the representatives appointed by the several constituent District Councils and four members to be nominated and appointed by the Governor.

It was prescribed that ordinary meetings of the General Council should be held before the 15th January in each year at the office of the Magistrate, Butterworth, and should be presided over by the Chief Magistrate or in his absence by the Magistrate of Butterworth.

The Chief Magistrate was empowered in his discretion at any time to convene special meetings of the General Council for the transaction of such business as might be laid before it.

The Proclamation laid down that at every meeting of the General Council the Chairman should explain the business to be considered ; that after discussion the representatives of the several districts should by voting record their opinion on the subject under consideration, and that the Chairman, after consultation with the other Magistrates present, should decide upon the action to be taken and should give the necessary instructions.

For the financing of the General Council, the Governor was empowered to levy an annual rate, of not less than 10/- in any year, upon every Native adult male residing in any area under the jurisdiction of the Council and upon every Native woman, widowed or unmarried, occupying either alone or with her family any separate portion of land or any hut in any such area.

The General Council was authorised to undertake and carry out or to assign to any District Council any work or services which might be sanctioned by the Governor, and, subject to Government approval, to appoint at suitable salaries officers, including auditors, for the transaction of its business.

The nature of the ordinary undertakings which it was intended should fall within the purview of the Council was indicated in the section providing for the appropriation of its revenue. The purposes for which appropriation of the revenue was contemplated included the construction and maintenance of roads and bridges ; the eradication of noxious weeds ; the establishment and maintenance of industrial and agricultural schools for Natives and providing generally for the educational requirements of the people ; the eradication of scab ; the establishment and maintenance of pounds ; afforestation ; the provision of an adequate water supply ; the acquisition of land for any of these purposes or for any purpose approved by the Governor ; the prevention or suppression of infectious or contagious diseases ; the prevention, removal and abatement of nuisances ; and generally all undertakings arising out of the administration of local affairs.

Further, special powers were vested in the General and District Councils to deal with the following matters under such regulations as might from time to time be approved by the Governor :—

(1) the control and management of locations and commonages ;

(2) the regulation of grazing rights upon commonages ;

(3) the enclosing of arable lands by occupiers ;

(4) the regulation of the number, position, and locality of huts and kraals upon commonages ;

(5) the regulation or prevention of beer drinking and Native dances ;

(6) the prevention of trespassing on commonages or in forests not under the control of the Forest Department ;

(7) the regulation of the cutting of wood from such forests ;

(8) the provision and regulation of public outspans ;

(9) such other matters as might from time to time be approved by the Governor.

Like the Glen Grey Act, the Proclamation made it unlawful for any councillor on pain of losing his seat to accept any salary, fee or reward for any duty or service performed by him in his capacity as such, except in accordance with a tariff framed by the Governor, or to contract with the Council or to have any interest direct or indirect in any contract entered into with the Council.

Proclamation No. 227 of 1898 made provision for the extension to the District of Butterworth of the system of individual tenure for Natives initiated by the Glen Grey Act and it followed that Act in providing for the establishment of location boards for the control and management of location commonages.   It substituted too in so far as the Butterworth

District Council was concerned the Glen Grey system under which the location boards, instead of the headmen, made recommendations for the appointment of councillors by the Governor.

Similar changes took place as regards the Nqamakwe and Tsomo District Councils by virtue of the application of the provisions of Proclamation No. 227 of 1898 to these Districts by Proclamations Nos. 41 of 1902 and 22 of 1904 respectively.

The District Council system was extended to the Kentani District by Proclamation No. 319 of 1898, which incidentally laid down that the number of the members of the Transkei General Council nominated and appointed by the Governor under Proclamation No. 352 of 1894 should be increased from four to five.

The Council system was attended by conspicuously successful results in the districts to which it had been applied and its beneficial effects in the direction of improved roads, the construction of dipping tanks, the establishment of plantations, the provision of improved educational facilites, etc., became year by year increasingly evident to the Natives themselves. This led the people of several districts, not in the Transkei proper but in Tembuland and East Griqualand, to ask for the extension of the system to themselves and in this connection it should be pointed out that from the very beginning the Government adopted and consistently maintained the policy of refraining from forcing councils upon the people in advance of their fitness or desire for them.

By 1903, it seemed that the time was ripe for the application of the system to the districts of Umtata, Mqanduli and Engcobo, in Tembuland, and Tsolo, Qumbu, Mount Frere*, Mount Fletcher and Umzimkulu in East Griqualand.

This was effected under Proclamation No. 152 of 1903*, which superseded Proclamation No. 352 of 1894 and provided for

(a) the establishment of District Councils in thirteen* districts, viz. the five districts to which Proclamation No. 352 of 1894 had been applied and the additional eight* districts specified above ; and

(b) the establishment of the *Transkeian Territories General Council* consisting of the *Chief Magistrate of the Transkeian Territories*, the

---

* It should be noted that the operation of Proclamation No. 152 of 1903 in respect of the district of Mount Frere was suspended by Proclamation No. 166 of 1903.

Mount Frere ultimately came in under the Council system by virtue of Proclamation No. 8 of 1910.

Magistrates of the various districts concerned, two representatives from each District Council nominated by the District Council for appointment by the Governor and one representative from each district nominated and appointed by the Governor.

Beyond making necessary adjustments having regard to the greatly increased field of the General Council, e.g. providing that the annual ordinary sessions of the Council should take place at Umtata instead of at Butterworth, the Proclamation introduced no radical changes but merely reiterated provisions which had previously been operative and which have already been indicated. The system of appointment of district councillors was left unchanged, i.e. the nomination and appointment of two in each district by the Governor and the nomination of four, by the headmen in communally occupied districts and by the location boards in surveyed districts, for appointment by the Governor.

The Districts of Willowvale and Elliotdale were brought under the council system by Proclamation Nos. 394 of 1903 and 114 of 1904 respectively.

Important changes were introduced by Proclamation No. 322 of 1906, which provided for the abolition of location boards in the surveyed districts, placed the general control and management of locations in such districts under the District Council and, in view of the abolition of the location boards, provided new machinery for the nomination in districts surveyed under Proclamation No. 227 of 1898 of the four district Councillors who previously had been nominated by the location boards for appointment by the Governor. The Proclamation laid down that in such districts the Council ratepayers of each location should, at a meeting held by the Magistrate, select from among the registered holders of land in the location three representatives and that the representatives of the several locations so selected should, at a further meeting to be held by the Magistrate, nominate four of their number for appointment to the District Council by the Governor, to whom the right of vetoing any such nomination was reserved.

Proclamation No. 211 of 1913 made provision for the extension to such unsurveyed districts as might desire it of the principle of four of the members of the District Council being nominated by representatives of the ratepayers, while Proclamation No. 48 of 1925 made this principle of general application.

The council system was extended to Mount Ayliff by Proclamation No. 69 of 1907 ; to St. Marks by Proclamation No. 83 of 1909 ; to

Matatiele by Proclamation No. 95 of 1911 ; and to Xalanga by Proclamation No. 310 of 1924.

Xalanga was the nineteenth district to be included under the jurisdiction of the Transkeian Territories General Council and the position then was that of the twenty districts comprising the Transkeian Territories, exclusive of Pondoland, nineteen fell under the Transkeian Territories General Council, the remaining one, Mount Currie, being preponderatingly European and containing only one small Native location.

From time to time throughout the years regulations had been framed, amended and revised in regard to the general administration of affairs falling within the purview of the general and district councils, e.g. regulations in regard to the procedure at meetings ; for the administration of council finances ; for the management and control of council, industrial and agricultural institutions ; for the management of council plantations ; for the payment of sessional and transport fees ; for the carrying out of dipping operations, etc., etc.

As these regulations were scattered throughout numerous different proclamations and government notices, it was decided in 1927 to consolidate and revise the council legislation generally. This was effected under *Proclamation No. 250 of 1927*, which consolidated and amplified the law regarding the establishment and constitution of district councils and the Transkeian Territories General Council, and under *Government Notice No. 1607 of 1927*, which consolidated the regulations for the administration of council affairs generally.

While Proclamation No. 250 of 1927 was far more elaborate and detailed than its predecessors, it introduced no radical changes. It may be noted, however, that it reiterated a provision which had been operative since 1905 for the audit of the accounts of the General Council by the Controller and Auditor-General and that, while taking due cognisance of the fact that, in terms of section *eleven* of the Natives Taxation and Development Act, all local tax and Native quitrent collected within its area of jurisdiction was payable to the Council, it provided for the imposition by the Governor-General when deemed necessary of a rate of more or less general application and also of a special stock rate upon the owners of cattle.

2. IN PONDOLAND

Pondoland was annexed to the Cape Colony by Proclamation No. 339 of 1894, issued under the provisions of Cape Act No. 5 of 1894, on the

D

25th September, 1894, that is considerably later than the remaining Native territories beyond the Kei.

The Pondos have always shown themselves to be more hide-bound by tribal ties and traditions, more conservative and less progressive than the other Transkeian Native tribes and it was not until the council system had been operative for a number of years in the Transkei proper, Tembuland and East Griqualand that there was any evidence that the Pondos were ready and willing to accept it.

The council system was introduced into Pondoland in 1911, when, under Proclamation No. 169 of that year, district councils were established for the three districts comprising what is known as Western Pondoland, viz. Libode, Ngqeleni and Port St. John's, and a general council, known as the " Pondoland General Council," was constituted for these three districts and such others as might from time to time be brought within the scope of the proclamation.

As might naturally be expected, the Pondoland District and General Councils were constituted on lines analogous to those of the Transkeian Territories, and, with the same purposes and ideas in view, were assigned similar duties and functions. An important difference existed, however, in the provisions for the appointment of councillors, the Pondoland proclamation, in recognition of the fact that the tribal system and traditions were more deeply rooted in Western Pondoland than elsewhere, providing for the nomination by the Paramount Chief of Western Pondoland, for appointment by the Governor-General, of four of the six councillors in each district council, the remaining two being nominated and appointed by the Governor-General. The chief's nominations were, however, made subject to veto by the Governor-General.

The proclamation laid down that the General Council should consist of three representatives from each council district, that the Magistrates of the various council districts should be entitled to attend and take part in its deliberations and that sessions of the council should be convened and presided over by the Chief Magistrate.

It was provided that of the three representatives of each district, one should be nominated and appointed by the Governor-General and the remaining two should be district councillors nominated by the Paramount Chief of Western Pondoland for appointment by the Governor-General.

For many years the Natives of Eastern Pondoland, comprising the districts of Bizana, Flagstaff, Lusikisiki and Tabankulu, consistently opposed the extension of the council system to themselves, but ultimately their objections were overcome and an important step forward was made when under the provisions of Proclamation No. 166 of 1927, which amplified and amended Proclamation No. 169 of 1911, the Pondoland General Council was reconstituted by the incorporation of these four districts, each of which was at the same time provided with its own district council.

This proclamation introduced a modification in so far as the selection of councillors for the Eastern Pondoland District Councils was concerned, laying down that of the six members of each such Council two should be nominated and appointed by the Governor-General, two should be nominated by the Paramount Chief of Eastern Pondoland and two by representatives of the people, the right being reserved to the Governor-General to veto these nominations. Similarly as regards the General Council, the proclamation stipulated that of the three representatives from each Eastern Pondoland district only one should be nominated by the Paramount Chief for appointment by the Governor-General, and that the remaining two should be nominated and appointed by the Governor-General but that one of them must be a member of the council of the district concerned holding that position by virtue of his having been nominated by the representatives of the people.

Proclamation No. 166 of 1927 provided further that the Paramount Chiefs of Eastern and Western Pondoland should be additional members of the General Council, with the former as an additional member of the Lusikisiki and the latter as an additional member of the Libode District Council.

The sessions of the Pondoland General Council were held annually at Port St. John's, as soon as practicable after the termination of the annual session of the Transkeian Territories General Council and lasted usually for about a week.

Proclamation No. 169 of 1911 conferred upon the Pondoland General Council the same power to levy an annual general rate upon the people as was enjoyed by the Transkeian Territories General Council and for many years this formed almost the exclusive source of the Council's revenue, the rate being uniformly assessed at 10/- per head per annum.

The Natives Taxation and Development Act, however, introduced the same financial changes as regards the Pondoland General Council as have already been noted in respect of the Transkeian Territories General Council. That Act provided that all local tax and quitrent collected from Natives living within the area of jurisdiction of the Council should be paid over to it, and, without expressly abolishing the provision for the levy of a council rate upon the people, laid down that it should not be deemed necessary for the Governor-General to impose an annual rate on behalf of the Pondoland General Council.

3. The United Transkeian Territories General Council

A very important step forward was taken when under the provisions of Proclamation No. 279 dated the 18th November, 1930, the Transkeian Territories General Council and the Pondoland General Council were amalgamated with effect from the 1st January, 1931, into a general council styled the United Transkeian Territories General Council.

This combined organisation now functions for all districts in the Transkeian Territories with the exception of Mount Currie.

Proclamation No. 279 of 1930 laid down that the seat of the United Transkeian Territories General Council should be at Umtata and that its meetings should be convened at that place from time to time by the Chief Magistrate of the Transkeian Territories upon dates to be fixed by him; it vested in the amalgamated body all powers previously enjoyed by the constituent councils in their respective areas of jurisdiction and provided for the transfer of all property, assets and liabilities of the old councils to the new body; it prescribed that all officers and employees of the Transkeian Territories General Council and the Pondoland General Council should become officers and employees of the United Transkeian Territories General Council and that as such they should retain all their existing and accruing rights.

Amalgamation in the first instance took the form of merely combining the two general councils (with their subordinate district councils) as previously existing and constituted under Proclamation No. 169 of 1911 (as amended) and Proclamation No. 250 of 1927. It was realised at the time that it would be both desirable and necessary to frame a fresh constitution for the amalgamated body, but it was considered that this essential work would best be undertaken by a committee specially appointed for the purpose at the first session of the United Council. This took place in 1931, when a recess committee, consisting of four magistrates and eight Native members of the Council, was appointed for the purpose.

The proposals of the recess committee were submitted to the United Council at its 1932 session and with certain amendments were adopted by that body. The revised constitution adopted by the Council was then submitted to the Government for consideration and, after having been approved subject to certain minor amendments, was promulgated under Proclamation No. 191 of 1932.

A copy of this Proclamation is included as Appendix " E."

The proclamation introduced no radical change as regards the constitution of district councils or the method of appointment and tenure of office of district councillors. It, however, brought the District Councils of Western Pondoland into line with those of Eastern Pondoland by reducing from four to two the number of members of each such council to be nominated by the chief and by giving representatives of the people the right to nominate two.

It provided, too, that the Chief of Tembuland should be an additional member of the Umtata District Council.

Corresponding changes were made by the proclamation as regards the General Council in that firstly, it gave the Pondoland District Councils the right each to nominate one of their number for appointment to the General Council and reduced from two to one the number from each such District Council to be nominated by the Chief of Western Pondoland in so far as Western Pondoland District Councils were concerned and by the Governor-General in so far as the Eastern Pondoland districts were concerned.

A further modification introduced by the proclamation is that it provides for the holding of six instead of four ordinary meetings of District Councils during the course of the year, such meetings to take place in the months of January, March, May, July, September and November.

The position then to-day is that there is one General Council and twenty-six District Councils functioning under it in the Transkeian Territories.

Each District Council consists of six Native members with the magistrate of the district as chairman.

Of the six Native members two are nominated and appointed by the Governor-General and in districts outside Pondoland the remaining four are nominated by an electoral college representative of the residents of the various locations for appointment by the Governor-General. In the Pondoland districts only two are nominated by representatives of the people the remaining two being nominated by the Chief of Eastern or of Western Pondoland as the case may be.

The Chiefs of Tembuland, Eastern Pondoland and Western Pondoland are respectively additional members of the Umtata, Lusikisiki and Libode District Councils.

The United Transkeian Territories General Council consists of the Chief Magistrate, who is chairman and chief executive officer, the magistrates of the districts in which there are district councils, the chiefs of Tembuland, Eastern Pondoland and Western Pondoland *ex officio* and three Native representatives from each district council.

Of these three Native representatives, one is nominated and appointed by the Governor-General and in districts outside Pondoland the remaining two are nominated by the district council concerned for appointment by the Governor-General. In Pondoland districts only one representative is nominated by the district council, the third being nominated by the Chief of Eastern or Western Pondoland as the case may be.

Representatives on the General Council are nominated and appointed annually and hold office for the calendar year.

The really important changes introduced under the revised constitution of the United Transkeian Territories General Council were the following :—

(1) Under section *twenty-one* of the proclamation, definite legislative recognition was afforded of the following matters as falling within the functions and powers of the General Council :—

(a) the initiation and consideration of any matter relating to the economic, industrial or social condition of the Native population of the Union or any part thereof in so far as it affects the Natives within the area of the jurisdiction of the Council ;

(b) the consideration of any proposed legislation or existing law which specially affects the Native population of the Union in so far as it affects the Natives within the area of jurisdiction of the Council ;

(c) the consideration of any specific matter submitted to it by the Governor-General or by the Minister ;

(d) the passing of resolutions on any such matter.

(2) The proclamation provided for the establishment of a standing Executive Committee, consisting of the Chief Magistrate together with three Magistrates and four Native members, which should be responsible

for the administration and control of all Council affairs failing within the following categories :—

Establishments :   The appointment, discipline and dismissal of pensionable officers.

Education :   Scholarships.

Agriculture :   (i) Establishment of new agricultural institutions.

      (ii) New agricultural institution buildings.

      (iii) Acquisition and disposal of farms.

      (iv) Establishment, acquisition and disposal of plantations.

Public Works :   Consideration of tenders for any service, the lowest tender for which is over £100.

General :   The institution of legal proceedings.

To appreciate the full significance of this step, it must be realised that previously the General Council, though a most important and influential body representative of over a million Natives resident between the Kei and Umzimkulu rivers, and having a large establishment of its own to say nothing of a revenue of approximately £160,000 per annum with an equivalent expenditure, was in essence purely advisory and that, while it certainly voiced Native opinion, it had no real power of its own. All actual power, authority and responsibility in connection with Council affairs was vested in the Chief Magistrate as the chief executive officer of the Council, a state of affairs which led a judge of the Supreme Court in certain proceedings in which the Council was involved to give utterance to the dictum that the Chief Magistrate was the Council.

This position has been definitely changed by the establishment of the Executive Committee.

As we have seen, the Executive Committee consists of eight members. Five of these form a quorum and four of them must be Native members of the General Council. Each Native member holds office for a period of three years unless he sooner becomes subject to some disqualification referred to in section *thirty-one* of the proclamation, in which case his seat becomes vacant and the vacancy must be filled by the nomination of a member of a district council by the General Council if then in session, or if it be not then in session by the Executive Committee itself, in which case the person nominated holds office temporarily pending confirmation of his nomination by the General Council.

The three magistrates, who are members of the Executive Committee, are selected by the Chief Magistrate and must be from districts in which the proclamation is in force. These members hold office for a definite period, but may from time to time be changed by the Chief Magistrate in his discretion, an unavoidable provision having regard to the necessity for staff changes and transfers from time to time.

The Executive Committee must meet at least once in every two months and the Chief Executive Officer may convene such additional meetings as he may from time to time deem necessary. In cases of urgency, the Chief Executive Officer may himself deal with any matter which should in the ordinary course be dealt with by the Executive Committee, but in such event he must report the action taken by him to the Executive Committee at its next meeting.

Questions arising in the Executive Committees are determined by a majority of votes of the members present. In the case of an equality of votes the Chief Executive Officer has a casting as well as a deliberative vote. In the event of any decision of the Executive Committee being contrary to the views of the chairman, he may reserve the matter at issue for decision by the Minister.

The Executive Committee is empowered to make rules for the conduct of its proceedings. Such rules must, however, be approved by the Minister.

For the rest, Proclamation No. 191 of 1932 largely reiterates provisions contained in Proclamation No. 250 of 1927, e.g. it makes the Chief Magistrate the Chief Executive Officer of the Council ; it provides for the appointment by the Governor-General of a secretary and treasurer for the Council who is made responsible to the Chief Magistrate for the collection of all revenue and other dues accruing to the Council, for the disbursement of its funds, and generally for the management of its affairs ; it authorises the appointment of such other officials as may from time to time be necessary ; it lays down that the accounts of the Council shall be audited by the Controller and Auditor-General ; it empowers the Governor-General to impose, when deemed necessary for any council purpose, a rate of more or less general application and to levy a special stock rate upon the owners of cattle.

The proclamation also reiterated a provision, which appeared in Proclamation No. 152 of 1903 and was repeated in Proclamation No. 250 of 1927, viz. that the Chief Magistrate should, in consultation with the magistrates of the council districts, deliberate upon the various matters dealt with by the General Council at any session and be responsible for giving the necessary directions or applying for the necessary authority in regard to any such matter.

This provision had long since resulted in what is known as the " official conference "—a conference of the various Magistrates of council districts held annually at Umtata, with the Chief Magistrate as chairman, immediately after the Bunga (annual session of the General Council) and lasting ordinarily about three days, of which one day is usually devoted to council business.

At this conference, the proceedings and resolutions of the General Council are brought under review and are carefully considered by the officials, who in their turn by voting record their opinions thereon. Finally, after the conclusion of the official conference, the Chief Magistrate refers to the Secretary for Native Affairs all matters dealt with at the Council session and requiring submission to the Government, advising him in respect of each item of the resolution passed by the Council, of the views adopted by the official conference and of his own considered opinion and recommendation.

GENERAL REMARKS ON TRANSKEIAN COUNCIL SYSTEM

Functions

From what has been said above, it will be appreciated that the Transkeian General and District Councils are constituted as auxiliaries to the administration, their primary and most important function being to associate the people with the control of local funds, to give them a voice in the conduct of affairs intimately affecting their own interests, to train them to constitutional methods of expressing their wishes in regard to general and local policy and to keep the Government and its officers in touch with Native feeling.

Questions are brought before the General Council by motions introduced by magistrates or individual councillors and also on submission from district councils and on reference by the Government. Considerable use is made by the Council in its proceedings of the " committee " system and generally the debates cover a wide range of subjects, including the revision of laws particularly affecting the Native population, e.g. Native marriage and inheritance, land tenure, education, stock disease regulations, the control of commonages and forests, etc.

In local administration the various district councils stand to the General Council in the relation of individual parts of a single body. They are the executive organs of the General Council, which distributes among them such duties as road maintenance, dipping operations and supervision of commonages, but remains financially responsible for their actions. Strictly speaking, they have no separate income or expenditure, but there is one common treasury into which all revenues flow and which is chargeable with the cost of the different services authorised. This arrangement has the twofold merit of allowing for local variations and ensuring, under central control, the accumulation of funds which enable the undertaking of projects beyond the means of any single district organisation. Generally speaking, district councils are responsible for the initiation of expenditure proposals which are collated and laid before the General Council in the form of annual estimates of expenditure. These estimates, after revision by the Treasurer, are considered and voted upon by the General Council and are ultimately submitted for the approval of the Governor-General.

Operations·

The operations of the General Council cover a very wide field and embrace the construction of bridges, causeways and dams ; the combating of soil erosion ; the maintenance of some four thousand three hundred miles of roads at a cost of approximately £60,000 per annum ; the construction and maintenance of dipping tanks of which there are now 588 for cattle and 867 for sheep in the twenty-six council districts ; the dipping of cattle ; the establishment and upkeep of wattle plantations ; the subsidising of the provision of hospital services for Natives ; the establishment and maintenance of agricultural schools and experimental farms for the teaching of agriculture to Natives and the improvement of stock-breeding ; the employment of Native agricultural demonstrators by means of whom a steady and continuous campaign is waged in the interests of agricultural development amongst the people ; the subsidising on the pound for pound basis of the " group " fencing of Native arable allotments ; the publication of a Native agricultural journal (*Umcebisi Womlimi Nomfuyi*), and the institution of school competitions for the eradication of noxious weeds.

The expenditure on council services for the first year after the Transkeian Territories General Council, as distinct from the Transkei General Council, came into being was £37,687. The estimates of the United Transkeian Territories General Council for the current financial year (1932-1933) are :—

General Account £150,238
Dipping Account 52,387

Total £202,625

From the 1st July, 1903, to the 30th June, 1932, the Council revenue in the Transkeian Territories amounted to £2,686,311 (which it must be borne in mind was all contributed by the Natives themselves), and the expenditure to £2,666,210. These figures, which do not include receipts and disbursements in respect of cattle dipping accounts, afford some indication of the development which has taken place and the far-reaching results which have been achieved.

The items of expenditure included in the figure specified above are the following: Scholastic education £466,696 10s. 1d.; Agricultural schools and farms £266,904 11s. 1d.; Industrial Institutions £32,675 1s. 3d.; Plantations, soil reclamation, dam construction, fences, sheep dipping tanks, agricultural shows, Native agricultural demonstrators, etc. £570,758 3s. 6d.; Public works £918,909 18s. 0d.; Public Health £59,977 7s. 2d.; Council buildings and land £44,220 17s. 7d.; Administrative establishments £128,933 14s. 4d.; Sessional expenditure £67,533 3s. 7d.; Audit £8,600 10s., and stationery, printing, surveys, pensions, etc. £101,000 6s. 9d.

The expenditure for the period from the 1st July, 1903, to the 30th June, 1932, on all council services, including dipping operations, amounted to £3,166,034. The total expenditure since the inception of the council system in the Transkeian Territories to the 30th June, 1932, is as follows :—

Transkei General Council
(1 : 1 : 1895 to 30 : 6 : 1903) £75,280 16 1
Transkeian Territories and Pondoland General
Councils and United Transkeian Territories
General Council 2,666,210 3 4
Dipping Accounts 499,823 17 6

£3,241,314 16 11

Establishment

It will be gathered from the figures furnished above that the Council has a considerable establishment of its own. This establishment is organised as follows :—

(a)   Administrative and Accounting Branch ;
(b)   Agricultural Development Branch ; and
(c)   Engineering Branch.

(a)   *General Administrative and Accounting Branch*

As previously stated, the Chief Magistrate is the chief executive officer of the General Council, while in addition the Treasurer is likewise a full-time Government official, viz. the chief clerk on the Chief Magistrate's establishment.   Much of the general administrative work of the Council is accordingly performed in the Chief Magistrate's office but the detailed work is carried out by the Council's own officials, the following staff being employed in this connection : an accountant, an assistant accountant, both Europeans, and six clerks, of whom three are Europeans and three are Natives.   In addition, a Native clerk paid by the General Council is attached to the Magistrate's staff in each council district for the performance of district council work.   In one district, Engcobo, there are two such clerks.

(b)   *Agricultural Development Branch*

The United Transkeian Territories General Council has taken over the entire control of the agricultural education and development of the Natives in the Transkeian Territories and its activities in this direction are centred in its Agricultural Development Branch at the head of which is the Council Director of Agriculture.   The Director of Agriculture is assisted by a general staff with headquarters at Umtata consisting of two European agricultural supervisors, a European plantation supervisor, two Native clerks and a messenger.   A third agricultural supervisor is stationed at the Flagstaff school of agriculture and in addition there is a general district staff consisting of some twenty plantation foremen and approximately one hundred Native agricultural demonstrators.

The General Council has established plantations in the districts of Butterworth, Engcobo, Idutywa, Matatiele, Mqanduli, Nqamakwe, Tsomo and Xalanga, and in charge of each is a Native foreman who works under the general direction and supervision of the European plantation supervisor referred to above.

Agricultural Demonstrators

The system of inculcating improved methods of agriculture amongst the Native population by practical work carried out in the locations by specially trained Natives, known as agricultural demonstrators, is so important and has been followed in the Transkeian Territories with such successful results as to deserve more than passing comment.

Native agricultural demonstrators employed by the General Council are selected from students who have completed a two years' course and have obtained a diploma at one of the Council schools of agriculture.

On first appointment such demonstrators must undergo a period of special training at one of the agricultural schools. The period of such training depends upon the circumstances of each case, but is seldom longer than six months.

During this period, demonstrators are required to perform such duties as may be placed upon them by the principal of the school of agriculture. While so employed, they are instructed in general farm work, and particularly in the methods which should be followed in demonstration work amongst Natives, namely, cultivation of lands, rotation of crops, vegetable gardening and general handling of stock and wool, etc.

After the completion of a sufficient period of training, a demonstrator is appointed to a district on probation for one year, and is placed on the fixed establishment of the General Council at the expiration of that year if his services, conduct and efficiency are satisfactory.

The general nature and scope of their duties is sufficiently indicated in the accompanying excerpt from a pamphlet issued in January, 1930, by the then Transkeian Territories General Council to the various demonstrators in its employ :—

"The main duties of demonstrators may be summarised as shown below. It should be clearly borne in mind that the list of duties enumerated is not exhaustive and the following remarks are not intended to be regarded as rules or regulations, but are intended to serve as a guide to demonstrators in the execution of the work entrusted to them.

(i) *Livestock etc.*

Advice should be freely circulated and demonstrations given as to the proper methods of animal-husbandry to be observed, the class of animal from which to breed good stock, the best method of castrating, the treatment of disease, etc. "Quality, not quantity" should be the sum total of a demonstrator's advice on matters concerning livestock. The evils of the overstocking of the commonages should be emphasised. The provision of winter feeding for livestock should be urged, especially the collection and storage of mealie stalks, the making of silos, the planting of barley, lucerne, etc. The people should on all occasions be advised to eliminate from their commonages donkeys and boer goats. Stock-owners should be persuaded to fatten and sell all surplus cattle and small stock. It is better that their sale price should be banked than that such stock should die of old age or poverty. The benefits of the dairying industry, especially the sale of cream, should be pointed out. The breeding for sale of suitable types of pigs should be stressed. Lastly the rearing of poultry and formation of egg-circles should be advocated.

(ii) *Wool*

The Natives should be strongly encouraged to breed a better class of sheep, and demonstrators should assist sheep-owners to procure good rams from the Council's Agricultural Institutions, etc., and show them how to class their wool. Natives who live close together and have the same class of wool for sale should be persuaded to work on a co-operative basis by combining to sell and thereby obtain better prices for their wool.

(iii) *Agriculture*

Demonstrators are appointed to assist Native ratepayers *inter alia* to make the most of arable and grazing lands. They should teach the best methods of cultivation and endeavour to stimulate production in every possible way. Their advice should be available as to the selection of seed, the type of seed to be planted, the places where it may be procured, the methods of combating cutworm and the mealie stalk-borer and other insect pests, and so on. The advantages accruing from market-gardening should be pointed out.

(iv) *Agricultural Shows*

The educational value of shows should be brought home to the people, who should be persuaded to exhibit at the shows which serve their district. Demonstrators must advise Natives what to exhibit and assist them in selecting the exhibits for the various classes.

(v) *Use of Agricultural Implements*

The care and use of all agricultural machinery should be explained and demonstrated wherever possible. Where a community desires to purchase improved implements, the demonstrator should be in a position to advise as to what implements are required and as to where they can be obtained.

(vi) *Fertilisers*

The advantages accruing from the use of fertilisers, and where necessary, agricultural lime, should be brought home to allotment-holders. When kraal or green manure is not available, the demonstrator should encourage the use of prepared fertilisers. They should point out to the people that by the purchase of fertiliser in bulk through Farmers' Associations, (i.e. on a co-operative basis), this commodity can be procured more cheaply than otherwise.

(vii) *Farmers' Associations, etc.*

As farmers' associations and agricultural co-operative thrift and credit societies are of great value to the Natives, demonstrators should make a point of advocating and encouraging the establishment of these bodies wherever possible, and should endeavour to lecture to the members on agricultural subjects at their meetings.

(viii) *Lectures*

A demonstrator's primary duty is not to preach but to demonstrate agriculture ; there are occasions, nevertheless, when much good can come of a few words spoken at the right time. Meetings should therefore be held at chiefs' and headmen's kraals and at schools from time to time, but it should not be necessary for these to be called oftener than once a month.

(ix) *Caravan Tours*

Upon notification by the Director of Agriculture of the dates on which meetings will be held by the officers taking part in the periodic caravan tours, demonstrators will be expected to circulate this information as widely as possible, and, in fact, to act as advertising agents, to ensure a good attendance of people at each meeting. They themselves must, of course, attend the meetings held in their districts.

(x) " *Umcebisi wo-Mlimi no-Mfuyi* "

All demonstrators are furnished with free copies of the Council's agricultural journal. They must endeavour to procure as many subscribers as possible to this paper, and may assist by collecting their subscriptions and remitting them to the Director of Agriculture.

(xi) *Noxious Weeds*

It is the duty of agricultural demonstrators to report to the Magistrates of their districts the presence of all proclaimed noxious weeds wherever found by them in the execution of their duties. In order to prevent the placing of difficulties in the way of the efficient performance of the duties of demonstrators, the Magistrate will treat such reports as confidential and not disclose the source of information, nor will the demonstrators be called as witnesses in cases where criminal proceedings have resulted from the Police having instituted enquiries in consequence of any such report. They should bear in mind, nevertheless, that serious notice will be taken if established weeds are discovered in situations which ought, by the exercise of proper diligence, to have been noticed by them.

(xii) *Soil Erosion*

Natives should be advised how to prevent or combat soil erosion by the erection of weirs across sluits and dongas, the planting of trees and grasses, and fencing. The " stitch-in-time " policy should always be strongly advocated. Magistrates should be advised of places on the location commonages where reclamation work is necessary.

(xiii) *Dams and Irrigation*

Although the General Council is bearing the whole cost of construction of domestic and stock dams on location commonages, demonstrators should nevertheless advise the people how to make these structures and how to carry out small irrigation schemes. Magistrates should be advised of suitable sites for dams, etc.

(xiv) *Winter Short Courses*

Winter short courses are held at the Council's Schools of Agriculture and it should be the duty of demonstrators to make these as widely known as possible and to advise Native agriculturists to attend.

(xv) *School Gardens*

The advice and assistance of a demonstrator must be placed at the disposal of Native school managers and principals who desire their help in teaching children the proper methods of agriculture by means of school gardens.

(xvi) *Diaries and Reports*

Each demonstrator must keep a daily dairy of his work and travelling, giving details of the lands ploughed, the acreage of each. plot, the name of the owner, and as much other information as possible from an agricultural point of view. A general report must be added at the end of the diary for the month, furnishing a summary of the month's work, giving details of weather conditions during the month and the condition of the stock and crops in the locality where the demonstrator has been employed. When the demonstrator attends the Magistrate's Office to receive his salary, he must produce his diary to the Magistrate for inspection and also leave with that officer the copy which will be transmitted by the Magistrate to the Director of Agriculture.

(xvii) *Care and Custody of Implements*

Each demonstrator is supplied with a set of agricultural implements, and must keep a proper list of these. He is responsible for the implements handed over to him and if any loss or damage occurs which may be due to his neglect or default he may be called upon to replace such implements or make good the damage. The following rules in the keeping of the stock lists must be observed :—

(a) Immediately any new machinery or implements are received in stock they should be entered in the list.

(b) The demonstrator must produce the list at any time when called upon by the Magistrate, Director of Agriculture or any other duly authorised officer.

(c) In the event of a demonstrator leaving the Council service this list should be produced and checked by the officer who takes his place.

(d) A " remarks " column should be included in the list and in this will be entered the reasons for striking any articles off the list. No articles may be struck off the list without the authority of the Director of Agriculture.

(xviii) *Records of Production*

Records must be kept of all plots worked by the demonstrator. In addition, for the purpose of comparison, records must be kept of the yield of plots worked by the owner which adjoin those plots worked by the demonstrator. These records must include acreage in each case, the quantity of seed sown, the amount of labour on each plot— including hoeing—and the actual yield. In July each year a return must be sent through the Magistrate giving details as above for the previous half year in respect of mealies, vegetables, etc., and in January of each year giving details of winter crops, vegetables, etc.

(xix) *Demonstrators' Conference*

Once a year, conferences of demonstrators will be called (usually at the Schools of Agriculture) when these officers may consider and discuss freely and openly the problems and difficulties which have occurred during the year in their work. In addition they will at these conferences be kept in touch with the activities of the Council's agricultural institutions and the modern methods of agriculture, and will receive a refresher course to enable them more efficiently to perform their duties. Demonstrators should note that subjects relating to their conditions of appointment (e.g. salary, discipline, animal transport, etc.) should not be discussed at these conferences which are limited to the objects named above.

(xx) *General*

Demonstrators are supervised by and receive instructions and advice from the Director of Agriculture and the Agricultural Supervisors as to the best methods to be adopted in the locality where the demonstrator is employed. They must remember that success depends not alone on the possession of expert knowledge but also on the manner in which such expert knowledge is applied. A practical demonstration is generally of more use than many explanations. Much must inevitably be left to the initiative, ability and efficiency of each demonstrator, who must do all in his power to develop and foster agricultural and pastoral progress in his area."

At least three (in most cases four) agricultural demonstrators are now employed in every district falling under the jurisdiction of the United Transkeian Territories General Council and the following excerpt from the report of the Director of Agriculture submitted to the Council at its 1932 session testifies to the beneficial results attending their efforts:

"The Agricultural Supervisors report good progress in the work carried out by the 86 demonstrators in the field, with a few exceptions, and the progress made by the people in contact with their operations, resulting in the purchase of better implements, better tillage and cultivation, and the use of good quality seed purchased from the schools of agriculture and seedsmen. In this latter respect progress has been very marked in the southern area, where only in a few cases have demonstrators used poor seed, Teko Yellow being the variety of seed most generally used. In some of the locations it is grown almost exclusively.

Their increased use of fertiliser obtained through demonstrators is a most healthy sign of progress, supplies through these officers amounting to $22\frac{1}{2}$ tons in the northern area alone, while one trader in the Mount Frere District of the central area sold 7 tons to the people. The use of kraal manure is being practised to a greater extent than in former years.

There are some very remarkable cases of individual effort on the part of some of the demonstrators resulting in progressive steps being taken by the people. The essential part of success is that the people must give themselves up wholeheartedly to the new methods, and take a pride in their agricultural operations and the increased yields which will result.

In some instances farmers are feeding their oxen on surplus grain harvested in order to maintain the condition of draught animals, are co-operating in the purchase of implements and collecting money to fence lands, buying grain-tanks to store surplus maize, using horses and mules for planting and cultivation, and growing wheat, potatoes and other crops in rotation.

This progress is the outcome of agricultural education at, and radiating influence of, the schools of agriculture, and actual demonstration work in the field.

Conservatism amongst the people in some areas is still evident, and is very forcefully evinced in connection with the difficulty we have in even obtaining sufficient plots for demonstrators to work in the first season after their location in some areas ; but this difficulty usually disappears after a year's work in any particular area, as a result of observations made by the people on demonstration work as a whole."

Agricultural Institutions and Farms

In addition to general agricultural administration throughout the districts, the following special agricultural institutions and farms maintained by the Council fall under its Agricultural Development Branch :—

Tsolo School of Agriculture in the Tsolo district ; Teko School of Agriculture in the Butterworth district ; Flagstaff School of Agriculture in the Flagstaff district ; Mbuto farm in the Tsolo district ; Nzulweni farm in the Mqanduli district ; the Butterworth experimental farm, and the Cala Agricultural Depôt.

(i) *Tsolo Agricultural School*

The School of Agriculture at Tsolo was started in 1913 with four students. At present there are fifty-two students. The question of providing accommodation for ten additional students is under consideration. Every year more applications for admission to the school are received than it is possible to accept. A very high standard of training in agriculture is provided at the institution and excellent results have been obtained both on the theoretical and on the practical side.

The staff of the institution consists of a principal, three European and two Native lecturers with a Native boarding house master, a Native matron and a Native clerk.

Winter vacation courses are held in connection with the school, which are attended by Native farmers from the surrounding districts and, in fact, from so far afield as Matatiele.

The amenities of the institution include a library, debating society and sports club.

In order to encourage the Natives to breed a hardier type of cattle more suitable to the conditions obtaining in the majority of districts in the Transkeian Territories, a stud herd of Afrikander cattle has been introduced at the Tsolo School of Agriculture.

A limited number of stock, well-bred cattle, sheep, pigs and poultry, are kept at the school and sales are effected to Natives desirous of improving their own stock. One thorough-bred stallion is kept which is made available to Natives for stud purposes on payment of a small fee of ten shillings in the case of local tax payers and one pound in the case of Natives other than local tax payers.

Crops grown by the students under the direction of the staff include mealies, pumpkins, beans, peanuts, sunflowers, oats, wheat, teff, millet, potatoes and chou moellier, and in addition there are extensive orchards and vegetable gardens and a large plantation.

The area of the Tsolo School of Agriculture property is 1,641 morgen.

(ii) *Teko School of Agriculture, Butterworth District*

The Teko School of Agriculture in the Butterworth district was established by the General Council in 1922 to meet the position created by the fact that the Tsolo institution could no longer cope with the demands made upon it by Natives desirous of obtaining agricultural training. The position to-day is that this school is likewise taxed to its utmost capacity. There are fifty-six students on the roll and the question of providing facilities for ten additional students is at present under consideration.

As with the Tsolo institution, there are more applications for admission to this school than can be accepted.

The institution is run on very much the same lines as the Tsolo one and the staff maintained is the same as at Tsolo, viz. a European principal, three European lecturers and two Natives, a boarding master, a matron and a clerk, the last mentioned three being Natives.

The school enjoys the same amenities as the Tsolo institution but naturally the type of farming carried on there is that most suited to the surrounding coastal districts and differs somewhat from the highveld farming at Tsolo.

Winter vacation courses are held as at Tsolo and the school authorities co-operate in so far as possible with neighbouring Native farmers' associations by sending out members of the staff at convenient intervals to the surrounding districts to lecture on various subjects of particular interest to the local agricultural community.

Well-bred cattle, sheep, pigs and poultry are kept at the farm and the services of pedigree animals, including a stallion, are made available to Natives for stud purposes on payment of a small fee.

Crops grown include mealies, beans, potatoes, pumpkins, millet, cow-peas, sunflowers, mangels, lucerne, barley, oats, teff, Sudan grass and vegetables. A type of mealie carefully propagated at this school from the ordinary German yellow type in order to suit territorial conditions has met with much success and is now well known by the distinctive name of the Teko Yellow mealie.

The area of the Teko School of Agriculture property is 641 morgen;

(iii) *Flagstaff School of Agriculture*

The Flagstaff School of Agriculture was opened on the 5th August, 1930. It had long been felt that there was urgent need for the establishment of a third school of agriculture in the Transkeian Territories and it was considered that this should be located in Pondoland having regard to the fact that the majority of the Pondoland districts are remote from the Tsolo and Teko agricultural schools.

Land of average fertility was selected for the institution and an area of 690 morgen was specially granted by the Government to the Pondoland General Council for the purpose.

Buildings of the most modern type were erected and the total cost of the institution, which was met entirely from the funds of the Pondoland General Council, amounted to approximately £20,000.

This agricultural school is conducted very much on the same lines as the Tsolo and Teko institutions and it carries the same staff.

The number of students is at present forty-six.

Suitable orchards and a plantation have been laid out and beans, teff, millet, potatoes, oats, mangels and vegetables are grown.

As at the other agricultural schools a good class of stock and poultry is kept at the institution.

(iv)   *Mbuto Farm, Tsolo District*

This property, which comprises an area of 1890 morgen near Tsolo formerly known as the " Tsolo Remount Farm," was acquired by the Council from the Government many years ago and is utilised primarily as a sheep experimental farm.

A flock of approximately 2,750 sheep of a fine type is maintained on the property and the main object is to make the services of stud rams available to Natives and to dispose of as many well-bred animals as possible from time to time to the people at actual cost price.

A manager (European) and an assistant manager (European) are employed on the farm which is conducted on modern up-to-date lines as an object lesson to the Natives.

While the main object of Mbuto is the development and improvement of sheep farming amongst the Natives, the agricultural side has not been neglected and considerable quantities of maize are grown and in addition there are extensive wattle plantations upon the property.

(v)   *Nzulweni Farm, Mqanduli District*

This property was acquired by the Council as a cotton experimental station.   The cotton growing venture did not prove a success and, in fact, the Council paid rather dearly to establish the fact that conditions in the coastal districts of the Transkeian Territories are not suitable for the cultivation of cotton on a commercial basis. A European manager was employed upon the farm for many years but upon his retirement on pension in 1929 it was considered advisable to replace him by a Native demonstrator and to convert the property into a centre for the demonstration of good farming methods, for which purpose it is utilised to-day. The chief crops now grown there are maize, tobacco and fruit.

(vi) *Butterworth Experimental Farm*

This property, which comprises approximately 90 morgen adjoining the Butterworth municipal area, was originally used for the purposes of an industrial institution, but as this did not prove successful it was subsequently utilised for seed production, poultry breeding and vegetable growing, supplies of vegetables being regularly sold at the Butterworth market. The farm is under the charge of a Native manager and serves to demonstrate intensive methods of agriculture.

(vii) *Cala Agricultural Depôt*

The Cala Agricultural Depôt was established in 1927 when a favourable opportunity presented itself for the acquisition by the Council of a suitable area of ground in the Xalanga District for the purpose. It is used as a centre for the demonstration of intensive methods of farming and for the production of seed wheat and mealies for distribution amongst the people at cost price. The depôt is in charge of a Native agricultural demonstrator.

General

In addition to its numerous other activities, the Agricultural Branch of the Transkeian Territories General Council edits a Native agricultural journal known as the *Umcebisi Womlimi Nomfuyi*. This journal is published every second month and serves a most useful and valuable purpose. The subscription is one shilling per annum, or twopence per copy, and the number of Native subscribers is rapidly approaching three thousand. Informative articles are published in every issue by technical and expert officers of the Council and the correspondence columns are widely used for the discussion of difficulties experienced by agriculturists.

Numerous Native agricultural shows are held under the aegis of the General Council and it may be mentioned in this connection that there are no less than twelve show-holding agricultural societies in the Territories. These shows serve not only to promote keen competition amongst the Natives but are of immense value to them from the educative stand-point as the judges and Government and Council experts, who are invariably in attendance, not only point out faults and furnish advice as to how they may be remedied but give lectures to the exhibitors and visitors on agricultural matters.

A Central Show is now held annually at Umtata after the district shows have been held. This enables prize-winners at the local shows to compete among themselves, but is not limited to such prize-winners. The Central Show is proving a valuable aid to the raising of the standard of exhibits and to improvement in agriculural development generally.

Important work is being carried out in combating soil erosion in the districts and steady progress has been made in this direction. The work is carried out under the direction of the magistrates of the districts concerned, who obtain any necessary advice and assistance from the Council Director of Agriculture and his staff. The total expenditure of the Council on soil reclamation work up to the 30th June, 1932, amounted to £22,907 and an annual provision of approximately £6,000 is voted by the Council for the purpose.

Other activities undertaken by the Council in connection with the agricultural development of the people include the following :—

(i)   Motor caravan demonstration tours, conducted for the purpose of penetrating to every corner of the Territories to teach and demonstrate proper methods of agriculture and animal hus-bandry.

(ii) Farmers' associations, the formation of which has been urged and encouraged by the Council's agricultural staff. At the end of 1931 there were thirty-three small farmers' associations and eleven district associations.

(iii) Ploughing and maize-growing competitions, which have been established by the Council's agricultural staff, and towards which the Council contributes prizes.

(iv) The provision of threshing machines to enable the Natives to thresh their wheat at a small charge.

(c)   *Engineering Branch*

The general staff of the engineering department of the General Council consists of a qualified civil engineer, three assistant engineers, three road inspectors (with headquarters respectively at

Umtata, Butterworth and Flagstaff), one European and one Native clerk, a permanent foreman of works, a motor mechanic and a Native caretaker-storekeeper. In addition numerous gangs of Natives, with overseers, are employed on the various works undertaken from time to time.

The work of the branch consists for the most part of :—(1) the construction and maintenance of roads, bridges, causeways, buildings and cattle and sheep dipping tanks ; (2) the furnishing of expert advice to the people in regard to the building of small dams, the carrying out of minor irrigation schemes and the construction of water furrows ; and (3) the preparation of plans and specifications for the erection of Council buildings and works and calling for tenders therefor.

As some indication of the extent of these operations, it may be mentioned that during the financial year 1931-1932, nine bridges were under construction at an estimated cost of £8,600 and two causeways at a cost of £450, while the amount provided for the construction and maintenance of roads (exclusive of causeways) for the year was £60,570. £1,500 was provided for sheep tank construction and repairs, £2,750 for cattle tank repairs, £10,533 for cattle tank construction and £2,275 for various buildings during the same financial year. Much of the building construction programme at the Flagstaff School of Agriculture was carried out departmentally by the Engineering Branch which, in addition, prepared all the plans, specifications and bills of quantities in connection with the work.

The Council provides motor transport at the schools of agriculture, for public works where desirable, and for the use of members of the field staff. It has at present six motor cars, two car-trucks and twenty-six motor lorries and trucks.

Pension Fund

Having briefly reviewed the work of the various branches of the United Transkeian Territories General Council, it remains to be stated that the Council has for the benefit of its permanent employees its own pension and gratuity fund, established in the first instance by the Transkeian Territories General Council on the most modern and up-to-date methods under Proclamation No. 143 of 1921. The number of council employees contributing to the pension fund is at present one hundred and eighty-eight and the amount of the fund is approximately £30,000.

Subsidies

The Council subsidises the following hospitals in the Transkeian Territories having regard to the services rendered to Natives at these institutions :—

Butterworth Hospital : Amount of subsidy for financial year 1931-1932 £540
Sir Henry Elliot Hospital, Umtata :   ,,   ,,   ,,   £2722
All Saints' Hospital, Engcobo :   ,,   ,,   ,,   £140
Kokstad Hospital :   ..   ,,   ,,   ,,   £143
Holy Cross Hospital, Lusikisiki :   ,,   ,,   ,,   £500
Tayler Bequest Hospital, Matatiele :   ,,   ,,   ,,   £118
St. Barnabas Hospital, Ngqeleni :   ,,   ,,   ,,   £213
Sulenkama Hospital, Qumbu :   ,,   ,,   ,,   £204
St. Lucy's Hospital, Tsolo :   ,,   ,,   ,,   £352

The Council's vote for Public Health also provides for meeting half the cost of treating Native tubercular patients from the Transkeian Territories at the Nelspoort Sanatorium, and for an annual grant of £70 to the South African (Native and Coloured) Health Society, in return for which the Society provides each district councillor and Native principal teacher in the Territories with a copy of the *Health Society Magazine*.

The General Council maintains a maximum number of fifty scholarships in operation, which are awarded to promising Native students to permit of their receiving higher education at the South African Native College at Fort Hare. The value of the scholarships, which ordinarily run for five years, is £30 per annum. Fifteen of these scholarships are held by Pondoland students.

Large Stock Dipping Operations

From the 1st July, 1915, cattle dipping operations in districts which fell under the jurisdiction of the Transkeian Territories General Council have been paid for from funds contributed by the Natives by means of stock rates. The Magistrate and District Council of each district are responsible for carrying out the dipping operations and, subject to control by the Chief Magistrate and co-operation with the Veterinary Sub-Department of the Department of Agriculture, they take the necessary steps for suppression of East Coast Fever.

In Pondoland the cost of cattle dipping operations was for very many years met from the funds of the Pondoland General Council and this constituted a heavy drain (approximately £15,000 per annum) upon the Council's resources.

When, however, the Pondoland General Council amalgamated with the Transkeian Territories General Council in the United Transkeian Territories General Council, the people accepted the principle of a special stock rate for the dipping of large stock and provision for the imposition of such a rate in Pondoland was made in the " amalgamating " proclamation, No. 279 of 1930.   Since then the cost of dipping large stock in Pondoland has been met from the proceeds of this stock rate and not from Council funds.

The construction of cattle dipping tanks and major repairs thereto are arranged for and supervised by the Engineering Branch of the General Council, minor repairs being carried out by members of the dipping staff as part of their ordinary duties.

The dipping staff employed by the United Transkeian Territories General Council, (excluding tank labourers and the dipping staff in the Idutywa District, where dipping operations are controlled by the Idutywa Native Dipping Committee which functions without reference to the Council) is as follows :—

European Dipping Supervisors ..	29
Native Dipping Supervisors ..	9
Native Assistant Dipping Supervisors	30
Dipping Foremen	288
	356

C

OTHER FORMS OF LOCAL GOVERNMENT

Other forms of local government operative in certain Native areas prior to the passing of the Native Affairs Act, No. 23 of 1920, were—

1. Boards of Management under the Mission Stations and Communal Reserves Act, No. 29 of 1909 (Cape), and

2. Native Reserve Boards constituted under Ordinance No. 6 of 1907 of the Orange Free State.

1. BOARDS OF MANAGEMENT UNDER THE MISSION STATIONS AND COMMUNAL RESERVES ACT, No. 29 OF 1909, OF THE CAPE OF GOOD HOPE

The Cape Mission Stations and Communal Reserves Act, No. 29 of 1909, was passed " to provide for the better management and control of certain mission stations and certain lands reserved for the occupation of certain tribes or communities and for the granting of titles to the inhabitants of such stations and reserves."

The necessity for the Act lay in the fact that from time to time the Government in order to afford them facilities for carrying on their work had granted certain lands to missionary societies in trust for the Natives or Coloured persons in occupation thereof, the areas in question thereafter being administered by the local representative of, and under rules and regulations framed by, the Society concerned.

In the course of time, disputes between the missionary body on the one hand and the Native or Coloured community on the other arose in many instances and so frequent did these become that it was considered advisable to create machinery for the separation, when desired, of the religious from the secular interest, in other words, for a definition of rights as between the Society and the people. To this end, it was provided that the Act might be applied by Proclamation to any such mission station provided that the trustees consented and the wishes of the people had been ascertained by consultation in a manner to be prescribed by regulation.

Upon the application of the Act to any mission station, a grant outright is, after due enquiry by a commissioner specially appointed for the purpose, made to the Missionary Society concerned of the land actually occupied by it for church, school, residential and other purposes, and the remaining extent of the mission station is then divided into separate holdings and allotted to the Coloured or Native residents, existing lines of occupation being followed as far as possible and due provision being made for commonage. Particulars of allotments are recorded in a register kept for the purpose.

For the control and regulation of the affairs of the Native or Coloured community thus established, a Board of Management is provided by the Act. The Board consists of ten persons, of whom six are elected from the registered occupiers and three appointed by the Governor-General (one of whom is nominated by the Missionary Society) with the Magistrate of the District *ex officio* as Chairman. The members of the Board hold office for twelve months but are eligible for re-appointment on expiration.

The Board is vested with certain of the duties and functions of a Village Management Board, e.g. the control of roads, fences, sanitation, water supply and use of the commonage, and it has power, subject to the approval of the Governor-General, to make regulations in regard to such matters. In addition, the Act specifically authorises the Board to levy a rate of not less than ten shillings a year upon each adult male resident of or female property owner in the mission station for the purpose of defraying the costs of administration.

The Act makes provision for the introduction of a system of individual tenure by the Governor-General consequent upon the adoption of a resolution in favour thereof by the board of management and ratification of such resolution by the majority of the registered occupiers present at a public meeting convened specially for the purpose of considering the matter.

Upon the introduction of the individual tenure system, survey is effected and the allotments are granted under title, free of quitrent, to the registered occupiers, who thereupon, of course, become registered owners.

Eight mission stations have now been brought under the operation of the Act, viz. Shiloh, in the District of Queenstown ; Goshen, in the district of Cathcart ; Mamre, in the District of Malmesbury ; Enon, in the district of Uitenhage ; Zoar in the district of Ladismith ; Pniel, in the district of Paarl ; Genadendal, in the district of Caledon ; and Ebenezer Kolonie in the district of Van Rhynsdorp.

Up to the present only one of these Mission stations, Goshen in the district of Cathcart, has been surveyed for the purposes of individual tenure.

It should be noted that of the mission stations enumerated above only two are occupied solely by Natives, viz., Shiloh and Goshen ; that Enon is a mixed settlement of Coloured people and Natives and that the remainder are purely Coloured communities. The Native Affairs Department has, however, been made responsible for the general administration of the Act wheresoever applied.

Act No. 29 of 1909 also provided for the application of its principles in a slightly modified form to the so-called communal reserves in Namaqualand, which are Coloured communities established by virtue of the activities of missionary organisations in that part of the country. There are four such communal reserves, viz. Concordia, Komaggas, Leliefontein and Steinkopf, comprising in all an area of approximately 1,155,500 morgen.

Each of these communal reserves has been proclaimed under the Act and is administered by its own Board of Management and under its own regulations.

2. NATIVE RESERVE BOARDS UNDER ORDINANCE NO. 6 OF THE ORANGE FREE STATE

The Natives Reserves Ordinance, No. 6 of 1907, of the Orange Free State provides for the establishment, within such areas as the Governor may proclaim as Native Reserves, of local boards consisting of a Chairman and Vice-Chairman (Europeans) and not less than five or more than seven Coloured* members. Members are nominated to the Board by the Governor and hold office for a term of three years. Board meetings must be held at least once per quarter and minutes of the meetings are to be kept and questions decided by a majority of the members present.

The Ordinance authorises the Boards to deal with matters of local interest, such as roads, fences, sanitation, water rights, dipping tanks, schools, etc., and section *ten* thereof empowers them, subject to the approval of the Governor, to make regulations on a variety of topics, including the following :—

(a) the grazing and watering of cattle on common lands and the fees, if any, payable therefor by the inhabitants and visitors respectively ;

(b) the issue of licences and permits for brick-making, quarrying, digging and excavating ground, gravel or stone and for cutting and removing wood upon the Reserves and the fees payable for the same ;

(c) the establishment and regulation of residential locations within the Reserves and the control of the same ;

(d) afforestation, sanitation and the abatement of nuisances ;

(e) the supply, use and distribution of water.

For the purpose of providing the boards with adequate funds for the discharge of their duties and responsibilities, the Ordinance empowered them to levy a location tax, not exceeding one pound in any year, on each Coloured male resident of the reserves between the ages of sixteen and sixty.

The basis of the boards' finances was, however, as with the Glen Grey District Council and the Transkeian Territories General Council, changed by the Natives Taxation and Development Act, which, as amended by the Natives Taxation and Development (Amendment) Act, No. 37 of 1931, provided that all local tax collected from Natives resident within the area of jurisdiction of any such board should, subject to its estimates of expenditure for the tax year having been approved by the Governor-General, be paid over to it, and, while not repealing the provision for the levy of the location tax referred to above, stipulated that no such tax should be levied without the express consent of the Minister of Native Affairs.

---

*For the purposes of Ordinance No. 6 of 1907 and other O.F.S. laws, Natives are included under the term " Coloured."

There are only three Native reserves in the Orange Free State, viz. Witzieshoek in the Harrismith district and Thaba 'Nchu and Seliba in the district of Thaba 'Nchu. All three of these have been proclaimed under the provisions of the Ordinance and are administered by boards constituted thereunder. The chairman of the Witzieshoek Board is the Assistant Native Commissioner (formerly known as the Commandant) stationed in the reserve, while the Native Commissioner, Thaba 'Nchu, is chairman of the Thaba 'Nchu and Seliba bodies.†

Each reserve has its own set of regulations promulgated under the Ordinance. The Witzieshoek regulations are restricted in their ambit but those of Thaba 'Nchu and Seliba have a wide scope dealing *inter alia* with such matters as the eradication of noxious weeds, the quarrying of stone and making of bricks within the reserves, the allotment and registration of land for cultivation or homestead purposes, the restriction of grazing, the forfeiture of rights to lands on account of non-beneficial occupation and the control of commonage.

D

COUNCILS UNDER THE NATIVE AFFAIRS ACT NO 23 OF 1920

The Native Affairs Act, No. 23 of 1920, to which reference has already been made, empowered the Governor-General on the recommendation of the Native Affairs Commission to establish a local council for the whole or any portion of any area set aside as a Native area by Parliament.

The Act stipulated that the members of any such Council should not exceed nine in number and that they should all be Natives but that an officer in the public service might be designated by the Minister of Native Affairs to preside at the meetings of and generally to act in an advisory capacity to any local council.

Powers

A local council has statutory power within its area of jurisdiction to provide :—

---

†The northern portion of the farm " Bofulo," which formerly was included in the Seliba Reserve, has recently been proclaimed a separate reserve for the purposes of Ordinance No. 6 of 1907, which was applied to it in modified form by Proclamation No. 29 of 1933. (Vide page 28 *supra*.)

The reason for the separate proclamation of this area is that a " Coloured " as distinct from a Native community is resident thereon.

(a) for the construction and maintenance of roads, drains, dams and furrows and for the prevention of erosion ;

(b) for an improved water supply ;

(c) for the suppression of diseases of stock by the construction and maintenance of dipping tanks and in any other manner whatsoever ;

(d) for the destruction of noxious weeds ;

(e) for a suitable system of sanitation ;

(f) for the establishment of hospitals ;

(g) for improvement in methods of agriculture ;

(h) for afforestation ;

(i) for educational facilities ;

and generally for any such purposes which can be regarded as proper to local administration, as may be committed to it by direction of the Governor-General.

Further, for carrying out any of the purposes indicated above or committed to them by the Governor-General, local councils are expressly authorised by the Act to acquire and hold land or interests in land. In addition, they are empowered, subject to the approval of and to revision by the Governor-General, to make bye-laws in regard to any such matter and to prescribe the fees which shall be payable for any service rendered.

To provide local councils with the " sinews of war," the Act laid down that they might levy a rate not exceeding one pound in any one year upon each adult male Native ordinarily resident within their respective areas of jurisdiction.

Further, section *eleven* of the Natives Taxation and Development Act, No. 41 of 1925, provides for the payment to any local council, subject to its estimates of expenditure in respect of the tax year having been approved by the Governor-General, of the amount of local tax and Native quitrent collected within its area of jurisdiction.

In addition, local councils are entitled to all fees collected in terms of their respective bye-laws and fines recovered for contraventions of the same.

Regulations

The Act authorises the Governor-General to make regulations applying either generally or in particular areas :—

(a) providing for the consultation of the inhabitants of areas for which a council is to be established, and for the selection or election of members of such councils ;

(b) providing for the periods of office and remuneration of such members ;

(c) prescribing the procedure of councils and the conduct of their business ;

(d) providing for the appointment and duties of officers of councils;

(e) prescribing the method according to which rates and fees shall be collected and brought to account, the exemptions which may be allowed, and the penalties to be imposed on persons failing to pay such rates and fees,

and generally for the better carrying out of its provisions relating to local councils.

Regulations dealing with these topics are contained in Government Notice No. 50 of 1930, as amended by Government Notice No. 931 of 1932.

These regulations lay down the procedure to be followed for the consultation of the people concerned in regard to any proposal or recommendation for the establishment of a local council ; they specify disqualifications preventing any person from being appointed as a member of a council and the circumstances under which a sitting member shall lose his seat ; they prescribe the mode of procedure where the constitution of any council provides for the election of any number of its members ; they provide that local councils shall enter upon office on the 1st October in every second year, that members shall be elected or nominated, as the case may be, for a period of two years and that ordinarily meetings of councils shall take place on the first Wednesday in the months of January, March, May, July, September and November in each year ; they empower the chairman at any time on seven days' notice to members to convene a special meeting of any council for the transaction of particular business ; they stipulate that two-thirds of the members of a council shall constitute a quorum ; they lay down the procedure for the transaction of business at meetings and provide for the recording of minutes, copies of which must, with the decisions arrived at, be forwarded to the Secretary for Native Affairs at the conclusion of each meeting ; they specify the fees payable to members for attendance at meetings and for the performance of other council duties ; they make provision for the appointment of a treasurer for each council who ordinarily must be a member of the public service designated by the Minister ; they empower councils, subject to the Minister's

F

approval, to make any other appointments suitable and necessary for the exercise of their powers and the discharge of their duties ; they provide for the timely preparation and submission for approval of annual estimates of revenue and expenditure ; they lay down detailed rules for the guidance of council officers in the discharge of duties involving the receipt, custody, banking or payment of council funds and the keeping of books and accounts, and, lastly, they provide for the annual audit of the accounts of each council by the Controller and Auditor-General of the Union.

Amendments

The Native Affairs Act of 1920 came into operation on the 5th August of that year and as soon as practicable thereafter the Native Affairs Commission, which adopted the principle that local councils should be established wherever possible, proceeded to this end to hold consultative meetings with Natives at various centres and to submit recommendations to the Government. In the light of these discussions and recommendations, it soon became apparent that there were certain difficulties which must be overcome before the establishment of local councils could satisfactorily be proceeded with.

In the first place, it was found that the provisions of the Act of 1920 were hardly suitable for all the areas where it was considered that councils might with advantage be established. The stage of development reached by certain communities, though it might justify a certain degree of participation in the administration of local affairs, did not permit of the delegation of the comparatively extensive powers contemplated by the Act. It was, therefore, felt that provision should be made for the establishment of local councils with more limited powers in areas where it would not be expedient to apply the available provisions.

Secondly, the provision in the Act restricting the establishment of councils to areas which had been recognised as such by Parliament, i.e. to areas scheduled under the Natives Land Act, No. 27 of 1913, complicated the position, since these areas are not in all cases compact blocks such as are desirable for definition for local council purposes. Further, this restriction prevented the application of the system to land, adjoining its recognised location, acquired and occupied by a Native tribe or community subsequent to the passing of the Natives Land Act.

The first difficulty indicated above was met by the enactment of the Native Affairs, 1920, Amendment Act, No. 27 of 1926, which provides that if the Native Affairs Commission reports to the Governor-General that in its opinion the condition or the stage of development of the inhabitants of any area for which it is proposed to establish a local council is such that the exercise by such council of any powers under the principal Act should be subject to the approval of the Minister, the Governor-General in issuing a proclamation establishing any such council may prescribe accordingly.

It is interesting to note that the Legislature did not contemplate that any such limitation upon the powers of a council should be permanent but made provision for its withdrawal when the Commission considers that a sufficiently advanced stage of development has been attained to permit of the Council concerned exercising the full powers contemplated under the Act of 1920.

To meet the second difficulty referred to, the Act was further amended by the Native Affairs Act, 1920, further Amendment Act, No. 15 of 1927, the effect of which is to permit of the inclusion under a local council of any area, adjoining a scheduled Native area, which the Governor-General may by Proclamation declare to be a Native area for local council purposes.

Councils Established

Since these obstacles have been removed, the establishment of local councils has proceeded apace and up to the present the following have been constituted with full powers under Act No. 23 of 1920 :—

Middledrift Local Council under Proclamation No. 3 of 1927.
Tamacha ,, ,, ,, ,, No. 4 of 1927,
as amended by Proclamation No. 78 of 1932.
Peddie Local Council under Proclamation No. 127 of 1927
Victoria East ,, ,, ,, No. 128 of 1927.
Mafeking ,, ,, ,, No. 211 of 1927,
as amended by Proclamations Nos. 252 of 1927
and 77 of 1931.
Keiskama Hoek Local Council under Proclamation No. 34 of 1928.
Herschel ,, ,, ,, ,, No. 219 of 1930.
East London ,, ,, ,, ,, No. 77 of 1932.

The following local councils have been established with powers restricted as provided by Act No. 27 of 1926 :—

Zebediela's Location Local Council under Proclamation
No. 324 of 1927,
as amended by Proclamation No. 258 of 1930,

Mpahlele's Location Local Council under Proclamation
No.   19 of 1928.

Sekukuni's Location   ,,   ,,   ,,   ,,   No.   62 of 1928.

Msinga District   ,,   ,,   ,,   ,,   No. 284 of 1928,
as amended by Proclamation No.   86 of 1929.

Bakeberg Masibi's Location Local Council under Proclamation
No.   5 of 1929,
as amended by Proclamation No. 158 of 1932.

Ramagopa's Location Local Council under Proclamation
No. 258 of 1929.

Moiloa Reserve Location Local Council under Proclamation
No. 280 of 1929.

Molietzie's Location Local Council under Proclamation
No. 307 of 1929.

It should be noted that each proclamation establishing a local council carefully defines its area of jurisdiction, lays down the number of members of which the council shall consist and states how many of such members are to be nominated by the Governor-General and how many, if any, are to be elected by representatives of the people in accordance with the regulations.

Act No. 23 of 1920 provides for the establishment not only of local but also of general councils, laying down that the Governor-General may, upon the recommendation of the Native Affairs Commission, constitute a general council whenever it appears that in any two or more local council areas the powers conferred upon those bodies can be more advantageously exercised by a body with jurisdiction over all those areas.   It is prescribed that a general council so constituted shall consist of such number of representatives from each of the constituent local councils as the Governor-General may determine on the advice of the Commission and that an officer of the public service may be designated by the Minister of Native Affairs to act as chairman of and in an advisory capacity to such general council.

A general council may exercise such of the powers conferred upon local councils by the Act as are allocated to it by the Governor-General upon the advice of the Commission and immediately upon such allocation it automatically becomes incompetent for the constituent local councils to continue to exercise those powers.

Up to the present no such general council has been established.

V

SPECIAL FUNDS ADMINISTERED BY THE DEPARTMENT FOR THE BENEFIT OF NATIVES

Germane to the question of local government amongst the Natives is the fact that special funds and trusts have been established and are administered by the Department for their benefit ; and, having discussed the different systems of local government operative in Native areas, it is now proposed to furnish a brief account of these special funds and trusts, of which the following are in existence :—

1. The British Bechuanaland Fund.
2. The Orange Free State Imperial Grant-in-Aid.
3. The Natal Native Trust and the Natal Mission Reserves Account.
4. The Putile Trust.
5. The Umnini Trust.
6. The Zululand Native Trust.
7. The Native Development Account.
8. Various Tribal Trust Funds.
9. Director of Native Labour : Native Estates Account.

1. THE BRITISH BECHUANALAND FUND

The British Bechuanaland Fund was constituted prior to the annexation of British Bechuanaland to the Cape Colony. It had its origin in the fact that under British Bechuanaland Proclamation No 62 dated the 25th April, 1889, it was proposed to vest the various Bechuanaland Native Reserves by title in trustees, who would be responsible for the general welfare and development of the reserves and, in the process of carrying out their duties, would receive certain revenues and would have to undertake certain expenditure, and would, moreover, have to be paid some remuneration for their services. The Proclamation accordingly made provision for the establishment of a separate fund for each Native Reserve, into which all revenue accruing to the Reserve would be paid and from which the expenditure incurred in respect of that Reserve would be met.

Proclamation No. 62 of 1889 was repealed by B. B. Proclamation No. 220 of 1895, which, while abandoning the proposal to vest the reserves in trustees (this idea had been carried out only as regards three of the reserves), made provision for the continuance of the special reserve funds.

Section *seven* of this Proclamation is still operative and reads as follows :—

" All moneys due as compensation in respect of surface damage occasioned by prospecting, digging, or mining for precious stones, or precious and other minerals, or by the construction of railways or other public works in any Native reserve, and all sums receivable therein or therefrom as subscription, interest, licence moneys, rents and profits accruing to the chief and people thereof shall be collected and recovered by the Civil Commissioner of the Division in which such reserve is situated, and shall by him be duly accounted for and dealt with as the Governor shall from time to time by regulations direct.   And the said funds shall be devoted exclusively to the direct and indirect benefit of the chief and people of such reserve in such manner and in such proportion as the Governor shall from time to time direct."

Regulations framed under this section were published under Government Notice No. 360 of 1914 and are as follows :—

" 1.   All amounts so collected shall be carried by the Civil Commissioner of the division or by any divisional receiver of revenue acting on his behalf to the credit of the Department of Native Affairs.

2.   Any amounts accruing to the chief and people of any Native reserve in respect of money so credited will be refunded by the Secretary for Native Affairs from time to time as required, and in each case the moneys so drawn shall be used exclusively for the benefit of the chief and people concerned in such manner as the Governor-General shall direct.

3.   A separate account shall be kept by the Secretary for Native Affairs of all moneys received and expended as above in respect of each Native reserve."

The main items of revenue accruing to the fund are trading rents, mineral lease and licence fees, grazing fees, shooting-permit fees, interest on investments, and money derived from the sale of sand and stone for building purposes

The main items of expenditure may be classified under the following heads : fencing, dipping, inoculation of stock, local works and salaries, a national secretary and assistant secretary being employed.

The revenue accruing to any particular reserve is expended exclusively for the benefit of that reserve.

The total amount standing to the credit of the fund as a whole at the 31st March, 1932, was £5,513 2s. 4d.

2. THE ORANGE FREE STATE IMPERIAL GRANT-IN-AID

After the conclusion of the Anglo-Boer War, a grant of £2,000,000 was made by the Imperial Government for the payment of compensation for war losses in the Orange Free State. Of this amount, £171,000 was assigned as compensation for Natives.

After all claims against the £171,000 so assigned had been met, there was an unexpended balance of approximately £27,124 and this sum was re-allocated by the Imperial Government to the Orange Free State Administration, subject to the condition that it should be devoted to the general advancement and benefit of the Native population by way of education or otherwise.

For many years the money was invested, grants to approved Native scholastic institutions occasionally being made from it, until in 1920 with accumulated interest the fund amounted to £39,000.

The Natives urged upon the Government that this money should be utilised for educational extension, and, in pursuance of this idea, arrangements were made with a view to devoting the annual interest to the payment of grants to approved institutions throughout the Union in respect of each Native pupil domiciled in the Orange Free State receiving at such institution industrial training or instruction in any standard above Standard IV.

The grant was fixed at £15 per annum per pupil, but subsidies on this basis constituted such an inroad upon the fund that it subsequently became necessary to reduce the grant to £12 per pupil and the number of pupils in respect of whom grants might be made to ninety-four.

In addition, grants and loans from this fund have from time to time been made to different Native educational institutions for building and development purposes, e.g. to the Stofberg Gedenkschool, to the Moroka Institute for Girls and to the Lovedale Institution. Loans have also been made during the past two years to various municipalities in the Orange Free State and to the Nederduitse Gereformeerde Kerk, Witzieshoek, for the building of schools for Natives. On the 31st March, 1932, a sum of £15,249 belonging to the fund, was out on loan. These loans carry interest at 5 per cent per annum and are repayable over a period of twenty-five years.

At the close of the financial year 1931-1932 the capital amount of the fund stood at £27,499 5s. 10d.

3. (a) THE NATAL NATIVE TRUST

In 1860, the then Lieutenant Governor of Natal, Mr. John Scott, pressed for the issue of some form of documentary title in respect of the lands which had been set aside for Native location purposes, considering that they should be secured to the Natives in a form far more binding than the mere permissive possession under which they held them. His proposal was that documentary titles should be issued conveying the land to trustees on behalf of the tribe concerned in each instance, one of the trustees to be the chief of the tribe. (This procedure had previously been adopted as regards the Umnini location, which in 1858 was set aside for the occupation of the Amatuli tribe who were required to remove in that year from what is now Durban).

The proposal was strongly opposed by the Natal Legislative Council which ultimately appealed to the Secretary of State for the Colonies in the matter.

The Secretary of State concurred in the policy of land tenure outlined by the Lieutenant Governor, whose proposals were, however, ultimately adopted only in a modified form, when under Royal Letters Patent dated the 27th April, 1864, the Natal Native Trust was constituted, the Trustees being the Governor and the Executive Council of the Colony for the time being. A copy of the Letters Patent appears in Appendix " F."

Various deeds of grant were then issued, under which 2,262,066 acres of land, comprising the great bulk of the Natal Native locations, were conveyed to the Natal Native Trust, the trustees of which were specifically authorised by the Letters Patent to " grant, sell, lease, or otherwise dispose of the same lands, in such wise as they shall deem fit, for the support, advantage or well-being of the said Natives, or for purposes connected therewith."

Certain nineteen Mission Reserves, comprising 144,192 acres, seventeen of which, with the intention of facilitating religious and educational work by approved religious denominations amongst the Natives, had between the years 1862 and 1887 been granted under title to various Missionary Societies in trust for Natives (with the Secretary for Native Affairs as a co-trustee), were in 1903, by the Natal Mission Reserves Act, No. 49 of that year, brought under the Natal Native Trust subject to certain conditions.

Act No. 1 of 1912 empowered the Governor-General to delegate to the Minister of Native Affairs the administration of all such matters as were at the date of Union administered by any legally constituted Native Trust, but at the same time very materially restricted the powers vested in the trustees by providing that no lands held by any such Trust should be alienated or in any way diverted from the purpose for which they were set apart without the special authority of Parliament, signified in the case of land, the alienation or diversion of which might be required for church, school, trading or public purposes, by a resolution of both Houses and in the case of all other land by a special Act.

The delegation of authority referred to in the preceding paragraph was duly made by the Governor-General, and was notified for general information under Government Notice No. 1601 of 1912.

The main activities which have been undertaken by the Natal Native Trust are afforestation, the establishment of certain irrigation works and fencing.

Afforestation

Prior to 1905 a small experimental timber plantation, in extent about 11 acres, had been established by the Trust near Henley in the Zwartkop location, District of Pietermaritzburg.

Observing the success which had attended this experiment, Sir George Leuchars, then Minister of Native Affairs for Natal, set aside additional land at Taylors in the same location for timber planting, with the result that at the date of Union there were some 500 acres of Trust land under exotic timber. Forty additional acres were planted in 1911, approximately two hundred acres in 1912, and some four hundred acres in 1913 and 1914.

The rigid economy necessitated by the outbreak of war in 1914 resulted in the stoppage of further extension work until 1917 when planting operations were resumed. Since then steady progress has been made each year until at the present date there are considerably over 2,000 acres of Natal Native Trust land under exotic timber, the principal varieties planted being Blue and Saligna Gums, Cypressus lusitanica, Cryptomeria japonica, Eucalyptus paniculata, resmifera and tereticornis, pines of several species and deodar cedar.

Complete records of all areas planted, with stock maps of the various blocks, are kept and data as to the rates of growth and suitability of the different species are recorded. All the plantations are fenced in where necessary and provided with such bridle paths and roads as to permit of their being given the requisite care and attention.

In addition, it should be mentioned that valuable indigenous forests are to be found on Trust land in the Bulwer, Alfred, Port Shepstone and Inanda areas and, in a lesser degree, in the Umzinto, Umlazi and Krantz-kop districts. Valuable species known to exist in these forests include the following : Real and bastard yellowwood (Podocarpus elongata and Podocarpus Thunbergii), Sneezewood (Ptaeroxylon utile), Camdeboo stinkwood (Celtis Kraussiana), " Mfuce " (Rhus longifolia) and Natal Mahogany (Trichilia emetica). It is considered that £200,000 is a conservative estimate of the value of matured timber available in indigenous forests belonging to the Trust to-day.

The expenditure incurred by the Natal Native Trust in the maintenance of afforestation during the financial year 1931-1932 amounted to £1,596 3s. 6d., while the revenue derived during the same period from the sale of exotic timber growing in the Zwartkop location plantations was £2,368 7s. 3d.

Irrigation Works

The Natal Native Trust has established two irrigation settlements, more generally referred to as " irrigation works," for Natives.

The Tugela River Irrigation Works were constructed in 1898 with the object of bringing under irrigation an area of 1929 acres of Trust land on the Tugela River in the Msinga District.

The works, which comprise a weir of rubble masonry in cement, a main furrow on the right bank of the Tugela, twelve and a half miles long, and a distributary to the left bank of the river, six and a half miles long, were constructed at a total cost of £53,026 14s. 9d., the capital sum being obtained from the following sources :

Voted by the Natal Government	£25,071	15	2
Natal Native Trust Funds	10,701	0	8
Loan Funds	17,253	18	11
	£53,026	14	9

The Mooi River Irrigation Works were undertaken in 1902 to bring under irrigation 1773 acres of Trust land in the Mpofana location in the Msinga District.

The works originally comprised a concrete weir and a furrow thirteen miles long on the left bank of the river and cost £33,174 19s. 6d., of which £1,000 was granted by the Natal Government, £2,607 11s. 10d. was made available from Trust funds and the balance, £29,567 7s. 8d. was borrowed from Loan funds.

Subsequently, a further furrow was constructed at Keates Drift in connection with these works at a cost of £2,321 17s. 9d., which was met from Trust funds.

The amount voted by the Natal Government in respect of each scheme was in the nature of an out and out grant, carrying no interest and not being repayable.

The amounts obtained from loan funds are re-payable subject to the conditions laid down in Natal Act No. 27 of 1902.

That Act authorised the Natal Native Trust to raise a loan of £50,000 upon debentures, the principal sum secured by the debentures to bear interest at a rate not exceeding 4% per annum and to be re-paid within forty years from the 1st July, 1902.

It was laid down that a sinking fund should be established for the repayment of the loan upon maturity, that the Trust should half-yearly from the date of the raising of the loan pay into this fund a sum of money not less than one per cent of the capital amount of the loan and that the sinking fund should be invested in approved securities but might be utilised by the trustees from time to time for buying in the debentures. The loan of £50,000 was duly raised in the manner prescribed and was appropriated as follows :

£29,567   7   8   to the cost of the Mooi River Works.
£17,253   18 11   to the cost of the Tugela River Works.
£3,178   13   5   for the construction of East Coast Fever fences.

Total   £50,000   0   0

Contributions towards the Sinking Fund were made regularly in terms of the Act until 1921, when owing to the favourable position of the fund further contributions were suspended. The position as regards the sinking fund at the 31st March, 1932, was that £19,400 worth of the debentures had been redeemed while an amount of £25,011 7s. 7d. was invested with the Public Debt Commissioners.

The irrigation plots at both settlements are as nearly as possible each two acres in extent but " corner " and " end " plots range from one to two and three-quarters of an acre in area. The plots are let to individual Natives at rentals which vary according to the value of the land but which on an average are assessed at £2 per acre per annum. During the financial year 1931-1932 the revenue derived from the Tugela Works amounted to £1,502 6s. 11d. and from the Mooi River Works to £1,104 8s. 5d. The cost of maintaining the settlements for the same period amounted to £2,496 13s. 7d. and £1,590 19s. 5d. respectively, to which must be added interest charges on debentures amounting to £866 0s. 10d. and contributions to the Sinking Fund (being interest on the amount invested with the Public Debt Commissioners) amounting to £620 16s., leaving a deficit of £2967 14s. 6d. chargeable against the general Trust Account. This considerable deficit is to be ascribed to the fact that, owing to the general economic and financial depression, the revenue from the works fell to a very low figure during the financial year 1931-1932 and does not represent the normal state of affairs.

The irrigation works have proved a great boon to the plot holders. There are 1015 plots at the Tugela works and 926 at Mooi River. The estimated annual value of the crops grown by the Natives on these holdings is £16,500 in respect of the Tugela works and £11,600 in respect of the Mooi River works.

The principal crops grown are mealies, peas, sweet potatoes and beans.

Regulations for the control and administration of Trust irrigation works in the Natal Province have recently been promulgated under Proclamation No. 195 of 1932.

Fencing

The Natal Native Trust is the " owner " of the extensive Natal locations for the purposes of the Fencing Act, No. 17 of 1912, and as such must, subject to the provisions of that Act, undertake liability for half the cost of the construction and maintenance of fences between the locations and adjoining properties.

Private owners of land adjoining Native locations are increasingly realising the necessity for the erection of adequate stock proof fences between their properties and their Native neighbours as a means of preventing trespass of stock and minimising disputes, etc. The result is that year by year the Trust is faced with an increased liability in this connection. The amount contributed by the Trust towards the cost of dividing fences during the financial year 1931-1932 was £666 16s. 11d.

In addition, the Trust is compelled from time to time to face expenditure under the Act in connection with the erection of fencing for the prevention of the spread of animal diseases, notably East Coast Fever. Reference has already been made to the fact that, from the loan of £50,000 authorised under Act No. 27 of 1902 an amount of £3,178 13s. 5d. was applied towards the cost of East Coast Fever fencing.

General

The Natal Native Trust lets various trading sites in the different locations, receiving an annual income of approximately £1,500 in this connection.

The income of the Trust for the year ended the 31st March, 1932, amounted to £10,870 12s. 3d. and its expenditure to £9,121 16s. 4d., leaving an excess of revenue over expenditure amounting to £1,748 15s. 11d.

3. (b) NATAL MISSION RESERVES ACCOUNT

The Natal Mission Reserves Act, No. 49 of 1903, in providing for the transfer to the Natal Native Trust of the trusts under which the various mission reserves had previously been held, empowered the Trust to exact rent from the Natives resident on the reserves and to make charges " for the supply and use of water which may be led or of any other conveniences which may be provided by them for public purposes on the reserve."

Section *ten* of the Act laid down that half of the revenue derived by the Trust from the lease of store sites on any mission reserve, from Native rents, etc., and a quarter of any moneys received in respect of prospecting and mining upon any reserve should be paid to the missionary society associated with that reserve and must be applied to the purposes of Native education and industrial training in accordance with the requirements of the Natal Education Department. It stipulated further that the balance of the revenue received by the Trust should be applied to works of general utility and for the benefit of the reserve from which the money was collected.

These provisions of the Act necessitate the keeping by the Department in connection with the finances of the Natal Native Trust of a separate Mission Reserves General Account with a subsidiary account for each individual mission reserve.

A few store sites are leased in the various reserves, the gross revenue in this connection being approximately £500 per annum.

The great bulk of the revenue of the mission reserves is, however, derived from the rentals paid by the Native residents themselves.

In this connection it may be mentioned that no rent was paid by the mission reserves residents prior to 1890. In 1888, however, a rule was passed requiring the payment of rental by newcomers as a condition of their being granted occupational rights in the reserves but this rule was only enforced in 1890. Originally the rental was assessed at 10s. per hut per annum but later the charge was increased to 30s. per hut per annum.

In 1904, under the provisions of Act No. 49 of 1903, the payment of rental was made general and the tariff was increased to £3 per hut per annum. In 1906, amending regulations were promulgated under the Act reducing the annual charge to 30s. per annum and permitting of further reductions being conceded in cases where this rent might be considered unduly heavy.

Finally, by the consolidated regulations for the administration of the Mission reserves published under Government Notice No. 621 of 1919, a uniform tariff of £1 per hut per annum was prescribed.

The total revenue collected from the various mission reserves during the financial year 1931-1932 amounted to £7,049 9s. 9d., of which a sum of £2,832 5s. 1d. represented the share due to the various Mission Societies, while during the same period an amount of £3,806 5s. 10d. was expended by the Trust for the benefit of the various Reserves.

Reference has already been made to the fact that a proclamation, No. 275 of 1929, was issued under the special powers of edictal legislation vested in the Governor-General by section *twenty-five* of the Native Administration Act, No. 38 of 1927, providing for the establishment of a Local Council for any one or more of the Natal mission reserves and for the establishment of a General Council in respect of three or more Local Councils so established.

This proclamation modifies section *ten* of the Mission Reserves Act by providing that the Natal Native Trust shall, after payment of the amounts specified in that section to the missionary bodies, and after re-payment of any advance made or expense incurred by it, pay the remainder of the revenue received by it in respect of any reserve to the general council exercising jurisdiction over that reserve and, in the event of there being no such general council, then to the local council established for such reserve.

No local or general council has as yet been established under the proclamation.

4. PUTILE TRUST FUND

The Putile Trust was constituted under an Indenture dated the 8th September, 1878, and in it was vested the Putile Location in the Estcourt district, measuring 13,054 acres.

On the 28th February, 1908, the Governor of Natal appointed the trustees of the Natal Native Trust to be the sole trustees of the Putile Fund, with the result that the affairs of this Trust are now administered in the same manner as those of the Natal Native Trust.

There is an amount of over £1,900 belonging to this fund invested with the Public Debt Commissioners and the fund derives a revenue of £25 per annum in respect of lease rents.

The value of the fund as at the 31st March, 1932, stood at £1,986 5s. 10d.

5. UMNINI TRUST FUND

The Umnini Trust was constituted under an Indenture dated the 27th May, 1858, for the benefit of the Amatuli Tribe which was removed from Durban in that year and settled in the Umlazi District on the Natal South Coast. The Umnini location, measuring 7,977 acres, was set aside for the occupation of the tribe and was vested in the Trust. Three trustees were appointed, viz. the Secretary for Native Affairs and his successors in office (as Chairman), the Chief of the tribe and his successors in that office and an unofficial member.

The Umnini Trust does not fall under the purview of Act No. 1 of 1912 and the trustees to-day are the Chief Native Commissioner, Natal, (Chairman), the Chief of the Amatuli tribe and Mr. Percy Saville.

The Trust receives the benefit of local tax collections within the location under the provisions of Act No. 41 of 1925, but for the rest its only regular source of revenue consists of lease rents in respect of certain lots in the location which produce a return of £11 per annum.

The funds of the Trust are utilised for the most part in the construction and maintenance of dipping tanks.

The amount standing to the credit of the Umnini Trust account at the 31st March, 1932, was £328 14s. 3d.

6. ZULULAND NATIVE TRUST

Zululand was annexed to the British Crown piece-meal between 1887 and 1897 (Proclamation dated 14th May, 1887 ; Proclamations IX —1885 and XIII—1885 ; Proclamations X—1897 and XIV—1897). By Natal Act No. 37 of 1897 the territory was annexed to the Colony of Natal and given the name of the Province of Zululand.

The annexation was assented to by the Imperial authorities on condition *inter alia* that no grants of land should be made for five years and that in the meantime a Joint Land Commission (Imperial and Colonial) should mark off Native locations which would be inalienable without the consent of the Secretary of State. This Commission, consisting of Mr. (later Sir) Chas. Saunders, Colonial Commissioner, and General Dartnell (subsequently replaced by Mr. N. H. Beachcroft), Imperial Commissioner, submitted its final report under date the 18th October, 1904. The recommendations of the Commission were accepted and ultimately, following the Natal system, the twenty-one Native reserves demarcated by the Commission—embracing a total area of 3,887,100 acres—were, under a Deed of Grant of the Governor of Natal, dated the 6th April, 1909, vested in the Zululand Native Trust for the use and benefit of the Natives, the trustees being the Governor and members of the Executive Council of Natal.

A copy of the Deed of Grant appears in Appendix " G."

The trustees were precluded from alienating any of the lands granted without the previous consent of the Secretary of State for the Colonies or under the authority of a special Act of Parliament.

The Zululand Native Trust falls under the purview of section *two* of Act No. 1. of 1912 and of the delegation of authority made thereunder, so that its affairs are now administered by the Minister of Native Affairs.

The main sources of revenue of the Zululand Native Trust are lease rents in respect of trading sites within the reserves, some of which were in existence prior to annexation, lease rents in respect of the Impapala Lands (to which further reference will be made in the Chapter dealing with Land Administration), prospecting fees, sales of wood, fees for game permits and interest on invested funds.

Fencing comprises a very considerable and ever increasing item of the expenditure of the Trust, which is the owner for the purposes of the Fencing Act, No. 17 of 1912, of the various reserves with their far-flung boundaries.

Grants from the funds of the Trust have from time to time been made in favour of various hospital institutions, e.g. a grant of £3,062 was made in 1928 towards a hospital erected at Empangeni by the Natal Provincial Administration on the understanding that special provision would be made for twenty beds to be retained for the treatment of Natives.

The Zululand Native Trust too provided the requisite funds for the erection of adequate buildings for the *Zululand National Training Institution*, which was established in the neighbourhood of the Mahashini Royal Kraal, Nongoma, in August, 1918, for the express purpose of providing a suitable course of training for the sons of chiefs and indunas in Natal with the object of fitting them for the discharge of the important duties, which, as leaders of their people, they would in the future be called upon to perform.

The institution buildings, which are valued at £2,210, were all erected by Natives, most of them being of a substantial nature and constructed of sandstone. They include a school (with three classrooms), carpenter's shop, three dormitories, principal's house, staff quarters, and the usual buildings required at an institution of this nature.

There is an adequate water supply—and the Ivuna stream which flows through the property provides bathing facilities for the students.

Electric light has been installed throughout the institution.

The property consists of some 300 acres, of which 100 are arable and suitable for growing the large range of crops which are cultivated. In addition there is a subsidiary farm, Tokazi, some 300 acres in extent,

G

which is worked by the institution.   About 100 acres of this farm are under cultivation (a portion being under irrigation).

An orchard with several varieties of fruit has been established.

The nucleus of a herd of pure-bred Red Poll cattle has been established and a herd of White Zulu cattle has been collected for experimental purposes.

From its inception the institution has stressed agriculture in its curriculum and since the appointment of the Director of Native Agriculture in 1928 considerable development in this direction has taken place.

The institution was opened with two students and the number has steadily increased from year to year until at present there are some sixty students from different parts of the Union in residence.

The staff consists of two Europeans, viz. the principal and a lecturer in agriculture and farming, and six Natives, including a head teacher, three assistant teachers, a building instructor and a farm manager.

Two distinct syllabuses have been drawn up to meet the educational standards of students.   The more advanced course is designed to meet the needs of students who have had previous education and comprises the ordinary syllabus of the Natal Education Department (Native Branch) up to Standard VI with special additional instruction in Native law and administration.   The less advanced course is of three years duration and is intended for students who have had no previous education.

Under both courses agricultural as well as industrial training is emphasised and the pupils receive practical instruction in better methods of farming — stock and agricultural — in carpentry, building, roadmaking and tree planting.

On the moral side, the virtues of discipline, cleanliness, punctuality and loyalty are inculcated.

The institution receives an annual subsidy from the Native Development Account.

The revenue of the Zululand Native Trust for the financial year 1931-1932 amounted to £3,154 11s. 4d. and the expenditure for the same period to £1,335 16s. 1d., resulting in an excess of revenue over expenditure amounting to £1,818 15s. 3d.

As at the 31st March, 1932, the balance of the Trust stood at £20,289 6s. 9d., of which an amount of £17,512 16s. 11d. represented funds invested with the Public Debt Commissioners.

7. NATIVE DEVELOPMENT ACCOUNT

The establishment of the Native Development Account under the provisions of the Natives Taxation and Development Act, No. 41 of 1925, may be regarded as the direct outcome of the Financial Relations Fourth Extension Act, No. 5 of 1922, which *inter alia* withdrew entirely from the Provincial Councils the power of imposing direct taxation upon the persons, lands, habitations and incomes of Natives ; and, while leaving the immediate control of Native education with the various Provincial Administrations and providing for the annual expenditure by them in this connection of an amount not less, or not proportionally less, than the figure reached during the financial year 1921-1922, laid down the principle that funds for further development should be met by special subsidies from the central Government granted on condition of their being spent according to the requirements of the Government. The Act definitely stipulated that such subsidies should be paid " out of the revenues derived from the direct taxation of the persons, lands, habitations, or incomes of Natives under any law now in force or which may be hereafter enacted, but shall not exceed in the aggregate a sum specifically appropriated each year by Parliament for the purpose."

The anomalies, inequalities and diversities of the systems of direct taxation of the Natives then operative in the various Provinces had long called for some effort towards uniformity and co-ordination, and the cognate problem of finding funds to provide for the extension of the educational facilities so much desired by the great bulk of the Native people rendered more urgent the necessity of a complete revision of the legislation dealing with taxation.

The problem was in the first place to decide upon a system which would afford the easiest and most equitable means of collection, having regard to the conditions under which the great majority of the Native people live, and in the second place to fix the rate, with due consideration of the economic position of the taxpayer, at such a figure as would provide revenue for general State purposes commensurate with that which had previously been derived from Native taxation, and, in addition, funds for educational purposes. After much discussion, the conclusion was arrived at that these two desiderata would best be achieved by making the tax a poll tax of £1, of which four-fifths should accrue to the general revenue, while one fifth should be ear-marked for Native education. This became the " general tax " under the Natives Taxation and Development Act, No. 41 of 1925.

There emerged, however, during the discussions the views that funds were required for beneficial services to the Natives other than education, and that Natives who were living on land provided and set aside for their occupation by the State were under a greater obligation than those who were not. These views took shape in the suggestion that Natives living in locations and reserves might well be required to contribute a supplementary amount which should be devoted to the benefit of the Natives living in the area of collection. This suggestion was embodied in the Act in the provision for the payment of a " local tax " of 10s. in respect of every hut or dwelling in a Native location (as defined under section *nineteen* of the Act) within the Union by the occupier thereof unless such occupier were the holder of an allotment under quit-rent title in that location. (For the " local tax " is substituted, in so far as allotments held under individual tenure on quitrent conditions in surveyed locations are concerned, the quitrent paid by the registered holders).

Sections *eleven* and *twelve* of the Act provide for the disposal of the proceeds of the taxes. In effect four-fifths of the general tax accrues to the Consolidated Revenue Fund for general State purposes ; the local tax and Native quitrent collected in any area falling under the jurisdiction of an approved general or local council or board are paid to that body ; and the local tax and Native quitrent collected elsewhere are paid into a special fund termed the " Native Development Account," which also absorbs the remaining one-fifth of the general tax.

Section *thirteen* of the Act, as amended by section *eight* of Act No. 37 of 1931 and by section *nine* of Act No. 25 of 1932, lays down that the amounts standing to the credit of the Native Development Account shall be applied at the discretion of the Minister, in consultation with the Native Affairs Commission, to any one or more of the following purposes :—

" (a) for the maintenance, extension and improvement of educational facilities amongst Natives ;

(b) for the further development and the advancement of the welfare of Natives ;

(c) for the payment to Divisional Councils in the Province of the the Cape of Good Hope in areas for which no local council exists under the Native Affairs Act, 1920, of the special hut tax payable to such Divisional Councils under section *twenty-five* of the Native Locations Amendment Act, 1899 (Cape of Good Hope) and of any rates or portion thereof levied in terms of section *one hundred and eighteen* of the Divisional Councils and Roads Ordinance, 1917 (Ordinance No. 13 of 1917), of the

Province of the Cape of Good Hope, or of such sums as may be agreed in lieu thereof ; but if such a local council is established such local council shall be liable to the Divisional Council for such sums as may be fixed in accordance with the provisions of section *thirteen* of the Native Affairs Act, 1920."

The section provides further for the expenditure of the proceeds of local tax and quitrent paid into the Development Account in such areas within the Province in respect of which they have been collected as may be prescribed. The areas prescribed by the Governor-General under the section were notified for general information under Government Notice No. 573 of 1932, and are as follows :—

Area No. 1

The Province of the Cape of Good Hope, excluding—

(a) the Transkeian Territories ; and

(b) British Bechuanaland (comprising the Magisterial Districts of Gordonia, Kuruman, Mafeking, Taung and Vryburg).

Area No. 2

The Transkeian Territories.

Area No. 3

British Bechuanaland (comprising the Magisterial Districts of Gordonia, Kuruman, Mafeking, Taung and Vryburg).

Area No. 4

The Province of the Transvaal.

Area No. 5

The Province of the Orange Free State.

Area No. 6

The Province of Natal, excluding Zululand.

Area No. 7

Zululand.

Finally, the section contains specific provision for the repayment from the Native Development Account to the Exchequer Account, in such instalments as the Minister of Finance may prescribe, of the total of the advances made by the Central Government to Provincial Administrations during the financial years 1923-1926 for the improvement of Native teachers' salaries. Here it may be mentioned that this total was ascertained to be £223,643, of which a sum of £44,728 was repaid during the financial year 1926-1927 and the balance of £178,915 is, with the approval of the Treasury, being paid off in annual instalments of £25,560. The final payment should accordingly be made during the financial year 1933-1934.

The provisions indicated above necessitated the division of the Development Account into two funds, viz. :—

(1) Native Development ' A ' Account—*the General Fund*—into which is paid the one-fifth of the general tax received from the Consolidated Revenue Fund and which is utilised for educational purposes and for the general welfare of Natives ; and

(2) Native Development ' B ' Account—*the Local Fund*—into which are paid the local tax and quitrent collections. From this fund are paid over the amounts due under section *eleven* of the Act to the various Native councils and boards and for the rest the fund is utilised to meet local expenditure for the benefit of the Natives within the areas of collection as prescribed under Government Notice No. 573 of 1932 referred to above.

It remains to be added that the readjustment of financial relations between the Union Government and the Provinces under the Provincial Subsidies and Taxation Powers (Amendment) Act, No. 46 of 1925, necessitated the fixing of a basis upon which grants in respect of Native education should be made by the Central Government for the future. The principle laid down in the Financial Relations Fourth Extension Act, No. 5 of 1922, was retained, and the grants were fixed at an amount equal to the relative expenditure of each Province for the financial year 1921-1922. The Act (No. 46 of 1925) provided for the payment to the various Provinces from the Consolidated Revenue Fund for the financial year 1925-1926 of the following amounts in this connection :—

Cape of Good Hope	£240,000
Natal	49,000
Transvaal	46,000
Orange Free State	5,000
	£340,000

The Act further laid down that, commencing with the financial year 1926-1927, an annual contribution of £340,000 should be made from the Consolidated Revenue Fund to the Native Development Account, and that grants to the Provinces in respect of Native education, i.e. for the maintenance, extension and improvement of education facilities among Natives and for the adjustment of salaries of Native teachers, should be defrayed from that account, subject to conditions to be prescribed by the Governor-General after consultation between the Minister of Native Affairs and the Administrator concerned.

These conditions were published under Government Notice No. 1507 of 1927 and they provide for the submission of draft estimates of expenditure by each Provincial Administration to the Secretary for Native Affairs for the consideration of the Minister, not later than the 30th November in each year, on a prescribed form showing (a) for the previous completed year, (b) for the current year, and (c) for the year in respect of which the estimates are submitted the expenditure incurred or to be incurred under appropriate sub-heads and items.

The draft estimates must be accompanied by a memorandum giving such information as may from time to time be required by the Minister, who, of course, is empowered to approve or refuse to approve of any proposed item of expenditure. Issues from the Native Development Account are made to the Provincial Administrations on account of approved services upon their requisitions from time to time but are strictly limited to the grants authorised by the Minister and to amounts required for expenditure within the period covered by the requisition. Expenditure on services other than those for which estimates have been approved is permitted only with the special authority of the Minister and all unexpended balances must be surrendered to the Native Development Account at the end of each financial year, when, in addition, an audited statement of its expenditure on Native education must be rendered by each Province to the Secretary for Native Affairs.

It is not too much to say that the establishment of the Native Development Account was an event of far-reaching importance, the beneficial effects of which, even at this early stage, have made themselves felt. The existence of this fund has permitted of steps being taken for the promotion of the interests of the Natives, notably in the directions of education and agricultural development, which would not otherwise have been possible. In 1921, the sum of £340,000 was spent on Native education throughout the Union ; by 1931 this expenditure had increased to £600,000. Without the help of the Native Development Account such progress would not have been possible.

The account came into being with the commencement, on the 1st January, 1926, of the Natives Taxation and Development Act, No. 41 of

1925, and the revenue up to the end of the 1925-1926 financial year, i.e. to the 31st March, 1926, amounted to £15,083 2s. 10d. of which £9,000 2s. 0d. accrued to the General and £6,083 0s. 10d. to the Local Fund.

For the financial years 1926-1927, 1927-1928, 1928-1929, 1929-1930, 1930-1931 and 1931-1932, the figures were as follows :—

	General Fund			Local Fund		
(including annual grant of £340,000 from the Central Government for Native education)						
1926-1927	£564,531	10	4	£230,805	5	8
1927-1928	£572,957	19	3	£247,519	0	3
1928-1929	£577,290	13	0	£257,308	13	9
1929-1930	£585,973	12	2	£265,702	0	1
1930-1931	£590,051	4	3	£269,996	13	8
1931-1932	£569,397	13	0	£241,959	5	7

Up to the 31st March, 1932, the total revenue received by the General Fund accordingly amounted to £3,469,202 14s. 0d. and that of the Local Fund to £1,519,373 19s. 10d.

General Fund

The great bulk of the General Fund revenue has naturally been utilised for subsidising Native education, grants totalling £3,256,811 6s. 4d. having been made to the different Provinces up to the 31st March, 1932.   From this sum must, however, be deducted unexpended balances, amounting to £65,152 8s. 0d., surrendered by the Provincial Administrations from time to time.   The grants over the period were allocated as follows :—

Cape Province	..	£1,970,662	0	0
Natal Province	..	582,980	0	0
Transvaal Province	..	507,454	0	0
Orange Free State	..	195,715	6	4

In addition, up to the end of March, 1932, an amount of £172,528 had been refunded from the General Fund to the Treasury in respect of the sum of £223,643 advanced to the various Provincial Administrations during the financial years 1923-1926, to which reference has already been made.

For the rest, the revenue of the General Fund has been mainly applied to furthering Native agricultural development.   In this connection the following items are of particular interest :—

(a) The farms Fort Cox (originally a military outpost used against the Natives in the early Kafir wars) and Florida in the King William's Town district were acquired in 1926 and 1929 respectively for the purpose of establishing a Native agricultural school for the benefit of the Natives in the Ciskei. The necessary buildings were proceeded with as soon as practicable and in addition a considerable amount of money was spent in fencing, installing plant for light and ensuring an adequate water supply.

The institution was formally opened by the Minister of Native Affairs on the 6th of September, 1930, and at present carries a full complement of students, of whom some eighty-five are in residence.

The staff consists of the Assistant Director of Native Agriculture for the Cape Province, as principal, two European lecturers, a European clerk who also lectures, a Native lecturer, a Native instructor in carpentry and a Native clerk with a married Native couple as boarding master and mistress.

The objects of the institution are :—

(i) To give a thorough, practical and theoretical training in general agriculture and stock-farming to young Native men so as to enable them to make better use of their own land subsequently or to take up posts as skilled agricultural labourers. A percentage of the most successful students are given employment as agricultural demonstrators in the Native areas.

(ii) To produce reliable seed, good rams, bulls and poultry, etc., for sale at reasonable prices to established Native farmers in the area served by the institution.

The course is of two years duration. The farm offers facilities for instruction in general agriculture, representative of Eastern Province conditions. All the practical work on the farm is carried out by the students themselves under the supervision of the staff.

Lectures and demonstrations are given in the following subjects :— General Agriculture, Cattle, Horses, Sheep and Wool, Pigs, Poultry, Dairying, Veterinary Science, Horticulture, Agricultural Entomology, Botany and Chemistry in relation to general agriculture and stock, Farm Bookkeeping, and Agricultural Economics. Intensive farming and the relationship thereto of pasture management, feeding and control of stock, soil erosion, etc., are stressed.

The total amount expended on the Fort Cox Agricultural School, that is in acquiring the land, erecting the necessary buildings and fencing, and providing the requisite light and water installations, up to the 31st March, 1932, was £25,044 8s. 3d.

(b) Some ninety Native agricultural demonstrators are employed by the Department in different locations in the Ciskei, British Bechuanaland, the Transvaal and Natal at salaries ranging from £60 to £190 per annum.   These men are performing excellent work among the people and are paid from the Native Development ' A ' Account.

Local Fund

Of the revenue which accrued to the *Local Fund* of the Native Development Account from the date of its inception to the 31st March, 1932, an amount of £1,014,544 0s. 6d. was, in terms of the Act, paid over to the various Native Councils and Boards ; £312,529 4s. 5d. was expended in connection with the dipping of stock ; £7,265 2s. 0d. was paid to various Divisional Councils in the Cape Province in lieu of the special hut tax payable to them by Natives under section *twenty-five* of the Native Locations Amendment Act, 1899 (Cape); £6,416 11s. 9d. was spent in connection with the erection and maintenance of location fencing, and sums amounting in the aggregate to £45,878 11s. 1d. were advanced to various Native tribes, communities, scholastic institutions and chiefs, for approved purposes, these advances being repayable in annual instalments and carrying interest at a reasonable figure.

It should be mentioned that an amount of £4,400 annually voted by Parliament for the welfare of Natives in Natal has since 1927 been paid to the Native Development Account (Local Fund) and is utilised for subsidising the Zululand National Training Institution and for the grant of financial assistance to certain mission hospitals.

Section *four* of the Financial Adjustments Act, No. 36 of 1924, provided that any rate levied under section *eight* of Act No. 20 of 1911 (i.e. for the purpose of recovering advances made for the construction and maintenance of dipping tanks in Native areas) should as from the 1st April, 1923, be placed to the credit of a separate account, entitled the " Native Dipping Tanks Account," to be applied to meet the cost of construction, maintenance, supervision and any other charges connected with dipping tanks, and, generally, with the eradication of stock diseases in Native reserves, mission stations or locations not under the control of a Native Council.

This separate dipping tanks account was maintained until the 31st March, 1928, when it was closed, the collection of dipping levies other than arrears having ceased. The balances were incorporated in the Local Fund of the Native Development Account which now bears the expenditure of dipping in Native areas (other than Council areas) and into which miscellaneous dipping revenue is paid.

Sixty-five European dipping supervisors were employed and paid from this fund as at the 31st March, 1932, their salaries ranging from £180 to £270 per annum.

Regulations governing the financial administration of the Native Development ·Account, made by the Governor-General in terms of paragraph (h) of sub-section (1) of section *sixteen* of Act No. 41 of 1925, were published under Government Notice No. 89 of 1932, a copy of which appears in Appendix " H."

8. Tribal Trust Funds

In the Transvaal what are known as Tribal Trust Funds have been established in various districts under the control of local officers of the Department.

Originally these funds were instituted for the purpose of extinguishing tribal debts and reorganising the finances of the tribes concerned. Owing to dilatoriness in meeting their obligations in respect of land purchase, etc., imprudence and mismanagement of tribal moneys, certain tribes had become yearly more and more involved until, with the consent of the chiefs and people, their affairs were investigated and taken in hand by Departmental officers, with the result that by reason of the assistance and protection thus afforded, the tribal finances were in many cases in the course of a few years placed upon a solvent and satisfactory basis.

The usual course adopted was to induce the tribe concerned to agree to the imposition upon the tribesmen of a *purely voluntary levy*, the amount of which was assessed by the chief and people themselves and the proceeds of which were paid into a special banking account opened in the name of the tribe. This account was made subject to the control of a board consisting of the local representative of the Department and the chief and councillors of the tribe.

Efforts in this direction were attended with such success that in the course of time the system became more or less generally applied, e.g. whenever a Native tribe embarked upon the purchase of land. It was found, however, in a large number of cases that the fact of the special levy being purely voluntary rendered it possible for the less scrupulous tribesmen to evade their moral obligations thus subjecting their more public-spirited brethren to an inequitable burden.

To deal with the position thus created and to place the whole matter of these tribal levies and funds upon a proper basis, special provision was made in section *fifteen* of the Natives Taxation and Development Act, No. 41 of 1925. That section as amended by section *nine* of Act No. 37 of 1931 reads as follows :—

" (1)   When a Native tribe or community voluntarily makes application for the levy of a special rate for the benefit of such tribe or community and the Minister is satisfied that the majority of tax-payers of such tribe or community desires such a levy and the Minister approves the purpose for which it is to be imposed, the Governor-General may levy such rate upon every member of such tribe or community who is a tax-payer and any rate so imposed shall be recoverable as if it were a tax imposed under this Act and shall for the purposes of the provisions of subsections (1) to (4), both inclusive, of section *nine* be deemed to be such a tax.

(2)   The proceeds of any such rate as is levied under sub-section (1) of this section shall be paid into a special account in the name of the tribe or community concerned to be administered by the Minister in accordance with regulations made under this Act."

Regulations framed under the Act for the collection and administration of tribal levies were published under Government Notice No. 349 of 1927.

These regulations make provision for the printing of face value receipt forms with counterfoils or duplicates, which are to be stocked, recorded and issued to approved tribal collectors by the local district officer of the Department. Collectors must furnish such security as the district officer may deem necessary and must account to him for all moneys received by them. The travelling expenses of collectors, together with such remuneration for their services as the tribe may by resolution grant to them, are, subject to the approval of the Minister, defrayed from the proceeds of the levy.

The district officer must pay into a special banking account, at such bank as the Minister may approve, to the credit of the levy all moneys received by him on account of the levy whether directly or through collectors.

Disbursements of the proceeds of any levy can be made only by cheque signed by the district officer and countersigned by the chief and only for the express purposes for which the levy was imposed and for such purposes incidental to the collection and administration of the levy as may be sanctioned by the Minister.

District officers of the Department are required to keep a separate account for each levy under their control and must enter therein all receipts and payments on behalf of such levy. These books and accounts must be closed off and submitted to audit by some person approved by the Minister annually, and a copy of the audited statement must be rendered to the Secretary for Native Affairs. Further, any officer of the Control and Audit Department inspecting the district officer's accounts shall have access, if he so desire, to the books of any levy and may audit them.

District officers are required to submit to the Department half-yearly statements of the revenue and expenditure of any tribal levy under their control.

Suitable penalties are prescribed in the regulations for misappropriation of or failure to account for the proceeds of any levy.

Up to the 31st March, 1932, *eighty-six* tribal levies had been imposed under Act No. 41 of 1925, upon various Native tribes, the great majority being tribes in the Transvaal.

9. THE NATIVE ESTATES ACCOUNT (DIRECTOR OF NATIVE LABOUR)

In 1903, the Transvaal Administration made special arrangements to facilitate the administration of the estates of Native labourers employed on the Witwatersrand. Whenever the death of a Native labourer was reported, enquiry was at once instituted by the Native Affairs Department regarding the effects and money left by the deceased and the amount of wages or other assets accruing to the estate. The amounts realised were paid into a Native Estates Account especially established in the Johannesburg office of the Department for the purpose. All available particulars of identity were then sent to the local officer in charge of the district in which the deceased lived with a view to ascertaining the heir to the estate, to whom, when traced, payment of the assets was made. If no heirs or next of kin could be traced, the estates were treated as derelict and the assets handed over to the Master of the Supreme Court.

Upon the establishment of the Government Native Labour Bureau in 1907, the Director thereof was made responsible for the administration of this estates account and he continued to be so responsible after Union.

The Native Labour Regulation Act, No. 15 of 1911, empowered the Governor-General to make regulations *inter alia* for the administration of the estates of deceased Native labourers. The regulations framed under that Act and published under Government Notice No. 1988 of 1911 provide for the payment by the employer to the Director upon the death of a Native labourer in any labour district of all wages due to the deceased and any money or goods belonging to the deceased which may be in his possession. The Director, after deducting any amounts due by the deceased on account of advances or other claims, must, in the absence of any will or other testamentary disposition by the deceased, transmit the balance to the magistrate of his district of origin for distribution according to law. Any unclaimed amount must be returned to the Director to be dealt with by him in accordance with the law governing the estates of deceased persons.

All such moneys pass through the Native Estates Account, some idea of the magnitude of the operations of which will be gathered from the fact that on an average it deals with Native estates of an aggregate value of over £50,000 per annum, though the value of each individual estate is small.

VI

NATIVE LAND ADMINISTRATION

Native land administration will now be considered from the following aspects :—

A. The occupation and tenure of land specially set aside for Natives.

B. Native occupation and tenure of land other than that specially set aside for them.

C. The general land policy initiated under the Natives Land Act, No. 27 of 1913, and subsequent developments.

A

THE OCCUPATION AND TENURE OF LAND SPECIALLY SET ASIDE FOR NATIVES

Under this heading fall to be considered :

1. Land tenure under the Natives' own tribal system.

2. The establishment of Native locations and reserves in the several Provinces and the different systems of land administration (exclusive of individual tenure) operative therein.

3. The application to Native locations and reserves of European ideas of individual tenure of land.

4. The acquisition by non-Natives of land or rights to and interests in land in areas set aside for Native occupation.

1. Land Tenure under the Natives' own tribal system

The Cape of Good Hope Commission on Native Laws and Customs of 1883 found that according to Native custom the land occupied by a tribe is theoretically regarded as the property of the paramount chief, who in relation to the tribe is a trustee holding it for the people, who occupy and use it in subordination to him on communistic principles.

Under the tribal system the basic idea of land tenure was occupation by the tribe as a whole and land was not regarded as a negotiable or commercial asset, the idea of actual legal ownership of the soil not having been developed.

Each tribesman ordinarily received from the chief, or a petty chief acting on his behalf, a homestead allotment for residential purposes and an arable allotment for cultivation—polygamists obtaining a separate land or arable allotment for each wife. The remainder of the tribal holding was utilised as common pasturage, from which, as the members of the tribe increased and fresh households were formed, further portions were allotted to the additional households.

The tribesman though, as previously stated, not in the juristic sense the " owner " of the land allotted to him, yet possessed certain permanent and exclusive rights therein which were recognised under Native law, e.g., he could cultivate it or not as he pleased but no one else had the right to do so ; any crops reaped belonged to him personally and there was no sharing of the fruits among the tribe as a whole ; and though possibly upon his death the land theoretically reverted to the chief, in actual practice the heir of a particular house succeeded to the deceased's rights over the land allotted that household, just as he had to assume responsibility for the maintenance of that house, the system of inheritance being based upon primogeniture.

The so-called " communal " tenure of land under the tribal system must accordingly be understood in the sense indicated above and not as indicating tenure in common.

2. The establishment of Native Locations and Reserves in the several Provinces and the different systems of land adminis-tration (exclusive of individual tenure) operative therein

As various tracts of land in the Union of South Africa from time to time came under European domination and extensive areas were appro-priated for European settlement, some provision had to be made for the large Native population which remained subsequent to annexation and this naturally took the form of the reservation for their occupation of definite areas styled Native locations or reserves.

Cape

Ciskei. Thus, in that tract of country in the Cape Province lying between the Great Fish River and the Kei, usually referred to as the "Ciskei," after each of the numerous Kafir wars fresh dispositions of land were made, loyal tribes being rewarded by the allocation of additional lands to them, rebellious tribes having their holdings very much reduced, if not altogether taken away, and additional areas, after each conflict, being thrown open for European occupation. As the result of the adjustment effected after the 1877-1878 war, the Ciskeian Native locations were demarcated more or less as they exist today.

Griqualand West was annexed to the British Crown under a proclamation dated the 27th October, 1871, and in 1877 a Commission was appointed to establish locations for the Natives, some fifty farms in separate blocks, comprising a total area of 159,821 morgen, being set aside for the purpose.

Provision was made for the annexation of the territory to the Cape Colony under Cape Act No. 39 of 1877, which, however, was only brought into operation by Proclamation No. 124 dated the 15th October, 1880.

In the meantime, in 1878, the Natives had broken into rebellion and most of them had abandoned their locations and fled to British Bechuanaland, thus forfeiting the lands which had been reserved for them. After the rebellion, a number of them were permitted to return and to reoccupy the locations under the direction and supervision of Mr. Matabili Thompson.

Finally, in 1898, a Commission was appointed to consider the question of concentrating the Natives, who were then very much scattered and in occupation of land far in excess of their requirements. On the recommendations of this Commission, the locations were reduced to an area of 87,355 morgen, and, except for one or two subsequent minor adjustments, demarcated as they exist to-day.

Immediately upon the annexation of *British Bechuanaland* on the 30th September, 1885, a Commission was appointed " to enquire into and decide upon the various questions connected with the land settlement " of the territory including Native reserves. The report of this Commission was submitted on the 29th May, 1886, and was accepted *in toto* by the authorities. It made generous provision for Native reserves.

The territory was annexed to the Cape Colony under the Bechuanaland Annexation Act, No. 41 of 1895 (Cape), section *seventeen* of which

H

provided that the Native reserves should be inalienable except by Act of Parliament.

Certain of the Native reserves were confiscated under Cape Act No. 17 of 1897 by reason of a rebellion which took place in 1896-1897.

Further, an adjustment of certain of the reserve boundaries was effected under Cape Act No. 8 of 1908, while an additional reserve, 19,021 morgen 290 square roods in extent, consisting of the farms Police, Bogogobo and Khuis, was established in the Gordonia district under the provisions of the Natives Land Adjustment Act, No. 36 of 1931.

For the rest, the Bechuanaland reserves remain to-day more or less as demarcated by the Land Settlement Commission of 1885.

The Transkeian Territories consist of the districts of Butterworth, Idutywa, Kentani, Nqamakwe, Tsomo and Willowvale, comprising the territory of the Transkei; the districts of Elliotdale, Engcobo, Mqanduli, St. Marks, Umtata and Xalanga, comprising the territory of Tembuland; the districts of Matatiele, Mount Ayliff, Mount Currie, Mount Fletcher, Mount Frere, Qumbu, Tsolo and Umzimkulu, comprising the territory of East Griqualand; the district and territory of Port St. Johns (recognised for council purposes as portion of Western Pondoland,) and the districts of Bizana, Flagstaff, Libode, Lusikisiki, Ngqeleni and Tabankulu comprising the territory of Pondoland.

The districts of Maclear and Elliot were formerly included in the Transkeian Territories, the former forming portion of East Griqualand and the latter a portion of Tembuland but as has already been pointed out (*vide* page 9 *supra*) they were in effect excised from the Territories under the provisions of Act No. 12 of 1913.

The Transkei, consisting of what was previously known as Fingoland and the Idutywa Reserve, was annexed to the Cape Colony by Proclamation No. 110 of 1879 issued under the provisions of the Transkeian Annexation Act, No. 38 of 1877. The District of Butterworth was included in the Transkei by Proclamation No. 229 of 1883 and Gcalekaland (the Willowvale and Kentani districts) by Proclamation No. 53 of 1891.

East Griqualand comprising the territory previously known as " Nomansland " was annexed to the Cape Colony by Proclamation No. 112 of 1879 likewise issued under the provisions of Act No. 38 of 1877. In East Griqualand were subsequently included the Xesibe country (now portion of the Mount Ayliff district) by Proclamation No. 174 of 1886 issued under the provisions of the Xesibe Country Annexation Act, No. 37 of 1886, and the Rode Valley (likewise today a portion of the Mount Ayliff district) by Proclamation No. 201 of 1887 issued under the provisions of the Rode Valley Annexation Act, No. 45 of 1887.

The Port St. John's Territory was annexed to the Cape Colony by Proclamation No. 215 of 1884 issued under the Walfish Bay and St. John's River Territories Annexation Act, No. 35 of 1884. This territory, formerly known as the St. John's River Territory, when annexed consisted of a strip of land, about 5,000 morgen in extent, on the west bank of the Umzimvubu river, which the Government, recognising the strategic importance of Port St. John's, purchased, with all sovereign rights over the waters and navigation of the Umzimvubu, from the Pondo Chief Nqwiliso. After annexation a small European settlement was established there and remains in existence to-day. The boundaries of the territory and district were subsequently extended by the inclusion therein for administrative reasons of Native locations which previously formed portions of adjoining Pondoland districts. These locations, however, remained in Native occupation.

Tembuland, comprising the territories previously known as Tembuland, Emigrant Tembuland and Bomvanaland, was annexed to the Cape Colony by Proclamation No. 140 of 1885 issued under the provisions of the Tembuland Annexation Act, No. 3 of 1885. Gcalekaland (the districts of Willowvale and Kentani) was likewise annexed under Proclamation No. 140 of 1885 but was subsequently, by Proclamation No. 53 of 1891, included in the Transkei.

Pondoland, comprising East and West Pondoland, was annexed to the Cape Colony by Proclamation No. 339 of 1894 issued under the Pondoland Annexation Act, No. 5 of 1894.

These various areas comprising the Transkeian Territories were annexed to the Cape Colony not with any idea of territorial aggrandisement but in the interests of peace, order and good government and, as regards certain of them, at the request of the Natives themselves.

Thus, while annexation was necessary, there was no intention of depriving the Natives of their land and for the most part what was Native territory prior to annexation remained such after annexation, the areas concerned being administered as Native dependencies rather than as integral portions of the Cape Colony.

Such European occupation as does exist to-day can be accounted for as follows :—

(a)   The establishment of a European settlement at Port St. John's as has been explained above.

(b)   Pre-annexation concessions by Native chiefs. For example, certain European farmers prior to the annexation of Tembuland, on the invitation of the Tembu Chief Gangelizwe, established themselves near Umtata in that territory and after annexation were allowed to remain.

(c)   The establishment for military reasons in the early days of a " buffer " settlement in the Transkei by the allotment to Europeans of the farms in the Entlhambe ward of the Butterworth district.

(d)   The settlement by Sir Philip Wodehouse in 1863 of Adam Kok's Griquas from Phillipolis in the Orange Free State in what was then an uninhabited portion of Nomansland and to-day constitutes the districts of Umzimkulu, Mount Currie and Matatiele. Large tracts of land in these districts were allotted to these people, the great bulk of which eventually passed into the hands of Europeans.

(e)   Confiscations and adjustments effected as the result of rebellion. Thus the insurrection of 1880 resulted in the allotment to Europeans of portion of the district of Xalanga extending along the base of the Drakensberg mountains adjoining the district of Wodehouse ; in the establishment for European occupation of a reserve of twenty-three thousand morgen around the seat of the Tsolo magistracy ; in the setting aside for European settlement of what constitutes today the Maclear district ; and in the giving out of farms to Europeans in the district of Matatiele.

(f)   The establishment of townships or villages at the seats of the various magistracies.

For the rest the Native territories remain intact and are administered as Native reserves today.

Natal and Zululand

Natal was brought under British sovereignty in 1843 and it was not long before a Commission, consisting of Messrs. W. Stanger (Surveyor-General), Theophilus Shepstone (Diplomatic Agent), Lieutenant Gibb, R.E., the Reverend N. Adams and the Reverend D. Lindley (American Missionaries), was appointed to demarcate locations for the Natives. The Commission regarded the Natives as the aboriginal inhabitants of the country and set apart for their use large tracts of land amounting in the aggregate to more than two million acres. This extent was regarded by successive Government Commissions (the Land Commission of 1848 and the Commission of 1852-1853, consisting of twenty-four members and known as the " Kaffir Commission ") as excessive, but the land was pointed out to the Natives for their permanent use and formed the basis of the subsequent grants of Native locations to the Natal and various subsidiary Native Trusts which have already been discussed.

Zululand. The circumstances of the establishment of the various Native reserves in Zululand have already been reviewed in dealing with the Zululand Native Trust.

Orange Free State

When the emigrant farmers settled in what subsequently became the Orange Free State, they found the country almost free of Natives, the inhabitants having some years previously been decimated and dispersed by Mosilikatze's forces in their flight from Tshaka's rule.

There are only three Native reserves in the Orange Free State, viz. Witzieshoek in the Harrismith district and Thaba 'Nchu and Seliba in the district of Thaba 'Nchu, their total extent being 74,290 morgen.

The Witzieshoek Reserve was assigned to the tribe of Paulus Mopeli, a Basuto Chief, as a location, when after the defeat of the Basutos by the Orange Free State in the 1865-1866 war he and his subjects tendered their submission to and requested to be accepted as subjects of the Republic.

The Thaba 'Nchu and Seliba Reserves are situate in the Thaba 'Nchu district, formerly known as the Moroka ward, where a Barolong tribe which had been driven out of Bechuanaland by Mosilikatze's forces was allowed to settle by the Basutos in 1829.   On the advent of the Voortrekkers, the acting Chief of these Barolongs, Moroka (who held the position of regent during the minority of the heir to the chieftainship), entered into friendly relations with them. He subsequently assisted them in their war with the Basutos and was recognised by the Republic as a friend and ally and dealt with as an independent chief. After Moroka's death internecine strife broke out in the tribe owing to his son, Samuel, desiring to usurp the chieftainship. In consequence of these disturbances, the President of the Orange Free State, then Sir John Brand, intervened and, in the interests of order and good government, annexed the territory by Proclamation dated the 12th July, 1884.

Moroka had parcelled out a considerable portion of his territory in farms to his sub-chiefs, or " captains," and their immediate followers ; he had also made grants to Europeans. Land certificates or deeds of grant were made out with the intention of issuing them, but they were never actually issued except to some Europeans.

After the annexation of the territory, the Free State Government caused full enquiry to be made by a commission concerning these grants. By resolution of the Raad passed on the 23rd June, 1885, and by Government Notice dated the 30th *idem*, it recognised all *bona fide* grants made by Moroka and title deeds were subsequently issued to both European and Native grantees on certain conditions. Twenty were issued to Europeans and ninety-five to Natives. After these grants had been made, there still remained a considerable number of Natives who were scattered over the rest of the " Ward " and, after full consideration and enquiry, the Government set aside seven farms, constituting what are now known as the Seliba (17,658 morgen) and the Thaba 'Nchu (6,632 morgen) reserves, for occupation by these Natives.

Transvaal

In the *Transvaal*, prior to its first annexation to the British Crown in 1877, no definite locations had been set aside for Native tribes, though under Volksraad resolution, Article 124, dated the 28th November, 1853, commandants of the Republic were instructed when necessary to grant land for occupation by Natives and their descendants, conditionally upon good behaviour and obedience.

The arrangements concluded under the Pretoria Convention of 1881 for the retrocession of the Transvaal stipulated (in Article 21) for the appointment of a standing Native Location Commission, the main duty assigned to which was to reserve to the " Native tribes of the State such locations as they may be fairly and equitably entitled to, due regard being had to the actual occupation of such tribes."

A Location Commission was immediately appointed in terms of this stipulation and at once embarked upon its labours.

The Convention of Pretoria was in 1884 superseded by the Convention of London, which in effect continued the provision for a Native Location Commission though permitting changes in the constitution and personnel of the Commission.

The labours of the Republican Location Commission were recorded in a duly authenticated register. Their recommendations were submitted to the Executive Council for approval and appear generally to have been acted upon and many of the existing locations were assigned by the Republican Government in accordance with these recommendations.

After the Anglo-Boer war, many questions affecting locations in reference to boundaries, mineral and trading contracts, control, compensation due to private landowners and to missionaries, etc., forced themselves upon the attention of the Crown Colony Government, and on the 19th August, 1905, a Location Commission was appointed, with the following terms of reference :—

"(a) To make recommendations as to the boundaries, where undefined, of existing locations granted to Native tribes ;

(b) to investigate the claims to locations on the part of other tribes in respect of promises made to them by the late Government, and to report on the extent and where such locations, if any, should be granted ;

(c) to ascertain what, if any, other tribes claim locations within the meaning of the Conventions of 1881 and 1884, and to recommend where, and to what extent, such should be granted ; and

(d) to report on any questions arising out of these terms of reference."

This Commission in May, 1907, submitted final reports dealing with the locations throughout the Transvaal, excepting only Sekukuni's and those in the districts of Rustenburg, Lichtenburg and Marico, which had already been dealt with by the Commission under the Republican Government.

By Executive Council Resolutions Nos. 2043 of 1906 ; 46, 56, 129, 839 and 1230 of 1907 ; and 58 and 61 of 1908, the reports of the Commission were adopted.

With a few modifications, specially authorised under Union Acts Nos. 28 of 1925 and 34 of 1927, the Transvaal Native locations exist today as established in pursuance of the recommendations of the two Location Commissions mentioned.

The extent of land formally reserved for Native location purposes in each Province is approximately as follows :—

Cape	6,000,000	morgen.
Natal	2,997,000	,,
Transvaal	905,000	,,
Orange Free State	74,290	,,

Having briefly sketched the main events leading up to the establishment of the various Native locations and reserves in the Union as they exist today, we will now consider the different systems of land administration applied in the several Provinces to communally occupied Native areas.

Cape

The following is an excerpt from the report of the South African Native Affairs Commission 1903-1905 : (pages 14 and 15, paragraphs 81, 82 and 83)

" 81.   The policy followed by the Government of the Cape Colony in respect of Native land tenure has been, to begin by adopting the communal system of occupation observed by tribes in their independent state, and, by gradually adapting it to the changing conditions of life attendant upon the march of civilisation, while at the same time establishing a just and sound administration of their personal as well as tribal affairs, to prepare the way for recognition by the people of the advantages of an individual system tending towards assimilation of European methods. Upon peaceable annexation of territory where tribes continued in occupation as before, or upon conquest of territory upon which loyal tribes or clans were in the early days located as a means of protection to the settler population from the frequent raids and disturbances created by those beyond the frontier, the rights and obligations pertaining to the land passed to or have been assumed by the Crown.   In the first case, then existing lines of occupation were recognised, and in respect of later annexations the people were assured of full protection in the enjoyment of their rights in the land without, in most instances, any formal act of reservation or insistence upon any special conditions other than fealty to the Crown.   In the other case of allied tribes under Government rule being located on conquered territory, the land was sub-divided into locations and reserves and set apart for the use of the tribe either by Proclamation (as, for example, the Herschel Reserve), or by title (as in Fingoland), or without such formal reservation (e.g. the Ox Kraal and Kamastone Locations), subject always to the express or implied condition of forfeiture for rebellion."

" 82.   The initial step of importance in the administration of land matters has been the registration of occupiers for hut or, as it might properly be called, land tax purposes.   Thereafter, the sub-division of the whole tribal area into locations has been effected, boundaries being at first widely fixed, and subsequently demarcated according as circumstances permitted."

" 83. In this process the tribal influence of the chief has been kept under control and, according to his character, utilised. The power of allotting lands has been vested in the Governor, but in general has continued to be exercised by the headmen subject to the decision of magistrates in cases of dispute."

In so far as the *Cape Province proper* was concerned, the following statutes dealing with Crown Native locations held under the so-called communal tenure were passed by the Cape Parliament :—

Act No. 2 of 1869, which made provision for the collection of hut tax in Native locations.

Act No. 10 of 1870, which provided for the management of Native locations and for the regulation of rights of commonage. This was repealed by Act No. 29 of 1881.

Act No. 6. of 1876 passed to provide for the better and more effectual supervision and management of Native locations.

Act No. 8 of 1878 amending and amplifying the provisions of the Native Locations Act, No. 6 of 1876.

Act No. 37 of 1884, which purported to " provide for the better and more effectual supervision of Native locations and for the more easy collection of hut tax," repealed Acts Nos. 2 of 1869, 6 of 1876 and 8 of 1878 and was itself repealed by the Native Administration Act, No. 38 of 1927.

Communally occupied locations in the Cape Province proper are to-day administered under the regulations contained in Proclamation No. 302 of 1928 (as amended by Proclamation No. 398 of 1931) which was promulgated under the special legislative powers vested in the Governor-General by section *twenty-five* of the Native Administration Act.

These regulations provide *inter alia* for the demarcation, occupation and registration of homestead and arable allotments, the standard area of the former being half a morgen and of the latter four morgen; the allotment of land by the Native Commissioner (who in practice would doubtless, except in cases of dispute, content himself with confirming dispositions made by the headman) ; the occupation of land in locations for public purposes ; the transfer of allotments by entry in the land registers subject to the approval of the Native Commissioner or other responsible official ; the cancellation of rights to allotments under certain circumstances; the making of bricks, the quarrying of stone and the construction of aqueducts by allotment holders on commonage land ; the building on commonage land of tanks or enclosures for the dipping or cleansing of live stock ; the temporary occupation of commonage land for special purposes with the approval of the Native Commissioner, and the demolition of unauthorised buildings and the removal of unauthorised persons from the district.   The proclamation further specifies offences in respect of commonage, provides for the preservation of pasturage, trees and thatching grass, prohibits the fouling of water-places, deals with the question of the unauthorised occupation of allotments in locations and provides penalties for breach of the regulations.

The following points are particularly worthy of mention :—

(a)   Under paragraph (b) of sub-section (2) of section *four* not more than one homestead allotment and one arable allotment may be allotted to any person, provided that to a person married under Native custom to more than one woman, one homestead and one arable allotment may be allotted for the purposes of each polygamous household.

(b)   In sub-section (7) of section *seven*, it is laid down that the rights of occupation in respect of allotments are not hereditable and automatically terminate upon the death of the holder, but that the widow, heirs or dependents of the deceased shall have first claim to re-allotment of the land should the Native Commissioner consider that they require the same.

(c)   Section *twenty* provides that the proceedings in all cases relating to possession and cancellation of allotments shall be in the nature of administrative action and not subject to the rules governing judicial procedure.   In such cases, the parties have the right of appealing to the Chief Native Commissioner within fourteen days after the decision of the Native Commissioner but have no further right of appeal.

Proclamation No. 302 of 1928 does not apply to the British Bechuanaland reserves which are still administered under the provisions of British Bechuanaland Proclamation No. 220 of 1895, the internal administration resting for the most part in the hands of the chiefs themselves.

In the *Transkeian Territories* the same general lines of policy as regards the administration of communally occupied locations have been followed as in the Cape Province proper.   In fact these principles were, by virtue of the system of edictal legislation operative there, developed in the Transkeian Territories to a degree which was not possible in the Ciskei until the passing of the Native Administration Act, No. 38 of 1927.

Upon annexation, the communal or tribal tenure of land was continued. However, in order to provide better means of keeping in touch with the people and of control, the tribal lands were sub-divided into wards or locations with a headman over each, the headman being made in the course of time directly responsible to the Magistrate, a disposition which has had the effect of restricting the arbitrary exercise of power on the part of chiefs.

Under the general regulations framed at the time of annexation the sole right of allotting land was vested in the Governor. Subsequent regulations have placed this duty in the hands of Magistrates. In point of practice, however, the headmen of the various locations actually allot lands in their respective areas subject to the confirmation of the Magistrate, which is readily given except in disputed cases requiring investigation.

All the locations in twenty out of the twenty-seven districts comprising the Transkeian Territories are occupied under communal tenure and by degrees the allotment and registration of land in these locations have been placed upon a proper basis with the result that it may fairly be claimed that the system operates satisfactorily to-day.

The regulations for the administration and control of Transkeian communal locations are contained in Proclamation No. 143 of 1919 as amended by Proclamations Nos. 18 of 1920, 24 of 1922 and 198 of 1926. The provisions of these Proclamations are very similar to those of Proclamation No. 302 of 1928 referred to above in dealing with the Cape Province proper, the last mentioned having in point of fact actually been based on the former.

Natal

(a) Locations

Reference has already been made to the institution of the Trust system in respect of the tenure of Native locations and reserves in Natal and Zululand as also to the provisions of Act No. 1 of 1912.

As regards the actual internal administration of these locations and reserves, the cardinal principles of policy followed in Natal were (a) the recognition of the Native system of law and (b) the adoption of the tribal system of control with the Governor as Supreme Chief.

The effect of this policy was to perpetuate the original tribal system of land tenure and to militate against the introduction of individual tenure.

Natal Act No. 37 of 1896 was passed " for the better management of Native locations."

Under section *three* of this Act the Governor was authorised to make rules to regulate the use and occupation of lands set apart as Native locations, while in section *four* it was laid down that such rules might provide for

(a) the apportionment of land in locations for use and occupation by Natives ;

(b) the admission of Natives to locations ;

(c) the removal of Natives from locations ;

(d) the removal of Natives from one location to another location, or from one part of a location to another part of a location ;

(e) the definition or alteration of boundaries of lands in locations allotted for the use and occupation of tribes ;

(f) the allotment of lands in locations for kraal sites, and for cultivation, pasturage and commonage ;

(g) all matters relating to roads, by-roads, fences, water-courses, woods, and streams, and the use of water, wood, clay, and stone ;

(h) the preservation of health and observance of decency ;

(i) the powers, authorities, and duties of the inspectors to be appointed under the provisions of the Act ;

(k) the duties of chiefs, district headmen, and kraal heads in locations, and with regard to the distribution of people therein, the allotment of kraal sites and sites for cultivation, and the removal of kraals, in locations, and

(l) generally for carrying out the provisions of the Act.

Section *nine* provided that nothing in the Act should be construed as in any way limiting the powers of the Supreme Chief.

Rules framed under sections *three* and *four* of Act No. 37 of 1896 were published under Government Notices No. 697 of 1896 and No. 49 of 1902.

The Natal Locations Act, No. 37 of 1896, was not extended to Zululand, where the reserves after annexation continued to be occupied under the tribal system of tenure with little or no interference from the Government. Paragraph (g) of clause *three* of the conditions of the Zululand Native Trust Deed of Grant vested the trustees with authority in reference to the allotment of land in the reserves for kraal sites and cultivation but these powers were very rarely exercised.

By Proclamation No. 123 of 1931 (which was issued under the special legislative powers vested in the Governor-General by section *twenty-five* of the Native Administration Act) the Natal location rules published under Government Notices Nos. 697 of 1896 and 49 of 1902 were repealed and fresh regulations were promulgated applicable to the Zululand reserves as well as the Natal locations but not to the mission reserves.

These regulations, which took effect from the 1st July, 1931, leave the allotment of land in locations for arable and residential purposes in the hands of the chiefs subject to the right of the Native Commissioner, with the approval of the Chief Native Commissioner, to intervene where abuse exists and subject to any limitation which may be prescribed by the Minister as regards the extent of allotments ; they provide for the definition, when considered necessary by the Minister, of areas in locations to be used exclusively for residential and cultivation purposes respectively ; they permit of the introduction, where deemed desirable, of the system of registration of allotments ; they make provision for the cancellation of rights to and the surrender of allotments under certain circumstances ; they authorise the making of bricks, the quarrying of stone, the cutting of grass and the construction of aqueducts on commonage land by allotment holders and, with the approval of the Minister, by persons other than allotment holders ; they provide for the building on commonage land of tanks or enclosures for the dipping or cleansing of stock, for the temporary occupation of commonage land for special purposes with the approval of the Native Commissioner, for the demolition of unauthorised buildings and the removal of unauthorised persons from locations ; they prescribe what shall be deemed to constitute offences in relation to the occupation of commonage land. The regulations contain detailed provisions as regards the grazing in locations of stock belonging to persons other than Native residents and define the privileges to which traders, missionaries and others are entitled in this connection.

A special chapter of the regulations relates to the shooting of game in locations and another to the protection and disposal of trees, timber and forest produce.

Proclamation No. 123 of 1931 was amended by Proclamation No. 160 of 1932.

(b) *Mission Reserves*

Reference has already been made to the grant between 1862 and 1887 of special reserves in Natal—known as Mission Reserves—to various missionary bodies in trust for Natives with the object of promoting missionary activity amongst the people and to the circumstances under which the trusts were transferred to the Natal Trust by Act No. 49 of 1903.

The Society named in the original deed of grant of each reserve was under Act No. 49 of 1903 granted the exclusive right of carrying on missionary work in that reserve.

The Act provided that the reserves should be retained for occupation solely by Natives but that the Natal Native Trust should have the right to grant temporary and conditional occupation of store sites, as also prospecting and mining rights, where such would not interfere with the rights and well-being of the Natives or the work of the missionary body concerned.

The financial provisions of the Act have already been discussed in dealing with the Natal Mission Reserves Account (*vide* page 93 *supra*).

The Act empowered the Governor to set apart any reserve or portion of a reserve for exclusive occupation by Native converts ; to decide what powers, if any, should be exercised by Native chiefs in mission reserves ; to define boundaries ; to remove tribes or portions of tribes from mission reserves, and from time to time ·to make regulations for the use and occupation of the reserves and for all purposes of the Act, the following topics being specifically enumerated :—

"(a) The admission of Natives to the reserve.

(b) The lease and hire of land and the conditions to be imposed with regard thereto.

(c) The appropriation of land for the purposes of cultivation, pasture and commonage.

(d) All matters relating to roads, by-roads, fences, pounds, watercourses, woods and streams, and the use of water, wood, clay and stone.

(e) The charges to be made for rent, the agistment of cattle, and for other things for which a charge is authorised by this Act.

(f) The preservation of health and observance of decency.

(g) The maintenance of order and any other matter or thing necessary to be done or be prohibited in the interests of the people living in the Reserve.

(h) The education and industrial training of children living on the Reserve.

(i) For the preservation of game."

Regulations framed under these powers were published under Government Notices Nos. 574 of 1904 and 488 of 1906. These were, however, repealed by Government Notice No. 621 of 1919, under which amended and consolidated regulations were promulgated.

The regulations published under Government Notice No. 621 of 1919 provide *inter alia* for the Chief Native Commissioner, Natal, on behalf of the Minister to direct and control the administration of the Act and regulations on each reserve ; for the appointment of inspectors to control the reserves under the directions of the Chief Native Commissioner ; for the reduction of the rental payable to a uniform rate of £1 sterling per hut per annum ; for the keeping of registers of tenants ; for the admission of Natives to the reserves ; for the allotment of lands ; for the erection of buildings and the removal and demolition of unauthorised buildings ; for the grazing of stock and the provision of commonage ; for the preservation of order and decency ; for the prohibition of heathen practices and beer drinks ; for the attendance of children at schools ; for the preservation of game; for the prevention of the manufacture and sale of intoxicating liquor in the reserves and for the appointment by the Minister of an advisory board to assist in the administration of any reserve.

Eleven such advisory boards have been established. Each consists of five members who hold office for one year. The members are nominated annually at a public meeting of the inhabitants of the reserve and their appointments are confirmed by the Chief Native Commissioner.

Act No. 49 of 1903, when enacted, applied to seventeen mission reserves specified in the schedule which had actually been granted to various missionary bodies. It contained a provision empowering the Governor to grant to the Natal Native Trust " any lands which have heretofore been delimitated as Native mission reserves for, but have not been transferred to, any ecclesiastical body." In terms of this provision the two remaining mission reserves, Emmaus and Ehlanzeni, were subsequently transferred to the Trust and are administered under the Act.

The provisions of section *two* of Act No. 1 of 1912, previously referred to, automatically apply to the mission reserves by virtue of the fact that they were vested in the Natal Native Trust at the date of Union.

Any local or General Council which may ultimately be established for any mission reserve or reserves under the provisions of Proclamation

No. 275 of 1929, to which reference has already been made, will have power within its area of jurisdiction to levy upon the inhabitants a special rate for the dipping of stock and the maintenance of dipping tanks and to deal with and make by-laws in respect of any of the following matters :—

(a) the construction and maintenance of roads, fences, drains, dams, furrows and prevention of erosion ;

(b) an improved water supply ;

(c) the suppression of diseases of stock by the construction and maintenance of dipping tanks and in any other manner whatsoever ;

(d) the suppression of noxious weeds ;

(e) sanitation ;

(f) the preservation of public health by the establishment or maintenance (wholly or in part) of hospitals, nursing or other institutions and in any other manner whatsoever ;

(g) the improvement in methods of agriculture ;

(h) the control and regulation of the grazing of stock ;

(i) afforestation ;

(j) education facilities.

Appended is a schedule of the various mission reserves, indicating in respect of each its extent and the missionary body by which it was previously held or (in respect of Emmaus and Ehlanzeni) for which it was intended.

Mission Reserve.	Extent in acres.	Missionary body.
Amahlongwa	6,965	American Board of Commissioners for Foreign Missions in Natal.
Amanzimtoti	8,077	,, ,,
Ifafa	6,209	,, ,,
Ifumi	7,498	,, ,,
Inanda	11,500	,, ,,
Isidumbeni	5,500	,, ,,
Itafamasi	5,500	,, ,,
Mapumulo	8,196	,, ,,
Table Mountain	5,623	,, ,,
Umsunduzi	5,595	,, ,,
Umtwalumi	12,922	,, ,,
Umvoti	6,207	,, ,,

Mission Reserve.	Extent in acress.	Missionary body.
Umlazi	7,521	Church of England in Natal.
Emmaus	5,476	Berlin Mission Society.
Ehlanzeni	11,000	Hanoverian Missionary Society.
Etembeni	5,939	,, ,,
Umpumulo	12,000	Norwegian Mission in Natal.
St. Michael's	6,300	Roman Catholic Missions.
Indaleni	6,164	Wesleyan Missionary Society.

Orange Free State

The Orange Free State Native locations are all communally occupied and the allotment of land for residential and cultivation purposes is effected by the chief at Witzieshoek and by headmen in the Seliba and Thaba 'Nchu reserves

It has already been pointed out in discussing the system of local government under Ordinance No. 6 of 1907 that the reserve boards have power, subject to the approval of the Governor, to frame regulations in respect of a variety of topics, among which are included certain aspects of land administration.

No special land regulations have been framed under the Ordinance in so far as the Witzieshoek reserve is concerned but, in terms of the regulations published under Government Notice No. 1049 of 1916, any allotment of land made by a headman in the Seliba or Thaba 'Nchu reserve is subject to the approval of and must be recorded in a special register kept for the purpose by the chairman of the board, i.e. the Native Commissioner. The Thaba 'Nchu and Seliba regulations deal too *inter alia* with the making of bricks and quarrying of stone within the reserves, the forfeiture of rights of occupation of allotments on account of non-beneficial occupation and the control of commonage.

Under Government Notice No. 228 of 1930 restrictions were placed upon the grazing of stock upon the commonage of the Thaba 'Nchu reserve, the regulations providing that residents might depasture only ten head of large and twenty head of small stock free of charge and that in respect of any excess over these numbers grazing fees should be charged at the rate of 2s. per head of large and 3d. per head of small stock per annum.

Mention has already been made of the protection afforded to the Native reserves in the Orange Free State by section LII. (3) of the Royal

I

Letters Patent which prohibited their alienation or diversion from the purposes for which they were set apart otherwise than in accordance with " a Law passed by the Legislature," a safe-guard which was re-affirmed under section *one hundred and forty-seven* of the South Africa Act.

Transvaal

The land reserved for Native location purposes in the Transvaal may be divided into two classes (which in some cases co-exist in one location) as follows :—

    A. Land belonging to the Natives themselves ; and

    B. Land not belonging to them.

Class " A " includes :—

(1) land acquired by tribal or joint purchase and subsequently reserved as " locations " on the recommendations of the Republican Location Commission ; thus, most of the recognised locations in the Rustenburg, Pretoria and Marico districts were actually purchased by the tribes concerned ; and

(2) land to which the Natives, on annexation to the Transvaal, retained their original proprietary right, e.g., the Kunana Reserve in the Lichtenburg district.

Under class " B " fall :—

(1) Crown land specially reserved for location purposes under section *twelve* of the Crown Land Disposal Ordinance, No. 57 of 1903 (Transvaal), e.g. most of the locations in the Northern Transvaal ; and

(2) privately-owned land expropriated for location purposes, of which an interesting example is Mothiba's location in the Pietersburg district referred to in the Appellate Division case " Mathiba and others vs. Moschke " (A.D. 1920—page 354).

Location land in the Transvaal, like that in the Orange Free State, was protected from alienation by a provision in the Letters Patent which was re-affirmed under section *one hundred and forty-seven* of the South Africa Act.

The basic law upon which rested the administration of Native affairs in the Transvaal for over forty years was Law No. 4 of 1885, which was repealed by the Native Administration Act No. 38 of 1927. No provision was made in that law, or in any Transvaal legislation prior to

Union, regulating the tenure of land in the Native locations, nor in point of fact has any been made since Union. The original tribal system of communal occupation accordingly continues in operation, the allotment of land in the locations rests entirely in the hands of the chiefs and the only avenue of official intervention in matters of this nature has been under and by virtue of the powers of the Paramount Chief (vested formerly in the State President, after annexation in the Governor and subsequent to Union in the Governor-General).

Transvaal Law No. 3 of 1898, Article *three*, provided that no obligation or contract entered into by a Native chief, by which either his tribe or the ground granted to him as a location might in may way be bound, should be valid unless approved by the Executive Council. Law No. 3 of 1898 was repealed by the Native Administration Act, No. 38 of 1927, but upon it are based the very useful provisions contained in section *three* of that Act (*vide* page 21 *supra*), which, of course, apply not to the Transvaal alone but throughout the Union.

3. THE APPLICATION TO NATIVE LOCATIONS AND RESERVES OF EUROPEAN IDEAS OF INDIVIDUAL TENURE OF LAND

Cape

(a) *Ciskeian Districts other than Glen Grey*

Allotments have been granted to Natives in surveyed locations in the Ciskei from time to time since 1855 and today there are locations held under individual tenure in the districts of East London, King William's Town, Victoria East, Fort Beaufort, Peddie, Stutterheim, Queenstown, Herschel and Glen Grey. Though the statement is made in the report of the South African Native Affairs Commission, 1903-1905, that the policy of the Cape Government as regards land tenure was to begin by adopting the communal system of occupation and, by gradually adapting it to the changing conditions of life attendant upon the march of civilisation, to prepare the way for recognition by the people of the advantages of an individual system, evidence is not lacking to show that in the early days the necessity for inculcating European ideas and methods amongst the Natives by a *gradual process* was not sufficiently appreciated.

When the earliest grants were made the Natives neither desired nor understood the European system of individual ownership of land, which was entirely different from their own customs and ideas. The change was introduced before the people were ripe for it and consequently the earlier Native location surveys did not prove a success. The conditions inserted in the title deeds were unsuited to the needs of the Natives in their then stage of development with the result that certain of them were never enforced and remained for the most part a dead letter, e.g. the stipulation that the common rights of the whole location should be subjected to the management of a Municipality. No special protection was afforded the Natives under their conditions of title with the result that the land could be mortgaged without let or hindrance and could be sold in execution for debt.

As further grants were made from time to time, additional conditions, which experience had shown to be desirable or necessary, were inserted in the title deeds issued and more particulaily was this the case after the passing of Act No. 40 of 1879, which made statutory provision for the survey and grant of allotments in Native locations subject to such conditions as the Governor might deem fit and as might be approved by both Houses of Parliament. The result was an entire absence of uniformity as regards the conditions under which these allotments were held.

Mr. M. C. Vos, formerly Secretary for Native Affairs, who was in 1922 appointed to enquire into and report upon the system under which Native allotments had been surveyed for individual tenure and the system of registration of ownership or occupation of such allotments, remarks as follows on the earlier surveys (U.G. 42—'22 page 1) :—

" The failure of the system in the early days was largely due, as far as the Natives were concerned, to (1) the preference to tribal or common tenure, due in a great measure to the deep-seated aversion of the chiefs to individual tenure, as it would gradually and surely sap their control over the people ; (2) to the dislike of the Native to being tied down to definite and permanent sites for dwelling or gardens ; (3) reluctance to pay the cost of survey and title ; (4) unsuitability of allotment caused by surveyors not consulting the interests of the future occupants so much as their own convenience in the survey, and to this cause must be assigned the reason of the unwillingness to take up title and to the large numbers which had to be cancelled owing to the lots being utterly unsuitable for tillage."

The greatest defect, however, of the systems of individual tenure applied in Native locations prior to the passing of the Glen Grey Act of 1894 was the absence of provision for a simple and inexpensive method of transfer. The result was that these small allotments, the average extent of which was less than five morgen, could be transferred only by means of a formal transfer deed, necessitating the employment of a qualified conveyancer and the payment of transfer duty and legal costs amounting in many instances to more than the actual value of the land to be transferred. Add to the prohibitive cost of transfer the fact that, speaking generally, the Natives themselves did not appreciate the necessity when transferring their land to do more than hand over the actual title deed to the new owner and it will be readily understood that in only a very small percentage of cases was the transfer of allotments, not held under the Glen Grey system of tenure, registered, though the allotments undoubtedly frequently changed hands. Mr. M. C. Vos, when investigating the position in 1922, found that of 1,448 lots in the Kamastone location only 389 were occupied by persons registered as the owners thereof.

With the effluxion of time, the position became aggravated to such an extent that it was considered necessary to make special provision in the Native Administration Act of 1927 to put matters right. To this end the Governor-General was given power under section *eight* of the Act to appoint commissioners to investigate the question of the occupation and ownership of allotments in surveyed locations and provision was made whereby persons found by the commissioners to be entitled to allotments might become registered as the owners thereof on payment of a fee of £1 in each case.

Thus, where an allotment has changed hands several times without transfer ever having been effected, it would in the ordinary course be necessary for each successive transfer to be registered by formal deed, involving the payment of heavy conveyancing fees and transfer duty in respect of each transaction, and, in most cases, very heavy penalties in respect of overdue transfer duty as well. In many instances too, transfer could be passed only under the authority of an order of the Supreme Court, the cost of obtaining which would obviously be prohibitive. Under the provisions of the Native Administration Act, however, the Natives are absolved from the necessity of all this expense, and an allotment, no matter how often it has changed hands without transfer having been passed, can be registered in the name of the person who is found to be entitled to it subject to payment by him of an inclusive fee of £1. Any person who feels aggrieved by the finding of a commissioner has under sub-section (9) of section *eight* of the Act the right to appeal to a board of three persons appointed by the Governor-General.

Commissioners were duly appointed for the various districts concerned and commenced holding their investigations. In the meantime, the Government's proposals as regards Ciskeian land matters, which had been made known to the people, had been the subject of considerable misrepresentation and suspicion on the part of a section of the population, who refused to accept the assurance that they were intended entirely for their own benefit and assistance and construed them as an indirect and veiled attack upon their franchise rights.   The upshot was that, with a view to challenging the validity of sections *seven* and *eight* of the Native Administration Act, a Native of the King William's Town district, named Ndobe, refused to produce his title deeds when called upon to do so by the commissioner in the course of his investigations.   He was then formally subpoenaed by the commissioner, under the provisions of sub-section (3) of section *eight*, to produce the documents and on his refusal to comply was prosecuted for contempt and fined 2s. 6d.   He appealed against the conviction to the Eastern Districts Local Division of the Supreme Court on the grounds that the Native Administration Act contains such provisions as would fall within the purview of section *thirty-five* of the South Africa Act, that it should accordingly have been passed at its third reading by a majority of both Houses of Parliament sitting together, that it was not so passed and is therefore invalid.

The Eastern Districts Court confirmed the conviction, ruling that the Act was not such a measure as was contemplated under section *thirty five* of the Act of Union.   Ndobe then made application for and was granted leave to appeal to the Appellate Division.   Here again the decision went against him and he then made application for leave to appeal to the Privy Council.   Before this application could be heard Ndobe died.

Investigations by the various commissioners under section *eight* of the Act were suspended by the Government pending the outcome of Ndobe's appeal to the Supreme Court.   They were, however, resumed after the Appellate Division had given judgment against Ndobe, have been proceeding steadily ever since and in the case of a number of locations have been completed.

The Board of Appeal contemplated under sub-section (9) of section *eight* of the Act, to which reference has already been made, was appointed under Government Notice No. 945 of 1932 and consists of Messrs. M. G. Apthorp (Chief Native Commissioner for the Ciskei), R. D. H. Barry (President of the Native Appeal Court, Cape and Orange Free State) and J. G. Freislich (Magistrate and Native Commissioner, King William's Town) with the first-mentioned as chairman.

It would obviously have been futile to incur considerable expense in placing the question of the ownership of land in the Ciskeian locations on a proper basis unless steps were at the same time taken to prevent any recurrence of the former chaotic state of affairs and to ensure sound and efficient administration of these locations for the future.

To this end the following measures were adopted :—

(a) By Proclamation No. 119 dated the 12th March, 1931, promulgated under the provisions of section *six* of the Native Administration Act, No. 38 of 1927, a Native Deeds Registry was established with effect from the 1st April, 1931, in the office of the Chief Native Commissioner at King William's Town, with the Chief Native Commissioner as Registrar. This registry is modelled on the lines of that established in the office of the Chief Magistrate at Umtata under Proclamation No. 196 of 1920, concerns itself with the registration and custody of Native titles only and has already met with a large measure of success.

(b) Under and by virtue of the general legislative powers vested in the Governor-General in respect of scheduled Native areas by section *twenty-five* of the Native Administration Act, certain much needed reforms not actually dealt with in the Act itself were introduced by Proclamation No. 117 dated the 12th March, 1931.

First and foremost, is the provision of a cheap and simple procedure for the transfer of allotments. Transfer is subject to the approval of the Governor-General (who has power to delegate and has delegated his functions in this connection to the Chief Native Commissioner) and is effected by the Chief Native Commissioner, in his capacity as Registrar of Deeds, by endorsement on the title deed on payment of a fee of 2s. 6d. Thus the necessity for the preparation of formal deeds of transfer by qualified conveyancers, with the attendant heavy costs, has disappeared. In addition, the proclamation expressly provides that transfer duty shall not be payable in respect of the transfer of these Native allotments.

Secondly, uniformity as regards the conditions of tenure of allotments in surveyed locations in the Ciskei outside the district of Glen Grey was achieved under the proclamation, which prescribed certain conditions under which they should all be deemed to be held. While these conditions are not irksome and do not interfere with an owner in the occupation and enjoyment of his property, they introduced certain necessary safeguards in the interests of the Natives themselves, e.g. they provide that an allotment shall not be liable to execution for debt other than a debt due to the Government or one secured under a mortgage bond duly registered.

Thirdly, Proclamation No. 117 of 1931 has made it possible for additional allotments to be granted in the various locations so as to provide for the descendants of existing owners, who previously could not obtain lots otherwise than by succession or transfer.

Fourthly, provision is made under the proclamation for the surrender by registered holders of unsuitable allotments, e.g. such as are useless owing to erosion or other cause, and for the grant of fresh ones in substitution therefor.

Finally, the proclamation definitely lays it down that no allotment in a surveyed Native location may be sold in execution to a European.

(b) *The Glen Grey System of Individual Tenure*

The report of the Cape Native Affairs Commission of 1910 contains the following passage (G. 26-1910, page 20 paragraph 58) :—

> " The Glen Grey Act No. 25 of 1894 and the Transkeian Proclamations developed from it, constitute the best adaptation of the European system of rigidly defined individual allotments to the requirements of the Native people. The Act, while providing for the survey and issue of title to all arable land, does not require the survey of dwelling sites, and admits of the issue of title to a building plot only where there is a desire on the part of the intending grantee to carry out substantial structural improvements."

The essential features of the Glen Grey system of tenure may be summarised as follows :—

(1) The grant is subject to payment of perpetual quitrent at the rate of 15s. per five-morgen allotment, which is the average, and 3s. for every additional morgen, and survey expenses including cost of title.

(2) The land is inalienable without the Governor-General's consent.

(3) The land is hereditable according to the law of primogeniture as observed by the Natives themselves, power of disherison for good cause and after due enquiry being conceded. (This principle has by section *twenty-three of* the Native Administration Act No. 38 of 1927 been made of general application to all land in locations held in individual tenure upon quitrent conditions by Natives).

(4) The principle of " one man one lot " is applied.

(5) Transfer of the land upon approval of the Governor-General or according to the table of succession is effected by simple en-

dorsement of the title deed upon payment of a registration fee of 2s. 6d., the deed then being forwarded by the Magistrate to the Registrar of Deeds for registration.

(6) The land cannot be subdivided or sub-let.

(7) Rights of way and rights of expropriation for public purposes are reserved, mineral rights being subject to the provisions of the Mineral Law of the Cape Province.

(8) The grant is liable to forfeiture for non-fulfilment of conditions, particularly for :—

  (a) Rebellion.

  (b) Conviction of theft.

  (c) Non-beneficial occupation.

  (d) Non-payment of outstanding instalments of survey expenses or quitrent, after summary process of distraint.

(9) The value of the land cannot be counted for the purpose of qualifying for the franchise.

(c) *Transkeian Districts*

The Glen Grey system of individual tenure was extended to the District of Butterworth in the Transkeian Territories by Proclamation No. 227 of 1898 and later to the Districts of Nqamakwe, Tsomo, Idutywa, Umtata and Engcobo. A somewhat modified but essentially similar system was applied to the District of Xalanga by Proclamation No. 241 of 1911.

The cardinal features of the system have already been indicated but it should be mentioned in so far as the Transkeian Territories are concerned that, by taking advantage of the edictal system of legislation operative there, it has been practicable to introduce modifications and improved methods from time to time with a facility which would not otherwise have been practicable.

A deeds registry for Native titles under the individual tenure system as applied in the Transkeian Territories was established in the office of the Chief Magistrate at Umtata by Proclamation No. 196 of 1920 and has functioned most satisfactorily. Over 50,000 title deeds are registered in this deeds registry and grants, transfers, etc. are expeditiously handled.

Regulations for the general management and control of surveyed locations in the Transkeian Territories are contained in Proclamation No. 174 of 1921 (applicable to the districts surveyed under Proclamation

No. 227 of 1898) and Proclamation No. 170 of 1922 (applicable to Xalanga). Both of these proclamations were amended by Proclamation No. 217 of 1925.

(d) *General Remarks*

Considerable misgivings have been felt as to the success of the various systems of individual tenure. The survey of the locations has been an expensive process, the Natives are not able to appreciate the value of exact measurement, and the surveys have not in all instances been carried out in a way to meet the conservative habits of those for whom the allotments were intended. The Survey Commission, which reported in 1921, recommended that some simpler form of survey should be employed where Native allotments were in question, and Mr. M. C. Vos was appointed to go into the question and submit a scheme with this object. His report (U.G. 42 of 1922), which has already been referred to, is a valuable synopsis of the history of individual tenure, and contains suggestions for a simpler system of defining the boundaries of Native allotments.

Natal

No system of individual tenure is operative in the Natal locations and Zululand reserves, but in the early days certain lots in three mission reserves were granted by the Trustees (before the trusts were transferred to the Natal Native Trust) in freehold to Natives. Thirty-four lots were so granted in the Amanzimtoti, one hundred and fifty-five in the Umvoti, and twenty-six in the Ifumi Mission Reserves.

In 1918 the Minister of Native Affairs, in the exercise of his powers under Act No. 1 of 1912, authorised the general survey of the Ifafa and Amanzimtoti Mission Reserves into small holdings, and lots, in extent approximately 13 acres, were surveyed for monogamous residents with adequate provision of commonage. The holdings were not granted under title but a leasehold form of tenure was introduced, a ticket of occupation being issued for each lot carrying a minimum annual rental of £1 sterling.

These principles, it may be stated, were decided upon after careful consideration and investigation and after close consultation with the missionary bodies concerned, as well as with representatives of the Native residents.

The cost of carrying out the survey operations was borne from mission reserve funds, and advisory boards, as contemplated in Government Notice No. 621 of 1919, have been constituted to assist in the administration of the areas.

Proclamation No. 275 of 1929, which has already been referred to as providing for the establishment of local and general councils for the mission reserves, empowers the Minister, on a resolution adopted by the Local Council of any such reserve and by a majority of the rent-payers present at a special meeting held for the purpose, to cause steps to be taken in respect of that reserve :—

(a) for the sub-division and survey of the reserve into arable lots, building lots, residential areas and commonage ;

(b) for the transfer, subject to conditions, from the Natal Native Trust of arable lots and building lots to approved applicants ; provided that the claims of registered rent payers occupying land in the reserve shall receive first consideration.

In so far as *Zululand* is concerned, the only attempt at introducing anything in the nature of a system of individual tenure has been in respect of certain three farms, usually known as the " Impapala Lands," in the District of Eshowe, occupied by a community of Christianised Natives who migrated there in 1886. These farms, which are 2,638 acres in extent, were surveyed into eight-five lots comprising 1,944 acres and thirteen commonages comprising 694 acres. The lots vary in extent from nine to thirty-five acres and certificates of occupation were issued in respect of them in 1912 under the authority of resolutions of both Houses of Parliament.

A rental of 2s. per acre per annum was made payable under the certificates which stipulated further for the repayment of the costs of survey in annual instalments of 10s. The rental was in 1925, with the concurrence of both Houses of Parliament, reduced to 1s. per acre per annum, subject to a minimum annual charge of £1.

The certificates of occupation carry no definite legal rights of succession, though administratively the rights of the next of kin are invariably recognised, and transfer is permitted only with the consent of the Government. The lots can be used for residential and agricultural purposes only and must be occupied by the registered holder or a member of his family for a period of not less than six months in each year.

The settlement was vested in the Zululand Native Trust and constituted a scheduled Native area under the provisions of Act No. 28 of 1925.

Transvaal and Orange Free State

No attempt has up to the present been made to introduce any form of individual tenure in the Transvaal and Orange Free State Native locations.

4. THE ACQUISITION BY NON-NATIVES OF LAND OR RIGHTS TO AND INTERESTS IN LAND IN AREAS SET ASIDE FOR NATIVE OCCUPATION

The most common and at the same time the most important phases of European activity in areas specially set aside for Native occupation are trading and missionary enterprise and numerous applications are from time to time received from Europeans for permission to occupy sites in Native locations for these purposes.

Other directions in which European activities manifest themselves in Native areas are as regards the obtaining of concessions over location land for industrial purposes, e.g. for the exploitation of natural products such as Dobo Grass or the Euphorbia, the negotiation of mineral contracts, and the acquisition of servitudes—whether under the Irrigation Act or otherwise—over Native land.

As regards *trading* in Native locations, there is diversity of practice and procedure in the different Provinces.

In the Transkeian Territories, the occupation of trading sites is governed by Proclamation No. 11 of 1922, which contains elaborate provisions to prevent over-trading, to prohibit trading monopolies and undesirable practices, to regulate the issue of licences and generally to give the Government adequate control over the activities of traders.

The system of edictal legislation operative in the Transkeian Territories has enabled the Government to crystallise into law in those Territories wholesome restrictions which are administratively applied in so far as possible in other parts of the country, e.g., for the prevention of over-trading, the restriction that, save under exceptional circumstances, a trading station shall not be established in a Native location at a distance of less than five miles from any existing trading site ; for the prevention of monopolies, the restriction upon the acquisition by the holder of a trading site of any other trading concern within a radius of twenty miles of the first-mentioned site ; to ensure a suitable type of trader, the provision making the occupation of any fresh trading site or the alienation of any existing trading site subject to the approval of the Governor-General.

The tenure of trading sites in the Transkeian Territories was for many years under certificates of occupation issued on the authority of the Governor-General and subject to more or less precarious conditions. In 1919, however, the Government accepted a recommendation put forward by the Select Committee on Native Affairs that the survey and grant under title of trading sites in the Transkeian Territories be authorised upon the application of the holders. The necessary provision to this end was made in Proclamation No. 11 of 1922 and many of the traders took advantage thereof with the result that to-day they hold their sites under formal deeds of grant. It may be mentioned that there are more than six hundred and fifty trading stations in the Transkeian Territories alone.

In the Cape Province proper, trading sites in communally occupied locations are either held under certificates of occupation issued under the provisions of Act No. 30 of 1909, or, subject to the concurrence of both Houses of Parliament, are granted outright under the Crown Lands Disposal Act, No. 15 of 1887. In the surveyed locations grants under Act No. 15 of 1887 are made.

It may be added that traders in the Ciskeian locations have during recent years been accorded the same facilities as their Transkeian brethren to obtain title in respect of their trading sites.

In Natal, trading sites in Native locations are leased by the particular Trust concerned to the trader in each instance and the procedure adopted when the establishment of a store in any location is considered desirable is to call for tenders for the lease of the site. Here again the Department is at pains to ensure that only persons of suitable character obtain such trading rights, to prevent over-trading with its attendant malpractices and to avoid the creation of monopolies. In terms of section *two* of Act No. 1 of 1912, leases to Europeans of Trust land for trading purposes must be ratified by resolution of both Houses of Parliament.

The procedure as regards the occupation of trading sites in the Transvaal is, in so far as Crown Native locations are concerned, much the same as in Natal. Tenders are invited and the sites are leased by the Government to the successful tenderer on a yearly basis, a prescribed form of trading permit being issued by the Department. There is no requirement necessitating the ratification of such leases by Parliament.

In so far as tribally owned locations are concerned, however, the acquisition of trading rights is a matter for negotiation by the would-be trader with the Natives of the tribe in question. No such tribal contracts can be entered into without the approval of the Minister of Native Affairs and they must accordingly be submitted to the Department, upon which is imposed the duty of carefully scrutinising the relative agreements with a view to protecting the interests of the Natives.

All cessions from European to European of trading rights in scheduled Native areas in the Natal, Transvaal, and Orange Free State Provinces are subject to the approval of the Governor-General under section *one* of the Natives Land Act, 1913, a requirement which enables the Department to exercise a wholesome surveillance over such transactions.

Enough has been said as regards the occupation of trading sites in Native areas to indicate the principles upon which applications by Europeans generally for land rights within such areas are dealt with by the Department. The paramount consideration is the promotion of the welfare of the Natives themselves, and, where such privileges are granted, every precaution is taken to protect the interests of the Natives and to preclude interference with their rights.

As regards the *occupation of sites for church, school, and mission purposes in Native areas*, the policy of the Department is largely based upon certain recommendations which were put forward by the Select Committee on Native Affairs in 1925 and were accepted by the Government. Those recommendations were as follows :—

"With regard to applications by Churches or religious bodies for sites or other privileges depending upon Government recognition, that as a general rule permission shall only be granted to Churches long established and enjoying universal public recognition and in all other cases before any application is considered by the Native Affairs Department a report shall be submitted by the Native Affairs Commission in regard to the applicant body as to the demand for its existence, its stability, its capacity both financially and educationally, and its general fitness for religious work amongst Natives."

At the same time, the Department is concerned in so far as possible to prevent proselytism and unhealthy sectarian rivalry and to this end a restriction, known as *the three miles radius rule*, has been imposed by virtue of which in the ordinary course no denomination is permitted to occupy a church or school site in a Native location or reserve within a distance of three miles from any existing mission station. In so far as Native areas in the Transvaal and Natal are concerned, the radius requirement has recently been extended to five miles.

The standard area, occupation of which is permitted for church and school purposes in Native locations, is half a morgen, but where exceptional circumstances exist to justify such a course the occupation of larger extents is authorised.

All applications for church and school sites, and they are very numerous, are dealt with by the Department under the respective laws of the different Provinces. The provisions of Act No. 1 of 1912 necessitate the submission of such applications in so far as Natal locations and reserves are concerned for the approval of both Houses of Parliament.

As an indication of the extent to which missionary work is undertaken amongst the Natives, it may be mentioned that there are more than eighteen hundred approved church and school sites in the Transkeian Territories alone.

Prospecting activities in Crown Native locations are not generally encouraged and applications for permission to prospect for precious stones in such areas are consistently refused. In several locations in the Cape Province all prospecting has definitely been forbidden by Proclamation

In so far as the Transvaal Province is concerned, permission to prospect in Crown Native locations can be obtained only with the approval of the Minister of Native Affairs. Having regard to important mineral discoveries in this Province, e.g. platinum, the Government has felt that it would not be justified in adopting an attitude which might have the effect of preventing the exploitation of assets of national importance and so a limited number of prospecting permits have been issued in respect of precious and base metals. The policy adopted in this connection is designed, on the one hand, to prevent the influx of large numbers of irresponsible Europeans into Native locations and to avoid the creation of monopolies on the other. It has accordingly been laid down that two permits may be issued in respect of any given area of location land, conferring a three months' prospecting right, against payment in advance of a fee of £10, the question of the renewal of such permits being dependent upon whether, during the period of their availability, *bona fide* prospecting has been carried out to the satisfaction of the Department.

As regards tribally-owned locations or lands, the matter of the acquisition of prospecting rights is (unless the mineral rights are held by some person other than the tribe), one for negotiation by the prospector with the chief and tribe concerned. Such agreements usually provide

for the exercise by the prospector, on payment of a reasonable consideration, of prospecting rights for a period of six months renewable up to a
year or two years, during which the prospector is given the option either
to enter into a perpetual mineral lease in respect of the property concerned
on a rental and royalty basis or to purchase the mineral rights outright.
These contracts fall under the purview of section *three* of the Native
Administration Act, No. 38 of 1927, and accordingly require, in so far as
the tribal interest is concerned, firstly to be adopted by a majority of the
tribesmen present at a general meeting of the tribe convened for the
purpose of considering the matter, and, secondly, to be approved by the
Minister of Native Affairs.   It is accordingly the function of the Department to all intents and purposes to act as the agent of the Natives in matters
of this nature, which not infrequently involve interests running into
thousands of pounds, so as to ensure that they receive an equitable *quid
pro quo* and that their interests are adequately protected in each instance.

The *mineral rights* in respect of the various locations and reserves in
the Natal Province are for the most part owned by the Trusts in which
those locations and reserves are respectively vested.   The Natal Mines
and Collieries Act, No. 43 of 1899, contains special provisions in regard
to prospecting and mining on Native Trust land.   No prospecting may
be undertaken without the permission of the Trust concerned and,
speaking generally, the same policy is followed as in the case of the Transvaal locations.

The conditions under which permits are issued to prospect on Trust
land in Natal are prescribed by Government Notice No. 1538 dated the
25th September, 1931, which reads as follows :—

    " It is hereby notified for general information that from and after
        the date hereof a charge of £3 sterling (three pounds) per
        permit will be made in respect of the issue of permits to enter
        and prospect for minerals, metals or precious stones upon land
        vested in any Native Trust, the affairs of which are administered
        under the provisions of Act No. 1 of 1912, and that the follow-
        ing conditions will be inserted in all such permits :—

    (1)   The permit holder shall be in possession of prospecting permits
        as required by law.

    (2)   The permit holder is expressly forbidden to trespass in Native
        kraals and lands.

    (3)   All open workings must be properly protected and, if dangerous
        to human life or to stock, must be filled in to the level of the
        surface when abandoned.

(4) All questions as to the permit holder's rights to wood, water and grazing shall be settled by the Native Commissioner in consultation with the chief and the tribe of the location.

(5) Any breach of the conditions of this permit or any misbehaviour or disreputable conduct in the location on the part of the permit holder, his employees or persons directly connected with him, shall entail the immediate cancellation of this permit.

Government Notice No. 2174 dated the 28th November, 1930, is hereby withdrawn."

B

NATIVE OCCUPATION AND TENURE OF LAND OTHER THAN THAT SPECIALLY SET ASIDE FOR THEM

Land occupied by, but not specially reserved for, Natives may be either :—

1. Land privately owned by Natives ; or
2. Crown land ; or
3. Land owned by non-Natives,

and it is proposed to deal with this topic under these headings.

1. LAND PRIVATELY OWNED BY NATIVES

Cape

In the Cape Province there has never been any bar to the acquisition of land by Natives. The Native is as free to purchase land as the European and no legal obstacle exists to prevent him from doing so to-day. The restrictions imposed by section *one* of the Natives Land Act, No. 27 of 1913, were held by the Appellate Division of the Supreme Court in the consolidated appeals of " Thompson and Stilwell *versus* Kama " (A.D. 1917, p. 209) not to apply in respect of the Cape Province.

It is estimated that, exclusive of lots held under individual tenure in Native locations, the area of land privately owned by Natives in the Cape Province is approximately 260,000 morgen.

Natal

In the Natal Province there was, prior to the passing of the Natives Land Act, 1913, no general restriction upon the acquisition of land by Natives though it was prohibited in certain cases, e.g. in certain townships in Zululand.

K

Generally speaking, however, Natives were free to buy land in t. same manner as Europeans, and, in fact, in many instances Crown lan were allotted to Natives on the same basis and conditions as to European

The effect of the Natives Land Act on the acquisition of land by Natives in Natal will be considered in dealing specifically with that Act.

It is estimated that the approximate extent of land privately owned by Natives in Natal is 150,000 morgen.

Orange Free State

In the Orange Free State, Natives were by article six of Part I of Chapter XXXIV of the Law Book debarred from purchasing land. This prohibition was absolute except as regards the Moroka Ward (the district of Thaba 'Nchu), in respect of which the rights of the Natives were guaranteed in the Proclamation issued by the State President, Sir John Brand, upon annexation of the territory.

The grants of land made by Moroka prior to annexation to both Europeans and Natives have already been mentioned (*vide* page 118 *supra*), as has also the fact that the Government in recognition of such of these grants as could be proved to be *bona fide*, issued title to twenty European and ninety-five Native grantees.

The Native owners were, however, debarred from disposing of their land to Natives other than their parents or brothers, sisters, children, or direct descendants—*vide* Part II of Chapter XXXIV of the Law Book, articles 11-16.

The Moroka Ward Land Relief Act, No. 28 of 1924, repealed these provisions and made it lawful for any Native who is the registered owner of land in the Moroka Ward, with the approval of the Governor-General, to sell, let, or transfer any right, title or interest in such land to any *bona fide* member of the Barolong tribe, who, being domiciled in the Orange Free State, is approved by the Minister of Native Affairs after consultation with the tribe located in the said ward. In other words, the effect of the Act was to permit a Native landowner in the Moroka Ward to sell to any other reputable Barolong domiciled in the Orange Free State and not merely to some member of his immediate family as had previously been the case.

It is regrettable to record that, owing largely to the improvidence and lack of foresight of the owners, many of the original ninety-five Native-owned farms in the Moroka ward have already fallen into the hands of

Europeans, and it would seem to be merely a matter of time before a similar fate will overtake the rest, as the large majority of them are very heavily bonded, while year by year the financial position of the owners seems to become more and more involved.

The area of Native-owned land in the Thaba 'Nchu district is estimated at 80,000 morgen.

Transvaal

As regards the Transvaal, the Pretoria Convention of 1881, in stipulating that Natives should be allowed to acquire land, prescribed that the grant or transfer of such land should be made to and registered in the name of the Native Location Commission in trust for the Natives concerned.

The Republican Government subsequently appointed the Superintendent of Natives (who occupied a position corresponding to that of Minister of Native Affairs) to take the place of the Location Commission as trustee of Native land so acquired and under the Crown Colony Government this trust vested in the Commissioner for Native Affairs.

In consequence of the definite provision in the Convention of Pretoria and the resultant practice of vesting Native land in trust, it was for a long time considered that no Native could hold land in his own name in the Transvaal but that title must necessarily vest in the Commissioner for Native Affairs in trust for the actual owner. This view was, however, exploded by the decision of the Supreme Court in *Ex parte Tsewu* (1905 T.S.C. 130) which definitely established the right of individual Natives to acquire and take transfer of immovable property in the Transvaal.

This decision of the Supreme Court removed all difficulties which previously existed, or were thought to exist, regarding the acquisition of land by Natives and from that date until the passing of the Natives Land Act, 1913, there were no restrictions upon Native land purchase in the Transvaal, except that

(a) the conditions of title issued in respect of erven in certain townships expressly debarred acquisition by Natives ; and

(b) no Coloured person could acquire fixed property in mining stand townships or on proclaimed fields or public diggings under the Gold Law or under the Precious Stones Ordinance.

The effect of the Natives Land Act on the acquisition of land by Natives in the Transvaal will be considered in dealing specifically with that Act.

In the early days there were very few instances of land purchase by individual Natives in the Transvaal, tribal acquisition being the general rule.

After the decision of the Supreme Court in *Ex parte Tsewu*, however, there manifested itself amongst the Natives a growing tendency to acquire land in individual or partnership title as opposed to tribal acquisition.

Individual purchase of land by Natives is unobjectionable and is to be encouraged but it is only in very exceptional cases that an individual Native has the means to negotiate the purchase of any considerable extent of land. Such purchases can under present conditions be effected only by co-operative effort and yet it must be recognised that there are very serious drawbacks to the acquisition of property by a large number of individual Natives in co-partnership in undivided shares. There is no adequate supervision over such lands which inevitably develop into uncontrolled locations. Further, the individual co-purchasers die or dispose of their rights and no steps are taken to effect transfer of their undivided shares to the heirs or purchasers, as the case may be, a state of affairs which will inevitably lead to disputes and litigation in the future.

Various expedients have from time to time been attempted with a view to overcoming the difficulty, but the Department has ultimately come to the conclusion that the only satisfactory course is to insist upon co-operative land purchase by any number of Natives in excess of six being effected on a tribal as opposed to a partnership or communal basis.

The practice to-day is to register all land tribally purchased by Natives in the name of the Minister of Native Affairs in trust for the tribe concerned, a course which can be insisted upon by virtue of the fact that such acquisitions are subject to the approval of the Governor-General. This registration is a formality and the Minister does not purport to exercise any active rights of ownership by virtue thereof but the system has the great advantage of ensuring reference to the Department in respect of any matter or transaction affecting such land and thus enabling it to prevent exploitation of the Natives and to afford them a measure of protection they would not otherwise enjoy.

2. CROWN LAND OCCUPIED BY BUT NOT SPECIALLY RESERVED FOR NATIVES

Cape

In the *Cape Province* there are various areas of Crown land, of an estimated total extent of 150,000 morgen, which have not been reserved as Native locations but are occupied by Natives.

Prior to the passing of the Natives Taxation and Development Act, No. 41 of 1925, the Natives resident upon these lands were called upon to pay hut tax. Hut tax was, however, abolished under Act No. 41 of 1925 and such Natives now pay local tax by virtue of the provision contained in section *nineteen* of that Act, which includes within the definition of " Native location " for local tax purposes any Crown land occupied by Natives under communal conditions other than land for which rent is payable to the Government.

Natal

The law relating to the occupation by Natives of Crown land in the Natal Province is contained in Ordinance No. 2 of 1855, Law No. 41 of 1884 and Act No. 48 of 1903.

Ordinance No. 2 of 1855, which took effect on the 1st of August, 1855, was passed " to prevent unlicensed squatting and to regulate the occupation of land by the Natives," and contained provisions relating to both Crown and privately owned land.

Under section *one* Magistrates were required to remove all Natives from Crown land and under section *two* penalties were prescribed for unlicensed squatters.

The provision was, however, apparently never enforced and remained practically a dead letter.

Law No. 41 of 1884 was passed " to provide for the collection of rent from Native Squatters or Occupiers of Crown lands." To this end it laid down that Magistrates should give notice to all Natives resident on Crown land in their respective districts that from and after the 1st July, 1886, an annual rental of £1 per hut would be charged for the use and occupation of such land, (the charge being however made variable by the Governor to meet the circumstances of any particular case) ; that the field cornets, or other officers specially appointed for the purpose, should furnish lists of the Natives occupying Crown land in their respective wards to the Magistrates, and that further squatting on Crown lands should not be permitted without the permission of the Governor in each instance.

This Law further provided that Native squatters should remove from Crown land after having been given six months' notice in writing, which notice, however, could be given only in the month of January in any year, and that the removal of any Native disregarding such notice might be summarily effected.

Under Act No. 48 of 1903 the rental payable by Native squatters on Crown land in Natal was increased to £2 per hut per annum and this charge is still operative to-day.

The estimated extent of Crown land occupied by Natives in the Natal Province is 800,000 morgen.

Orange Free State

Under Article *nineteen* of Chapter CXXXIII of the Orange Free State Law Book, Natives are forbidden to reside on Government land without written permission from the Magistrate of the district. In actual fact, apart from the Native reserves, there is no appreciable occupation of Crown land in the Orange Free State by Natives.

Transvaal

The squatting of Natives upon Crown land in the Transvaal was prohibited by the Republican Government under Volksraad Resolution No. 359 of 1891. It was, however, not found practicable to enforce the prohibition, with the result that in 1899 the Superintendent of Natives recommended that the restriction be withdrawn.

Under the Crown Colony Government, the residence of Natives upon Crown land was regulated by Executive Council Resolution No. 1,104 of 1903, which prescribed a rental of £1 per annum for each adult male so resident. This charge covered the right to reside and cultivate on Crown land, entitled the squatter to sufficient wood and water for domestic purposes and included the right to depasture stock, the number of which was not restricted.

Matters continued on this basis until 1921, when the position was reviewed by the Executive Council and it was decided that the annual charge of £1 was entirely disproportionate to the benefits enjoyed and that it should be re-assessed upon an economic basis.

The revised tariff decided upon was laid down in Executive Council Resolution No. 34 dated the 12th February, 1923, and is as follows :—

" An annual rental of thirty shillings (30s.) for each adult male which shall include the right to graze ten head of great stock or twenty head of small stock, and a further grazing rent of ten shillings (10s.) for each five additional head of great stock and two shillings and six pence (2s. 6d.) for each ten additional head of small stock."

These charges took effect from the 1st January, 1924, and are still operative.

A condition of the tenancy is that should either party—the Government on the one hand or the Native on the other—wish to terminate it three months' notice must be given, provided that in any case the Native shall have the right to reap his standing crops.

It may be added that under Executive Council Resolution, No. 1,633 of 1905, the Native Affairs Department was made responsible for the collection of rentals from Natives in occupation of Crown land in the Transvaal and this arrangement still continues.

It is estimated that the area of Crown land, not reserved for location purposes, occupied by Natives in the Transvaal is 1,500,000 morgen.

3. Occupation by Natives of Land Owned by Non-Natives

From the very nature of things, wide variations are to be found in the conditions under which European-owned land in rural areas is occupied by Natives.

The most common forms of tenure are, however, the following :—

(a) Occupation by Natives as full-time servants. Natives permanently employed by a farmer are frequently given, in addition to their monthly wage, the right to cultivate a plot of land for their own benefit and to depasture a limited number of stock upon the property.

(b) Occupation by Natives who are not full-time servants but who, in consideration of their being granted the right to reside upon a farm, and to cultivate and to depasture their stock upon the property, undertake to render free service to the owner for a certain period in each year. The period stipulated varies from sixty to one hundred and eighty days but is usually ninety days. In many instances the stipulation as to service includes not only the kraal head but extends to members of his family as well. This form of tenure obtains in all of the Provinces.

(c) Occupation under a system of metayage, the Native being granted residential, cultivation and grazing rights upon the property on condition of his rendering to the owner a share— usually one half—of the crops reaped by him. This form of tenure was prevalent in the Orange Free State prior to the passing of the Natives Land Act, 1913.

(d)   Occupation on a rent paying basis under informal agreement. The Native tenant is granted residential and cultivation rights and the right to depasture stock upon the property on payment of an annual rental—usually £2 sterling per annum but often more—plus grazing fees, which are usually fixed at three shillings per head of large and six pence per head of small stock per annum.   This form of tenure obtains especially as regards large blocks of Company-owned land in the Transvaal.

(e)   Leasehold occupation by Natives—whether tribes, syndicates or individuals—under formal agreements of lease.   This formal leasing of land to Natives has always been prohibited in the Orange Free State but takes place, though to no very great extent, in the other Provinces.

In the past, the general term " squatting " has been loosely used to connote the occupation by Natives—no matter what the nature of the tenure—of land owned by non-Natives.   To-day, however, the tendency is to restrict the application of the term to occupation under metayage or on a rent-paying basis.

It will readily be appreciated that certain of the forms of tenure indicated above are peculiarly susceptible of abuse, as tending to encourage the evil of absentee landlordism, to facilitate the creation of small uncontrolled locations, to tempt the European owner to take the easy course of living on rents or produce received from Native tenants instead of developing his property himself, to retard the progress of the Native owing to insecurity of tenure, to restrict or cause an unequal distribution of the supply of labour and, last but not least, to promote desultory methods of labour amongst the Natives instead of bringing out the best that is in them.

It is not surprising therefore that each of the pre-Union legislatures found it necessary to enact legislation to regulate the residence of Natives on privately owned property in rural areas so as to guard against these manifold evils.

The laws operative in this connection in the various Provinces differ considerably in detail but were all passed with the same main objects in view.

Legislation on the subject was first introduced in so far as the Cape was concerned by the Native Locations Act, No. 37 of 1884, which dealt with locations on both Crown and privately owned land.   The provisions of this Act relating to privately owned land were repealed by Act

No. 30 of 1899, which in turn was replaced by the Private Locations Act, No. 32 of 1909, which is operative to-day.

The Transvaal and Orange Free State Governments passed laws on similar lines after consultation in 1895. The Free State Law is, however, more detailed and has been more strictly applied than that of the Transvaal, which proved unsuitable for the requirements of the Province and has never been consistently enforced.

The Natal Law on the subject is contained in Ordinance No. 2 of 1855 and this too has been honoured in the breach rather than in the observance thereof.

The salient features of the laws of the various Provinces are briefly indicated hereunder.

Cape

The Private Locations Act, No. 32 of 1909, lays down that no person may establish a private location on his property without a licence, a private location being defined as any number of huts or other dwellings on any private property occupied by one or more Native male adults *who are not servants*.

The Act classes adult male Natives who may reside on private property under four heads :—

(a) *Servants*—Natives continuously employed by the owner or his representatives. No licence is required in respect of such Natives.

(b) *Labour Tenants*—Natives male adults who are not required to work continuously by the proprietor but whose labour is *bona fide* required from time to time in connection with the farming operations, trade, business or handicraft carried on by the proprietor on the property.

(c) *Ordinary tenants*—Native male adults residing on the property who are neither servants nor labour tenants nor exempted Natives.

(d) *Exempted Natives*—certain classes of Natives specified in the Act whose occupation of the property is not deemed to constitute a private location, e.g. Native owners and joint owners, sole lessees under *bona fide* written leases paying certain prescribed rentals, etc.

Under the Act the occupation of private property by labour or ordinary tenants must be licensed.

The licence is an annual one having effect from the 1st January in each year. The fees payable are 10s. per annum for each labour tenant and £2 per annum for each ordinary tenant, provided that if the location be established after the 1st July in any year only half the fees specified are payable for a licence for the unexpired portion of the year.

The Act lays down the procedure to be followed in regard to the issue of licences. The formalities prescribed are

(a) written application to the Inspector who must submit the application with his report thereon to the Magistrate ;

(b) advertisement of the application for general information so as to permit of the lodging of objections ;

(c) submission of the application by the Magistrate to the Divisional Council. At this stage the procedure varies according to whether the application is for labour or for ordinary tenants.

In the case of *labour tenants* the Divisional Council need only be consulted, and discretion is given the Magistrate, after consultation, to grant or refuse to grant a certificate authorising the issue of a licence. Should, however, the Magistrate refuse to grant the certificate, the applicant may appeal to the Minister of Native Affairs.

In the case of *ordinary tenants*, the *consent* of the Divisional Council and thereafter of the Governor-General must be obtained before the Magistrate may issue a certificate authorising the issue of the licence.

The Magistrate may summarily renew licences for either labour or ordinary renants upon expiration unless he has learnt of some reason against such renewal, in which case he may require the application to be treated in the same way as one for a new location.

Available statistics reflect a steady and satisfactory decrease in the number of Natives resident on privately owned property as ordinary or labour tenants.

Thus in 1907 there were 1,107 private locations carrying a total population of 35,418. In 1926 there were 458 private locations consisting of 622 ordinary and 1,051 labour tenants with a total population of 12,507. In 1931 the figures were 138 locations, 389 ordinary and 555 labour tenants ; total population 6,630.

Transvaal

The law regarding the residence of Natives on privately owned farms in the Transvaal is contained in :—

(a)   Law No. 21 of 1895 read in conjunction with the Natives' Land Act, 1913, and Act No. 26 of 1926 ; and

(b)   the Native Service Contract Act, No. 24 of 1932.

(a)   *Law No. 21 of 1895*

The basic principle of this law is that not more than five Native householders may· be allowed on any one farm, except with the express permission of the Government.   Special provision was made, however, under Article *three* whereby an owner of more than one farm might concentrate upon any one farm a quota of five families for each farm owned by him up to but not exceeding twenty-five families.

The object of the law was largely defeated by Article *four*, which provided that every White person of full age living on a farm as lessee, tenant or " bywoner " should have the same right as the owner to keep five families provided the owner permitted it.

Article *five* reads as follows :—

" Every portion of a farm, provided it is separately transferred to the name of a white owner, shall be considered as a farm for the purposes of this law, provided, however, that portions of the same farm transferred to the same person, even if separately transferred, shall only be considered as one farm."

Under Article *nine* the number of families which might reside on farms owned by Natives was likewise restricted to five.

The law made no provision whatever for the payment to the Government of any fees, whether by licence or otherwise, in respect of the residence of Natives on farms.

It was never found practicable, either under the Republican regime or subsequently, generally to enforce the restrictions imposed under the Law.

Act No. 27 of 1913

The Natives Land Act, 1913, modified the Squatters Law, No. 21 of 1895, in three important directions.

(1) Proviso (a) to section *six*, in distinguishing between the " farm labourer " and the ordinary squatter, introduced a new element quite foreign to the principles of Law No. 21 of 1895. It laid down that " nothing in any (such) law or in this Act shall be construed as restricting the number of Natives who, as farm labourers, may reside on any farm in the Transvaal," a farm labourer being defined under the Act as a Native, who, in consideration of his being allowed to reside upon a farm, renders the owner at least ninety days service per annum but no valuable consideration whatsoever other than labour.

(2) Proviso (c) to section *six* legalised, pending further provision by Parliament, occupation which may have been, and in innumerable cases undoubtedly was, illegal under Law No. 21 of 1895. The object of this proviso was in so far as possible to retain the *status quo* pending the further legislation contemplated in the Act.

(3) Section *one* of the Act restricted the right of an owner for the future to allow Natives to reside on or occupy his ground except as servants or farm labourers.

Act No. 26 of 1926

This Act brought certain contracts between landowners and their Native tenants, viz., those whereby any Native or any member of his family is permitted to occupy or cultivate land in return for services to be rendered by him, within the ambit of the Masters and Servants Law.

(b) *Act No. 24 of 1932*

The Native Service Contract Act, No. 24 of 1932, is dealt with in a subsequent portion of this chapter (*vide* page 159 *infra*).

Natal

The law regarding the residence of Natives on privately owned land in the Natal Province is contained in:—(a) Ordinance No. 2 of 1855 as modified by the Natives Land Act, 1913, and Act No. 26 of 1926 ; and (b) the Native Service Contract Act, No. 24 of 1932.

(a) *Ordinance No. 2 of 1855*

Section *six* of the Ordinance provided that no owner or occupier of land should permit more than three Native families to reside on his land without rendering to the Magistrate a return in the month of January in each year showing the number of Native men, women and children residing on the land, the number of their huts or dwelling houses and the nature of any agreement he had concluded with them.

Section *five* provided that no Native should reside on land belonging to any person not occupied by him personally or by his mandatory or representative, except with the written permission of the Lieutenant Governor, or the Colonial Secretary or the Secretary for Native Affairs or the Magistrate. Section *three* provided for the summary removal by order of the Magistrate of Natives unlawfully residing on farms.

No limitation was imposed by the Ordinance regarding the number of Natives who might, with the permission of the owner, reside upon privately owned land in Natal nor was any provision made for payment of licence or other fees in respect of the residence of Natives on such land.

The South African Native Affairs Commission, 1903-1905, found that Ordinance No. 2 of 1855 was largely a dead letter and had never been enforced to any appreciable degree.

Act No. 27 of 1913

The Natives Land Act modified the law regarding squatting in Natal in the following important directions :—

(1) Under section *one* it restricted the right of a European owner to lease land to Natives within the meaning of the term lease as defined in the Act ;

(2) Proviso (c) to section *six*, designed to maintain the *status quo* pending the passing of the further legislation contemplated in the Act, applies to Natal as well as to the Transvaal.

Act No. 26 of 1926

The remarks made in this connection as regards the Transvaal apply equally regarding Natal.

(b) *Act No. 24 of 1932*

The Native Service Contract Act is, as previously stated, dealt with in a subsequent portion of this chapter (*vide* page 159 *infra*).

Orange Free State

The law regulating the residence of Natives on privately owned farms in the Orange Free State is contained in Chapter CXXXIII of the Law Book as amended by Law No. 4 of 1895 and modified by the Natives Land Act, 1913.

The basic principle of the " squatting " policy of the Orange Free State was identical with that adopted by the Transvaal under Law 21 of 1895, viz. that in the ordinary course not more than five Native families should be permitted to reside on any one farm (vide Article 9 of Law 4 of 1895).

Article *ten* of Law 4 of 1895 lays down that each separate piece of land separately registered and each undivided portion of such piece of land, provided it is registered in the name of a White person, shall be considered to be a farm.

Article *twenty-one* of Chapter CXXXIII of the Law Book prohibits the keeping of more than two heads of families of Natives on any farm or portion of a farm not occupied by a White person.

Heads of families are defined as persons having one or more wives or a family but do not include persons over 60 years of age who have no children fit for work (vide Article *twenty-two* of Chapter CXXXIII of the Law Book).

Under Article *eleven* of Law 4 of 1895, it was provided further that the following persons might be kept on a farm without being regarded as heads of families for the purposes of the quota allowed :

(a)   Single persons hired by the occupier of the farm.

(b)   Heads of families temporarily hired for definite work on the farm, e.g., dam-making.

(c)   Coloured persons temporarily hired by a White person who has accepted under contract a piece of work to be done on the farm.

Under Article *twelve* of Law 4 of 1895, the owner of a farm or his representative may apply to the landdrost for permission to keep more than five heads of Coloured families on his farm and, if the landdrost is satisfied after due enquiry that more servants are required for the working of the farm or for carrying out special works thereon, he may authorise such owner to keep more than five but not exceeding fifteen heads of Coloured families on the property. This privilege may, however, be withdrawn under Article *fifteen* when circumstances no longer warrant an increased number of families.

Under Article *fourteen* the owner must pay an annual fee of £5 in respect of each head of a Coloured family he is allowed to keep in excess of *ten*. No other fees are payable under the Law.

Act No. 27 of 1913

The Natives Land Act, 1913, made Natives, who are resident on privately owned farms in the Orange Free State and who enjoy the benefits of sowing and depasturing stock on such farms, subject to the provisions of Ordinance No. 7 of 1904, the Master and Servants Law, thereby re-establishing a position which had existed prior to the repeal of Chapter CXI of the Law Book (the old Master and Servants Law of the Orange Free State).

THE NATIVE SERVICE CONTRACT ACT NO. 24 OF 1932

The intention of the Native Service Contract Act, No. 24 cf 1932, as expressed in its preamble, was to amend the Transvaal and Natal law relating to masters and servants, to amplify the Natives Land Act, 1913, and to impose a tax on certain owners of land and to provide for other matters incidental thereto.

The Act provided that it should take effect from a date to be prescribed by the Governor-General by proclamation in the Gazette. By Proclamation No. 54 of 1933 it was brought into operation on the 10th March, 1933. All of its provisions are applicable to the Provinces of the Transvaal and Natal, sections *one*, *seven*, *eight*, and *ten*, only, apply in the Orange Free State and the measure has no application at all in the Cape Province.

Of the provisions which are applicable to the Orange Free State :—

(i) Section *one* deals only with the interpretation of various terms used in the Act.

(ii) Section *seven*, which contains the amplification of the Natives Land Act referred to in the preamble, was designed to overcome a very serious difficulty encountered in prosecutions instituted against non-Native land owners under that Act, viz., that of establishing the fact that such a land owner is an actual party to any occupation by Natives of his land in contravention of the provisions of the Act. To meet this difficulty, the section places upon the owner the onus of proof which in the ordinary course would rest upon the Crown. It provides that "if in any proceedings against a person other than a Native on a charge of having been a party to an agreement or transaction with a Native for the sale or lease of any land to such Native in contravention of any provision of the Natives Land Act, 1913 (Act No. 27 of 1913), or any regulation made thereunder, it is proved that such Native is or was residing on or using or cultivating such land and that such person is or was the owner thereof or that he exercises or exercised any measure of control or management thereover, such person shall be presumed to have been a party to such agreement or transaction unless the contrary is proved."

(iii) Section *eight* makes it obligatory upon land owners, when called upon so to do by a Magistrate, to furnish such information as may be required concerning Natives resident upon or using their land or in regard to any matter relating to such residence or use.

(iv) Section *ten* is a general penal clause.

From what has been said above, it will be appreciated that the Native Service Contract Act affects the Orange Free State only in so far as the operation of the Natives Land Act in that Province is concerned, while, as previously stated, the Cape Province is entirely outside its ambit.

The essential features of the Act are contained in the provisions applicable to the Transvaal and Natal. These are as follows :—

(a) The prohibition upon the employment of or the issue of a pass to any male Native domiciled in the Union to proceed to a place other than his home unless such Native produces a document of identification in a form prescribed by regulation, coupled with the further provision that, should it appear from such document of identification that the Native is domiciled in the Transvaal or Natal on land outside a location, no person shall employ him during any period unless he further produces a labour tenant contract between himself and the owner of such land or a statement signed by such owner or his agent to the effect that such Native is not obliged to render him any service during such period.

The object of these provisions is obviously to ensure in so far as possible that Natives residing as labour tenants on privately owned farms will not evade their service obligations to their landlords.

(b) The prohibition of the employment of any male Native under eighteen years of age, unless such Native produces, in addition to the identification document, a statement or statements in writing signed by the owner (or his agent) of the land whereon the guardian of such Native is domiciled and by such guardian to the effect that such Native has his permission to enter into a contract of service during any period specified in such statement or statements.

(c) The prohibition upon the employment of any female under eighteen years of age unless she produces a statement in writing signed by her guardian to the effect that she has his permission to enter into a contract of service for any period specified in such statement.

(d)   The authority granted under section *three* to the guardian of any Native, male or female, between ten and eighteen years of age, on his or her behalf to enter into a labour tenant or other service contract with the owner of the land on which such guardian is domiciled.

The object of the provisions referred to under (b), (c) and (d) above is to counteract the ever-growing tendency on the part of juvenile Natives of both sexes to flout parental authority, control and discipline, and to leave their homes in quest of the meretricious attractions of life in the towns.

(e)   The provision contained in section *nine* making land owners in any area, which may from time to time be proclaimed by the Governor-General in the Gazette, liable to an annual tax of five pounds in respect of every able-bodied male Native (other than a chief, headman, minister, evangelist, or marriage officer) over eighteen and under sixty years of age domiciled on their land, who in any such year does not during a period of not less than six months in the aggregate, or such shorter period or periods of not less than three months in the aggregate, as the Governor-General may by proclamation prescribe, render service to such owner under a service contract or work as a school teacher.

The tax is not payable

(i) if the services of such Native were not available to the owner during a sufficient period or periods in the year to exempt him therefrom and such owner could not take any reasonable steps to ensure that his services would be available ;

(ii) for any year in respect of a guardian of three or more Natives who in such year have each, under a service contract, served the owner of the land whereon such guardian is domiciled for the prescribed period or periods referred to above.

The intention of section *nine*, which it should be emphasised is to apply only to areas specifically proclaimed thereunder, is to place further obstacles in the way of anything in the nature of " kafir farming " and to compel European owners to keep upon their farms only such Natives as are necessary to meet their *bona fide* labour requirements.   No area has yet been proclaimed under section *nine*.

Such are the main features of the Native Service Contract Act.

Incidental provisions subsidiary to the main principles contained in the Act are the following :—

L

(a)   The provision for the execution and attestation, at the option of the parties, of labour tenant or other service contracts (if recorded in duplicate in a form prescribed by regulation) before a "competent office:," e.g., a Magistrate, Justice of the Peace, Commissioner of Oaths, etc., (Section 4 (1)).

(b)   The provision whereby *either* party to a labour tenant or other service contract, under which a Native binds himself to render service to any other person during any period in excess of one month, may demand that the name and place of residence of the employer, the duration of the contract and the wage stipulated therein be endorsed by a competent officer upon such Native's document of identification (Section 4 (2) and (3)).   Such an endorsement would to all intents and purposes have the same effect as a written contract.

(c)   The limitation to three years of the period of operation of any labour tenant contract, whether oral or written, and the provision that in the absence of any express stipulation as to its period of duration any such contract shall be deemed to have been entered into for a period of one year with tacit relocation from year to year thereafter, subject to the right of either party to terminate it at the end of any such year provided he gives at least three months' notice of his intention to do so (Section 5 (1) (3) and (4)).

(d)   The reciprocal rights given under section 5 (6) to Natives and their landlords, upon change of ownership or control of the land occupied or used by such Natives under labour tenant contracts, to terminate such contracts on three months' notice.

(e)   The right given to a labour tenant, upon termination of his contract from whatever cause, to tend his standing crop until maturity and thereafter to reap and remove it (Section 5 (7)).

(f)   The provision giving a labour tenant preference over his employer as regards the use of manure in any kraal or stable on land used or occupied by such labour tenant so long as such manure is used to fertilize land which the labour tenant is entitled to cultivate under his contract. (Section 5 (9).)

(g)   The provision in section 5 (11) for the joint termination by the employer of labour tenants contracts entered into with Natives of the same kraal or household upon the default of any one of them.

(h)   The much discussed " whipping " clause—section *eleven*— which reads as follows :—

" Any contravention by a male servant who is or appears to be not more than eighteen years of age of any provision of the law relating to masters and servants shall be punishable by the Court on conviction by a whipping not exceeding five strokes in substitution for any punishment provided for such contravention in such law."

It may be remarked in passing that this provision would apparently apply not only to Natives but to any servant under the Transvaal and Natal Masters and Servants Laws.

Special mention must be made of section *six* of the Act which empowered the Governor-General to make regulations prescribing :—

" (a) the form or nature of any documents of identification referred to in section *two* or of a service contract to be entered into in writing in terms of section *three*, the particulars to be set forth therein and the persons by whom and conditions upon which any such document may be issued ;

(b) the form of any contract referred to in section *four*, the particulars to be set forth therein, the manner in which such forms shall be made available to the public, and the charges (if any) to be made therefor."

Regulations made under section *six* of the Act were published for general information under Government Notice No. 1453 in Government Gazette No. 2071 dated the 4th November 1932. A copy of the Government Notice appears in Appendix " I."

It is clear from the provisions of section *two* of the regulations that they were framed in definite contemplation of the Act being brought into operation on the 1st July, 1933, and the obvious intention of the Government in promulgating these regulations so long beforehand was to allow of the necessary arrangements being made for the issue to Natives in the meantime of identification documents as prescribed thereunder, which they would be required to produce when in search of employment after the Act had been brought into force.

In order to avoid hardship upon the Natives, the regulations were framed with the idea that other forms and documents which they are required from time to time to carry and produce should in so far as practicable be combined with or merged in the documents of identification and to this end the principle of elaborating the form of the general tax receipt and making it serve as the holder's identification document was adopted. Consequently three forms of documents of identification, as set forth in the first, second and third schedules to the regulations, have been prescribed.

The First Schedule form is to be issued to adult Natives otherwise than in connection with the payment of tax, e.g., to the Native who is exempt from the payment of tax or (as an *interim* measure) to the Native who holds the ordinary tax receipt, or to the Native who has not previously paid tax but has become liable therefor and wishes to undertake employment so as to enable him to earn money to pay his tax, or to the Native who has lost a document of identification (tax receipt) issued in the form prescribed in the Second Schedule and applies for a new one.

The Second Schedule form is to be issued to adult Natives upon payment of the general tax for which they are liable under Act No. 41 of 1925. This is the form which will be in general use when, after the necessary preliminary work has been done, the regulations are in full swing and it will serve the dual purpose of document of identification and tax receipt as well.

The Third Schedule form is to be issued to Native juveniles (under eighteen years of age) on the application of their guardians or, if there be none such, in the discretion of the issuing officer (the receiver of Native tax) on their own application.

First and Third Schedule documents of identification are valid for three years from the date of issue or until the issue to the holder of another document of identification (e.g., a Second Schedule document). A Second Schedule document of identification is valid until another such document is issued to the holder but the period of validity will not extend beyond the year following the year of issue.

A special provision to meet the difficulties of the *interim* period, that is the period which must inevitably lapse before the regulations are in full working order, is contained in the proviso to sub-section (1) of section *two* of the regulations, which lays down that during the period commencing on the 1st July and ending on the 31st December, 1933, any receipt issued between the 31st December, 1931, and the 1st July, 1933, to any Native, for the payment of the general tax imposed by Act No. 41 of 1925, shall be deemed to be the document of identification of such Native, if he has not been furnished upon or after the last-mentioned date with a document of identification in the form of the First Schedule or Second Schedule.

The forms of identification documents all contain a warning to employers and make provision for endorsements in terms of the Act and for recording particulars of labour tenant or service contracts which may be entered into by the holder.

The regulations prescribe also :—

(a) the forms of labour tenant contract and service contract which may be entered into, in terms of section *three* of the Act, for a period in excess of one year, between the guardian of a Native juvenile, on behalf of such juvenile, on the one hand, and the owner of the land whereupon such guardian is domiciled on the other hand ; and

(b) the forms of labour tenant and service contracts for the purposes of sub-section (1) of section *four* of the Act.

The forms of labour tenant and service contracts referred to under (a) above figure respectively as the fourth and fifth schedules to the regulations, while those referred to under (b) are set forth in the sixth and seventh schedules respectively.

C

THE GENERAL LAND POLICY INITIATED UNDER THE NATIVES LAND ACT, NO. 27 OF 1913, AND SUBSEQUENT DEVELOPMENTS

The principle of territorial segregation or separation of land rights between the European and Native races in South Africa was after careful consideration strongly and almost unanimously advocated by the South African Native Affairs Commission, 1903-1905 (vide paragraphs 191 *et seq.* of the report of that Commission) and the passing of the Natives Land Act, No. 27 of 1913, was the initial step in the direction of the practical application of that principle in the Union.

The Act was designed as an *interim* measure and it was intended to check the indiscriminate occupation of land by Europeans and Natives with its attendant evils, and, by temporarily restricting the further acquisition of land by Natives, so far as that could be done without undue hardship, to maintain the *status quo* as regards the ownership and occupation of land pending the passing of a definite, comprehensive and final measure, which, based upon the report of the Commission for the appointment of which provision was made in section *two* of the Act, would lay down permanent lines of territorial segregation, i.e. permanent Native areas outside of which Natives would not be permitted to acquire land.

In furtherance of these objects, the Act provided that, except with the approval of the Governor-General, a Native might not acquire from a person other than a Native, nor a person other than a Native from a Native, any land or interest in land in any area outside the Native areas described in the schedule to the Act, and that, without such approval, no person other than a Native might acquire any land or interest in land in a scheduled Native area.

These scheduled Native areas, it may be mentioned, comprised the then existing Native reserves and locations throughout the Union and, in addition, much land privately owned by Natives.

The functions of the Commission, to which reference has already been made, were to enquire into and report upon :—

(a) what areas should be set apart as areas within which Natives should not be permitted to acquire or hire land or interests in land ; and

(b) what areas should be set apart as areas within which persons other than Natives should not be permitted to acquire or hire land or interests in land.

The Act stipulated that the Commission should consist of not less than five members and that it should complete its enquiry and present its reports and recommendations to the Minister within two years after the commencement of the Act.

This Commission, commonly known as the Beaumont Commission, was appointed on the 27th August, 1913, and consisted of Sir W. H. Beaumont, General S. W. Burger, Col. W. R. Collins, Col. W. E. M. Stanford and the Honourable C. H. Wessels, with Sir W. H. Beaumont as chairman.

Its enquiries were delayed by the war but it ultimately submitted its report on the 2nd March, 1916.

In the following year, the further legislation foreshadowed in Act No. 27 of 1913 was introduced into Parliament in the shape of the Native Affairs Administration Bill. The Native areas recommended by the Beaumont Commission were embodied in a schedule to the Bill, which, after the second reading was referred to the Select Committee on Native Affairs.

After hearing a vast amount of evidence from both Native and non-Native sources, the Select Committee found that the recommendations of the Beaumont Commission could not be accepted in their entirety, and recommended the appointment of " Local Committees " to revise the recommendations of that Commission. Local Committees were accordingly appointed in respect of (1) the Cape Province (excluding Griqualand West and British Bechuanaland), (2) the Orange Free State (excluding the districts of Hoopstad and Boshof), (3) Natal, (4) the Eastern Transvaal, and (5) the Western Transvaal (including Griqualand West, British Bechuanaland and the districts of Hoopstad and Boshof in the Orange Free State).

The reports of the various Local Committees were furnished in 1918, and the proposals put forward were received with the same antagonism as had been evinced in many quarters on the part of both Europeans and Natives towards the recommendations of the Beaumont Commission as embodied in the Native Affairs Administration Bill.

The Government accordingly decided that, before proceeding with the segregation clauses of the Native Affairs Administration Bill, it should deal with certain other principles embodied in that Bill, viz., the appointment of a permanent Native Affairs Commission as an instrument for dealing with Native policy and the establishment of councils in Native areas. The necessary legislation was, as we have already seen, subsequently introduced to this end and became law under Act No. 23 of 1920.

This decision rendered it imperative that the Government should by administrative action, i.e., by obtaining the approval of the Governor-General under section *one* of the Natives Land Act, relieve the disabilities of Natives as regards the acquisition of land. To this end it was laid down by General Botha in 1918 that the Governor-General's approval, which previously had been granted only in cases of hardship, should be sought in respect of the acquisition or lease of land by Natives in areas recommended for Native occupation by a local committee as well as by the Beaumont Commission, and, subsequently by General Smuts in 1922, that Local Committee areas were to be regarded as areas in which Natives could buy or lease land. The policy adopted by General Smuts in this connection was subsequently endorsed by the present Government.

In 1926, the Honourable the Prime Minister, General Hertzog, laid upon the table of the House and published for general information in Government Gazette Extraordinary No. 1570 dated the 23rd July, 1926, his series of Bills, generally known as the " Native Bills," consisting of the Representation of Natives in Parliament Bill, the Union Native Council Bill, the Natives Land (Amendment) Bill and the Coloured Persons' Rights Bill.

These Bills were, with certain minor modifications, formally introduced into Parliament and read a first time in 1927. After the first reading, they were referred to a large and representative Select Committee which functioned during the 1927 and 1928 sessions.

In January 1929, three of the Bills, viz., the Natives Parliamentary Representation Bill, the Coloured Persons' Rights Bill, and the Natives Land (Amendment) Bill, which had been re-cast in the light of discussions which had taken place in the Select Committee, were re-introduced and read a first time. The two former, having regard to their provisions, required to be dealt with by both Houses of Parliament sitting together in accordance with sections *thirty-five* and *one hundred and fifty-two* of the South Africa Act, 1909, and were passed in second reading. At the third reading, before the Joint Session, however, the Natives Parliamentary Representation Bill failed to secure the requisite two-thirds majority and under the circumstances the Coloured Persons' Rights Bill and the Natives Land (Amendment) Bill were not proceeded with.

The Natives Parliamentary Representation Bill and the Coloured Persons' Rights Bill were re-introduced during the 1930 session of Parliament and were read a first time before a Joint Sitting of both Houses which referred them to a Select Committee on which both Houses were represented. The Select Committee was unable to complete its work during the session and at the termination thereof suggested that it be afforded an opportunity of resuming its deliberations during the following session.

In 1931, in accordance with this recommendation, a Joint Select Committee, consisting of twenty members of the House of Assembly and seven members of the Senate, was appointed " to consider the question of making special provision for the representation of Natives and Coloured Persons in the Parliament and Provincial Councils of the Union and for the acquisition of land by Natives."

This Joint Select Committee resumed the work of the 1930 Select Committee on the Natives Parliamentary Representation Bill and also considered the Natives Land (Amendment) Bill as introduced in 1929, (A.B. 22—'29). It reported in due course that it had made substantial progress in regard to the question of the representation of Natives in Parliament as well as the question of the acquisition of land by Natives, but had been unable in the time available to deal with that of making special provision for the representation of Coloured persons in Parliament. It recommended that the Government be requested to take into consideration the advisability of appointing a Commission, composed of the members of the Committee, as soon as possible during the recess in order to continue and complete the work of the Committee. This recommendation was adopted by resolution of both Houses of Parliament, but circumstances precluded the Committee from functioning as a Commission during the recess as had been contemplated.

The Joint Select Committee was re-appointed during the 1932 session with the same terms of reference. At the close of the session in reporting progress, it intimated that it was not yet in a position to submit a report and again recommended that its members be appointed to function as a Commission during the recess to continue and complete its work.

This recommendation was adopted and the Select Committee members were duly appointed as a Commission for the purpose in view. The Commission, several of the members of which were unfortunately unable to attend, sat at the Union Buildings, Pretoria, from the 4th to the 17th November, 1932, and, when furnishing its report, it submitted an amended series of Bills for consideration.

At the commencement of the last session of Parliament, the Joint Select Committee was re-appointed and the Commission's report was referred to it.

Under date the 2nd March, 1933, the Joint Select Committee reported to Parliament as follows :—

"Your Committee has to report that owing to the probable early prorogation of Parliament and the limited time that has been at its disposal during the present Session, it has been unable to make any appreciable progress in the consideration of the matters referred to it.

Your Committee begs to recommend that the Government take into consideration the advisability of the publication of the reports and proceedings of the Select Committee of the Joint Sitting of both Houses of 1930, the reports and proceedings of the Joint Select Committees of the Sessions 1931, 1931-'32 and 1933, together with the Report of the Commission of 1932 and the Bills which emanated from that Commission and submitted to your Committee."

The cardinal features of the Natives Land (Amendment) Bill as introduced in 1929 were its provisions for :—

(a) the removal, in respect of certain areas, defined in the first schedule to the Bill and termed " Released Areas," of the restrictions imposed by the Natives Land Act, 1913, upon the acquisition of land by Natives ;

(b) bringing the Cape Province into line with the remaining Provinces (Reference has already been made to the decision of the Appellate Division of the Supreme Court in the combined appeals of Thomson and Stilwell *versus* Kama laying it down that the restrictions imposed by section *one* of the Natives Land Act, 1913, do not, having regard to the provisions of sub-section (2) of section *eight* of the Act, apply in the Cape Province) ; and

(c) the establishment of a Natives Land Purchase and Advances Fund.

The released areas defined in the first schedule to the Natives Land (Amendment) Bill are based upon the areas recommended by the various Local Committees of 1918, with certain necessary modifications.

In the meantime, pending the enactment of the further legislation contemplated on the Native land question, the Government does not hesitate to supply by administrative action indispensable requirements which it was originally intended should be met by the legislation foreshadowed in the Natives Land Act, 1913.

In the first place, it readily recommends for the approval of the Governor-General under section *one* of that Act transactions whereby Natives are to acquire land or interests in land within the areas defined in the first schedule to the Natives Land (Amendment) Bill, 1929, and thus affords relief from the restrictions imposed by section *one* of the 1913 Act.

Secondly, special financial provision is made annually for the purchase of land by the Government for Native occupation and this money is utilised for the settlement in recognised Native areas of evicted and landless Natives on rent-paying conditions assessed on such a basis as to afford a small rate of interest on the capital expenditure involved. Considerable extents have from time to time been acquired for this purpose in the Piet Retief, Glen Grey, Pietersburg, King William's Town, Peddie, Lichtenburg and Taung districts, the total capital outlay over the period from 1st April 1918, to the 31st March 1932, having been approximately £260,000.

One far-reaching and important feature of the Natives Land Act, 1913, is that the restrictions imposed by section *one* necessitate the submission of each specific transaction involving the acquisition by Natives of land or interests in land from non-Natives, or *vice versa*, to the Department, which is consequently in a position to exercise a healthy supervision over such contracts and to afford the Natives protection against exploitation by unscrupulous individuals on the one hand and against their own foolishness on the other—foolishness which has in many instances in the past led them to embark upon ambitious schemes of land purchase which they were entirely unable to carry through and which accordingly involved them in heavy losses.

Before submitting transactions involving the acquisition of land by Natives for approval under Act No. 27 of 1913, the Department concerns itself to ascertain in each case whether the purchase price and terms and conditions of sale are fair and reasonable and whether the Natives' financial position is such that they may reasonably be expected successfully to negotiate the purchase.

The schedule to the Natives Land Act, 1913, has been amended by Acts Nos. 28 of 1925, 34 of 1927, and 36 of 1931.

The extents of the Native areas scheduled under the Natives Land Act, 1913, as amended, and of the released areas scheduled under the Natives Land (Amendment) Bill are approximately as follows :

Province.	Approximate Extent in *morgen* of scheduled Native Areas under Act No. 27 of 1913.	Approximate Extent in *morgen* of released areas scheduled under Natives Land (Amendment) Bill.
Cape	6,127,000	1,500,000
Natal	2,997,000	275,000
Transvaal	1,232,000	4,900,000
Orange Free State	74,290	79,000
	10,430,290	6,754,000

VII

NATIVE DEVELOPMENT AND TAXATION

In this chapter certain topics closely allied to the question of Native land administration, viz., Native agricultural development, the dipping of stock, fencing and taxation, are considered.

A

NATIVE AGRICULTURAL DEVELOPMENT

Mention has already been made of the appointment in the Department early in 1929 of a Director of Native Agriculture with a view to promoting agricultural development and education in the various Native areas throughout the Union.

The Department was fortunate in being able to secure for this post the services of Mr. R. W. Thornton; who had previously been Director of Field and Animal Husbandry in the Union Agricultural Department.

Except in council areas, very little had previously been done in the way of organised effort to inculcate amongst the large masses of the Native population an appreciation and knowledge of modern scientific methods of agriculture and stock-raising. This apparent neglect is to be attributed in large measure to lack of funds and in a smaller degree, perhaps, to an undue emphasis upon the purely scholastic side of education in so far as the Natives were concerned.

The natural result was that until recently little was done in most of the Native areas to combat primitive and wasteful methods of cultivation, to encourage the use of fertilisers and to check soil erosion and over-stocking with their attendant evils.

The establishment of the Native Development Fund had the effect of making available funds which could be utilised to deal with the problem on a systematic and organised basis and the appointment of the Director of Native Agriculture was the first move in the campaign.

Mr. Thornton's initial step after his appointment was to make a survey of conditions within the various Native areas with a view to deciding upon the most suitable and efficient organisation to meet requirements.

In pursuance of his recommendations, the Native areas in the Union have for the purpose of agricultural development organisation been divided into four groups, as follows :—

(1)   Transkeian Territories.

(2)   The Native areas in the Cape Province proper.

(3)   Natal including Zululand.

(4)   Transvaal including Bechuanaland and the Orange Free State.

In so far as the Transkeian Territories are concerned, it has been decided to leave matters in the hands of the United Transkeian Territories General Council which has an up-to-date and very efficient organisation of its own, as has already been shown in dealing with that Council. For the *Cape Province proper* an Assistant Director of Native Agriculture has been appointed with headquarters at the Fort Cox Agricultural School, of which he is also principal. In so far as the school is concerned he is, as has already been pointed out, assisted by a vice-principal, three European lecturers and six trained Natives. For the carrying out of the necessary extension work, forty-five Native demonstrators have been appointed, who work, each of course in his own prescribed area, under the surveillance of two European agricultural supervisors.

The duties of these Native agricultural demonstrators, all of whom are trained men, have already been indicated in dealing with the demonstrators employed by the United Transkeian Territories General Council.

For *Natal and Zululand* an Assistant Director of Native Agriculture has likewise been appointed. He has under his control two European Agricultural supervisors, a European supervisor of irrigation settlements, several European forestry officers and twenty-eight Native agricultural demonstrators. He also exercises supervision over two small agricultural and cane demonstration farms and the Zululand National Training Institution, of which an account has already been furnished.

The fourth division, comprising the *Transvaal, British Bechuanaland and the Orange Free State*, falls under the immediate and direct control of the Director of Native Agriculture, no Assistant Director having been appointed in this area.

The field work in this division is carried out by eighteen Native agricultural demonstrators who function under two European supervisors.

The great bulk of expenditure in connection with the Agricultural Branch of the Department is met from the Native Development Account.

The salary of the Director is paid from the Departmental Vote, as is also portion of the salaries of the Assistant Directors, but the various lecturers, the European supervisors and the Native demonstrators are all paid from the Development Account.

Mention has already been made of the appointment of a Departmental engineer, with headquarters at Pretoria, to serve the requirements of the Transvaal, Bechuanaland and the Orange Free State. An engineer is likewise employed by the Department to serve the Native areas in the Natal Province, his headquarters being at Durban and his salary being paid from the Native Development Account.

These engineering sections function in close consultation with and under the control of the Director of Native Agriculture.

The Natal engineer has under him a staff of trained Native masons and all construction work in the Native areas in Natal and Zululand falls under his direct control. At present, this work is to great extent concentrated on the erection and repair of dipping tanks, but attention is also directed to the development of sources of water supply.

In the Transvaal and British Bechuanaland locations and reserves, a comprehensive boring programme has been undertaken by the Department and is at present in progress. The programme, which embraces the provision in various Native areas of one hundred and nine bore-holes adequately equipped with handpumps, windmills and reservoirs, is being carried out under the direct supervision of the Engineer at Pretoria. The actual drilling is undertaken by the Irrigation Department on behalf of this Department, but the erection of the windmills and pumps and the construction of the reservoirs are carried out by a trained field staff employed by this Department.

In addition, several small irrigation schemes are being developed in the Native areas, while well-sinking programmes have been authorised in the locations in the Barkley West and Douglas districts of the Cape Province.

B

THE DIPPING OF STOCK

Natives in the Native areas of the Union to-day own some 5,000,000 head of large stock, that is to say, approximately half the cattle of the.

country. In addition, the number of their small stock is estimated at 6,000,000 head.

It will, therefore, readily be appreciated that in a country which has been subject to the ravages of animal diseases, particularly East Coast Fever in cattle and Scab in sheep, to such an extent as South Africa, it is a matter of national importance to ensure the regular and efficient dipping of these vast herds of Native owned stock, as this alone can keep disease in check.

To this end the Native Affairs Department, working in co-operation with the Department of Agriculture, has assumed responsibility for the construction and maintenance of dipping tanks and the adequate supervision of dipping operations in Native areas.

Prior to the establishment of the Native Development Account under the provisions of Act No. 41 of 1925, the requisite funds for dipping had been raised in the different Native areas in a variety of ways, e.g., by voluntary levies ; by the imposition of special rates under the provisions of the Dipping Tanks (Advances) Act, No. 20 of 1911 ; by stock rates ; by imposing a definite charge in respect of each beast, etc.

The Native Development Account has, however, proved a boon in this as in so many other respects. The position to-day is that as regards scheduled Natives areas, other than (a) one or two locations in the Transvaal, such as Malaboch's, where voluntary levies are still in operation, and (b) areas falling under the jurisdiction of a council or approved board, the cost of the erection and maintenance of dipping tanks and the expenditure incurred in dipping operations, including the wages of European supervisors, Native assistant supervisors and Native foremen, are met from the Local Fund of the Native Development Account. In scheduled Native areas falling under a council or approved board, such expenditure is ordinarily met from the revenue of the council or board concerned, which revenue, as has already been pointed out, is derived almost exclusively from the proceeds of the local tax and Native quit-rent paid over to such body in terms of Act No. 41 of 1925 from the Local Fund of the Development Account.

The only exception to this rule is in respect of the districts falling under the jurisdiction of the United Transkeian Territories General Council. Dipping operations are carried out in those districts under the aegis of the Council but the cost, except as regards the dipping of small stock, is not met from the revenue of the Council but from the proceeds of a special rate levied for the purpose in each district on either a stock or poll basis.

C

FENCING

For the purposes of the Fencing Act, No. 17 of 1912, as amended by Act No. 11 of 1922, the Native Affairs Department is the " owner " of all Native locations, reserves or other land held in trust for any Coloured or Native community, except where such land is vested under registered title in any particular " person " or body, e.g., the Natal or Zululand Native Trust locations, tribally owned farms in the Transvaal, etc.

The Department is accordingly constantly faced with the necessity of contributing, under the provisions of the Act, half of the cost of the erection and maintenance of dividing fences between such lands and adjoining farms.

Farmers generally throughout the country are increasingly realising the importance and advantages of fencing and this is doubly the case as regards owners whose holdings adjoin Native reserves, as experience has taught them that the absence of adequate dividing fences leads to trespass by Native owned stock, facilitates the depredations of vermin, occasions boundary disputes and, not infrequently, results in stock theft.

The Department's liability as regards location fencing is accordingly an abiding and, indeed, an ever increasing one.

The Fencing Act makes provision for the ultimate recovery from the Natives of the particular area concerned in each instance of amounts which the Department is from time to time called upon to contribute in this connection. The normal procedure is for the money to be advanced from loan funds and thereafter for a special rate to be imposed by Proclamation upon the tribe or community concerned, which rate is assessed on such a basis as to provide for the re-payment of the amount involved, with interest at the rate of 4% per annum, over a number of years not exceeding eighteen in all.

Recourse is, however, not had to this procedure when the necessary refund is obtainable from some other source, e.g., from monies belonging to the tribe concerned, from Council funds, etc.

In the past, fencing charges have constituted a particularly heavy liability upon the inhabitants of small Native locations surrounded by European owners, but since the establishment of the Native Development Account relief has been afforded in such cases by virtue of the fact that the Minister has approved of the principle of local tax proceeds standing to the credit of any area in the Development Account Local

M

Fund being utilised, as and when available, to meet commitments in respect of the *erection* of external location fencing in such area.

Similarly, general and local councils have been given the option of undertaking liability in respect of the erection of external location fencing within their respective areas of jurisdiction. If a council is prepared to undertake this obligation, it refunds any amount which the Department, as " owner," is called upon to contribute in respect of the erection of fencing within its area. If the council is not prepared to accept the charge, a proclamation is issued providing for the recovery of the money from the location residents in the ordinary course.

The application of the principle of meeting liabilities for the erection of fencing from council funds or the Native Development Account has not been extended to costs incurred in respect of maintenance and repairs, as it is felt that any concession which might be made in this connection might have the deleterious effect of placing a premium upon destructive tendencies which have unfortunately manifested themselves among certain sections of the Native population in so far as fencing is concerned. Costs of fencing maintenance and repairs are accordingly uniformly recovered direct from the inhabitants of the particular location concerned.

Fencing charges in respect of Natal locations and Zululand reserves are borne by the Natal Native Trust and Zululand Native Trust respectively and, as has already been pointed out, constitute a considerable item in the annual expenditure of these bodies.

The following figures are furnished in respect of expenditure incurred in connection with the fencing of Native locations and reserves during the financial year 1931-1932 :—

£491 12s. 7d. advanced from the Departmental Loan Vote J.
£904 11s. 9d. paid from the Native Development Account.
£666 16s. 11d. paid by the Natal Native Trust.
£665 5s. 9d. paid by the Zululand Native Trust.
£183 2s. 7d. paid from the British Bechuanaland Fund.

In addition, payment of various fencing claims was effected by different councils and Native reserve boards in respect of areas falling under their jurisdiction, e.g., the United Transkeian Territories General Council, the Glen Grey District Council, the Seliba Reserve Board, the Middledrift Local Council, the Tamacha Local Council, the Victoria East Local Council, etc.

D

TAXATION

Prior to Union, each of the then existing Governments had its own system of Native taxation and the various systems differed materially as regards the amount of taxation imposed, the basis of its incidence and the method of its collection.

In the *Cape* a hut tax of 10s. per hut per annum was payable, under the provisions of section *eleven* of Act No. 37 of 1334, by residents of all Crown Native locations except where *quitrent* was payable in respect of allotments held in individual tenure in such locations.

In addition, for local Government purposes, Natives falling under the jurisdiction of the Glen Grey District Council, the Transkeian Territories General Council and the Pondoland General Council were liable to a general rate, assessed consistently at 10s. per annum.

In Natal a hut tax of 14s. per hut per annum was payable, under the provisions of section *two* of Law No. 13 of 1875, by all Natives resident in the territory with the exception of those living in houses of European construction, having only one wife and generally conforming to civilised usages.

In the *Transvaal* a poll tax of £2 per annum was levied on every adult male Native, under section *three* of Act No. 9 of 1908, with a remission of £1 in respect of municipal location residents and *bona fide* farm labourers.

In the *Orange Free State* a poll tax of £1 per annum was payable, under Ordinance No. 2 of 1904, by all male *Coloured persons* who had resided in the Province for a period of at least six successive months in the tax year.

In addition, the Native Reserve Boards established under Ordinance No. 6 of 1907 had power for local government purposes to levy a location tax, not exceeding one pound in any year, upon each Coloured male resident in the reserves between the ages of sixteen and sixty.

Thus, in the Cape and Orange Free State, purely Native communities paid taxation for local government purposes and in that way relieved the central government of expenditure, while this was not the case in the Transvaal and Natal.

The Cape practically adopted the " land " as the basis of its direct taxation in the form of hut tax and quitrent, reserving the " poll " tax for local government.

The Transvaal and Orange Free State imposed " poll " rates purely and simply.

The Natal hut tax was payable even although the hut was situate on privately owned land and it thus approximated to a poll tax.

Upon Union, these diverse systems necessarily continued in operation in the respective Provinces but it soon became apparent that they gave rise to serious anomalies and that the co-ordination and consolidation of the various taxation measures should be undertaken at the earliest practicable date to secure a more equitable distribution of the burden. In fact a draft consolidating measure was prepared by the Revenue Department as early as 1911.

The problem was, however, one of peculiar intricacy and complexity and, by reason of this fact and the succession of other more urgent matters demanding the attention of the Government, the question was held in abeyance until finally brought to a head by the enactment of the Financial Relations Fourth Extension Act, No. 5 of 1922, which had the effect of

(a) preventing Provincial Councils from imposing direct taxation on the persons, lands, habitations or incomes of Natives ;

(b) compelling Provincial Councils to make financial provision for Native education not less proportionately than that of 1921-22 ; and

(c) making the Central Government responsible—by implication— for the extension of Native education and obtaining funds therefor from the direct taxation of Natives.

As recurrent annual provision could not be made from the proceeds of the then existing Native taxation, it became essential that additional taxation should be imposed upon the Natives.

The whole question of Native taxation was accordingly thoroughly investigated, first by a Departmental Committee and secondly by the Native Affairs Commission. Conferences were held and discussions took place between the Department, the Treasury and the Revenue authorities and ultimately a bill was introduced into Parliament which subsequently became law as the Natives Taxation and Development Act, No. 41 of 1925.

The considerations, which resulted in the provision made in that Act for the payment of a " general " or " poll " tax of £1 per annum by all adult male Natives domiciled in the Union or who have resided therein for a continuous period of twelve months immediately preceding the date on which the tax becomes due (the 1st January in each year), and of a " local " tax of 10s. in respect of every hut or dwelling in a " Native location " by the occupier thereof (with certain exceptions specified in section *one* of the Natives Taxation and Development Act, 1925, Amendment Act No. 28 of 1926), have already been sufficiently indicated in dealing with the Native Development Account, as has the matter of the disposal of the proceeds of these taxes.

Act No. 41 of 1925 defines an adult Native as one who has reached the age of eighteen years and assigns a very wide meaning to " Native location," which is defined as follows :—

" Native location " means :—

(a) any land granted or reserved by or on behalf of the Crown for the habitation or use of Native communities ;

(b) Crown land occupied by Natives under communal conditions, other than land for which rent is payable to the Government ;

(c) land held by a missionary society or religious body carrying on educational or missionary work amongst Natives occupying such land, unless such land is specially exempted by the Governor-General ;

and includes also any area which the Governor-General may, by proclamation in the Gazette, declare to be a Native location for the purposes of this Act as he is hereby authorised to do, but does not include—

(i) urban or municipal Native locations under the control of a local authority ;

(ii) mission stations or reserves where rent or its equivalent is collected from Natives by the Government, by the Natal Native Trust or Zululand Native Trust or where a rate is levied for local purposes ;

(iii) such other lands as may be approved by the Minister."

The Act provides for exemption from the payment of tax, whether general or local, of :—

(a) any Native who satisfies the receiver of tax that he is indigent and is prevented from working by reason of age, chronic disease or other sufficient cause or that he is in necessitous circumstances and is prevented by causes not within his own control from earning sufficient to enable him to pay the tax ;

(b) any Native whose permanent home is outside the Union but who is residing within the Union to perform labour therein and produces proof that he has discharged his liability to pay the current taxes imposed under the law of the territory of his permanent home ;

(c) any Native who satisfies the receiver that, in consequence of his regular attendance at an educational institution approved by the Native Affairs Commission, he has been precluded from earning wages which would enable him to pay the tax.

In reference to clause (c) above, it may be mentioned that the educational institutions approved by the Native Affairs Commission are all such as are State-aided.

Any Native who is an income tax payer under the provisions of the Income Tax Act, No. 40 of 1925, is exempt from the payment of the general (but not the local) tax, if the income tax so paid by him amounts to not less than £1. If such income tax is less than £1, the Native is entitled to a corresponding abatement of the general tax.

A receiver of tax may in his discretion grant any Native an extension of time in which to effect payment of any tax due by him.

The Act makes provision with a view to ensuring the effective collection of tax by giving powers to call for the production of receipts, by authorising the distraint of the movable property of defaulters and by making failure to produce a receipt or to pay tax a criminal offence.

The statutory recognition accorded under section *fifteen* of the Act in respect of the imposition of voluntary levies upon Native tribes and communities has already been discussed (*vide* page 108 *supra*).

Administrative difficulties encountered in the administration of the Act have necessitated the passing of amending legislation under Act No. 28 of 1926 and Act No. 37 of 1931, but these enactments do not affect the basic principles which have been referred to above.

Generally speaking, it may be claimed that the Act has worked well and has been loyally accepted by the Natives, even in areas where the change has involved an increased burden. The Act has certainly to a very large degree removed glaring inequalities and anomalies which previously existed.

Particulars of the amounts collected in respect of general and local tax under the Act in respect of each financial year since it has been in operation are appended. As regards 1925-1926, it should be noted that the Act commenced on the 1st January 1926, and so was in operation only for three months during that financial year.

Province	1925-1926		1926-1927		1927-1928		1928-1929	
	General	Local	General	Local	General	Local	General	Local
Cape	17,716	1,692½	417,284	108,959	429,011	111,233	444,582	116,462
Tvl.	22,502	758	280,567	19,894	319,565	22,203	323,994	21,634
Natal	2,314	297½	322,273	57,304	305,805	55,720	311,119	55,898
O.F.S.	1,553		102,533	857	110,351	1,649	106,614	1,326
Total	£44085	£2748	£1122657	£187014	£1164732	£190805	£1186309	£195320

Province	1929-1930		1930-1931		1931-1932	
	General	Local	General	Local	General	Local
Cape	454,205	121,403	463,590	124,659	412,360	110,284
Transvaal	335,725	22,826	347,095	24,221	335,715	23,461
Natal	325,255	57,277	325,910	57,914	280,170	49,345
O.F.S.	111,335	1,423	106,690	1,275	107,245	1,253
Total	£1,226,520	£202,929	£1,243,285	£208,069	£1,135,490	£184,343

Regulations made under the powers vested in the Governor-General by section *sixteen* of the Natives Taxation and Development Act have been published under Government Notice No. 1596 of 1931.

VIII

NATIVES IN URBAN AND INDUSTRIAL CENTRES

The residence, employment and control of Natives in urban and industrial centres within the Union are regulated by the provisions of the Natives (Urban Areas) Act, No. 21 of 1923, as amended by the Natives (Urban Areas) Act 1923, Amendment Act, No. 25 of 1930 ; by the Native Labour Regulation Act, No. 15 of 1911, and, in a lesser dergee, by the Pass Laws.

A

NATIVES (URBAN AREAS) ACT, NO. 21 OF 1923, AS AMENDED BY ACT NO. 25 OF 1930

A significant and disturbing feature of recent years has been the rapidity with which the Native population in urban centres in the Union has increased, a state of affairs which is to be attributed mainly to a steady and ever-growing influx as a consequence of the demand for labour and the higher wages obtaining in industrial centres, combined with the meretricious attractions of town life, and, in a subsidiary measure, to the natural increase of what may be described as the permanent Native population in urban areas.

Before Union, the control and administration of matters affecting Natives in urban areas were vested in the local authorities having jurisdiction. These functions were exercised through regulations framed under statutory powers and subject, prior to promulgation, to Government approval.

The position, however, was unsatisfactory in that on the one hand the statutory powers were entirely inadequate for satisfactory administration, while, on the other, local authorities generally failed to appreciate that there existed a serious responsibility on their part to ensure proper and healthy conditions and decent amenities of life for that section of the urban population from which was derived the bulk of the labour supply.

Small wonder then that the conditions under which Natives lived in urban areas were uniformly unsatisfactory and formed the subject of adverse comment on the part of successive Commissions which found it within their province to touch upon the subject, e.g., the South African Native Affairs Commission, 1903-1905, the Assaults on Women Commission, 1913, and the Tuberculosis Commission of 1914. In fact, in some of the larger centres such as Johannesburg and Cape Town, these conditions approximated to those obtaining in the worst slum areas of Europe.

The influenza epidemic of 1918 afforded a startling revelation of the appalling state of affairs and of the clamant necessity for remedial legislation.

This legislation took shape in the Natives (Urban Areas) Act, No. 21 of 1923, the purpose of which as expressed in its preamble was " to provide for improved conditions of residence for Natives in or near urban areas and the better administration of Native Affairs in such areas ; for the registration and better control of contracts of service with Natives in certain areas and the regulation of the ingress of Natives into and their residence in such areas ; for the exemption of Coloured persons from the operation of pass laws ; for the restriction and regulation of the possession and use of kafir beer and other intoxicating liquor by Natives in certain areas and for other incidental purposes."

The Act fully recognised and entrenched the system of segregating in locations, for racial and social reasons, the Native population in European towns and villages, a system which had been adopted and was generally in vogue in three of the four Provinces for many years previously.

The essential principle of the Act is that, subject to adequate powers of governmental oversight and control, it places the responsibility for the accommodation and well-being of Natives in any urban area upon the local authority concerned, which is empowered, subject to the approval of the Minister after reference to the Administrator of the Province, to set aside land for locations or Native villages, to provide hostels,—within or without the limits of a location or Native village,—for Natives not living under family conditions, to provide dwellings in locations for Native families, to require employers of more than twenty-five Natives or employers of Natives on work of a temporary nature to provide or hire approved accommodation for their employees in locations, hostels or elsewhere, and to require Natives (other than certain exempted classes), who reside in but are not employed in the urban area, to remove therefrom .

The site of any new location or the extension of an existing location requires the approval of the Minister, which is given only when he is satisfied as to the suitability of the area set apart, the general plan and lay-out of the location and the provision made for water, sanitary and other necessary services. Details of the extent, boundaries and situation of each location must therefore be furnished and a permanent record thereof is kept.

Up to the present, approximately two hundred and seven locations, chiefly in the Cape and Orange Free State Provinces, have been gazetted under the Act.

In the Transvaal, locations are attached to nearly all urban centres. The great majority of them were established under the laws in force before the Act and were, therefore, in terms of sub-section (3) of section *twenty-seven*, duly constituted locations for the purposes of the Act. In Natal, the location system has not been extensively applied, and in this Province there are only nine locations defined under the Act, namely at Greytown, Vryheid, Louwsburg, Paulpietersburg, Pietermaritzburg, Dundee, Ladysmith, Utrecht and Durban.

The Act provides too that no location may be removed, curtailed or abolished except with the consent of the Minister and upon such terms and conditions as to compensation and otherwise as he may direct. When for any reason circumstances necessitate the curtailment or removal of a location, the Department is concerned to see that provision is made else-where for the accommodation of the Natives displaced, while, as regards determining the compensation payable, the accepted procedure is to appoint a valuation board consisting of an equal number of representatives of the local authority and of the Natives with the Magistrate of the district as umpire. The accepted basis of compensation is the award of an amount equivalent to the value of the dwelling which must be vacated, plus a percentage for the inconvenience and trouble occasioned by the removal and the expense to which the occupier is put as regards the erection of a fresh dwelling—usually of a better type—in the new location.

To ensure the observance by urban local authorities of their respon-sibilities in the direction of providing accommodation for Natives, the Act empowers the Minister in any case where he deems it necessary to order a public enquiry to be held, at which the urban local authority and any other person interested are entitled to be heard. If, as the result of any such enquiry, it appears to the Minister that the provision made for Natives in any urban area is inadequate or unsuitable for ordinary re-quirements, he may, by written notice given through the Administrator, direct the local authority within a specified time to make proper and adequate provision ; and, should the local authority fail to comply with the Minister's requirements, the latter may, after reference to the Administrator and after written notice to the local authority, assume control and carry out the necessary reforms at the expense of the urban community concerned.

Up to the present, it has proved necessary in only one case to appoint a committee of enquiry and in this instance the recommendations put forward by the committee were willingly accepted by the local authority concerned.

As a corollary to the establishment of locations in urban areas, the Act makes provision for enforcing the residence of Natives therein. In terms of sub-section (1) of section *five*, as amended by paragraph (a) of section *three* of Act No. 25 of 1930, the Governor-General may, whenever he deems it expedient, by proclamation in the *Gazette* declare that from and after a date to be specified therein all Natives within the limits of any urban area or any specified portion thereof shall reside in a location, Native village or Native hostel.

Certain classes of Natives are exempted from the operation of any such proclamation, the most important class being domestic servants for whom sleeping and sanitary accommodation to the satisfaction of the urban local authority has been provided by their employers.

No request by any urban local authority for the issue in respect of the area under its jurisdiction of a proclamation under the provisions of section *five* of the Act is entertained unless and until the Department is satisfied that adequate and suitable provision has been made for the accommodation of the Natives who under such proclamation would be required to reside in the Native location, village or hostel. Some sixty-two urban areas have up to the present had these segregation provisions applied to them. In this connection, it should be pointed out that in the Transvaal and Orange Free State compulsory segregation in locations was provided for under the laws in force prior to the commencement of the Act and that these provisions were, by sub-section (3) of section *twenty-seven* of the Act, continued in force until superseded by proclamation under section *five*.

The urban local authority having jurisdiction in any area proclaimed under sub-section (1) of section *five* may, in terms of sub-section (4) of that section as amended by section *three* of Act No. 25 of 1930, issue to the owner, lessee or occupier of any premises within the proclaimed area a licence permitting him to accommodate on such premises a specified number of Natives of one or other or each sex.

After an area has been proclaimed under sub-section (1) of section *five*, the urban local authority concerned must serve upon each Native (not being an exempted Native) whose removal from the proclaimed area is desired a written notice, calling upon him to take up, within one month from the first day of the month following the service of such notice, his residence in a location, Native village or hostel specified in such notice *in which accommodation is available for him*, and any Native who disregards such notice is guilty of an offence (sub-section (3) of section *five* of the Act as amended by section *three* of Act No. 25 of 1930).

Any owner, lessee, occupier or person in charge of premises (other than a Native hostel) in a proclaimed area, who, without being licensed thereto, permits any Native (not being an exempted Native) to reside thereon, is likewise guilty of an offence (sub-section (5) of section *five* of the Act as amended by section *three* of Act No. 25 of 1930.)

A far-reaching provision was that inserted as sub-section (6) of section *five* of the Act by section *three* of Act No. 25 of 1930. This empowers the Governor-General, in pursuance of a resolution adopted at a duly constituted meeting of the local authority of any urban area, the *whole* of which has been proclaimed under sub-section (1) of section *five*, by proclamation in the *Gazette*, to declare that from and after a date to be specified therein, no Native may enter that urban area for the purpose of seeking or undertaking employment or of residing therein except in accordance with conditions prescribed in such proclamation.

Only three urban areas have up to the present been proclaimed under this sub-section, viz., Kroonstad (Proclamation No. 431 of 1931), Steynsrust (Proclamation No. 90 of 1932), and Bloemfontein (Proclamation No. 91 of 1932).

A further direction in which urban authorities are assisted to cope with the responsibilities imposed upon them by the Act lies in the special powers conferred upon them by section *seven* of purchasing, and if necessary expropriating, land for location purposes, of borrowing money for the construction of dwellings and of advancing money or supplying material on credit to approved Natives to assist them in providing their own habitations.

Subsidiary principles embodied in the Act, in consonance with and in furtherance of its main object as regards the residence of Natives in locations, Native villages and Native hostels, are the following :—

(a)   The prohibition of the acquisition by non-Natives of lots or premises in any location or of any interest therein.   This provision is in conformity with the segregation idea and is designed to prevent non-Native landlordism in the locations.

(b)   The prohibition of the residence or congregation of Natives,—other than certain privileged classes,—within three miles of an urban boundary.   This provision is intended to reinforce the segregation policy by preventing the congregation under uncontrolled conditions on the outskirts of a town of Natives who should be residing in the town location.   It should be noted that the Governor-General may, by proclamation, increase the three mile limit to five miles in the case of any particular urban area should he deem it expedient.

(c)   The expenditure of all revenue derived from urban locations exclusively upon those locations.   To this end the Act provides for the keeping of a separate account, the Native Revenue Account, by each local authority having under its control a location, Native village or hostel and specifies in detail what moneys are payable into this account and what services are chargeable thereto.   The Minister is given control over these funds by virtue of the fact that the appropriation of moneys from them can take place only in accordance with estimates of expenditure approved in writing by him.   That the careful scrutiny and revision by the Department of these annual estimates of expenditure from the Native revenue accounts of urban authorities involve a tremendous volume of work will readily be appreciated.

(d)   The association with the local authority in the management of its location or Native village of a Native Advisory Board of not less than three Native members together with a chairman, who may be a European. When such a board has been established for any location or Native village and is performing its functions, it must be consulted in regard to any regulation which the urban local authority proposes to make for such location or village.

These boards have for the most part been found to work well and to be of practical assistance to the local authorities in keeping them in touch with the views and feeling of the Natives and with conditions generally in the locations.

(e)   The licensing by the Minister of Native Affairs of all officers appointed by urban local authorities to superintend Native locations. The object of this provision is to secure a satisfactory type of municipal officer for the administration of Native affairs.

(f)   The periodical inspection of municipal Native areas and conditions by competent Government officials.

(g)   The summary removal from urban or industrial areas to their homes or to a labour colony of Natives adjudged by a Magistrate or Native Commissioner, after due enquiry, to be idle, dissolute or disorderly persons.

(h)   The restriction of trading in urban locations and Native villages to Natives or to the urban local authority itself.   In this connection, special mention should be made of the fact that under section *twenty-two* of the Act, as amended by section *twelve* of Act No. 25 of 1930, the Minister can, after consultation with the Administrator and after due enquiry at which the urban local authority is entitled to be heard, direct an urban local authority to let sites to Natives for trading or business purposes within any location or Native village under its jurisdiction, subject to such conditions as he may prescribe.

Special provision is made in section *twelve* of the Act, as amplified by section *seven* of Act No. 25 of 1930, for a comprehensive system of control over Natives and their employers in urban, industrial and mining centres.

Areas are brought under the purview of section *twelve* by proclamation of the Governor-General and control is established primarily by means of the registration of service contracts.

In every urban or industrial area so proclaimed, every male Native, —not belonging to certain specially exempted classes—must carry and may be required to produce on demand either a permit to seek work or a duly registered service contract, in order to establish his right to be within the area.

If a Native fails to find employment within a prescribed period, he may be ordered to leave the proclaimed area, and, should he fail to comply with such order, he may be removed under section *seventeen* of the Act.

Natives under eighteen years of age and unaccompanied by a parent or guardian may be refused permission to enter the proclaimed area. Female Natives may likewise be prohibited from entering a proclaimed area unless they are in possession of a certificate of approval from the urban local authority concerned, which certificate must, however, subject to the necessary accommodation being available, be issued to any female who produces satisfactory proof that her husband, or, if she be unmarried, her father, has been resident and continuously employed in the proclaimed area for a period of not less than two years.

For the more effective control of Natives carrying on trade or business on their own account in a proclaimed area, section *twelve*, as amended, lays down that every male Native, who is not under a contract of service, may be required to register himself with a prescribed officer, to pay such fees and to carry such documents as may be prescribed and to produce such documents on demand by an authorised officer.

Natives not lawfully in a proclaimed area may be ordered to depart therefrom and if they fail to do so may be removed under section *seventeen* of the Act.

Monthly fees payable by the employers are imposed in respect of the registration of service contracts to cover the cost of the system, which has been applied to all the principal towns in the Transvaal, to Kimberley and Cape Town in the Cape, to Pietermaritzburg, Durban, Vryheid and Isipingo Beach in Natal, to Bloemfontein, Winburg, Parys, Heilbron, Kroonstad, Senekal, Wepener, Steynsrust, Petrus Steyn and Brandfort in the Orange Free State, and to rural industrial areas and circles in the Transvaal, Orange Free State and Cape Provinces.

Each of these proclaimed areas has its own series of regulations, made by the Governor-General under section *twenty-three* (1) of the Act, for the exercise of the powers conferred by section *twelve*, and, in so far as the Transvaal is concerned, these various series of regulations are actually administered by the Department. Outside the Transvaal they are administered by the urban local authority concerned in each instance.

As regards Kafir beer, the Act makes provision for either :—

(a) the grant to Natives in urban locations and Native villages of facilities for domestic brewing, subject to the urban local authority concerned (after consultation with or reference to the Native advisory board), acquiescing in this course ; or

(b) the enjoyment of a monopoly by an urban local authority in respect of the manufacture, sale and supply of Kafir beer within its area of jurisdiction. Such a monopoly must be authorised by the Minister and can be granted only in pursuance of a resolution passed in a prescribed manner by the local authority after consultation with or reference to the Native advisory board or boards concerned. Any such monopoly must be exercised in accordance with regulations laid down by the Minister.

Failing the adoption of either of these two alternatives, the manufacture, sale and supply of Kafir beer in any urban location, Native village or Native hostel is prohibited and this prohibition applies to any intoxicating liquor other than Kafir beer.

The municipal monopoly system is not operative outside Natal. In the Orange Free State the system of domestic brewing is fairly general. In the Transvaal, with a few exceptions, prohibition is the general rule, while in the Cape Province the balance between prohibition and domestic brewing is fairly even, prohibition being in force in the larger centres.

Section *eighteen* of the Amending Act, No. 25 of 1930, provides machinery whereby an urban local authority can take steps for the removal of the occupants from and the demolition of dwellings, in a location or Native village under its control, which for health reasons have been condemned by its medical officer. In such case, the occupants of the condemned buildings must be offered either :—

(a) the lease of other adequate housing accommodation in the same or some other location or Native village under the control of the urban local authority ; or

(b) compensation for the loss sustained by them as a result of the removal or demolition, together with the lease of a site in the same or any other location or village under the control of the local authority for the purpose of erecting a fresh dwelling thereon.

The Amending Act also contains in section *nineteen* provisions relating to curfew restrictions in urban areas. These are dealt with in a subsequent portion of this chapter in conjunction with the Pass Laws.

The Natives (Urban Areas) Act makes provision for the making of regulations upon a very wide and diverse range of topics in order to give effect to its objects and policy.

Regulatory powers are vested in the Governor-General in respect of more important issues such as the exercise of the powers of registration and control in areas proclaimed under section *twelve.*

The making of regulations on the more important aspects of the Kafir beer question, including powers of search and confiscation, is assigned to the Minister, while local authorities are empowered to prescribe regulations, which, however, must be approved by both the Administrator and the Minister, in regard to matters of a very wide scope pertaining to the administration of locations, Native villages and hostels;

N

For the guidance of local authorities, a series of model regulations for locations and advisory boards was drawn up by the Department and published under Government Notice No. 672 dated 22nd April, 1924. Local authorities have largely adopted this series as the basis of their regulations although it has been found necessary to amplify and modify them in certain respects to meet special local needs in certain cases. A copy of these model regulations appears as Appendix " J."

Regulations made by the Governor-General and by the Minister are administered by the Department, which is also charged with the duty of scrutinizing and revising regulations submitted for approval by the various local authorities.

Some two hundred and forty series of regulations have been promulgated for different urban areas and, as will readily be appreciated the work devolving upon the Department in this connection forms a most important feature of the administration of the Act.

The Act has been in operation for nine years and has undoubtedly resulted in an improvement of the conditions in urban locations generally, though much still remains to be achieved.

Since the commencement of the Act, loans, amounting approximately to £551,528, have been granted, for the specific purpose of providing housing accommodation for Natives, to various local authorities, through the medium of the Provincial Administrations, from funds provided by the central Government under the Housing Act, 1920. Particulars of these loans are as follows :—

Cape Province.

Aberdeen Municipality		£2,424
Adelaide	,,	5,000
Aliwal North	,,	16,000
Barkly East	,,	9,670
Burghersdorp	,,	5,982
Cambridge	,,	10,674
Cathcart	,,	1,000
Cedarville	,,	2,460
Cradock	,,	5,000
De Aar	,,	2,500
Dordrecht	,,	6,000
East London	,,	32,310
Grahamstown	,,	3,000

Cape Province (continued)

Hanover Municipality	1,500	
King William's Town	18,197	
Kimberley	,,	48,485	
Kokstad	,,	10,000	
Lady Grey	,,	3,963	
Matatiele	,,	2,897	
Middelburg	,,	7,895	
Molteno	,,	2,060	
Philipstown	,,	1,728	
Port Elizabeth	,,	25,000	
Umtata	,,	3,650	
Vryburg	,,	1,500	
Walmer	,,	5,499	£234,394.

Orange Free State.

Bloemfontein Municipality	£11,129	
Kroonstad	,,	1,740	
Smithfield	,,	1,170	£14,039

Natal.

Colenso Local Board	2,640	
Durban Municipality	63,634	
Estcourt	,,	2,000	
Ladysmith	,,	7,500	
Vryheid	,,	11,103	£86,877

Transvaal.

Balfour Municipality	200	
Barberton	,,	1,657	
Benoni	,,	21,290	
Boksburg	,,	11,306	
Brakpan	,,	40,161	
Brits	,,	3,000	
Ermelo	,,	1,000	
Germiston	,,	19,655	
Krugersdorp	,,	24,522	
Machadodorp	,,	1,300	

Transvaal (continued)

Pietersburg Municipality	3,612	
Pretoria ,,	30,000	
Springs ,,	36,222	
Vereeniging ,,	10,000	
Witbank ,,	11,293	
Piet Retief ,,	1,000	£216,218

Cape Province	£234,394
O.F.S. ,,	14,039
Natal ,,	86,877
Transvaal ,,	216,218
Total all Provinces	£551,528

In addition, certain of the larger urban local authorities, notably Johannesburg, Cape Town and Durban, have since the commencement of the Act expended very considerable sums of money in Native housing and in improving conditions in their Native locations.

The approximate amounts, which have already been expended or appropriated for expenditure in this connection by the three local authorities mentioned, are as follows :—

Johannesburg :	£1,100,000
Cape Town :	£300,000
Durban :	£170,000

In reference to the large towns, it may be stated briefly that Pretoria, Johannesburg, Pietermaritzburg, and Bloemfontein, have taken full advantage of the facilities granted under the Act.

In Pretoria the Act is in fullest operation and Natives not actually in employment are under strict control. A reception depôt for the residence of Natives seeking work has been established by the Government and a large hostel for the accommodation of male Natives has been provided by the Municipality.

In Johannesburg it has not been found possible, having regard to the magnitude of the task involved in providing accommodation in Native locations, villages or hostels, at once to effect, by proclamation under section *five* of the Act, the segregation of all Natives throughout the urban area and the problem is being dealt with piece-meal, limited portions of the urban area being proclaimed under the section as accommodation becomes available. The matter is being handled energetically by the local authority and satisfactory progress has been made as regards providing accommodation and cleaning up slums.

In Bloemfontein segregation was in force before the commencement of the Act, but the population of the location is in excess of the actual needs of the town. Efforts are being made to improve the position, but so many Natives have established permanent residence that the process of adjustment will be slow.

In Cape Town, where the municipality has taken over the Ndabeni Location from the Government, a certain amount of progress has been made, but segregation will not be fully effective until the Langa Township, in which it is intended ultimately to accommodate a population of approximately 8,000 Natives, is completed. Fair progress has been made with the provision of accommodation in the Township and as this becomes available Natives are removed thereto.

The Port Elizabeth Municipality has until recently administered the New Brighton Location under the Cape Act, No. 40 of 1902, which embodied segregation provisions. By Proclamation No. 47 dated the 16th February, 1933, the provisions of the Natives (Urban Areas) Act were, however, in terms of section *twenty-six* (b) thereof, extended to New Brighton.

East London continues the segregation principle of its own Municipal Act, and is providing new accommodation for Natives of an improved type to replace old condemned buildings.

In Durban, limited provision has been made by the local authority for Natives in the form of hostels and barracks and the position was unsatisfactory by reason of the number of Natives living in the smaller urban areas surrounding the borough. Legal provision for segregation exists, but the accommodation provided locally by the Corporation is insufficient for the number of Natives working in the Borough. Since the 1st August, 1932, however, the surrounding Health Board areas have been incorporated in the Borough. This should greatly facilitate and simplify control. The Corporation is now engaged in laying out a Native village on land acquired at Clairwood and this should substantially relieve the position.

In Pietermaritzburg hostels have been established and a location has been laid out in which municipal dwellings are being erected. The whole of the urban area has now been proclaimed for segregation purposes.

B

THE NATIVE LABOUR REGULATION ACT, NO. 15 OF 1911

The Native Labour Regulation Act, No. 15 of 1911, was passed " to regulate the recruiting and employment of Native labour and to provide for compensation to Native labourers in certain cases."

It was a comprehensive consolidating measure which embodied the best features of the pre-existing legislation of the various colonies on the subject and, while recognising the rights as well as the obligations of employers, afforded improved facilities and greater protection for Natives employed on mines and works.

The Act provided for the appointment by the Minister of Native Affairs of a special officer termed the " Director," upon whom it conferred wide powers and to whom it assigned important executive duties.

The following principles embodied in the Act ensure adequate supervision and control over the recruiting of Natives for labour purposes and the conditions under which they are employed :—

1. The licensing of persons engaged in recruiting and of compound managers.

2. The execution and attestation of written contracts between Native labourers and recruiters.

3. The appointment of Inspectors, with special powers, whose duty it is to enquire into and redress, if necessary, or otherwise to report to the Director any grievances brought forward by Native labourers.

Other special features of the Act are :—

4. The provision made for the proclamation of labour districts.

5. Its provisions as regards the payment of compensation in respect of personal injuries caused to Native labourers by accident arising out of or in the course of their employment.

Before proceeding to discuss the various principles referred to above in detail, it is necessary to point out that not every Native worker is a " Native labourer " for the purposes of the Act, which defines " Native labourer " as " a Native employed upon any mine or works or recruited under this Act or a prior law for labour upon any mine or works." [For definitions of " mines " and " works " reference should be made to section *two* of the Mines and Works Act, No. 12 of 1911, as amended by section *one* of the Mines and Works (Amendment) Act, No. 22 of 1931].

A Native therefore becomes a " Native labourer " as soon as he accepts or is recruited for employment on " mines " or " works " and it accordingly follows that while the recruiting and cognate provisions of the Act refer to all Natives, not excepting females, its remaining provisions relate almost exclusively to Native labourers.

To deal now with the main principles of the Act outlined above :

1.   *System of Licensed Recruiting*

The Act prohibits any person from exercising the calling of or acting as a *labour agent* (one who by himself or through Native canvassers known as " runners " recruits Natives for employment by another in work or labour of any kind within or outside the Union), *compound manager* (a person who has the superintendence and control of fifty or more Native labourers—otherwise than at their work—in any labour district) or *conductor* (one who escorts Native labourers to their destinations) unless he be duly licensed as such.   Further, subject to certain specified exemptions, no person may recruit Natives for employment by himself or on his own behalf on any mine or works or for employment outside the Union unless he be the holder of an employer's recruiting licence.

Licences under the Act are annual and discretion is vested in the Director as regards their issue, refusal or renewal, subject to an appeal to the Minister.   Licences are further liable to summary cancellation by the Minister upon his being satisfied, after a formal enquiry by a Magistrate, that the holder has been guilty of misconduct.

In addition, every Native runner employed by a labour agent must hold a permit from the Magistrate of the district concerned, who in his discretion may refuse to issue any such permit.

2.   *Execution and Attestation of Contracts*

In terms of section *twelve* of the Act, labour agents must enter into a written contract with every Native labourer recruited by them.   Each such contract must be attested by a Magistrate or other person specially appointed thereto by the Minister.

The attesting officer must in each instance satisfy himself that the Native concerned is apparently over eighteen years of age and that the terms and conditions of the contract are fully understood and accepted by him

In addition, the labour agent must satisfy the attesting officer that he has authority to enter into the contract on behalf of the person for whom, or organisation for which, he purports to recruit the Native.

Every Native labourer must be registered to the person on whose behalf he is employed or recruited.

3. *Inspectors of Native Labourers*

These officers are empowered by the Act, for the purpose of carrying out their duties, to enter any compound or other place occupied by Native labourers and are authorised to summon witnesses and examine them under oath.

All employers of Native labourers are obliged to afford inspectors holding enquiries every reasonable facility and, should they fail so to do, they render themselves liable to a heavy criminal penalty.

Inspectors are further given summary jurisdiction in respect of minor offences committed by Native labourers, e.g., neglect of duty, disobedience, etc., and, in the exercise of such jurisdiction, they may impose fines not exceeding forty shillings.

Inspectors have been appointed under the Act on the Witwatersrand for the performance of judicial functions and to act as Protectors of Natives, visiting the compounds, inspecting conditions under which they are accommodated, enquiring into complaints and putting forward their claims for compensation for injuries sustained or for disability due to phthisis or tuberculosis. In addition, seven inspectors have been appointed for the Transvaal (other than the Witwatersrand), Kimberley, Barkly West and the Orange Free State. Two inspectors have likewise been appointed for and are stationed on the Natal coal fields.

4. *Proclamation of Labour Districts*

Labour districts are proclaimed under the Act in respect of areas where large numbers of Natives are employed either in mining, industrial or other work.

The Act renders it compulsory for employers housing fifty or more Native labourers within a labour district to appoint a compound manager to supervise and control them, to investigate their complaints and attend to their lawful requirements. As all compound managers must be licensed by the Director, the latter is able indirectly to control such appointments.

In labour districts, stricter regulations are applied as regards the registration of contracts and the issue of registration certificates or passes. Close supervision is exercised by Government Inspectors and special regulations are in operation in regard to the housing and feeding of and the provision of hospital accommodation for Native labourers.

The chief of these districts, with the approximate number of Native males employed therein on the 31st December, 1931, are as follows :—

	On Mines	Otherwise than on Mines	Total
Witwatersrand	209,305	99,953	309,258
Heidelberg	5,381	2,722	8,103
Vereeniging	248	4,668	4,916
Rayton	1,402	397	1,799
Witbank	6,639	4,010	10,649
Breyten-Ermelo	1,883	—	1,883
Dundee	6,095	677	6,772
Vryheid	3,985	707	4,692
Kimberley (not proclaimed)	2,185	—	2,185
Orange Free State	2,594	—	2,594
Total	239,717	113,134	352,851

The territorial origin of these Natives was approximately as shewn hereunder :—

On 31/12/31	On Mines	Otherwise than on Mines	Total
Union of South Africa	124,890	101,979	226,869
British Protectorates, etc.	41,669	10,928	52,597
Portuguese East Africa	73,158	227	73,385
Total	239,717	113,134	352,851

The Natives employed otherwise than on Mines comprise those who voluntarily come forward from the Native Territories in search of employment, supplemented by more or less permanent residents in industrial areas who have become parly or wholly detribalised.

The labour supply on the Mines consists of :—

(a) Voluntary new Natives— Those who have come forward independently.

(b) Voluntary local Natives— Those who are already in the industrial area but change from one class of employment to another.

(c) Assisted voluntary Natives—Those who obtain an advance in the home district, to cover railfare and contingencies, but (subject to a time limit) are not required to enter into a contract of service until they have found a mine which they select and which at the same time is willing to receive them.

(d) Recruited Natives— Those who engage at their homes through labour agents for work on the Mines.

For the years 1930 and 1931 the labour engaged from the Union and Protectorates for employment on the Mines represented the following percentages under each heading of the total new labour engaged from the same sources :—

	Voluntary new	Voluntary local	Asstd. voluntary	Recruited
1930				
Gold Mines	30.30	12.67	11.92	45.11
Coal Mines	68.22	31.78		—
Diamond Mines	—	6.11		93.89
Others	58.74	41.26		—
1931				
Gold Mines	27.74	13.09	20.45	38.72
Coal Mines	72.69	27.31		—
Diamond Mines	—	5.98		94.02
Others	79.52	20.48		—

Thus, for the Gold Mines, which engaged in 1930, *157,262* Natives, and in 1931, *159,079* Natives, during the year 1930, *47,655* or upwards of 30.3%, and during 1931, *44,135* or upwards of 27.74% came forward as volunteers for the work without the urge of labour agents.

Recruited Natives from the Union are mainly engaged on contracts of 270 shifts, but in certain areas contracts are for 180 shifts. Those from Portuguese Territory are recruited for 313 shifts with the option of renewal for a period which, with the initial period, cannot exceed eighteen calendar months.

5. *Compensation*

The Act provides for the payment of compensation by the employer of any Native labourer in respect of any personal injury caused to such labourer by accident arising out of or in the course of his employment, other than such as is due to his own serious and wilful misconduct, and resulting in his permanent, total or partial incapacitation or in his death.

The compensation is payable to the Director and is assessed by him upon the following scale :—

For partial incapacitation, a sum of not less than £1 and not more than £20.

For total incapacitation for work, a sum of not less than £30 and not more than £50.

In the case of death, a sum of not less than £30 and not more than £50 [section 22 (2) (c) of Act No. 15 of 1911, as amended by section 2 (1) (f) of the Workmen's Compensation Act, No. 25 of 1914].

If an employer disputes his liability for compensation in any case, whether *in toto* or in respect of the Director's assessment thereof, the matter must be adjudicated upon by a Board consisting of three members, viz., the Magistrate of the district as chairman, a nominee of the employer and a medical practitioner nominated by the other two or, failing agreement as to such nomination, appointed by the Minister. The decision of the board is final.

Compensation received by the Director on behalf or in respect of any Native labourer is payable in the case of injury to the Native personally and in the case of death to his dependents.

The Act specifically lays down that its provisions as regards compensation are not to be regarded as debarring any Native labourer from claiming compensation under his rights at common law but that, if compensation under those provisions is recovered by the labourer or his dependents, no action shall lie against the employer for damages or compensation in respect of the same accident.

It must be pointed out that Native labourers under Act No. 15 of 1911 are not classed as " workmen " for the purposes of the Workmen's

Compensation Act, No. 25 of 1914, and that accordingly the scales of compensation laid down in the latter Act, which are far more generous than those prescribed by the former, are not applicable to them.

Thus arises the anomalous position that if a Native, who is a Native labourer as defined under Act No. 15 of 1911, is permanently injured as the result of an accident in the course of his employment, he receives compensation on a less generous basis than another Native, who, not being a Native labourer as defined under the Act, receives similar injuries in the course of his employment.

Provision for rectifying this anomaly is made under the Workmen's Compensation Bill (A.B. 44-'32) which was introduced and read a first time during the 1932 session of Parliament. This Bill contains a chapter specially relating to Native workmen.

It should be added that the payment of compensation to Native labourers in respect of phthisis or silicosis contracted by them while employed underground at the mines is governed by the provisions of section *thirty-five* of the Miners' Phthisis Acts Consolidation Act, No. 35 of 1925. The Director is given *locus standi* to put forward claims on behalf of Native labourers and the Act makes the compensation payable to him on their behalf.

The scales of compensation provided under that Act for Native labourers found to be suffering from silicosis are for practical purposes as follows :—

(a) If the disease is in the ante-primary stage, a sum equivalent to twelve times the Native's monthly earnings.

(b) If the disease is in the primary stage, a sum equivalent to eighteen times the Native's monthly earnings.

(c) If the disease is in the secondary stage, or if the Native is suffering from tuberculosis with silicosis, a sum equivalent to twenty-four times his monthly earnings.

(d) In the case of the death from silicosis of a Native, who has not received any benefit under (a) (b) or (c) above and who has dependents, a sum equivalent to twenty-four times his monthly earnings is payable to the Director for the benefit of such dependents.

It will be observed therefore that the scales of compensation under Act No. 35 of 1925 are far more generous than those prescribed under Act No. 15 of 1911.

The practice on the Mines is to pay each Native on the completion of thirty shifts worked. Before he is paid, he is weighed and the weight recorded. Any Native who shows a decrease in weight of six pounds either for the month or for a period is submitted to strict medical examination including the use of the stethoscope. Natives discharged from underground work or who go on leave are similarly medically examined. If there is any suspicion that a Native is suffering from silicosis or tuberculosis, there is an obligation on the manager to report the matter and a formal claim is submitted by the Inspector on behalf of the Native. Final decision as to whether the Native has or has not compensationable disease lies with the Miners' Phthisis Medical Bureau appointed by the Government under the Act.

The awards of compensation to Native labourers under Act No. 15 of 1911 and Act No. 35 of 1925 respectively, for the years 1930 and 1931 were as follows :—

A. Under Act No. 15 of 1911.

	1930	1931
No. of Cases	11,021	12,822
Compensation paid	£45,513	£47,563

B. Under Act No. 35 of 1925.

	1930	1931
No. of applications for benefits	1,701	1,920
Compensation paid	£57,100	£62,710

6. *Regulations*

Generally speaking the Native Labour Regulation Act, No. 15 of 1911, contents itself with laying down broad principles, leaving matters of detail to be dealt with in accordance with those principles by regulations, for the framing of which wide powers are conferred upon the Governor-General with a special provision that different regulations may be made in respect of different Provinces; districts or areas in the Union.

Comprehensive regulations framed under the Act were published under Schedule I to Government Notice No. 1,988 of 1911. This schedule has from time to time been amended by various Government Notices. The regulations are divided into three parts as follows :

Part   I—Regulations applicable to the whole Union.

Part   II—Special Regulations for the Orange Free State.

Part III—Special Regulations for the Transvaal.

In addition, certain of the labour districts proclaimed under the Act have their own special series of regulations designed to meet peculiar local conditions.

The general regulations deal with procedure as regards orders and appeals (sections 2-4); the issue, renewal and cancellation of licences and permits (sections 5-14); the duties of compound managers and conductors (sections 15-19); the attestation, registration and conditions of contracts with Natives and Native labourers (sections 20-35); the administration of the estates of Native labourers (sections 36-38); the keeping of books and, accounts by employers in respect of wages paid to Native labourers and the rendering of returns to the Director (sections 39 and 40); the registration of Native labourers to their employers (section 49), and the washing, drying and disinfecting of the clothing of Native labourers (section 50).

The provisions as regards the registration of Native labourers are important having regard to the fact that an employer of a Native labourer is defined in the Act as " the person to whom such labourer is registered under this Act or the regulations," so that a person who employs a Native labourer only becomes liable to the duties and responsibilities of an employer under the Act when that Native has been registered to him in the manner prescribed. The regulations for the various labour districts make a special feature of the registration of contracts by a special registering officer, including the issue of identification labour passports or employment certificates for retention by the employers and monthly passes or registration certificates (in respect of which a monthly fee is payable) to Native labourers. Outside labour districts, the provisions of section *forty-nine* of the general regulations apply in respect of registration.

In addition, section 12 (1) (a) of the Natives (Urban Areas) Act, No. 21 of 1923, provides that the registration of a contract of service under that Act shall be regarded, where the Native is a Native labourer under the Native Labour Regulation Act, 1911, as the registration of the Native to his employer for the purposes of the latter Act.

Under the regulations, no Native can be employed upon a Mine or " Works " unless and until he has been medically examined by an approved medical officer and certified as fit for the employment for which he is engaged.

Standards are laid down as to housing, feeding, medical treatment and hospital accommodation. Plans for all buildings to be used for the accommodation of Native labourers have to be submitted to the Director for approval and, if the buildings subsequently become unsuitable, they are condemned on the recommendation of the Medical Adviser.

The hospital accommodation and medical amenities on the Mines are now distinctly good.   Most of the Mines are equipped with modern hospitals which, in many cases, include X-Ray appliances, and the law requires that a medical officer shall be permanently employed with the necessary number of approved assistants.

The Director or any Magistrate has the power to cancel contracts of service in certain circumstances, where such agreements are regarded as inimical to the Natives' interests.

No Native can be discharged from his employment by reason of illness or injury unless and until his discharge is approved by a representative of the Director and the employer provides the necessary funds.

C
ADVANCES TO NATIVE LABOURERS : ACT NO. 18 OF 1921

A feature of the recruiting of Natives for work under contract, whether on the Mines or elsewhere, has always been the holding out to them of special inducements, in the form of advances in cash or in kind, to accept such employment.   Though the making of pecuniary advances to Native labourers proceeding to work under contract for six months or longer is unobjectionable in principle and in many instances is actually necessary for the purpose of providing for the maintenance of their families during the initial period of their absence, yet the practice is one which is easily susceptible of abuse, and it was recognised at an early stage that it should be brought under suitable restriction and control.

The Native Labour Regulation Act empowered the Governor-General, under section *twenty-three* (1) (e), to make regulations in this connection for the purposes of that Act, but it was found necessary to extend the control to every class of agent, employer and employment. Legislation was accordingly introduced and the Natives Advances Regulation Act, No. 18 of 1921 was enacted.

This Act empowers the Governor-General by proclamation in the Gazette to make regulations regulating or limiting the amount of advances (whether in cash or in kind) to any Native by or on behalf of any person (or his agent) who employs or desires to employ or contemplates the employment of such Native.   The Act provides further that different regulations may be made in respect of different provinces, districts or other areas of the Union and also in respect of different industries or classes of employment.

Regulations under this Act are contained in Proclamation No. 175 of 1921, as amended by Proclamation No. 231 of 1923. They limit any advance made in consideration of a Native accepting employment to £2, with the proviso that where the period of employment is to extend to nine months or longer the advance may be increased to £3.

Advances by an employer to a Native during the subsistence of a contract are limited to £2 sterling where the Native is employed on roads, railways and harbours or on mines and works, or on a sugar, tea or wattle plantation or on work controlled by a local authority, and in all other cases to £5 sterling or, in the Natal Province, one head of horned stock in kind.

Advances made under these regulations may be recovered by deductions from wages earned or to be earned by the Native and a penalty, not exceeding £50, is prescribed for contravention of the regulations.

D

GENERAL REMARKS ON NATIVE LABOUR SUB-DEPARTMENT

Organisation

Native affairs organisation in labour districts is under the Director of Native Labour who, through the Secretary for Native Affairs, is responsible to the Minister. The Director is also Chief Native Commissioner for the Witwatersrand.

On the Witwatersrand there are three Native Commissioners, who also act as Inspectors of Native Labour, one Assistant Native Commissioner, three Inspectors of Native Labour and ten relatively senior officers in charge of pass offices in the various districts.

The Native Commissioners and Inspectors visit places where Natives are employed, examine conditions of housing, feeding, medical attention, hospital administration, sanitation, etc., and afford Natives an opportunity of ventilating any grievances. At each mine a complaints book is kept by the licensed Compound Manager, which is viséed by the Native Commissioner or Inspector on his visits. Matters and messages of a domestic nature referred to the Director by Magistrates in the country are conveyed to the labourers through these officers, who also facilitate any arrangements that may be necessary in regard to such.

The Pass Officers act as Welfare Officers particularly in regard to Natives employed otherwise than on the mines ; complaints of any nature are investigated and, where necessary, these are referred to the Native Commissioner of the district.

The Director's staff on the Witwatersrand includes 152 Europeans and 153 Natives.

At each pass office there is established a branch of the Native Deposit and Remittance Agency. A sum of £14,323 was remitted on behalf of Natives during the year 1930 and £14,665 during the year 1931.

Natives who arrive from their homes are afforded accommodation free of charge at the Pass Offices whilst they are seeking employment. They are during this period medically examined and, where necessary, vaccinated.

All Natives, whether recruited or voluntary, who arrive on the Witwatersrand in search of employment on the mines are sent to a central depôt where they are medically examined, there being an examining staff of six medical officers. The central depôt is thoroughly well equipped with sterilizing plant, modern hospital accommodation, including an up-to-date X-ray plant, and all reasonable conveniences. Natives from the Cape Province come to the Reef by labour trains under the supervision of conductors employed by the Government. Similarly, Natives who are unfit to remain in employment on the mines are centralized at this depôt where they are medically examined by the staff above referred to and their final repatriation by the labour trains is subject to the issue by the Government Medical Officer of certificates of fitness to travel.

The death rates on Gold and Coal Mines for the years 1922 to 1931 were as shown hereunder :—

Death rate per 1,000 per annum

Year	Gold Mines	Coal Mines
1922	11.23	14.80
1923	11.60	15.58
1924	9.99	16.05
1925	8.61	15.73
1926	9.05	13.30
1927	11.72	14.67
1928	11.92	15.08
1929	10.50	15.06
1930	9.70	11.30
1931	8.93	12.06

o

Thrift

The policy of encouraging thrift amongst Natives has been followed. In addition to the departmental remittance agency referred to above, an approved system of depositing and remitting moneys by the mines is in operation on the mines themselves. Under this system, moneys are received from Native labourers (against receipts issued on the credit of the mine) on deposit during their period of employment or for remittance to their nominees. The individual mines retain 25 per cent of the moneys deposited wherewith to pay out current claims against the account. The balance of 75 per cent is invested in Government securities and the interest accruing is administered by a Board subsequently referred to.

A system of voluntary deferred pay in respect of British South African Natives was brought into operation in February, 1918, under which Natives from the Union and Protectorates can decide to receive their earnings, less 10s. paid in cash monthly at their place of employment, on their return to their homes. This system has grown much in favour with Natives. In 1919, 33.2% of the recruited Natives elected to come under the system ; in 1923, 30.2% ; in 1926 43.1%, and in February of 1930, 58%. Those from Cape Province for the same month represented 64.7% of the recruited Natives from that area. The amount paid out under the scheme up to February, 1930, exceeded one and a half million pounds.

As it was not considered practicable to pay very small sums in interest to the very large number of individual Natives concerned, a trust board, called the " Deferred Pay Board of Control," was formed, on which there are three Government and three Mining representatives with the Director of Native Labour as Chairman. The money in suspense is invested, as in the case of deposits, in Government securities and the accruing interest is administered by the Board which subsidises or finances undertakings particularly designed for the benefit of Natives, generally of the labour class. Grants made by the Board are subject to ministerial approval.

Accidents on the Mines

A special Committee known as " The Accidents Committee," was established by the Chamber of Mines some years ago. It includes in its membership, the Government Mining Engineer, the Chief Inspector of Mines, the Director of Native Labour, and representatives of the various sides of mining, administrative, medical, and technical.   The Committee is financed by the mining industry, it meets ordinarily once a month and has several sub-committees which consider special aspects.   The objects of the Committee are to place the incidence of accidents on the mines under the microscope and by its influence and propaganda to induce all concerned to take all possible precautions and to eliminate all avoidable risks.   The activities of this committee have been of the greatest advantage and it can claim to have done excellent work.   In spite of the increased depth of mining during recent years, the death rate from accidents on the Witwatersrand gold mines decreased from 3.81 per 1,000 in 1913 to 2.29 in 1928 and 2.52 in 1931.

Conclusions

Briefly speaking, it may be claimed that the results achieved by the Sub-Department of Native Labour during recent years include the general adoption of clean methods of recruiting, fair and careful consideration of legitimate grievances of Natives, greater attention to efficiency and the conservation of labour, improved status and responsibility of compound managers and of those in immediate control of Natives, vastly improved hospital provision with full-time medical officers on nearly all the mines, the substantial reduction of death rates from disease and accident, and greatly improved conditions of living for Natives in urban locations.

E

NOTE ON NATIVE LABOUR FROM PORTUGUESE EAST AFRICA

The gold-mining industry on the Witwatersrand has from its earliest days been to some extent dependent upon the introduction of alien Native labour.

An Industrial Commission of Enquiry appointed by the Transvaal Republican Government in 1897 found that the chief supply of Native labour to meet the increasing demands of the mines must come from the East Coast.

Arrangements were accordingly made with the Government of the Province of Mozambique whereby labour agents approved by the Republican authorites might obtain licences to recruit labour there for the

Transvaal mines and a properly controlled channel for the introduction of Native labour from the East Coast to the mines resulted.

These Portuguese East African Natives proved themselves the most satisfactory and efficient labourers on the mines and were as a general rule prepared to enter into contracts for longer periods of service than were the South African Natives.

The Native labour strength of the gold mines was dispersed during the South African war and its re-assemblage was found to be both tardy and difficult.   The gold-mining industry on this account established a co-operative recruiting association with a view to expediting the engagement and augmenting the supply of East African Natives for the mines and to eliminating the evils of competitive recruiting.   The Transvaal Government at the same time negotiated with the Portuguese authorities an instrument, known as the " Modus Vivendi, 1901," authorising recruiting operations.

The rehabilitation of the labour supply was, however, slow and there followed the introduction of large drafts of Chinese labourers under the Labour Importation Ordinance, No. 17 of 1904.   The repeal of this Ordinance by the Constitution Letters Patent on the grant of responsible government to the Transvaal necessitated the repatriation of the Chinese and the mining industry was thrown back upon the Native population for its labour.

In April, 1909, the Transvaal Government negotiated a fresh convention with the Mozambique authorities in order to secure a regular supply of labour from the East Coast.   This Convention was made operative for a period of ten years from the 1st April, 1909, and subject thereafter to termination by either Government on one year's notice. The Convention was denounced by the Union Government by notice dated the 1st April, 1922, negotiations for a new agreement being subsequently initiated.   As no agreement was arrived at by the 31st March, 1923, when the notice expired, the Convention in its old form lapsed on that date.   It was, however, arranged by the two Governments that Part I of the Convention, dealing with Native labour, should be prolonged provisionally subject to six months' notice.   In November, 1927, the Portuguese Government denounced this part of the Convention, which therefore under the provisional agreement terminated on the 1st June, 1928.

A fresh Convention was entered into between the Union Government and the Government of the Portuguese Republic at Pretoria on the

11th September, 1928, and the entry into the Union of Native labourers from the Colony of Mozambique is now governed by its terms.

This Convention was made operative for a period of ten years and subject thereafter to termination on the expiry of twelve months after denunciation by either Government. It is specially provided however that, five years after the date of signature of the Convention, either Government shall be entitled to call for a revision of its terms, whereupon, in default of mutual agreement, the Convention shall lapse six months after the date of receipt of notice of termination.

The Convention provides for a progressive reduction in the number of Portuguese Natives, who may be employed on the mines, to a maximum complement of 80,000 within the five years succeeding the date of the Convention. It limits the duration of contracts of service in respect of Portuguese Natives to a period of twelve months (313 shifts worked), subject to renewal at the option of the labourer for a further period of six months (156 shifts worked). The maximum period of service is thus restricted to eighteen months. The Convention further provides that, after the first nine months' service, payment of the wages of Portuguese Native labourers, to the extent of 1s. per shift, shall be deferred.

F

PASS LAWS

Pass laws based on various statutes are in operation throughout the Union, with the exception of the Cape Province (excluding British Bechuanaland and the Transkeian Territories), where the Natives, unless accompanied by livestock, enjoy entire freedom of movement.

Pass laws originally owed their inception to the necessity of securing control over the Native population and of providing a safeguard against crimes such as theft of stock. In the earlier days, their aim was principally directed against an influx of Natives from the neighbouring barbarian tribes and for the protection of the cattle and property of border farmers. As the country became more settled, however, they were utilized for enforcing contractual obligations between Natives and Europeans and for detecting deserters. Later, when the Natives began to seek employment in the large European urban and mining centres— more particularly the Witwatersrand—these laws, amplified and extended, were used to maintain order, to detect desertion, to identify on behalf of their relatives Natives who had become lost and to trace the heirs of those who had died leaving assets which should properly be distributed at their homes.

Little or no attempt was made prior to Union to deal with pass legislation on uniform lines and each government instituted its own system of control.

Thus in the Cape Province proper, while there was virtually no pass system, the purposes achieved by pass regulations in the other Provinces were largely served by the Vagrancy Act, No. 23 of 1879, as amended by Act No. 27 of 1889, whereby an owner, lessee or lawful occupier of any land, or his duly authorised representative, could apprehend as an idle and disorderly person, and take before the nearest magistrate or special justice of the peace, any person found without his permission wandering over his farm or loitering near any dwelling house, shop, store, kraal, or other enclosed place or loitering upon any road crossing such farm. The onus of proving his *bona fides* was placed upon the person arrested.

In British Bechuanaland, passes were (and still are) required under B.B. Proclamation No. 2 of 1885 by Natives when entering or leaving the territory.

In the Transkeian Territories, the law required any person leaving or entering any of the said Territories to be provided with a pass, but the proclamation on defining the persons required to produce their passes did not include Europeans. The inter-territorial movements of Natives within the Transkeian Territories were not, however, hampered by a strict enforcement of the regulations.

In the Transvaal, there were general pass regulations, special pass regulations for labour districts framed under the provisions of Proclamation No. 37 of 1901 as amended by Ordinance No. 27 of 1903, and, in addition, special pass regulations for urban areas framed under the Urban Areas Native Pass Act, No. 18 of 1909.

In the Orange Free State, there were general pass provisions in the Squatting Laws (Chapter CXXXIII of the Law Book and Law 4 of 1895), in Law 8 of 1899, in the Pass Laws Amendment Ordinance, No. 9 of 1906, and in the Pass Laws Supplementary Ordinance, No. 30 of 1906, dealing with inward and outward passes, travelling passes, trek passes and rural residential passes.

In addition, there was special provision in Law No. 8 of 1893 compelling Natives residing in urban areas to take out municipal residential passes.

The Natal laws provided for—(a) inward and outward passes, i.e., passes for entering or leaving the territory (Act No. 48 of 1884 and Act No. 52 of 1887 and the regulations framed thereunder, published under Government Notice No. 120 of 1910); and (b) identification passes (Act No. 49 of 1901, as modified by Act No. 3 of 1904, and the regulations framed thereunder, published under Government Notice No. 199 of 1904).

The question of co-ordinating and consolidating the various pass laws throughout the Union was referred by the House of Assembly to the Select Committee on Native Affairs in 1914. This Committee reported that it considered it inadvisable to attempt at that stage to legislate with a view to the consolidation of the pass laws in force in the different Provinces, but that such legislation should await the action to be taken by Parliament on the report of the Natives Land Commission then sitting. At the same time, the Committee recognised that there were certain defects in, and grievances under, the pass laws, which might be remedied as a temporary measure pending consolidating legislation, and it accordingly recommended for the consideration of the House a draft Bill, the text of which will be found in the Committee's report (S.C. 8A -'14). During the war period it was not found possible to introduce this amending Bill, but administrative action was taken to relieve the situation in certain directions.

An Inter-departmental Committee of Inquiry was appointed in December, 1919, which fully investigated the pass question in all four Provinces and presented a report to the Government (U.G. 41-1922). After consideration of the subject by the Native Affairs Commission, a Bill, embodying in the main the recommendations of the Committee and entitled the Native Registration and Protection Bill, was introduced into Parliament during the 1923 session as a complementary measure to the Natives (Urban Areas) Bill. The Bill was not proceeded with, but certain of its provisions were incorporated in the Natives (Urban Areas) Act, which introduced a measure of uniformity as regards urban and industrial areas by adopting (in section *twelve*) the principle of enforcing contractual obligations and of ensuring control over unemployed Natives in such areas by a system of registration of service contracts and of compulsory reporting. This system does not differ in essence from a direct pass system, as the employed Native must always be in a position to produce evidence of his contract of service and the unemployed Native of his having reported as prescribed. This Act repealed the Transvaal pass laws in their application to labour districts, the Transvaal Urban Areas Native Pass Act, No. 18 of 1909, and the Orange Free State Law No. 8 of

1893 in so far as that law related to Natives and Native locations. Further, sub-section (2) of section *twenty-seven* of the Natives (Urban Areas) Act authorises the Governor-General, in making any regulation for any urban or industrial area for the purposes of section *twelve*, to repeal in its application to that area so much of any law or regulation as he deems inconsistent with the operation thereof.

Special powers as regards pass laws and regulations were vested in the Governor-General by section *twenty-eight* of the Native Administration Act, No. 38 of 1927, which reads as follows :—

> " 28 (1) The Governor-General may, by proclamation in the Gazette—
>
> (a) create and define pass areas within which Natives may be required to carry passes ;
>
> (b) prescribe regulations for the control and prohibition of the movement of Natives into, within or from any such areas ; and
>
> (c) repeal all or any of the laws relating to the carrying of passes by Natives ;
>
> Provided that no area included in the Schedule to the Natives Land Act, 1913 (Act No. 27 of 1913), or any amendment thereof, shall be included within a pass area.
>
> (2) Such regulations may provide penalties for any breach thereof not exceeding a fine of five pounds or imprisonment with or without hard labour for a period not exceeding three months."

A draft proclamation designed to achieve the purposes indicated in paragraphs (a), (b) and (c) quoted above and to introduce a simple, uniform system of general application outside the scheduled Native areas has been prepared by the Department and is at present engaging the consideration of the Government.

G

NIGHT PASS REGULATIONS

Curfew or night pass regulations for Natives were prior to Union operative in respect of urban areas in the several Provinces.

In the *Cape*, by section *two* of the Local Authorities Increased Powers Act, No. 30 of 1895, local authorities were empowered to make regulations preventing Natives from being in streets, public places and thorough-fares between the hours of 9 p.m. and 4 a.m. without a pass from an employer or some person duly authorised to issue such passes.

The *Transvaal* Night Passes Ordinance, No. 43 of 1902, prohibited Natives from being abroad in any public place within any town council or health board area, or any other area proclaimed for the purposes of the Ordinance, between the hours of 9 p.m. and 4 a.m. without a pass.

In the *Orange Free State*, no specific curfew provisions existed but regulations were framed under the provisions of paragraph (a) of section *one* of Law 8 of 1893, sub-section (3) of section *one hundred and eight* of Ordinance No. 6 of 1904 and paragraph (c) of section *one hundred and twenty* of Ordinance No. 35 of 1903. These provisions were repealed by Act No. 21 of 1923 in so far as they related to Natives.

In *Natal*, curfew restrictions were imposed under section *two* of the Vagrancy Law, No. 15 of 1869, which made it an offence for Coloured persons (including Natives) to wander abroad in any borough, between such hours as the Corporation of such borough might fix, without being able to give a good account of themselves.

Reference has already been made (*vide* page 193 *supra*) to the fact that curfew provisions are contained in section *nineteen* of the Natives (Urban Areas) Act 1923, Amendment Act, No. 25 of 1930. That section, which is, of course, of general application throughout the Union, empowers the Governor-General, at the request of any urban local authority, by proclamation in the Gazette, to declare that no Native, male or female, shall be in any public place within the area controlled by such authority during such hours of the night as are specified in such proclamation unless such Native be in possession of a written permit signed by his employer or by a person authorised by such employer to issue such a permit to such a Native or by some person authorised by the urban local authority to issue such permits or by the officer in charge of any police station within such area.

Any Native contravening the provisions of any such proclamation is guilty of an offence, as is also any person who, without authority so to do, issues a "night pass" to a Native in a proclaimed area. No proclamation issued under the section applies within any location or Native village and the following classes of Natives are exempt from the operation of any such proclamation :—

(a) Natives who are the registered owners of immovable property, within the urban area concerned, valued for rating purposes at seventy-five pounds or more, so long as they continue to be the registered owners of and to be ordinarily resident on such property ;

(b)   In the Province concerned, Natives who hold letters of exemption granted under any law in force in the Province of Natal, the Transvaal or the Orange Free State ;

(c)   In the Province of the Cape of Good Hope, Natives who are registered parliamentary voters ;

(d)   Natives who are the registered owners or the *bona fide* purchasers of land in any such township as is defined in paragraph (i) of subsection (1) of section *eight* of the Natives Land Act, No. 27 of 1913 ;

(e)   Approved chiefs and headmen ;

(f)   Ministers of religion who are marriage officers, teachers whose salaries are paid or defrayed directly or indirectly in whole or in part by the Government or any provincial administration and interpreters of the various courts of the Union ; provided they are approved in such manner as may be prescribed.

Proclamations under section *nineteen* of Act No. 25 of 1930 have already been issued in respect of one hundred and eighty urban areas.   The curfew hours generally prescribed under these proclamations are from 10 p.m. to 4 a.m.

Section *twenty* of Act No. 25 of 1930, in providing for the repeal of the pre-existing curfew laws, laid down that regulations and provisions in force in any area under those laws immediately prior to the commencement of the Act, i.e., the 30th May, 1930, should continue in force for a period of twelve months after that date unless previously superseded by proclamation under section *nineteen*.

IX

RECOGNITION OF NATIVE LAW AND ALLIED TOPICS

In this Chapter we touch upon the question of the recognition of Native law and custom in the Union, proceed to consider certain allied topics, viz., the judicial system, marriage and inheritance in their relation to Natives, furnish a note on the exemption laws and finally give a brief account of the work of the Department on the ethnological side.

A

RECOGNITION OF NATIVE LAW AND CUSTOM

Prior to Union widely divergent policies had been adopted by the several Governments as regards the fundamental question of the recognition of Native law and custom, and, in so far as the Cape was concerned, different policies were followed in different parts of the Colony.

Cape Colony Proper. By the incorporation of British Kaffraria with the Cape Colony under Act No. 3 of 1865, the large body of Natives, together with the European population, then comprehended within the limits of that dependency, were brought within the pale of Cape Colonial Law, although no adequate machinery was provided for giving effect to this in so far as its application to Natives was concerned. No provision was made for the recognition of Native law and custom, which had prior to annexation been in operation, and thenceforward the Native population fell under European law, the principle being that Black and White should be regarded as equally subject to the laws of the Colony, which under the Charter of Justice of 1832 were to be applied by the Supreme Court in all civil and criminal causes affecting persons of any race or colour within the Colony.

Thus in the Cape Colony proper, in spite of the declared intention of the successive earlier Kaffrarian administrations, there was no straightforward recognition of Native law and in consequence the Administration was forced to the adoption of illogical and spasmodic makeshifts, such as the establishment of an extra-legal court at King William's Town to settle disputes under Native law on the understanding that the parties would submit to the decision ; the special retention by deed of grant of the Native law of succession in respect of allotments granted in individual tenure ; appeal to the Governor-General in cases of Native heirship in the districts originally constituting British Kaffraria ; and powers to lay down by proclamation the usages to be observed in regard to the administration and distribution of property in such Native locations as might be proclaimed. These were merely palliatives of conditions in which the Native social organisation operated on lines of its own out of harmony with the legal system.

The *Transkeian Territories*, as has already been explained, were always regarded as essentially Native and enjoyed special privileges as such. The various Annexation Acts of the different territories beyond the Kei recognised that " the Natives were not sufficiently advanced in civilisation and social progress to be admitted to the full responsibility granted and imposed respectively by the ordinary laws of the Colony to and upon other citizens thereof " and made them subject not to the ordinary laws but to a special system of edictal legislation which, while permitting of Native law and custom being accorded the widest possible measure of recognition, made Native law susceptible of definition, limitation and amendment by the Executive so that it could be moulded to meet the progress of the people, neither shackling their development on the one hand nor forcing the premature adoption of principles alien to their conception and experience on the other.

Native custom then has consistently been recognised in the Transkeian Territories, has been modified by Proclamation as necessity or expediency has demanded and has been applied in judicial proceedings at the discretion of the courts.

In *British Bechuanaland*, the operation of Native law was recognised under the Imperial regime and retained upon the annexation of the territory to the Cape Colony. By section *thirty-one* of B.B. Proclamation No. 2 of 1885 the chiefs were given exclusive civil jurisdiction in civil cases between Natives of their own tribes and by section *thirty-two* they were allowed to retain criminal jurisdiction except as regards certain serious crimes.

In *Natal* proper, Native law was not only recognised but was codified, first in 1878 and subsequently under Law No. 19 of 1891, so that the incidents of customary marriage, dowry and succession and generally of Native social organisation and discipline were provided for. The

Code, however, was rigid and could be amended by statute only, which militated against its ready adaptability to changing conditions.

In *Zululand*, the superseded Natal Code of 1878 was theoretically in force, as was laid down by the Appellate Division in 1921 in the case of *Ntuli versus Ntuli*, but Native disputes were to a considerable extent adjusted according to custom without deference to this Code.

In the *Transvaal*, by Law No. 4 of 1885 the laws, habits and customs observed among the Natives were continued in force in so far as they were not inconsistent with the general principles of civilisation. This limitation and the interpretations of the Supreme Court largely defeated the purpose of the law in that, for instance, marriages by Native law and custom were, by virtue of the element of polygamy, pronounced to be inconsistent with the general principles of civilisation and accordingly as nothing more than illicit unions. Principles of succession according to Native custom were recognised under section *seventy* of the Transvaal Administration of Estates Proclamation, No. 28 of 1902.

In the *Orange Free State*, principles of succession and guardianship according to Native custom were maintained under Law No. 26 of 1899, while in the Witzieshoek Native Reserve of that Province the Chief was authorised to hear minor civil cases according to Native law and custom. In such cases an appeal lay to the court of the Commandant at Witzieshoek as to a court of equity.

Such briefly was the state of affairs in the different Provinces at Union.

The Select Committee on Native Affairs of the House of Assembly, after carefully considering the question, reported in April, 1911, as follows :—

> " Your Committee recommend that legislation be introduced admitting of the recognition by Courts of Law of such Native laws and customs as are already embodied in the law in force within certain parts of the Union."

With the effluxion of time, it was increasingly recognised that the discrepancies and variety of conditions in regard to the application of Native law involved serious injustice to the Natives and provision was made to deal with the matter in the Native Administration Bill of 1917, which, for reasons already explained, was not placed upon the Statute book.

Ultimately, the necessary reforms were introduced in the Native Administration Bill, 1927, which was enacted as Act No. 38 of that year.

This Act, as amended by Act No. 9 of 1929, provides for the establishment of Native Commissioners' Courts and special Native Appeal Courts, for the settlement of disputes arising out of Native law and custom by chiefs and headmen and for the exercise by chiefs and headmen of a limited criminal jurisdiction in respect of offences punishable under Native law and custom. It contains special provisions as regards Native marriages and customary unions and regulates Native succession.

All of these matters are dealt with in subsequent portions of this chapter and for the moment it is sufficient to note

(a) the recognition accorded to Native law and custom in section *eleven* of the Act which reads as follows :—

" 11. (1) Notwithstanding the provisions of any other law, it shall be in the discretion of the courts of Native Commissioners in all suits or proceedings between Natives involving questions of customs followed by Natives, to decide such questions according to the Native law applying to such customs except in so far as it shall have been repealed or modified : Provided that such Native law shall not be opposed to the principles of public policy or natural justice : Provided further that it shall not be lawful for any court to declare that the custom of *lobola* or *bogadi* or other similar custom is repugnant to such principles.

(2) Where the parties to a suit reside in areas where different Native laws are in operation, the Native law, if any, to be applied by the court shall be that prevailing in the place of residence of the defendant " ; and

(b) that the Governor-General was by section *twenty-four* of the Act given power by proclamation to amend the Natal Code of Native law and to extend the operation of that Code or any amendment thereof to Zululand.

The revision of the Code was put in hand shortly after the commencement of the Native Administration Act.

The objects in view were the following :—

(i) to bring the Code into harmony with the existing practices and usages of the Natives in Natal in recognition of the changes and development which had undeniably taken place in the family life and customs of the people during the years which had elapsed since it was enacted ;

(ii) to consolidate the Native law in Natal which was contained in the original Code and in a number of amending statutes ;

(iii) to re-arrange the Code in proper logical and legal form, the original Code being archaic in form and language and very badly arranged ;

(iv) to bring the Code into harmony with the provisions of the Native Administration Act ; and

(v) to facilitate the application of the Code to Zululand.

The matter was in the first instance referred to a committee of experienced Natal Magistrates assisted by a recognised authority on Native law and custom in Natal, Professor F. B. Burchell, Professor of Law at the Natal University College.

The Committee devoted considerable time and unremitting labour to their task and freely consulted Magistrates, Natives and others well versed in Native law and custom. They were not called upon to undertake the very necessary work of re-arrangement but confined themselves to carefully examining the substantive provisions of the Code, as modified from time to time, and recommending in what directions it should be amended.

Upon receipt of their report and recommendations, the work of re-arrangement was undertaken in Pretoria and when this was completed further discussion on the draft revised measure took place in Pietermaritzburg.

The revised Code in draft form was published for general information under Government Notice No. 1796 of 1931. It was amended in certain respects in consequence of representations received from a variety of sources and was ultimately promulgated under Proclamation No. 168 of 1932 dated the 17th September, 1932.

The Revised Code is embodied in the schedule to the Proclamation, which

(a) substituted it for the schedule to Law No. 19 of 1891 (Natal) ;

(b) repealed antecedent Natal legislation ;

(c) laid down that the revised Code should commence and take effect from 1st November, 1932 ; and

(d) extended the operation of the revised measure to Zululand.

(Here it may be mentioned that the Code of 1878 had in its application to Zululand been repealed by the Native Administration Act, 1927.)

A copy of Proclamation No. 168 of 1932 appears as Appendix " K."

B

JUDICIAL SYSTEM PROVIDED FOR NATIVES

It must be emphasised in the first place that, generally speaking, Natives in both civil and criminal matters are subject to the ordinary laws of the land and that the ordinary courts, viz., Magistrates' Courts and the various divisions of the Supreme Court, are open to them.

In addition, certain special courts for the hearing of purely Native cases have been established for the benefit and in the interests of the Natives themselves, with a view to affording them a simpler and less expensive method of procedure, to having cases arising out of Native law and custom heard by officials experienced and well versed in such laws and customs and, in so far as Native chiefs' courts are concerned, to according a measure of recognition to purely Native institutions.

1.   CRIMINAL MATTERS

Dealing first with the administration of the criminal law, Natives are in the ordinary course prosecuted for criminal offences in exactly the same manner and in the same courts as Europeans.   Less serious offences are dealt with by a Magistrate's court (or the court of a special Justice of the Peace if the offence be one falling within the jurisdiction of and committed in the area of a special Justice of the Peace), while, as regards more serious crimes, preparatory examinations are taken by the Magistrate and the accused are tried before a Judge of the Supreme Court and a jury, or before a Judge with two Magistrates as assessors, in the ordinary course, except in so far as in Natal the jurisdiction of the Supreme Court is in respect of certain crimes excluded in favour of the Natal Native High Court—*vide infra.*

Reference is frequently made to the fact that it is not competent for Natives to serve on juries and that consequently the jury system militates adversely against a Native accused who, when a European is the complainant, is unlikely to receive impartial justice at the hands of a jury composed exclusively of Europeans.   The answer to this is that it is not necessary for any Native accused to be tried before a jury as Natives have, under section *two hundred and sixteen* of the Criminal Procedure and Evidence Act, No. 31 of 1917, the same right (a right of which they are invariably notified) as Europeans to elect to stand their trial before a Judge (who in his discretion may summon to his assistance two assessors to act in an advisory capacity) instead of being tried by jury.

The criminal jurisdiction and functions of the Supreme Court, whether as regards trial, review or appeal are the same in respect of Natives as in respect of Europeans, except that in Natal the jurisdiction of the Supreme Court as a court of the first instance is expressly excluded in respect of crimes cognisable by the Natal High Court.

While Natives are subject to the criminal law administered by the ordinary courts, there are the following special criminal tribunals for Natives :—

(a) *Native Chiefs' and Headmen's Criminal Courts*

(i) Section *twenty* of the Native Administration Act, as amended by section *six* (1) of Act No. 9 of 1929, empowers the Governor-General to grant to any Native chief or headman jurisdiction over members of his own tribe resident or being upon tribal land or in a tribal location within his area in respect of offences punishable under Native law and custom.

In the exercise of jurisdiction so conferred upon him, a chief or headman may impose a fine not exceeding two head of cattle or five pounds upon any person convicted by him of any such offence. An appeal against any such conviction lies to the Magistrate of the district.

Regulations governing the exercise by chiefs and headmen of this special criminal jurisdiction were framed under the section and published under Government Notice No. 2256 of 1928. A copy of this Government Notice appears in Appendix " L."

The policy of the Government is to confer this special criminal jurisdiction upon chiefs and headmen in Zululand and British Bechuanaland but not in the remainder of the Cape and Natal Provinces nor in the Transvaal and Orange Free State.

(ii) In *British Bechuanaland* Native chiefs were, by section *thirty-two* of B.B. Proclamation No. 2 of 1885, given jurisdiction according to Native law in all criminal cases arising exclusively between Natives of their respective tribes, other than cases of rape, murder, culpable homicide, pretended witchcraft and theft from other tribes. Chiefs were, however, debarred from inflicting any punishment involving death, mutilation or grievous bodily harm.

This jurisdiction was retained at annexation and was specially preserved under section *twenty-one* of the Native Administration Act.

Under section *two* of Act No. 7 of 1924, it is provided that appeals from the decisions of Native chiefs in British Bechuanaland, in both civil

P

and criminal cases, shall lie to the court of the Magistrate of the district, from whose decision there shall be a further appeal to the Griqualand West Local Division of the Supreme Court.

(iii) Under the revised Code of Native Law for Natal, chiefs and headmen :—

(a) have authority to require compliance by the people under their jurisdiction with their duties under Native law and m-- give orders for that purpose ; the enforcem--- ---to authority, of the duty of children to the--- --he obligations of the inmates of kraals to their --i- cular fall within the scope of their authori--- ---g these functions they may impose a fine --- ---o pounds for any defiance or disregard of thei---

(b) are, in carrying out the directions and ord-- Chief, his minor deputies and when so actin--- --- not exceeding two pounds for any act of de---- --- obedience to a lawful order ;

(c) in exercising their lawful judicial functions, a--- privileges of a court of law in respect of disc--- orders or contempt of court and may impose a--- ing two pounds for any such offence.

(b) *Native Commissioners*

Section *nine* of the Native Administration Act, No. 38 of 1927, reads as follows :—

" The Governor-General may, by proclamation in the Gazette, confer criminal jurisdiction upon a Native Commissioner in respect of any offence, subject to the jurisdiction of a Magistrate's court, committed by a Native within his area of jurisdiction and thereupon such Native Commissioner shall, for all purposes of the Magistrates' Courts Act, 1917 (Act No. 32 of 1917), or any amendment thereof, and of the Criminal Procedure and Evidence Act, 1917 (Act No. 31 of 1917), or any amendment thereof, be deemed to be a Magistrate's court or a Magistrate in connection with any proceedings relating to any offence committed by a Native. The jurisdiction so conferred upon a Native Commissioner shall be concurrent with the jurisdiction of the Magistrate's court and Magistrate concerned under the said Acts."

It should be noted that the section provides for conferring criminal jurisdiction upon *Native Commissioners* and not upon *Native Commissioners' courts* and that thereupon such Native Commissioners for all purposes of the Magistrates' Courts and Criminal Procedure and Evidence Acts are to be deemed to be Magistrates or Magistrates' courts in connection with any proceedings relating to offences committed by Natives. Questions of appeal and review and (as regards preparatory examinations taken by Native Commissioners) trials are accordingly dealt with by the Supreme Court in the ordinary course and not by the Native Appeal courts, which under section *thirteen* are given jurisdiction for the hearing of appeals in any proceedings from *courts* of Native Commissioners.

It is not the policy of the Government to confer criminal jurisdiction upon Native Commissioners, *qua* Native Commissioners. Criminal functions are, it is considered, under all ordinary circumstances appropriately exercised by Magistrates. Exceptions are, however, made in the following cases :—

(i) when a Native Commissioner (this term embraces also an Additional or an Assistant Native Commissioner) is stationed at a centre remote from the seat of magistracy, so that it is desirable for the convenience and in the interests of the community generally that he should exercise criminal jurisdiction over Natives ; and

(ii) where, in order to prevent congestion in the Magistrate's court, it is necessary that an additional forum should be provided for the trying of offences committed by Natives.

(c) *Natal Native High Court*

All crimes committed in Natal solely by *unexempted* Natives (i.e. by Natives not relieved from the operation of Native law) except those specified hereunder are, by section *one* of Natal Act 30 of 1910, cognisable by the Natal Native High Court, but without prejudice to the jurisdiction of Magistrates' courts.

The crimes excluded from the jurisdiction of the Natal High Court are :—

(i) criminal cases under the Insolvency laws ;

(ii) criminal cases arising out of the laws relating to electoral or municipal franchise ;

(iii) cases of crimes or offences created or defined by the laws relating to the following subjects including contraventions of such laws or of any by-laws, rules, or regulations made thereunder :—

Municipal Corporations, Townships, Villages, Immigration Settlements, Customs and Excise, Railways, Posts and Telegraphs, Stamps, Ports and Harbours, Licences other than those required under Native law, Mines ;

(iv) Private prosecutions (including cases under the laws relating to Masters and Servants) in which the complainant is not a Native.

The jurisdiction of the Supreme Court as a court of first instance is expressly excluded in respect of crimes committed by Natives (i.e. unexempted Natives) cognisable by the Natal Native High Court (vide section *one* of Natal Act 30 of 1910 read in conjunction with section *fifty-nine* (1) of Act 39 of 1926).

Under section *four* of Act No. 30 of 1910, the full bench of the Natal Native High Court may reserve any question of law for consideration by the Supreme Court, while an appeal lies from the judgment of the Native High Court (full bench) to the Natal Provincial Division of the Supreme Court upon the question whether any person is or is not a Native within the meaning of Act 49 of 1898. This is the only question upon which an appeal does lie from the Native High Court to the Provincial Division of the Supreme Court. In all other matters, appeal from the Native High Court lies to the Appellate Division in terms of section *one* of Act No. 1 of 1911.

2. CIVIL MATTERS

In civil as well as criminal matters, the ordinary courts of the land, i.e., courts of Special Justices of the Peace, Magistrates' courts, and the Supreme Court, are, generally speaking, according to the nature and exigency of the case, open to Natives and it must be noted that in so far as any non-Native is concerned in any case with a Native that case can be dealt with only by the ordinary courts.

Where, however, a Native Commissioner's court has been established for any area (vide page 230 *infra*), the jurisdiction of Magistrates' courts is ousted in respect of any civil suit between Native and Native in that area.

It should be pointed out that, save in so far as may otherwise be specially prescribed by a particular statute (e.g. in a case of succession which the law may specifically direct is to be decided according to Native Law), the ordinary courts are precluded from taking cognisance of Native law and custom and must decide all causes according to the ordinary law. Previously Magistrates' Courts in the Transkeian Territories and in Natal could try Native cases according to Native law and custom, but Native Commissioners' courts have been established throughout both the Transkeian Territories and Natal and consequently the Magistrates' courts there can no longer exercise jurisdiction in purely Native cases.

Native law and custom can be applied only in the special courts which, as previously stated, have been established for the benefit and in the interests of Natives.   These courts are :—

(a) *Native Chiefs' and Headmen's Civil Courts*

(i) Section *twelve* of the Native Administration Act, 1927, as amended by section *six* (1) of Act No. 9 of 1929, empowers the Governor-General to authorise any Native chief or headman recognised or appointed under the Act to hear and determine civil claims arising out of Native law and custom brought before him by Natives against Natives resident within his area of jurisdiction.   The Governor-General may at any time revoke such authority, which in any case cannot extend to the determination of any question of nullity, divorce or separation arising out of any marriage by civil or Christian rites.

Sub-section (2) of section *seventeen* of the revised Code of Native Law for Natal provides that for the purposes of section *twelve* of the Native Administration Act, 1927, the term " chief " shall be deemed to include a " chief's deputy," that is to say, any person appointed by a chief, with the approval of the Native Commissioner of the district concerned, to control any particular section of his tribe.

An appeal lies from the judgment of any chief or headmen exercising jurisdiction under this section to the *Native Commissioner*, whose court must to all intents and purposes hear the cause " *de novo* " as a court of the first instance.

Regulations framed under sub-section (5) of section *twelve* for courts of Native chiefs and headmen are contained in Government Notice No. 2255 of 1923, as amended by Government Notice No. 1312 of 1931. A copy of these regulations appears as Appendix " M."

(ii) Under section *thirty-one* of British Bechuanaland Proclamation No. 2 of 1885, Native chiefs have original and exclusive jurisdiction between Natives of their own tribes.   This jurisdiction was retained upon annexation of the territory to the Cape Colony and was, except as regards the determination of questions of nullity, divorce or separation arising out of marriages by civil or Christian rites, preserved by section *twenty-one* of the Native Administration Act, 1927.

Appeals from the judgments of Native chiefs in the exercise of their jurisdiction under B.B. Proclamation 2 of 1885 lie, in terms of section *two* of Act No. 7 of 1924, to the court of the *Magistrate* of the district concerned, from whose decision a further appeal lies to the Griqualand East Local Division of the Supreme Court.

(b) *Native Commissioners' Courts*

Section *ten* of the Native Administration Act, 1927, as amended by section *five* of Act No. 9 of 1929, provides that the Governor-General may by proclamation in the *Gazette* establish courts of Native Commissioners for the hearing of all civil causes and matters between Native and Native only but that no such court shall have jurisdiction in matters in which

(a) the status of a person in respect of mental capacity is sought to be affected ;

(b) is sought a decree of perpetual silence ;

(c) namptissement is sought ;

(d) the validity or interpretation of a will or other testamentary document is in question ; or

(e) a decree of nullity, divorce or separation in respect of a marriage (contracted according to civil or Christian rites) is sought.

When the parties to any proceedings do not both reside within the area of jurisdiction of the same court of Native Commissioner, the court within whose area the defendant resides has jurisdiction in the proceedings.

Regulations under sub-section (4) of section *ten* of the Act for Native Commissioners' courts, elsewhere than in the Transkeian Territories, are to be found under Government Notice No. 2253 of 1928, as amended by Government Notices Nos. 1313 of 1931 and 1078 of 1932. A copy of these regulations appears in Appendix " N." The main endeavour in framing these rules was to prescribe as simple, informal, and inexpensive a method of procedure as possible.

In so far as the Transkeian Territories are concerned, Proclamation No. 299 of 1928, which established courts of Native Commissioner throughout those territories, provided that the procedure and rules of Magistrates' courts as contained in Proclamation No. 145 of 1923 and any amendment thereof should be deemed, *mutatis mutandis*, to be regulations made under sub-section (4) of section *ten* of the Act for the courts of Native Commissioner so established.

Under section *nineteen* of the Act, a Native Commissioner's court is at liberty to call to its assistance, in an advisory capacity, such Native assessors as it may deem necessary.

Reference has already been made to the provisions of section *eleven* of the Act prescribing the law to be applied in Native Commissioner's courts, (*vide* page 222 *supra*) as also to the appellate jurisdiction exercised by such courts in respect of judgments given by Native chiefs and head-men in civil cases (*vide* page 229 *supra*).

It is the policy of the Government to establish courts of Native Commissioner, and *a fortiori* Native chiefs' courts, only in areas or centres where there are necessity and demand for such by reason of the existence of a considerable " non-detribalised " Native population. Where this condition does not exist, it is not considered that it is either necessary or expedient to introduce the special sanctions of Native law.

A necessary corollary is that the recognition of Native law and custom in the courts is similarly restricted.

(c) *Native Appeal Courts*

Sections *thirteen* to *nineteen*, inclusive, of the Native Administration Act 1927, deal with Native Appeal courts for the hearing of appeals in any proceedings from courts of Native Commissioners.

Two such courts have been established—the one for the Cape and the Orange Free State and the other for Natal and the Transvaal—under Proclamation No. 301 of 1928. The former has its headquarters at King William's Town and the latter at Pretoria.

Section *thirteen* provides that a Native Appeal court shall consist of three members, one of whom shall be president. The president is a full-time officer appointed by the Governor-General, while the members other than the president are, in terms of the section, appointed by the Minister from time to time as required and are selected from Magistrates, Native Commissioners and other qualified persons.

The decision of the majority of the members is the judgment of the Court.

Rules for the Native Appeal Courts, which sit as such times and places as the Minister by notice in the Gazette appoints, were framed under the provisions of sub-section (5) of section *thirteen* and published under Government Notice No. 2254 of 1928, a copy of which appears in Appendix " O."

Section *fourteen* of the Act provides for the settlement of conflicting decisions given by a Native Appeal Court within its area of jurisdiction by the preparation, on instructions from the Minister, of a special case to be argued before the Appellate Division of the Supreme Court to obtain its ruling on the point at issue, which ruling is final.

Section *fifteen* gives a Native Appeal court full powers to review, set aside, amend, correct, etc., any judgment of a Native Commissioner's court within its area of jurisdiction.

Section *sixteen* gives advocates and attorneys of the Supreme Court the right to appear in a Native Appeal court and also in a Native Commissioner's court.

Section *seventeen* divested the Natal Native High Court of jurisdiction in civil matters and provided for the abolition of the pre-existing Native Appeal court of the Transkeian Territories.

Section *eighteen* provides that appeals from Native Commissioners' courts shall lie only to a Native Appeal court, unless the Native Appeal court itself consents to an application for leave to appeal, upon any point stated by it, being made to the Appellate Division of the Supreme Court. For the rest, the decision of the Native Appeal court, save as regards the matter of conflicting decisions dealt with under section *fourteen*, is final and conclusive.

Section *nineteen* authorises a Native Appeal court, when it considers such a course desirable, to call to its assistance Native assessors in an advisory capacity.

It should be noted that Native Appeal courts constituted under section *thirteen* of the Native Administration Act have no jurisdiction as courts of the first instance or in respect of any criminal matter, other than their inherent jurisdiction to punish for contempt of court.

(d) *Native Divorce Courts*

Section *ten* of the Native Administration Act, 1927, Amendment Act, No. 9 of 1929, authorised the Governor-General by proclamation in the Gazette to establish special Native divorce courts which should be empowered to determine suits of nullity, divorce and separation arising out of marriages by Christian or civil rites (as distinct from customary

unions in respect of which Native Commissioners' courts have full jurisdiction) between Natives domiciled within their respective areas of
jurisdiction and to decide any question arising out of any such marriage
which is not cognisable by a Native Commissioner's court.

The Act provided further that the area of jurisdiction of any court so
established should coincide with that of a Native Appeal court established
under the Native Administration Act and that the president of the Native
Appeal court exercising jurisdiction in the same area should constitute
such court, which might in its discretion call upon two Magistrates to act
as assessors in an advisory capacity on questions of fact.

In accordance with these provisions, two divorce courts were established under Proclamation No. 271 of 1929, one for the Cape and
Orange Free State Provinces and the other for the Transvaal and Natal,
the court consisting in each instance of the president of the Native Appeal
court of the area concerned.

Rules for these special Native divorce courts, framed under sub-
section (4) of section *ten* of Act No. 9 of 1929, were published under
Government Notice No. 1976 of 1929. These regulations are at present
under process of revision and will in due course be superseded by an
amended series.

An appeal from the judgment of a Native divorce court lies to the
provincial or local division of the Supreme Court having jurisdiction and
must be noted and prosecuted as if it were an appeal from a judgment
of a Magistrate's court in a civil action.

The sole object of providing these special Native divorce courts
was to meet a very real and urgent need for an inexpensive forum for the
determination of matrimonial causes between Natives married according
to civil or Christian rites. There was therefore no intention whatsoever
of ousting the jurisdiction of the Supreme Court, which, indeed, was
specifically preserved by sub-section (7) of section *ten* of Act No. 9 of
1929. It is accordingly open to any Native, who wishes and can afford to
do so, to institute proceedings for divorce, separation, etc., in the Supreme
Court in the first instance rather than in a Native divorce court.

It should be noted that it is not competent for a Native divorce
court established under section *ten* of Act No. 9 of 1929 to adjudicate
upon any claim for damages in connection with any divorce proceedings
brought before it, as such a claim for damages would be cognisable by a
Native Commissioner's court.

C

MARRIAGE

In relation to Natives the term " marriage " is frequently used indiscriminately in respect of two entirely distinct and separate institutions, viz., a marriage in the strict legal sense according to European ideas and a conjugal relationship under Native custom which recognises polygamous unions.

The need for appropriate terminology to distinguish between these separate institutions was recognised by the Legislature when enacting the Native Administration Act, No. 38 of 1927, and the terms " marriage " and " customary union " were adopted. These terms were respectively defined as follows under section *thirty-five* of the Act, as amended by section *nine* of Act No. 9 of 1929 :—

> " Marriage " means the union of one man with one woman in accordance with any law for the time being in force in any Province governing marriages, but does not include any union contracted under Native law and custom or any union recognised as a marriage in Native law under the provisions of section *one hundred and forty-seven* of the Code of Native Law contained in the Schedule to Law 19 of 1891 (Natal) or any amendment thereof or any other law."

> "Customary Union" means the association of a man and a woman in a conjugal relationship according to Native law and custom, where neither the man nor the woman is party to a subsisting marriage."

It may be stated generally that prior to the passing of the Native Administration Act, 1927, marriages by Native custom or, to use the more appropriate term, " customary unions," were recognised in the courts only in the Transkeian Territories, the Province of Natal, and, to a very restricted degree, in British Bechuanaland. In other parts of the Union such alliances, while contracted by the vast majority of Natives, were regarded in the eyes of the law not as valid and binding but merely as illicit unions, with the result that the parties had no legal redress in matters arising therefrom, though in certain cases, e.g. under section *seventy* of Transvaal Proclamation No. 28 of 1902 and under article *twenty-eight* of O.F.S. Law No. 26 of 1899, children born of such unions enjoyed rights of succession to the parents.

Certain very important and far-reaching provisions were enacted in section *twenty-two* of the Native Administration Act and the following is a brief statement of the position as it exists to-day.

1. MARRIAGE (ACCORDING TO CIVIL OR CHRISTIAN RITES)

Throughout the Union it is competent for Natives to contract marriages according to civil or Christian rites.

In the *Cape Province,* including British Bechuanaland and the Transkeian Territories, such marriages must be contracted in accordance with the ordinary marriage laws, which are applicable to both Europeans and Natives.

In the *Orange Free State,* such marriages can likewise only be contracted in accordance with the ordinary marriage law of the Province, contained in Law No. 26 of 1899.

In the *Transvaal,* such marriages are not contracted under the marriage law applicable to Europeans but under the provisions of a special statute, the Coloured Persons Marriage Law No. 3 of 1897, as amended by Proclamation No. 25 of 1902, Proclamation No. 28 of 1902, Ordinance No. 39 of 1904 and Ordinance No. 19 of 1906.

Under this Law marriages must be solemnised before marriage officers, who are divided into two classes, viz. :—

(a) Civil marriage officers appointed under Article 2 of the Law. Under this group must be included Native Commissioners, Additional Native Commissioners and Assistant Native Commissioners in the Transvaal, as such officers are, by sub-section (4) of section *two* of the Native Administration Act, empowered, within their respective areas of jurisdiction, to solemnise marriages under Law No. 3 of 1897.

(b) Ecclesiastical marriage officers appointed under Article 6 of the Law.

The essential formalities of such marriages are :—

(1) Submission by the parties to a marriage officer of an application for the celebration of the marriage together with a certificate either from their parents or guardians, their " Kaptein " or chief, or the minister of their church, to the effect that there is no impediment to their marriage according to law.

(2) The publication of banns or the production of a special licence.

(3) A civil or religious ceremony, as the case may be, which must take place before witnesses between 8 a.m. and 4 p.m. (Certain

duties are placed upon civil and ecclesiastical marriage officers which need not be entered into here).

Marriages solemnised between Natives under the provisions of Law 3 of 1897 can only be dissolved by divorce in accordance with the ordinary law.

In *Natal* the position is somewhat complicated. Where both parties are Natives exempted from the operation of Native law, their marriage can be celebrated by civil or Christian rites under the provisions of the Marriage Ordinance No. 17 of 1846, that is to say, the ordinary marriage law of the Province.

No provision is made in the Natal law for the celebration, between Natives not exempted from the operation of Native law or between an exempted and an unexempted Native, of a marriage by ordinary (European) *civil* rites. In fact, civil marriage officers are expressly prohibited under section *one* of Law No. 46 of 1887 from solemnising marriage between any parties who being Natives are not exempted from Native law.

Provision for the celebration of marriages according to *Christian* rites between Natives, both of whom are or one of whom is subject to Native law, is contained in Law No. 46 of 1887 as amended by Act No. 44 of 1903, both of which statutes apply to Zululand as well as to Natal proper.

Natives desirous of contracting a marriage according to Christian rites under Law 46 of 1887 must apply to the Magistrate of the district for a licence, sign declarations giving particulars of their names, ages, tribe, etc., and pay a fee of 10s., whereupon the Magistrate explains the nature and obligations of the contract to them and issues the requisite licence which is valid for three months.

The consent of the father or guardian of an unexempted Native woman is necessary prior to the issue of a licence, but where such cannot be obtained, e.g. on account of death, insanity or absence, or is unreasonably withheld, the parties may petition the Governor who may authorise the issue of the licence.

No minister of religion may solemnise a marriage between Natives, one or both of whom may be subject to Native law, except upon production to him of the necessary licence. If the licence is forthcoming the marriage may be solemnised in the ordinary way.

In addition to the formalities prescribed for the celebration of marriages between Natives according to civil or Christian rites by the marriage laws of the various Provinces, certain further requirements, which are of application throughout the Union, are prescribed by section *twenty-two* of the Native Administration Act, 1927. These are as follows :—

(a) A male Native, who during the subsistence of a customary union between himself and any woman wishes to contract a marriage (according to civil or Christian rites) with any woman, must before doing so declare upon oath before the Magistrate or Native Commissioner of the district in which he is domiciled " the name of every such first-mentioned woman ; the name of every child of any such customary union ; the nature and amount of the movable property (if any) allotted by him to each such woman or house under Native custom ; and such other information relating to any such union as the said official may require."

(b) Before celebrating the marriage of any Native male, the marriage officer, civil or religious as the case may be, must first take from such Native a declaration as to whether there is subsisting at the time any customary union between him and any woman other than the woman to whom he is to be married ; and, if any such union does subsist, a certificate under the hand of the Magistrate or Native Commissioner that the requirement specified under (a) above has been observed must be produced to the marriage officer.

2. CUSTOMARY UNIONS (MARRIAGES ACCORDING TO NATIVE LAW AND CUSTOM)

Marriages according to Native law and custom are now recognised in all the Provinces of the Union *in so far as they conform to the definition of a " customary union " contained in section thirty-five of the Native Administration Act, 1927, as amended by section nine of the Native Administration Act, 1927, Amendment Act, No. 9 of 1929,* (vide page 234 *supra*), and provided, in so far as the Natal Province is concerned, that they have been contracted in accordance with the essential requirements prescribed under the Natal Code of Native Law.

This recognition of customary unions under the Native Administration Act is not *explicit*, but is *implicit* :—

(a) in the provisions of section *eleven*, which authorises Native Commissioners to take cognisance of Native law in so far as it is not opposed to principles of public or natural justice, and definitely lays down that the customs of *lobola* or *bogadi* (the delivery of cattle or other property by or on behalf of the intended male partner to the parent or guardian of the intended female partner under a customary union) or any similar custom shall not be deemed to be repugnant to such principles : and

(b) in the provisions of section *twenty-two*, which affords special protection to Native women and children in respect of property rights arising out of customary unions.

Polygamy is a feature of Native law and custom, but, from what has been said above, it will be gathered that polygamous relationships are recognised under the Native Administration Act only in so far as they are contracted by persons neither of whom is a party to a marriage according to civil or Christian rites.   A Native may contract a marriage during the subsistence of a customary union between himself and another woman but may not contract a customary union during the subsistence of his marriage.   In fact, under the Natal law, a Native who purports so to do renders himself liable to prosecution for bigamy.

The following special points should be noted in respect of *Natal* :—

(1) As has already been mentioned, customary unions to be recognised in the Natal Province must be contracted in accordance with the formalities prescribed in the Natal Code of Native Law.   The essentials of a customary union as laid down in sub-section (1) of section *fifty-nine* of the Code are :—

(a) the consent of the father or guardian of the intended wife, which consent may not be withheld unreasonably ;

(b) the consent of the father or kraal head of the intended husband, should such be legally necessary ;

(c) a declaration in public at the celebration of the union, by the intended wife to the official witness (i.e. a person specially appointed to attend at the celebration of customary unions) that the union is with her own free will and consent.

(2)   The partners under a customary union in Natal can be divorced or their union annulled only by order of a competent court.   The grounds for divorce, e.g., adultery, wilful desertion, etc., are specified in section *seventy-six* and those for a declaration of nullity, e.g., insanity at the time of marriage, the absence of any of the essentials of marriage, etc., in section *seventy-seven* of the Code.   A Native Commissioner's court has, under section *ten* of the Native Administration Act, jurisdiction to deal with any such matter.

(3) A Native who is exempt from the operation of Native law in Natal cannot contract a customary union as he is deemed to fall outside the operation of Native law.

3. PROPERTY RIGHTS IN RELATION TO CUSTOMARY UNIONS AND NATIVE MARRIAGES

Under Native law and custom females are regarded as perpetual minors. Married women are subject to their husbands and in all kraal matters to the kraal head.

A married woman may acquire and hold property (e.g., property donated by her father) for the use of the house to which she belongs but females may neither inherit nor bequeath. The property of each particular house devolves under Native custom upon one male person determined according to the law of primogeniture.

Customary unions accordingly confer no property rights as between the partners.

Prior to the passing of the Native Administration Act, 1927, community of property (unless specially excluded by ante-nuptial contract) ensued upon marriages between Natives according to civil or Christian rites, even if contracted by the husband during the subsistence of a customary union or unions to which he was a party, except :—

(a) in the Natal Province (including Zululand), where, if the husband were an unexempted Native, community of property did not ensue but Native law applied just as if the union had been contracted according to Native law and custom ; and

(b) in the Transkeian Territories, where it had been laid down by Proclamation No. 142 of 1910, as amended, that no marriage between Natives should produce the legal consequence of community of property, unless, in the case of a marriage not contracted during the subsistence of a customary union between the husband and any other woman, the parties had within one month previous to its celebration declared before the Magistrate of the district their intention and desire that community of property should follow upon their union, in which event community would apply except as regards immovable property held by the husband under title deed granted under the provisions of Proclamation No. 227 of 1898.

Proclamation No. 142 of 1910 laid down certain principles for the protection of women and children under customary unions inasmuch as it had been found that there was a tendency on the part of Native men, upon their embracing Christianity, to marry one wife (possibly an entirely new one) according to Christian rites and to " put away " and leave destitute other partners they might previously have had under customary unions.

Section *twenty-two* of the Native Administration Act was based on Transkeian Proclamation No. 142 of 1910, as amended, and made of general application throughout the Union the protective principles referred to. These principles are embodied in sub-sections (6) and (7), which read as follows :—

> " (6) A marriage between Natives, contracted after the commencement of this Act, shall not produce the legal consequences of marriage in community of property between the spouses : Provided that in the case of a marriage contracted otherwise than during the subsistence of a customary union between the husband and any woman other than the wife it shall be competent for the intending spouses at any time within one month previous to the celebration of such marriage to declare jointly before any Magistrate, Native Commissioner or marriage officer (who is hereby authorized to attest such declaration) that it is their intention and desire that community of property and of property and loss shall result from their marriage, and thereupon such community shall result from their marriage except as regards any land in a location held under quitrent tenure such land shall be excluded from such community."

> " (7) No marriage contracted after the commencement of this Act during the subsistence of any customary union between the husband and any woman other than the wife shall in any way affect the material rights of any partner of such union or any issue thereof, and the widow of any such marriage and any issue thereof shall have no greater rights in respect of the estate of the deceased spouse than she or they would have had if the said marriage had been a customary union."

It was, of course, to ensure the full operation of the provisions of these sub-sections that the pre-nuptial declarations by Native males previously referred to (vide page 237 *supra*), were made obligatory.

Rights under marriages in community of property contracted prior to the commencement of the Native Administration Act were specially preserved by sub-section (8) of section *twenty-two*.

Here it may conveniently be mentioned that the provisions of Chapter V of the Native Administration Act relating to marriage and succession (sections *twenty-two* and *twenty-three*) were by Proclamation No. 296 of 1928 brought into operation from the 1st January, 1929.

D

SUCCESSION

Prior to the passing of the Native Administration Act, the law relating to Native succession was entirely different in the several Provinces, and, in so far as the Cape was concerned, it varied in different parts of the Province.

The following is a brief review of the pre-existing laws in relation to :—

(1) the right of testamentary disposition, and

(2) intestate succession.

1. THE RIGHT OF TESTAMENTARY DISPOSITION

In the *Transvaal* and *Orange Free State*, Natives enjoyed full powers of testamentary disposition and could accordingly dispose of their property by will as they thought fit.

In the *Cape Province*, the rights of testamentary disposition enjoyed by Natives were limited in three directions, viz. :—

(i) As regards allotments held under the Glen Grey conditions of tenure—whether in the Glen Grey district itself, or in the Transkeian surveyed districts or in certain Ciskeian surveyed locations where the provisions of the Glen Grey Act as regards succession were applied by the conditions of title. Such allotments could not be devised by will but necessarily devolved upon one male heir determined by prescribed Tables of Succession based on Native law.

(ii) In *British Kaffraria* (comprising the districts of East London, King William's Town, Komgha, Stutterheim and portions of Victoria East and Cathcart), in so far as Natives who did not belong to certain privileged classes under the Hofmeyr Act, No. 39 of 1887, (e.g., registered voters, certificated teachers, ordained ministers, etc.,) were concerned, the power of testamentary disposition was, under Ordinance 10 of 1864, limited to such as had no wives or children or other direct issue and to property not acquired by descent according to tribal custom.

Q

(iii) In the *Transkeian Territories*, a Native could not devise by will any movable property allotted by him under Native custom to any wife or house.

In *Natal*, Natives who were exempt from the provisions of Native law were in the same position as Europeans and enjoyed full powers of testamentary disposition. Unexempted Natives were under Law No. 7 of 1895 given the right to dispose of their immovable property by will executed according to certain prescribed formalities but could not so dispose of their movable property.

2. INTESTATE SUCCESSION

Transvaal. Section *seventy* of the Administration of Estates Proclamation, No. 28 of 1902, provided as follows :—

" If any Native who shall not during his lifetime have contracted a lawful marriage or who being unmarried shall not be the offspring of parents lawfully married shall die intestate his estate shall be administered and distributed according to the customs and usages of the tribe or people to which he belonged . . . ."

In all other cases, the intestate estates of deceased Natives devolved according to the ordinary law of intestate succession.

Orange Free State. The ordinary law of intestate succession applied in the case of a Native dying intestate except that :—

(a) Article *twenty-eight* of the Orange Free State Marriage Law, No. 26 of 1899, recognised the right of " children born of heathen parents though the latter may not have been legally married to take by way of inheritance the lawfully acquired properties of such parents, where it shall be proved that such parents regarded one another as husband and wife and lived with one another as such."

(b) Chapter *LVI* of the Orange Free State Law Book, *relating exclusively to persons who were at the time of annexation of the Barolong territory, known as the Moroka ward, living in the said territory in a state of polygamy*, contained special provisions recognising the rights of children and wives of such polygamous unions.

Cape Province.

In the *Cape Province proper*, succession to the *devisable* property of a Native who died intestate was in accordance with the ordinary law, except in so far as such Native, not being a member of a privileged class under the Hofmeyr Act, was the holder of a certificate of citizenship under Act No. 17 of 1864 ; or was resident in a location proclaimed under section *six* of the Native Succession Act, No 18 of 1864 ; or was domiciled in British Kaffraria and died either unmarried or leaving a widow or issue in respect of a marriage under Native law and custom In all of these cases, devolution took place in accordance with Native law and custom.

In the *Transkeian Territories*, succession to the intestate estate of a Native was governed by Native law and custom.

In *British Bechuanaland*, the law provided that the intestate estate of any Native should devolve according to the ordinary law of the Cape.

Natal. Succession to the intestate estate of a Native who had been exempted from Native law was in accordance with the ordinary law of intestate succession.

The intestate estate of an unexempted Native devolved according to Native law and custom, such law and custom is so far as Natal proper was concerned being as defined in the Natal Native Code of 1891.

Paragraph (d) of section *three* of the Administration of Estates Act, No. 24 of 1913, provided that the provisions of that Act should not apply to Native estates, which therefore continued to be administered according to the laws previously in force in the respective provinces.

3. SUCCESSION UNDER THE NATIVE ADMINISTRATION ACT AND REGULATIONS THEREUNDER

The law relating to Native succession and the administration of the estates of Natives throughout the Union was consolidated and co-ordinated by section *twenty-three* of the Native Administration Act, 1927, as amended by section *seven* of Act No. 9 of 1929.

The section, as amended, reads as follows :—

" 23(1) All movable property belonging to a Native and allotted by him or accruing under Native law or custom to any woman with whom he lived in a customary union, or to any house, shall upon his death devolve and be administered under Native law and custom.

(2) All land in a location held in individual tenure upon quitrent conditions by a Native shall devolve upon his death upon one male person, to be determined in accordance with tables of succession to be prescribed under sub-section (10).

(3) All other property of whatsoever kind belonging to a Native shall be capable of being devised by will.

(4) Any dispute or question which may arise out of the administration or distribution of any estate in accordance with Native law shall be determined by the Native Commissioner, or where there is no Native Commissioner by the Magistrate of the district in which the deceased ordinarily resided, or in respect of immovable property by the Native Commissioner or, where there is no Native Commissioner, by the Magistrate of the district where such property is situate, and every decision of a Native Commissioner or Magistrate under this section shall be subject to an appeal to the Native Appeal Court herein before referred to, and the decision of such court shall, save as is provided in sections *fourteen* and *eighteen*, be final.

(5) Any claim or dispute in regard to the administration or distribution of any estate of a deceased Native shall, if any of the parties concerned is not a Native, be decided in an ordinary court of competent jurisdiction.

(6) In connection with any such claim or dispute, the heir, or in case of minority his guardian, according to Native law, if no executor has been appointed by a Master of the Supreme Court, shall be regarded as the executor in the estate as if he had been duly appointed as such according to the law governing the appointment of executors.

(7) Letters of administration from the Master of the Supreme Court shall not be necessary in, nor shall the Master or any executor appointed by the Master have any powers in connection with, the administration and distribution of

   (a) the estate of any Native who has died leaving no valid will ; or

   (b) any portion of the estate of a deceased Native which falls under sub-section (1) or (2).

(8) A Master of the Supreme Court may revoke letters of administration issued by him in respect of any Native estate.

(9) Whenever a Native has died leaving a valid will which disposes of any portion of his estate, Native law and custom shall not apply to the administration or distribution of so much of his estate as does not fall under sub-section (1) or (2) and such administration and distribution shall in all respects be in accordance with the Administration of Estates Act, 1913 (Act No. 24 of 1913).

(10) The Governor-General may make regulations not inconsistent with this Act :—

(a) prescribing the manner in which the estates of deceased Natives shall be administered and distributed ;

(b) defining the rights of widows or surviving partners in regard to the use and occupation of the quitrent land of deceased Natives ;

(c) dealing with the disherison of Natives ;

(d) prescribing the powers and duties of Native Commissioners or Magistrates in carrying out the functions assigned to them by this section ;

(e) prescribing tables of succession in regard to Natives ; and

(f) generally for the better carrying out of the provisions of this section.

(11) Any Native estate which has, prior to the commencement of this Act, been reported to a Master of the Supreme Court shall be administered as if this Act had not been passed, and the provisions of this Act shall apply in respect of every Native estate which has not been reported."

It will be observed that the effect of these provisions is to divide Native owned property into

(a) property which can be devised by will ; and

(b) property which cannot be so devised.

Non-devisable property falls under the section into two classes :—

(i) Movable property belonging to a Native and allotted by him or accruing under Native law and custom to any woman with whom he lived in a customary union or to any house. All such property upon his death must devolve and be administered under Native law and custom.

(ii)   Land in a location held by a Native in individual tenure upon quitrent conditions.   Such land, which is almost entirely restricted to holdings in surveyed locations in the Transkeian Territories and in a few districts, including Glen Grey, in the Ciskei, must upon the death of the owner, devolve upon one male person to be determined in accordance with prescribed tables of succession.

These tables of succession are based upon Native law and, except as regards the Transkeian Territories, are contained in Part II of the regulations framed under sub-section (10) of section *twenty-three* and published under Government Notice No. 2257 of 1928.   Part I of these regulations was repealed by Government Notice No. 1664 of 1929 (referred to hereunder) and a copy of Part II, as amended by Government Notice No. 946 of 1932, appears as Appendix " P."   As regards the Transkeian Territories, the tables of succession prescribed under Proclamation No. 142 of 1910, as amended, are still in operation.

The jurisdiction of the Master of the Supreme Court is entirely ousted as regards non-devisable property belonging to a Native.

Devisable property.   The Act gives Natives full power to devise by will any property other than such as falls within one or other of the two classes indicated above.

Testate Estates

Where a Native has died leaving a valid will, whether he purports to dispose of the whole or only portion of his property thereunder, his entire estate, save any non-devisable property therein, must, in terms of sub-section (9) of section *twenty-three*, be administered in all respects in accordance with the provisions of the ordinary law as set forth in the Administration of Estates Act, No. 24 of 1913.   (Section 3 (d) of this Act, previously referred to, was repealed by the Native Administration Act).

Intestate Estates

As regards the intestate estates of Natives, sub-section (3) of section *twenty-three* of the Native Administration Act, as originally enacted, expressly provided that any property in the estate of a deceased Native not devised by will should devolve and be administered according to Native law and custom.   This provision was, however, deleted when the section was amended by section *seven* of Act No. 9 of 1929.   The reason for this is to be ascribed to the fact that it is undesirable that it should be rigidly laid down that in any case where a deceased Native leaves no will his property should devolve under Native law, and, indeed, the provision which formerly existed in this connection would undoubtedly have given rise to anomaly and hardship as regards the estates of exempted and detribalized Natives. No definite provision was accordingly made under section *twenty-three* of the Act, as amended, as to the manner in which such of the property in the intestate estate of a deceased Native as does not fall under sub-section (1) or sub-section (2) of section *twenty-three* should devolve and be distributed, the matter being left to be dealt with in greater detail than could conveniently be laid down in the Act, by regulation under sub-section (10), which vests very wide powers in the Governor-General, notably under paragraphs (a), (d), (e) and (f). The regulations were published under Government Notice No. 1664 dated the 20th September, 1929, a copy of which appears in Appendix " Q."

Section *two* of these regulations is extremely important and reads as follows :—

" 2. If a Native dies leaving no valid will, so much of his property as does not fall within the purview of sub-section (1) or sub-section (2) of section *twenty-three* of the Act shall be distributed in the manner following :—

" (a) If the deceased was at the time of his death the holder of letters of exemption issued under the provisions of Natal Law No. 28 of 1865, the property shall devolve as if he had been a European.

(b) If the deceased had during his lifetime contracted a marriage in community of property or under antenuptial contract, the property shall devolve as if he had been a European.

(c) When any deceased Native resident at the time of his death in an urban or industrial area is not survived by any wife, partner, or child under a marriage or customary union and was at the time of his death living with any woman as his putative wife under such conditions as in the opinion of the Minister to render the application of Native law and custom to the devolution of his property inequitable or inappropriate, such property shall devolve as if the deceased and such putative wife had been married.

(d) If the deceased does not fall under any of the classes described in paragraphs (a), (b) and (c), the property shall be distributed according to Native law and custom."

The principle underlying these provisions is that Native custom should apply in respect of the devolution of the intestate estates of ordinary tribal Natives, but not as regards the estates of such Natives as live more or less according to European standards and ideas, as evidenced by the fact of their exemption from Native law or by their having availed themselves of special facilities and privileges provided under the ordinary common law, e.g. marriage in community of property or under ante-nuptial contract.

It will be noted that on equitable grounds special provision has been made under paragraph (c) of section *two* to meet the case of informal alliances contracted by otherwise unattached Natives resident in urban or industrial centres, while in reference to paragraph (b) of the section, it must be borne in mind that, by virtue of sub-section (6) of section *twenty-two* of the Act, community of property no longer ordinarily ensues upon a marriage between Natives. (*vide* page 240 *supra*).

It is not considered expedient that Native Commissioners, other Government officials or professional persons should ordinarily intervene in the administration of an estate which under the regulations is to devolve according to Native law and custom, nor should the parties be required ordinarily to prepare and file any documents arising out of the adminis-tration of any such estate.   In the vast majority of such cases, the estates would satisfactorily be dealt with by the people themselves under their recognised customs without any question or dispute.

Provision has accordingly been made in the regulations for the inter-vention of Native Commissioners in such cases only :—

> (a) where it is apparent that some inquiry is necessary ; or
>
> (b) where a definite dispute has arisen ; or
>
> (c) where the transfer of immovable property is involved.

All intestate estates of Natives devolving according to the ordinary common law principles of succession must, however, be administered under the supervision of the Native Commissioner (or, as regards any district for which no Native Commissioner has been appointed, of the Magistrate) of the district in which the deceased ordinarily resided, whose duty it is to ensure that distribution of the devisable property is effected in accordance with the ordinary common law principles of intestate succession and that any non-devisable property is dealt with in accordance with sub-section (1), or sub-section (2), of section *twenty-three* of the Act, as the case may be.

As regards intestate Native estates generally, it must be emphasized that the intention of the regulations is not to multiply formalities but to secure the expeditious and efficient administration and distribution of the property by as simple and inexpensive a procedure as possible.

To this end, very wide powers have been vested in Native Commissioners (notably under sections *three* and *four* of the regulations) with, of course, corresponding responsibilities.

Reports received up to the present indicate that the system now in operation as regards the administration of Native estates works well, is a great improvement on anything that existed in the past and gives general satisfaction.

E

NOTE ON EXEMPTION LAWS

Prior to Union, each of the constituent Colonies had enacted legislation providing for the exemption of specially qualified or otherwise deserving Natives from the operation of restrictions imposed by certain laws specially affecting the Native population, e.g. the pass laws.

In the *Cape*, the Hofmeyr Act, No. 39 of 1887, exempted Natives who were registered as Parliamentary voters from the operation of all laws differentially affecting Natives, e.g. the Liquor Laws.

In the *Transvaal*, letters of exemption and registration certificates, issued under Proclamation No. 35 of 1901 and Ordinance No. 28 of 1902 respectively, relieved the holders from the operation of the pass laws, including the Night Passes Ordinance.

In the *Orange Free State*, letters of exemption granted to certain classes under the Coloured Persons Relief Ordinance, No. 2 of 1903, conferred upon the holders immunity from the provisions and operation of any of the laws relating to passes.

In *Natal*, letters of exemption were issued under Ordinance No. 28 of 1865 and had a very far-reaching effect. Exemption was primarily from the operation of Native law, but the effect of Law 14 of 1888, which purported to define the word " Native " for the purposes of all antecedent laws and regulations, was to place exempted Natives in the same position as Europeans except as regards :—

(a) the liquor law ; and

(b) any statute passed subsequent to Law No. 14 of 1888 and containing a specific definition of " Native," e.g. the Natives Land Act, 1913.

The Native Administration Act repealed the exemption laws of the various Provinces (including the Hofmeyr Act " in so far as it is in conflict with the provisions of this Act ") and, as amended by section *eight* of Act No. 9 of 1929, contains the following provisions in section *thirty-one* :—

"31. (1) In any case in which he may deem fit, the Governor-General may grant to any Native a letter of exemption exempting the recipient from such laws, specially affecting Natives, or so much of such laws as may be specified in such letter : Provided that no such exemption shall be granted under this section from any provision of law regulating the ownership or occupation of land, or imposing taxation or controlling the sale, supply or possession of intoxicating liquor.

(2) Any such exemption may be made subject to any condition imposed by the Governor-General and specified in such letter.

(3) Any letter of exemption issued under any law included in the Schedule to this Act shall be deemed to have been granted under sub-section (1).

(4) Any letter of exemption granted under sub-section (1), or referred to in sub-section (3), may at any time be cancelled by the Governor-General without assigning any reason.

(5) The Governor-General may make regulations prescribing the forms of application for letters of exemption, the particulars to be submitted therewith, the method of registration of such letters, the fees which may be imposed, the form and issue of documents certifying the fact of exemption, the requirements as to the production of such documents and the penalties for wilfully false statements made in connection with any application for exemption."

No regulations under sub-section (5) quoted above have yet been promulgated.

F

NOTE ON THE ETHNOLOGICAL SECTION OF THE DEPARTMENT

The Ethnological Section was created in 1925, firstly, with a view to promoting scientific investigation and research into Bantu ethnology, sociology, philology and anthropology, and, secondly, in order that the Department might have at its disposal the services of an academically-trained anthropologist conversant with the ethnological and linguistic side of Native Affairs, accurate information in regard to which, it was realised, was likely to prove of the greatest assistance in the smooth and harmonious administration of tribal affairs and in the prevention of friction.

The activities of the section fall naturally into two categories, viz., routine work on the one hand and research on the other.

In so far as routine work is concerned, the ethnologist, whenever called upon, furnishes his opinion on questions of Native law and custom and on matters of an anthropological or other more strictly scientific nature. He participates in formal enquiries instituted by the Department into such matters as land and succession disputes and assists in any other matter in respect of which it is considered that his specialised knowledge will prove useful. The services of the Departmental ethnologist have from time to time been of assistance to other Government Departments and institutions, for instance to the Treasury for the purpose of deciding whether certain persons were to be classified as " Coloured persons " under the Old Age Pensions Act or not ; to the Department of Veterinary Services in respect of research in Native animal husbandry, and to universities and museums in various ways.

Research, however, constitutes and must necessarily constitute the most important part of the ethnologist's work. His investigations are conducted primarily with a view to obtaining information of interest to the Department and its officers. It has been proved time and again that when a dispute has arisen, it is too late to obtain impartial evidence on the point at issue. Definite information on law and history, previously collected, must on the other hand greatly facilitate an equitable settlement.

Research is therefore instituted into the history, divisions and groupings, affinities and relationships of the tribes, their languages and state of culture, and a study is made of former conditions in comparison with the present.

The findings are made available for reference and study by including them in the series of " Ethnological Publications " of the Department. This series was started in 1930, since when volumes have appeared from time to time. The Department is thus gradually building up a source of information for its own officers and at the same time contributing towards the scientific anthropological literature of South Africa.

Besides the collection and publication of information, an attempt is also being made to record photographically and cinematographically, in maps, diagrams and sketches, whatever would appear to be useful for reference in one way or another.

The Departmental Ethnologist in the course of his researches spends about half of the year in field work in the various Native reserves in different parts of the Union. His activities include also investigations in the archives, in museums, in mine compounds on the Witwatersrand and elsewhere, and in various industrial centres. They necessitate, from time to time, visits to mission stations and educational institutions and, for the purpose of comparison, to the territories adjoining the Union.

X

NATIVE EDUCATION

In no phase of Native life has the influence of the Missionary been greater than in the domain of education. Right from the very earliest times, as soon as the missionary had established his mission station and gained a few converts, his first and natural thought was to confer upon those converts a modicum of education if for no other purpose than to enable them to learn to read the Bible.

Thus with the church went the school and education walked hand in hand with religion. The mission stations became the centres of Native education throughout South Africa and the various pre-Union Governments, while assisting as regards the provision of land and by the grants of subsidies, were for the most part content to allow missionary societies to undertake this burden of responsibility towards the Native people and to bear the bulk of the expense involved.

With the effluxion of time, however, the necessities of expansion and development compelled the missionary to look ever increasingly to the Government for financial support for his schools, the Natives themselves became clamant for greater educational facilities and the European element demanded that the Government and not religious bodies should dictate the general policy to be followed as regards the education of the Native population. Thus gradually the whole question began to assume a national character and the Government assumed responsibility for subsidising Native schools in ever-increasing measure, the grants being made dependent upon conditions laid down by it as regards the attendance of pupils, the curriculum and inspection.

In such manner has arisen the system of State-aided Native primary education as it exists in South Africa to-day.

There are within the Union some three thousand two hundred Native primary schools attended by over a quarter of a million children. These schools are not Government institutions as the European schools are, but have been built and equipped by missionary enterprise, the salaries of the teachers being paid by grants from Government.

Primary education throughout the Union was in terms of section *eighty-five* of the South Africa Act placed under the several provincial administrations " for a period of five years and thereafter until Parliament should otherwise provide."

No separate organisation was established or existed for dealing with Native education, which, consequently, with European primary education, was relegated to the provincial administrations and was for some years financed from the provincial revenue funds.

In those years the financial relations between the central Government and the provincial administrations were periodically adjusted, but no subsidies specially ear-marked for Native education were paid by the Government to the provincial administrations.

No change was made upon the expiry of the initial quinquennial period specified in section *eighty-five* of the Act of Union.

In 1916, the Provincial Administration Commission report contained the following paragraph relating to Native education :—

" There is besides the all-important question of Native education that cannot in any sense be called ' higher education ' and it therefore falls under the provincial administration. In other respects, however, the South Africa Act was most careful to keep in the hands of the Union Government all matters of Native policy. Indeed the need for a consistent and uniform policy in Native affairs was one of the causes which led to the establishment of Union. Now it can safely be said that of all the influences which are at present affecting the Native in his relation to the European, education is one of the most potent. Yet the present division of education as between the Union and the Provinces leaves Native education in the hands of the Provinces divorced from all connection with the general Native policy of the country."

The previous system, however, continued unchanged until matters were brought to a head in 1921 by the action of the Transvaal Provincial Administration in imposing a direct tax on Natives under the plea that its increasing expenditure on Native education justified such a course.

The position was reviewed at the close of 1921 by the Financial Relations Conference, which arrived at the conclusion that the direct taxation of Natives should be entirely in the hands of the Central Government. The position thus created might have been met by the obvious course of transferring the control of Native education to the Central Government but the Conference came to the conclusion that the time was not ripe for such a change and the arrangements which have already been indicated in dealing with the Native Development Account (*vide* page 99 *supra*) were agreed upon, resulting in due course in the enactment of sections *nine* and *ten* of the Financial Relations Fourth Extension Act, No. 5 of 1922.

It has already been pointed out on page 180 above in dealing with Native taxation that the effect of these sections was that from the 1st April, 1922,—

(i) Provincial Councils were debarred from imposing direct taxation on the persons, habitations, lands or incomes of Natives ;

(ii) Provincial Councils were required to provide funds for Native education, not less proportionately to the whole sum spent on all education than was spent in the financial year 1921-22 ; and

(iii) the Governor-General was empowered to make grants to any Province for the extension and improvement of educational facilities amongst Natives, such grants to be made out of revenue derived from the direct taxation of Natives.

The Treasury, owing to the position of the Union finances, was unable to make available from *revenue* any grants such as those contemplated in the preceding paragraph, but agreed to find money as loans for this purpose.

The necessity for finding money for subsidising the further development and extension of Native education made it imperative for the Government to introduce legislation to impose additional direct taxation upon Natives. At the same time, the inequalities and anomalies of the then existing taxation laws of the various Provinces made the consolidation and co-ordination of these laws an urgent necessity.

The upshot was the enactment of the Natives Taxation and Development Act, No. 41 of 1925, and the establishment thereunder of the Native Development Account.

Sections *eleven* and *twelve* of that Act provided for the disposal of the local and general taxes imposed under the Act and section *thirteen* directed how the funds of the Native Development Account should be expended. These sections have already been fully dealt with on pages 100 and 101 above, to which particular attention is invited.

The provisions of section *three* of the Provincial Subsidies and Taxation Powers (Amendment) Act, No. 46 of 1925, relating to Native education, and of the regulations framed under that section, have likewise been considered in dealing with the Native Development Account—*vide* pages 102 and 103 *supra*.

To sum the position up very briefly—there is available for Native education to-day :—

(a)   A recurrent annual grant of £340,000 made by the Union Government under section *three* of Act No. 46 of 1925. This grant must be utilised exclusively for Native education and must be allocated to the various Provinces as follows :—

Cape :	£240,000
Natal :	49,000
Transvaal :	46,000
Orange Free State :	5,000

(b)   One fifth of the general tax collected from Natives under Act No. 41 of 1925. This money is paid in to the Development Account and is utilised mainly, but not exclusively, for Native education purposes. It may also be applied for the general welfare of Natives. The amount of £223,643 advanced by the Treasury to the Provincial Administrations during the financial years 1923-1926 is being refunded in annual instalments from this source.

(c)   Any money which may be specially voted for Native education by any provincial administration from its own revenue.

The provincial administrations retain the immediate administration and supervision of Native education but a measure of control is exercised by the Department by virtue of the fact that the money paid to the provincial administrations must be expended in accordance with prescribed conditions and requirements.

From the date of its constitution, the Native Affairs Commission has closely identified itself with the problems of Native education and in 1925 it was definitely associated with the control of the Native Development Account by section *thirteen* of Act No. 41 of 1925, which placed a statutory obligation upon the Minister of Native Affairs to consult the Commission as regards the application of funds standing to the credit of that Account. Since 1923, a series of conferences (usually held annually) has taken place on the question of Native education between the heads of the various provincial education Departments, the Native Affairs Commission and the Department.

As the result of these conferences, the following broad lines of policy have been laid down as regards Native education :—

(i) The main objects should be to provide *elementary education* for Native children, to extend facilities for such to as large a number of pupils as possible with the funds available and to bring about uniformity and improvement in the salaries of teachers.

(ii) The system of education should emphasize character training, habits of industry, use and appreciation of the vernacular, the official languages, health and hygiene, agriculture and other practical subjects.

(iii) To provide teachers for these schools, a limited number of students should be trained at approved training institutions. These institutions should be selected on a regional rather than on a denominational basis.

(iv) There should be established in certain areas (on a regional rather than on a denominational basis) a limited number of Native high schools designed :—

(a) to train men as farm demonstrators ;

(b) to train women as home demonstrators ;

(c) to offer vocational training to a limited number of Natives ; and

(d) to prepare students for admission to the South African Native College.

A scale of salaries for teachers in Native schools has been fixed and teachers have been placed on the minimum notch of their particular scales. It has not been possible to grant increments but the general position of the teachers has certainly been improved.

A statement, furnishing in respect of each Province for each year since the establishment of the Native Development Account the number of schools, the number of pupils, the amount of tax collected, the amount granted from the Account, and the cost per pupil, appears in Appendix " R."

Secondary Education

There are a number of institutions in the Union which endeavour to cater for the needs of the Native people in regard to secondary education, i.e. education beyond Standard IV, including industrial, agricultural and commercial education, preparation for the Ministry and the teaching profession. The leading institutions are :—

R

Cape Province : Lovedale, Blythswood, Healdtown, Bensonvale, St. Matthew's (Keiskama Hoek), Shawbury (Qumbu), St. John's College (Umtata), Buntingville (Umtata), Lesseyton (Queenstown), Peddie, Zonnebloem College, Tiger Kloof (Vryburg).

Natal Province : Adams Training Institution, Edendale, Amanzimtoti, Mariannhill, Ohlange, Modderspruit.

Transvaal Province : Kilnerton (Pretoria), Diocesan College (Pietersburg), Botsabelo (Middelburg).

Orange Free State Province : Thaba 'Nchu, Stofberg Gedenk.

Higher Education

There is only one institution which expressly caters for higher education of a University standard for Natives, viz. the South African Native College at Fort Hare which was opened in 1916 and has been eminently successful.

The College is entirely undenominational and Natives, Coloured and Indian students, both men and women, of all religions are admitted. The enrolment steadily increases year by year and students are drawn from the length and breadth of the Union and from Basutoland and other British Protectorates as well.

The College has now in active operation three different sets of courses of study, viz., Preparatory, Post-matriculation and Diploma Courses.

The preparatory courses are designed to prepare students (1) for the matriculation examination of the Joint Matriculation Board, and (2) for the College's own matriculation examination. The first is a temporary course intended only to be continued until the development of the College renders unnecessary the prosecution of university study elsewhere. The second provides the necessary preliminary training for entrance to the College courses proper, and is specially arranged for those preparing for the Ministry or for those who later will occupy the position of chiefs among their own people.

The post-matriculation courses are intended to train students preparing for university degrees or professional examinations and include a special course for higher teachers' certificates.

The diploma courses include (1) an arts course, comprising the usual subjects with the exception of the classical languages ; (2) a course in business training intended for those desiring to qualify for Government service or as clerks and interpreters ; and (3) a course in agriculture, which should be of great value, and which it is hoped will prove one of the strongest sides of the College's usefulness.

APPENDIX A

POWERS AND DUTIES OF CHIEF NATIVE COMMISSIONERS PRESCRIBED BY THE MINISTER OF NATIVE AFFAIRS IN TERMS OF SECTION 2 (1) OF ACT 38 OF 1927

1. *The Chief Native Commissioner* shall in the area for which he is appointed be the representative of the Department of Native Affairs and shall exercise the powers and carry out all duties imposed by any statute, proclamation, regulation, circular or special instruction.

2. He shall exercise supervision on behalf of the Department over Native Commissioners, Assistant Native Commissioners, Superintendents, Chiefs, Headmen and other officers of the Department in the exercise of the various duties assigned to them and shall immediately report to the Department any dereliction. He shall also bring to the notice of the Department, for the information of the Minister, any meritorious achievement deserving special mention on the part of any such officer.

3. It shall be his prime duty to watch over the interests of the Natives under his charge and to keep the Department advised of any action affecting such interests whether on the part of Government departments or private bodies or persons.

4. He shall carry out to the best of his ability the policy of the Government in Native affairs generally and shall secure a strict observance thereof on the part of all subordinate officers. Particular attention must be given to land administration which is one of the most important functions of district officers.

5. He will immediately report for the information of the Government any occurrence of political or administrative importance, serious affray, general disaffection or event of importance affecting the life of the tribes, as also information of anticipated disturbances or other undesirable actions.

6. He shall from time to time, as directed, visit the areas under his control, personally meet the officers employed therein and all important chiefs and headmen, and make himself thoroughly acquainted with the social, economic and other conditions of the people, the relationship of officials and people, and generally satisfy himself that the administration is properly conducted.

7. He shall promptly enquire into all reasonable complaints by Natives and take immediate steps to remedy such grievances as may be well founded.

8. He shall do his utmost to encourage friendly relations between European employers and Native servants especially in the rural areas and take such steps as may be necessary to enable his office to advise indigent and other Natives in regard to a market for employment.

9. He shall attend the annual congress or conference of the Agricultural Union in his area and give such assistance as may be necessary and desirable in the discussion of matters affecting Natives, especially in regard to wages, treatment and conditions of employment on farms so as to secure a more efficient and augmented supply of labourers.

10. He will give careful attention to the administration of local affairs by councils and tactfully encourage their creation in suitable areas where the chiefs are favourably disposed.

11. He shall keep himself informed in regard to the administration of the Urban Areas Act, 1923, in the towns in his area.

12. He shall interest himself in any desirable movement for the moral and material welfare of the Native, also in regard to agencies soliciting subscriptions or donations from Natives, instituting such enquiries into their *bona fides* as he may deem fit.

13. He shall submit to the Department with such comment as may be necessary all reports of importance from district officers, petitions or complaints from chiefs, headmen or other Natives requiring the attention of or necessary for the information of the Government.

14. He shall satisfy himself that all laws affecting Natives promulgated from time to time are duly notified to them by district officers.

15. He may suspend from duty for misconduct of a serious nature any chief or headman and shall immediately report such suspension to the Department for the confirmation or otherwise of the Minister.

16. He shall submit an annual report on his administration and conditions and events in his area in such detail as may be prescribed.

APPENDIX   B

GOVERNMENT NOTICE No. 2250 DATED 21ST DECEMBER, 1928

DUTIES ASSIGNED TO NATIVE COMMISSIONERS AND ASSISTANT NATIVE COMMSSIONERS BY THE MINISTER OF NATIVE AFFAIRS IN TERMS OF SECTION *TWO* (2) OF ACT No. 38 OF 1927.

It is hereby notified for general information that the Minister of Native Affairs has, under the authority vested in him by subsection (2) of section *two* of the Native Administration Act, 1927 (No. 38 of 1927), assigned to Native Commissioners and Assistant Native Commissioners the duties set out in the accompanying Schedule.

SCHEDULE

1.   Native Commissioners shall, subject to the authority of the Government, exercise general control over and supervision of the Native people residing in or for the time being in their areas, for their general and individual welfare.

2.   They shall communicate with the Department of Native Affairs through the Chief Native Commissioner.

3.   The Additional Native Commissioner in a magisterial district shall in addition to his judicial functions exercise, subject to any instructions that may be issued by the Native Affairs Department, the powers, duties and functions assigned to a Native Commissioner, under the general direction of the Native Commissioner of the district.

4.   Assistant Native Commissioners may be appointed for any defined portion of a district and therein they shall exercise judicial functions and under the direction of the Additional Native Commissioner such administrative functions as may be delegated to them by the Additional Native Commissioner of the district.

5.   Native Commissioners and Assistant Native Commissioners shall exercise such civil and criminal jurisdiction as may be conferred upon them by law, and in the settlement of civil suits and claims shall encourage Natives to avail themselves of the facilities provided by regulation for the simplified form of procedure in courts of Native Commissioner.

6.   They shall carry out all laws and regulations and the instructions of superior officers.

7.   As subordinate officers to the Chief Native Commissioner they shall loyally and to the best of their ability carry out his instructions.   They shall in their dealings with the Natives act in harmony with the policy of the Department and maintain frank and constant consultation with the Chief Native Commissioner, keeping him informed on all matters of importance in connection with administration generally.

8. They shall at all convenient times be readily accessible to the Native people collectively and individually and shall exercise patience and sympathy in the hearing of their representations.

9. They shall encourage the Native people to submit to them grievances and difficulties and to supply information in connection with their welfare, and they shall hear and determine such matters with due regard to Native law and customs and usages.

10. They shall convene quarterly meetings of the chiefs, headmen, and people for the purpose of acquainting them with new laws, and such instructions as it may be necessary to issue from time to time. The meetings shall afford the people the means of ventilating any grievances and difficulties they may have and of having them considered and disposed of. There shall be a mutual consultation, when necessary, between Native Commissioner and people on matters of administration, but officers shall avoid any semblance of committing the Government in any manner unless acting under specific orders to that end.

11. Minutes of the meetings, as provided in section *ten*, shall be recorded in a book kept for the purpose and a copy of such minutes shall be transmitted as soon as convenient after each meeting to the Chief Native Commissioner, together with any comments it may be desired to offer in regard thereto.

12. They shall at least once in every year visit the outlying portions of their areas after due notification of their intention to the chiefs and headmen. They shall meet the people if necessary and, as far as possible, settle any disputes and other matters requiring attention on the spot.

13. At the conclusion of such tours the Native Commissioner shall furnish a report to the Chief Native Commissioner on the more important matters dealt with and any unusual occurrences.

14. They shall encourage the people to avail themselves of the facilities afforded by the Government or bodies recognized by the Government for obtaining scholastic and other education.

15. They should recognize that one of the most important and difficult of their duties is the efficient and tactful administration of the laws and regulations relating to land. Officers are therefore required to devote much time and care in giving effect to these with a view specially to preventing illegal occupation of land, over-crowding and over-stocking and to promoting the proper and beneficial cultivation of the arable lands. These regulations in the areas not administered by chiefs are regarded by many Natives as irksome and an infringement of their ancient rights and privileges, and the successful application of the law depends in a great degree upon the personal interest and efforts of Native Commissioners.

16. They shall afford Natives such assistance and advice as they are able, with due regard to their judicial functions. They shall also and without delay bring to the notice of the Chief Native Commissioner any occurrences or matters in connection with which departmental intervention is considered necessary, and more particularly matters as between Natives and other races.

17. They shall make themselves acquainted with the laws and customs and the history of the tribes in their area and generally equip themselves in such a manner in regard to the Natives therein as to discharge in the best manner possible the functions entrusted to them.

18. They shall keep themselves informed of all political, social, economic and other influences and changes amongst the people, interesting themselves in such social movements as may benefit them and from time to time report to the Chief Native Commissioner matters of interest or importance. They shall assist Natives in all matters relating to their social and economic welfare.

19. They shall as far as possible act as the intermediary between all Government Departments and the Natives subject to such special instructions as the Minister may from time to time authorize.

20. They shall immediately bring to the notice of the Chief Native Commissioner any official action in the area which might be regarded as contrary to the interest of the Department of Native Affairs or the Natives.

21. They shall endeavour to ensure that Natives employed by the Government in their area are afforded every opportunity to acquire knowledge of their duties to make themselves efficient.

22. They shall take steps to secure that Natives, who frequently travel long distances to attend at their office, receive prompt attention. Great hardship is often caused by such persons not being asked their business and taken to the proper officer on arrival at the office.

23. They shall report to the Chief Native Commissioner any attempts to stir up strife, discord, dissatisfaction, enmity, or disloyalty amongst the members of the tribe or between the chief and members of his tribe or between Natives and the Government.

24. They shall exercise supervision over the collection of Native taxes so as to secure their due payment and maintain an efficient registration of taxpayers.

25. They shall assist in securing employment for Natives desirous of proceeding to work and maintaining a good understanding and better relations between masters and servants by improvement of efficiency and of the conditions of labour.

26. They shall keep a diary of their activities in connection with all important events and occurrences in their areas and shall record in a register such occurrences and their treatment.

27. They shall inquire into complaints in connection with the administrative acts of subordinate officers, chiefs, and headmen, and shall bring to the notice of a commissioned officer complaints against policemen or Natives.

28. They shall report to the Chief Native Commissioner in the month of January in each year upon the general condition of the Natives within their districts with special reference to the agricultural, industrial, and educational progress made by the people.

29. There may be established at the office of each Native Commissioner a Native labour bureau for the receipt and registration of applications from persons desirous of obtaining servants from the area and from Natives seeking to obtain employment, and for supplying information in regard to employers and servants and generally for facilitating the supply of labour and the obtaining of employment.

Such bureaux shall be administered under such rules as may be framed from time to time.

APPENDIX C

GOVERNMENT NOTICE No. 2251 DATED 21ST DECEMBER, 1928

DUTIES OF SUPERINTENDENTS OF LOCATIONS PRESCRIBED BY THE MINISTER OF NATIVE AFFAIRS IN TERMS OF SECTION *TWO* (6) OF ACT No. 38 OF 1927

It is hereby notified for general information that the Minister of Native Affairs has, under the authority vested in him by sub-section (6) of section *two* of the Native Administration Act, 1927 (No. 38 of 1927), prescribed for superintendents of locations the duties set out in the accompanying Schedule.

SCHEDULE

1. *Superintendents* shall, in the areas for which they are appointed, assist the Native Commissioners in the discharge of the duties assigned to them, and shall be subordinate to and under the control and supervision of such officer and shall efficiently carry out such orders and instructions as may be issued to them from time to time by the Government or by such officer aforementioned.

2. They shall at all convenient times be accessible to the people and no matter brought to their notice shall be deemed too trivial or unimportant to be heard.

3. They shall subject to such restrictions in regard to travelling as may be imposed by the Chief Native Commissioner move about the locations at frequent intervals in order to meet the people and deal with disputes and various matters on the spot.

4. They shall keep a diary in which shall be entered from day to day journeys undertaken, the time occupied, and generally the nature of the work done. Abstracts of such diaries shall be transmitted to the Native Commissioner concerned within seven days after the end of each month.

5. They shall promptly report to the Native Commissioner any matters of importance or any unusual occurrences taking place not only within their locations but elsewhere as may come to their knowledge.

6. They shall co-operate, but without unduly interfering with the performance of their ordinary duties, with inspectors of schools, bodies recognised by Government for managing schools, teachers and demonstrators in promoting scholastic education and industrial training.

7. They shall assist in the collection of taxes in such manner as may be required.

8. They shall promptly report to the officer concerned outbreaks of communicable diseases among the people and particularly occurrences of leprosy and smallpox, as also deaths from violence or unnatural causes.

9. They shall promptly report to the proper officers outbreaks of contagious and infectious diseases among large and small stock and shall co-operate in the measures taken for the eradication thereof.

10. They may impound stray stock, the owners of which cannot be ascertained.

11. They shall bring to the notice of chiefs and headmen the presence of noxious weeds in the locations and require them to take such steps as are provided by law for the eradication of such weeds. Should it be found that such orders have not been complied with, within a reasonable time, the fact shall be reported to the Native Commissioner.

12. They shall report to the Native Commissioner the presence of un-authorized persons in the locations or persons not domiciled in the locations or persons who are present for the purpose of disseminating undesirable propaganda among the Native people.

13. They shall devote special time, care, and patience in carrying out the land laws and regulations. Any serious complications and difficulties in this connection shall be submitted, without delay, to the Native Commissioner for instructions.

14. In areas in which the administration of land is vested in the Magistrate or Native Commissioner, the Superintendent will be required to prevent un-authorized occupation of land, encroachment thereon, the unauthorized entry of strangers or of stock into locations, and to provide for the preservation of land beacons and fences.

APPENDIX D

GOVERNMENT NOTICE No. 2252 DATED 21ST DECEMBER, 1928

It is hereby notified for general information that His Excellency the Officer Administering the Government has been pleased, under and by virtue of the powers vested in him by sub-section (7) of section *two* of the Native Administration Act, 1927 (No. 38 of 1927), to make the following Regulations prescribing the duties, powers and privileges of chiefs and headmen.

REGULATIONS PRESCRIBING THE DUTIES, POWERS AND PRIVILEGES OF CHIEFS AND HEADMEN

1. Chiefs shall be either appointed, or recognized, by the Governor-General.

2. Appointed chiefs shall be such persons as are appointed to exercise tribal government and control and to perform the administrative functions herein prescribed or required under any other law now in force or hereafter promulgated in and over any tribe or area assigned for the occupation of such tribe.

3. Recognized chiefs shall be such persons as are accorded by the Governor-General the rank and customary privileges of a Native chief in or over any tribe or portion of a tribe, but do not exercise any administrative or official authority on behalf of the Supreme Chief or the Government over any person or any land.

4. Headmen shall be such persons as are appointed by the Governor-General to control a minor tribe or location under the direction of a Native Commissioner but shall not include persons commonly called headmen or indunas appointed by chiefs to assist in the administration of their tribes.

5. In these regulations except when otherwise stated, chiefs shall mean appointed chiefs only.

6. *Chiefs and Headmen* shall carry out such lawful orders and instructions as may from time to time be given them through or by a Chief Native Commissioner, Native Commissioner, Magistrate, or Superintendent.

7. They shall comply with all laws and render such assistance as may be required of them by responsible officers of the Government in connection with the following matters :—

    (*a*) The registration of taxpayers and the collection of taxes and rates due by the people.

    (*b*) The dipping of large and small stock and the supervision thereof.

    (*c*) The prevention and eradication of animal diseases.

    (*d*) The collection of statistics.

    (*e*) The efficient administration of the laws relating to the allotment and registration of lands and kraal sites and to commonages and the prevention of illegal occupation of or squatting upon land.

    (*f*) The preservation of land beacons and fences.

    (*g*) The prevention, detection, and punishment of crimes and offences.

    (*h*) The supply of labour for agricultural and other purposes.

(*i*) Public health and sanitary measures.

(*j*) The eradication of noxious weeds.

(*k*) The preservation of game.

(*l*) The preservation of forests, monuments, historical objects, and public property.

(*m*) Such other matters as the Native Commissioner may from time to time prescribe.

Such requirements will, except in regard to the detection of crime and police administration, be made as a general rule through the Native Commissioner of the District in which such chief or headman resides.

8. They shall bring to the notice of their people all new laws, orders, instructions, and requirements of the Government communicated to them by the Native Commissioner or Superintendent.

9. They shall promptly report to the responsible officers of the Government the following occurrences :—

(*a*) Outbreaks of any notifiable disease amongst stock.

(*b*) Outbreaks of notifiable disease amongst persons.

(*c*) The deaths of persons from violence or other unnatural causes.

(*d*) The commission of crime and offences brought to their knowledge.

(*e*) The presence of strange persons in their areas unless such persons produce lawful authority to be therein.

(*f*) The unauthorized occupation of land, or encroachments thereon.

(*g*) The presence of a fugitive offender.

(*h*) The illicit introduction of arms, ammunition, and intoxicating liquor.

(*i*) Meetings for unlawful or undesirable purposes.

(*j*) The presence of strange stock in the area without lawful permit.

10. They shall prevent, so far as the law allows them to do so, veld burning, soil erosion, interference with *bona fide* travellers through their areas, the sale of poisons, love philtres, and the practice of pretended witchcraft or divinations, and the practice of Native customs which are contrary to the laws and principles of humanity and decency.

11. They shall render assistance to the educational authorities, teachers, demonstrators, and other officers employed by the Government or Native Councils established under Act No. 23 of 1920 in connection with the welfare of Natives and shall not manifest partisanship in the activities of the various religious bodies in church or school matters.

12. They shall at the request of the Native Commissioner or Superintendent convene meetings of their people and shall attend such meetings and endeavour to secure the attendance of all people thereat.

13. They shall in so far as they are able disperse or order the dispersal of all riotous or unlawful assemblies of Natives and may arrest and hand over to the police any person who fails to comply with such order.

14. They shall not, except when specially authorized under any law, try or decide any criminal charge.

15. They shall not become members or take any part in the affairs of any political association or any association whose objects are deemed by the Minister to be subversive of or prejudicial to constituted Government or good order.

16. They shall not absent themselves from their area of jurisdiction for a period in excess of seven days without the authority of the Native Commissioner and in case of absence beyond a period of one month without the authority of the Chief Native Commissioner and shall during such absence provide to the satisfaction of the Native Commissioner, without extra cost to the Government, for the proper performance of their duties.

17. They shall have and exercise in regard to any Native within the area of their jurisdiction such powers and authorities in connection with the arrest and custody of offenders as are conferred upon peace officers by Chapter V of Act No. 31 of 1917 or by any law relating to the theft of stock and produce or to the control of the sale of intoxicating liquor.

18. They shall have power to search without warrant any Native person or the kraal homestead or other place within the area of their jurisdiction occupied by a Native if there are reasonable grounds to suspect that stolen stock or produce or intoxicating liquor or arms or ammunition wrongfully obtained are hidden on such person or in such kraal or other place, and to seize and convey to the nearest police post any such stock or produce or intoxicating liquor or arms or ammunition so seized.

19. They shall impound or detain stray stock found in their areas of which the owners cannot be ascertained and in case of detention shall promptly report the fact to the Superintendent or Native Commissioner.

20. They may detain stock brought into their areas under unlawful or under suspicious circumstances, and shall promptly report the fact to the Superintendent or Native Commissioner.

21. They shall report to the district surgeon or Native Commissioner or Superintendent every untreated case of venereal disease or leprosy in their area.

22. *Chiefs* shall under the supervision of the Government exercise general administrative control over their respective tribes and over any other Natives residing within their areas of jurisdiction.

23. They shall be responsible for the proper allotment to the extent of the authority allowed them by law of arable lands and residential sites in a just and equitable manner without favour or prejudice.

24. They shall, subject to the instructions of the Supreme Chief, act as the upper guardian of orphans and minor children in the tribe in accordance with the Native law and custom prevailing.

25. They shall be responsible to the Government for the peace, order, welfare and administration of the tribe, and shall immediately bring to the notice of the Native Commissioner any conditions of unrest or dissatisfaction or any other matter of serious import or concern to the Government.

26. They shall enjoy the privileges conferred upon them by the long established and generally recognised customs and usages of their tribes, but otherwise shall not use any compulsion or other arbitrary means to extort or secure from any person any tribute, fee, reward, or present.

27. They shall be entitled to the loyalty, respect, and obedience of the members of the tribe.

28. They shall be paid such allowances, if any, as may from time to time be approved by or on behalf of the Minister.

29. The duties herein prescribed may be assigned by a chief with the approval of the Native Commissioner to any induna or similar representative nominated by him, but responsibility for the proper execution of such duties shall nevertheless rest upon the chief.

30. *Headmen* will receive allowances on the following scale :—

			Per annum.		
On first appointment	..	..	£12	0	0
After three years' good service	..	..	18	0	0
After six years' good service	..	..	24	0	0
After eleven years' good service	..	..	30	0	0
After sixteen years' good service	..	..	36	0	0

Special allowances may be approved by the Minister in the case of a recognized chief holding appointment as a headman.

31. Headmen in the Province of the Cape of Good Hope may with the approval of the Minister upon their retirement from service on account of age and infirmity be awarded an allowance according to the following scale, viz. :—

Per annum.

After fifteen (15) years' continuous good service   £6   o   o

After twenty-five (25) years' continuous good service 12   o   o

General.

32. Any infringement of any of the foregoing regulations and any neglect or disregard of any duty or obligation imposed by these regulations or any law whatsoever or of any order or instruction lawfully given and any misconduct or abuse of power shall, in addition to any penalty imposed upon him by any law, render a chief or headman liable to—

(*a*) suspension from employment and allowances for a stated period, or

(*b*) fine, or

(*c*) reprimand, or

(*d*) reduction of emoluments by the Minister, or

(*e*) summary dismissal from office by the Governor-General.

33. The Minister may, when he deems it necessary, order that an inquiry shall be held into any charge brought against any chief or headman and may give such instructions in regard to such inquiry as he may deem fit.

APPENDIX E

PROCLAMATION No. 191 OF 1932

UNITED TRANSKEIAN TERRITORIES GENERAL COUNCIL

Whereas the Transkeian Territories General Council and the Pondoland General Council voluntarily resolved to amalgamate ; and whereas such General Councils were duly amalgamated by Proclamation No. 279 of 1930 under the designation of " United Transkeian Territories General Council " ; and whereas it is desirable to consolidate and in certain respects to amend the law relating to the said United Transkeian Territories General Council ;

Now, therefore, under the powers and authorities vested in me by law, I do hereby proclaim, declare, and make known as follows :—

CHAPTER I

PRELIMINARY

1. This Proclamation is divided into nine chapters, which severally relate to the following subject matters :—

Chapter I : Preliminary (sections *one* to *three*).
Chapter II : District Councils (sections *four* to *sixteen*).
Chapter III : General Council (sections *seventeen* to *twenty-seven*).
Chapter IV : Administration (sections *twenty-eight* to *thirty-six*).
Chapter V : Officers (sections *thirty-seven* to *forty-two*).
Chapter VI : Audit and Finance (sections *forty-three* to *fifty-four*).
Chapter VII : Powers and Duties of Councils (sections *fifty-five* to *fifty-eight*).
Chapter VIII: Regulations (sections *fifty-nine* to *sixty-one*).
Chapter IX : General and Supplementary (sections *sixty-two* to *sixty-five*).

2. This Proclamation shall apply throughout the Transkeian Territories, exclusive of the District of Mount Currie, that is to say, throughout—

(a) the Districts of Butterworth, Idutywa, Kentani, Nqamakwe, Tsomo, and Willowvale, comprising the Territory of the Transkei ;
(b) the Districts of Elliotdale, Engcobo, Mqanduli, St. Marks, Umtata, and Xalanga, comprising the Territory of Tembuland ;
(c) the Districts of Matatiele, Mount Ayliff, Mount Fletcher, Mount Frere, Qumbu, Tsolo, and Umzimkulu, in the Territory of East Griqualand ;
(d) the Districts of Bizana, Flagstaff, Libode, Lusikisiki, Ngqeleni, Port St. John's, and Tabankulu, comprising the Territory of Pondoland.

3. Proclamations No. 169 of 1911, No. 86 of 1914, No. 138 of 1917, No. 166 of 1927, and No. 250 of 1927, are hereby repealed together with so much of any other law as may be inconsistent with or repugnant to the provisions of this Proclamation.

Chapter II

District Councils

4. Each council established under any prior law as a district council for the administration of local affairs within any district to which this Proclamation applies shall be deemed to be a district council duly established under the provisions of this Proclamation and each member of any such council duly appointed prior to the promulgation of this Proclamation shall for the remainder of his term of office be deemed to have been appointed under this Proclamation.

5. Subject to the provisions of section *eight*, each district council shall consist of six members of whom two shall be nominated and appointed by the Governor-General, and the remaining four shall be nominated and appointed as in section *six* or section *seven* provided.

6. (1) Each district shall be divided into four electoral areas (hereinafter referred to as sections) in such manner as the Chief Magistrate may approve and the local tax and Native quitrent payers in each section shall elect three representatives —

   (*a*) in an unsurveyed district from amongst the local tax payers and Native owners of farms domiciled in that section ; and

   (*b*) in a surveyed district from amongst the registered holders of allotments, local tax payers, and Native owners of farms domiciled in that section ;

and thereafter the several representatives in each district duly elected as aforesaid shall nominate—

   (i) in the Territories other than Pondoland, four of their number ;

   (ii) in the Territory of Pondoland, two of their number ;

   to be recommended to the Governor-General for appointment as district councillors.

(2) For the purposes of selection and subsequent nomination as in sub-section (1) provided, meetings of the local tax and Native quitrent payers in each section and of the representatives of the several sections respectively shall be called by the magistrate and shall be conducted in such manner as the Chief Magistrate may direct.

(3) The chief of Eastern Pondoland and the chief of Western Pondoland shall nominate two local nominees for appointment by the Governor-General as members of each district council within their respective areas.

7. Should the representatives of sections or the chief concerned, as the case may be, fail to nominate the requisite number of persons for appointment as members of any district council as in section *six* provided, or should the Governor-General deem it undesirable that any one or more of the persons nominated under that section should be appointed to any such district council, he may require the representatives of sections or the chief concerned, to nominate a sufficient number or, as the case may be, some other suitable person or persons, and should such requirement not be complied with within twenty-one days, he may appoint such person or persons as he may deem fit.

8. The chiefs of Eastern Pondoland, Western Pondoland, and Tembuland shall respectively be additional members of the Lusikisiki, Libode, and Umtata district councils.

9. The periods of office of a district council under this Proclamation shall be three years commencing on the first day of October of the year in which its members are appointed and its members shall, save as in sub-section (4) of section *ten* provided, be nominated and appointed for a period of three years.

10. (1) No person shall be capable of being appointed or of sitting as a member of a district council who—

(a) has at any time been convicted of any crime or offence for which he shall have been sentenced to imprisonment without the option of a fine for a term of not less than six months, unless he shall have received a grant of amnesty or a free pardon, or unless such imprisonment shall have expired at least five years before the date of his appointment ; or

(b) is an unrehabilitated insolvent ; or

(c) is of unsound mind, and has been so declared by competent authority.

(2) If a member of a district council—

(a) becomes subject to any of the disabilities mentioned in the last preceding sub-section ; or

(b) dies ; or

(c) becomes, in the opinion of the Minister, incapable of effective service on the council by reason of illness, infirmity, or other cause ; or

(d) becomes, in the opinion of the Minister, unfit by reason of misconduct or other cause to be a member of the council ; or

(e) fails to attend three consecutive meetings of such council ;
his seat shall thereupon become vacant.

(3) A member of a district council may, by writing under his hand addressed to the chairman thereof, resign his seat, which shall thereupon become vacant.

(4) (a) Whenever the seat of any member of a district council becomes vacant, it shall be filled as soon as possible for the unexpired portion of the period for which such member was appointed, by nomination by—

(i) such district council in the case of a people's nominee ;

(ii) the chief concerned in the case of a chief's nominee ; and

(iii) the Governor-General in the case of his nominee.

(b) For the purpose of this sub-section the provisions of section *seven* shall *mutatis mutandis* apply.

11. The magistrate of the district shall be *ex officio* chairman of the district council, shall preside at all its meetings, and shall be the local executive officer for the administration of affairs delegated to the district council.

12. Meetings of the district council shall be convened by the chairman thereof.

13. There shall be six ordinary meetings of the district council which shall respectively be held at the seat of the district magistracy during the months of January, March, May, July, September, and November in each year on such days as may from time to time be fixed by the chairman, who shall send notice of the day and hour appointed to each councillor at least fourteen days prior to any meeting ; provided that, subject to the provisions of sub-section (1) of section *eighteen*, the chairman may for good cause summon an ordinary meeting during a month other than the month in which such meeting would in terms of this section normally be held.

14. At any time the chairman of a district council, if satisfied as to the necessity therefor, may, and if instructed thereto by the Chief Magistrate, shall, call a special meeting of such council. At any such meeting only such business as the chairman may lay before it or approve shall be transacted.

15. (1) At each meeting of a district council the chairman shall inform the members present of the subjects to be discussed provided that at any ordinary meeting any councillor may, with the approval of the chairman, bring forward for discussion any matter within the scope of the council's functions. After discussion of each subject, the members of the council shall, by voting, record their opinions thereon. In the case of equality of votes the motion or amendment, as the case may be, shall be regarded as negatived.

(2) The chairman shall decide upon the action to be taken in regard to any matter dealt with by a district council as in sub-section (1) provided, and shall, if necessary, apply to the chief executive officer, secretary, treasurer, or other officer to whom the administration of any service may be assigned, for authority to carry out any proposal, or take such other steps as may be required.

16. The chairman shall, after each meeting, forward a minute of the proceedings and of the decisions arrived at to the Chief Magistrate, who shall bring before the General Council established under this Proclamation at its next session such matters as require to be dealt with by such council.

CHAPTER III

GENERAL COUNCIL

17. The General Council, which shall be styled the United Transkeian Territories General Council, shall consist of the Chief Magistrate, the magistrates of the districts in which this Proclamation is in force, and representatives of such districts appointed for each calendar year as hereinafter provided.

18. (1) At the November meeting in each year the members of each district council in the Territories of the Transkei, Tembuland, and East Griqualand shall nominate two of their number, and the members of each district council in the Territory of Pondoland shall nominate one of their number for appointment by the Governor-General to the General Council for the ensuing calendar year; provided that any member appointed to the Executive Committee as hereinafter prescribed shall be regarded, for the purpose of subsequent nominations by the district council concerned, as a nominee of such district council during the remainder of the term of office of the members of such district council.

(2) At the same time as members are nominated as in sub-section (1) provided, the chief of Eastern Pondoland and the chief of Western Pondoland shall each nominate a member of each district council within their respective areas of jurisdiction for appointment by the Governor-General to the General Council for the ensuing calendar year.

(3) The chief of Eastern Pondoland, the chief of Western Pondoland, and the chief of Tembuland shall *ex officio* be members of the United Transkeian Territories General Council.

(4) One member of each district council shall be nominated and appointed to the General Council by the Governor-General.

(5) If any district council or chief fails during the month of November to nominate the number of persons which such council or chief is under this section entitled to nominate, the Governor-General may himself nominate and appoint a sufficient number of persons to make good the deficiency.

19. All members of the General Council duly appointed prior to the promulgation of this Proclamation shall for the remainder of their term of office be deemed to have been appointed under the provisions of this Proclamation.

20. (1) No person shall be appointed or sit as a member of the General Council who is subject to any disability specified in sub-section (1) of section *ten* and the seat of any member shall become vacant by the operation of any such factor as is specified in paragraphs (*a*), (*b*), (*c*), (*d*), or (*e*) of sub-section (2) of that section.

(2) Any member of the General Council may, by writing under his hand addressed to the Chief Magistrate, resign his seat, which shall thereupon become vacant.

S

(3) Whenever for any cause the seat of any member of the General Council becomes vacant, such vacancy shall be filled in such manner as the Governor-General may direct.

21. (1) The functions and powers of the General Council shall include—

(a) the initiation and consideration of any matter relating to the economic, industrial, or social condition of the Native population of the Union or any part thereof in so far as it affects the Natives within the area of the jurisdiction of the Council ;

(b) the consideration of any proposed legislation or existing law which specially affects the Native population of the Union in so far as it affects the Natives within the area of jurisdiction of the Council ;

(c) the consideration of any specific matter submitted to it by the Governor-General or by the Minister ;

(d) the passing of resolutions on any such matter.

22. Subject to the provisions of section *fifty-seven* the area of jurisdiction of the General Council shall be—

(a) all land within the districts specified in section *two*, which falls within the definition of " Native location " in section *nineteen* of the Natives Taxation and Development Act, No. 41 of 1925 ; and

(b) all land within the said districts in respect of which Native quitrent is payable.

23. (1) There shall be held at Umtata one ordinary meeting of the General Council in every year, to commence on a date fixed by the Chief Magistrate, by whom such meeting shall be convened.

(2) Such meeting shall be presided over by the Chief Magistrate, or, in his absence, by the Assistant Chief Magistrate.

24. The Chief Magistrate may, at any time, upon being satisfied of the necessity for so doing, call a special meeting of the Council and at such meeting such business only as the chairman may lay before it or approve shall be transacted.

25. The Chief Magistrate shall, not less than twenty-one days prior to any meeting of the Council, cause the members of the Council to be informed of the date fixed for and of the business to be transacted at such meeting.

26. At every meeting the representatives of the several districts present shall, by voting, record their opinions upon the subject under consideration. In the event of an equality of votes, the motion or amendment, as the case may be, shall be regarded as negatived.

27. (1) The Chief Magistrate shall deliberate upon all matters dealt with at any session of the General Council in consultation with the magistrates of the districts to which this Proclamation applies and shall ascertain their views thereon. Thereafter he shall be responsible for giving any necessary directions or applying for any necessary authority in regard to any such matter.

(2) The Chief Magistrate may invite any official other than the magistrates referred to in sub-section (1) to be present at and participate in any such deliberations and the Native members of the Executive Committee established under section *twenty-nine* shall be entitled to attend and, subject to the approval of the Chief Magistrate, to take part in the deliberations.

CHAPTER IV

ADMINISTRATION

28. The Chief Magistrate shall be the Chief Executive Officer of the General Council.

29. The Chief Magistrate shall, together with three magistrates and four Native members appointed as hereinafter provided, constitute an Executive Com-

mittee responsible for the administration and control of such council affairs as are specified in the schedule to this Proclamation.

30.   (1) The Chief Magistrate shall from time to time appoint as members of the Executive Committee three magistrates of districts to which this Proclamation applies and may at any time in his discretion terminate, vary, or alter any such appointment.

(2)   The General Council shall, at its first meeting following any general appointment of district councillors, nominate from among its members, for appointment by the Governor-General as members of the Executive Committee, four Natives, who, subject to the provisions of section *thirty-one*, shall hold office until the appointment of their successors in like manner.

(3)   Notwithstanding anything in sub-section (2), the four persons nominated at the 1932 session of the United Transkeian Territories General Council shall, subject to the approval of the Governor-General, be the Native members of the first Executive Committee and shall hold office until their successors have been appointed as in sub-section (2) provided.

31.   (1) A Native member of the Executive Committee shall cease to hold office as such—

(a)   if he ceases to be a member of a district council ; or

(b)   if he fails without special leave of the Chief Executive Officer to attend three consecutive meetings of the Executive Committee.

(2)   If any vacancy occurs among the Native members of the Executive Committee the General Council shall nominate one of its members for appointment by the Governor-General for the unexpired period of office of the member whose position has become vacant :   Provided that should the General Council not be in session when the vacancy occurs the Executive Committee may appoint a member of a district council to hold office temporarily pending the ensuing session of the General Council.

32.   The Native members of the Executive Committee shall receive such remuneration as the Minister, after consultation with the General Council, shall determine ; provided that pending such determination, such members shall be paid for attendance and travelling in accordance with the tariffs laid down in paragraph (b) of section *one* and paragraph (a) of section *two* of Chapter IV of the regulations published under Government Notice No. 1607 of 1927.

33.   No member of the General Council shall be disqualified from sitting as such by reason of his appointment to the Executive Committee.

34.   (1) The Executive Committee shall meet every two months and at such other times as the Chief Executive Officer may determine.

(2)   Meetings of the Executive Committee shall be presided over by the Chief Executive Officer, or in his absence by the senior magistrate present.   Five members of the Executive Committee shall form a quorum.

(3)   Questions arising in the Executive Committee shall be determined by a majority of votes of the members present, and in case of an equality of votes, the chairman shall have also a casting vote ; provided that in the event of a decision being contrary to the wishes of the chairman the matter at issue may be reserved for decision by the Minister.

35.   The Executive Committee may make rules for the conduct of its proceedings, which shall, however, be subject to the approval of the Minister.

36.   Notwithstanding anything in section *twenty-nine*, the Chief Executive Officer may, where the circumstances are such as to render prompt action necessary, deal with any such matter as is in that section referred to without prior reference to the Executive Committee ; provided, however, that he shall report any action so taken by him to the Executive Committee at its ensuing meeting.

CHAPTER V

OFFICERS

37. (1) An officer to be styled the Secretary and Treasurer of the United Transkeian Territories General Council shall be appointed by the Governor-General.

(2) The said officer shall be responsible to the Chief Magistrate for the collection of all revenue or other dues accruing to the General Council, for the disbursement of its funds, and generally for the management of its affairs.

(3) The said officer in his capacity as Treasurer (hereinafter in that capacity referred to as " the Treasurer ") shall keep an account in the name of the General Council with a bank to be approved by the Minister.

38. The Governor-General may assign to and impose on officers of the public service such powers, functions and duties as he may think fit in connection with the administration of council affairs under this Proclamation.

39. Subject to the provisions of sections *twenty-nine*, *thirty-six*, and *forty* the Chief Executive Officer may—

(a) appoint persons, other than officers of the public service, for the discharge of such functions and the performance of such duties in connection with the administration of Council affairs as he may think fit;

(b) prescribe the salary, allowances and any other remuneration to be paid to any person appointed under paragraph (a) ;

(c) dismiss, fine, de-grade, or reduce the salary of any such person for failure to carry out his functions and duties to the satisfaction of the Chief Executive Officer or for any other reason ;

(d) require such security as he may from time to time deem necessary to be furnished by or on behalf of any officer appointed under this Proclamation for the administration of Council affairs.

40. Notwithstanding anything in section *twenty-nine*, section *thirty-six* or section *thirty-nine*, the Minister may direct that the appointment of any officer or class of officers for the administration of council affairs shall be reserved for his approval.

41. All officers appointed under the provisions of any law repealed by this Proclamation shall be deemed to have been duly appointed under this Proclamation.

42. The General Council or any district council shall be a " local authority " for the purposes of the Prevention of Corruption Act, No. 4 of 1918.

CHAPTER VI

AUDIT AND FINANCE

43. The financial year of the General Council, referred to in this Chapter as " the Council ", shall be the period from the 1st July to the 30th June.

44. The accounts of the Council, including those of collectors and sub-accountants, shall be audited by the Controller and Auditor-General of the Union, and each yearly certificate of discharge issued by the Controller and Auditor-General to the Treasurer shall be laid before the Council at its first session after such issue.

45. The Controller and Auditor-General, or any person duly authorized by him, shall have access to all records, books or documents of the Council for the purpose of carrying out his audit.

46. If it appear to the Controller and Auditor-General—

(a) that any deficiency has occurred in collecting or accounting for the revenues of the Council ; or

(b) that any moneys of the Council have been improperly paid or are not duly vouched ; or

(c) that any money, stamps, securities, stores, or other property of the Council are deficient ;

and if a proper explanation be not, within a period specified by him, furnished to him with regard to any such deficiency or improper payment or payment not duly vouched, the Controller and Auditor-General may surcharge against the person responsible therefor the amount of any such deficiency, improper payment, or payment not duly vouched. The amount of any such surcharge shall be a debt from the person against whom the surcharge is made.

47. The Controller and Auditor-General shall notify to the Treasurer any surcharge which may be made under the last preceding section, and the Council shall recover the amount thereof from the person liable to pay the same ; provided that, unless the Chief Executive Officer with the approval of the Minister otherwise direct, the amount of such surcharge which may be due from a person in the employment of the Council shall be recovered in equal monthly instalments by deductions from his salary not exceeding one-fourth of his monthly salary.

48. Every surcharge made by the Controller and Auditor-General shall be a debt due to the Council and recoverable as such, but if in the opinion of the Chief Executive Officer there are circumstances to justify such a course, relief may be granted wholly or in part from the surcharge, provided the authority of the Governor-General is first obtained.

49. The Council shall pay an audit fee to be fixed by the Treasury in consultation with the Controller and Auditor-General. Such fee shall not exceed the estimated cost of audit.

50. The Governor-General may levy a rate for any council purpose to be paid by every Native man or woman who shall be the occupier, either alone or with his or her family, either of any separate portion of land or of any hut, and also a rate to be paid by every other Native man domiciled in the area under the jurisdiction of the Council, and the Governor-General may from time to time make regulations defining the incidence of such rates in such area.

51. (1) The Governor-General may levy annually a stock rate, to be paid by all Natives owning cattle, or who for the time being are in charge of kraals and homesteads at which cattle are kept, in any area within the jurisdiction of the Council, which said rate shall be levied in respect of each head of cattle owned by any such Native or kept at any such kraal or homestead, on a date to be fixed by notice published in the *Government Gazette ;* and the Governor-General may from time to time make regulations prescribing the manner of assessment and collection of the said rate, and the method of registration of cattle for the purposes of the said levy.

(2) No such stock rate as is referred to in sub-section (1) shall be imposed in any district if the Governor-General has upon the request of the majority of the cattle owners therein and upon the recommendation of the district council thereof approved of dipping operations being carried out by the cattle owners independently of council control.

(3) The magistrate may from time to time convene a public meeting of the cattle owners in his district or a series of meetings of the cattle owners in different parts of his district in order to ascertain their desires as regards the dipping of their stock and the written certificate of the magistrate that the majority of cattle owners present at such meeting or meetings desire to be permitted to carry out dipping operations independently of the Council shall be deemed to constitute a request from the majority of the cattle owners in the district for the purposes of sub-section (2).

52. The provisions of section *nine* of the Natives Taxation and Development Act, No. 41 of 1925, or any amendment thereof, and the regulations framed

under the said Act, for the recovery of arrear taxes, shall apply *mutatis mutandis to* the recovery of any rate levied under the provisions of this Proclamation which may be in arrear for more than three months after the due date ; and the fees of the Messenger of the Court or other duly authorized officer, to cover all costs, shall be as prescribed in the said Act and regulations ; provided that in the case of a stock rate the owner of any cattle, which at the time of the accrual of the rate were kept at a kraal or homestead in charge of another person, shall be liable jointly and severally with such other person for the rate due in respect of such cattle, and in default of payment by such other person the arrear rate may be recovered from such owner in the manner prescribed by this section.

53.   The Governor-General may, upon the resolution of the Council and when he is satisfied that all available means have been used for the recovery of any arrear rate, arrear stock rate, or any other revenue due to the Council, and it is satisfactorily shown that there is no prospect of securing payment, direct that such amount shall be written off as irrecoverable.

54.   The local tax and quitrent paid to the Council under the provisions of section *eleven* of the Natives Taxation and Development Act, No. 41 of 1925, and all other moneys raised or received from any source for the purposes of the Council, shall, subject to the approval of and under such regulations as may from time to time be made by the Governor-General, be appropriated to—

(a) the expenses of the collection of council revenue ;

(b) the payment of the salaries of the lawfully appointed officers of the Council and of district councils and the cost of audit ;

(c) the payments authorized to be made to members of the Council and of district councils ;

(d) the construction, maintenance, preservation, repair, and improvements of bridges and roads ;

(e) the assertion by legal process of the rights of the public to any public road or right-of-way which the Council shall ascertain to exist, and shall find to have been closed or obstructed by any person or persons whatsoever ; provided that nothing in this paragraph shall be construed as requiring the Council to resort to such legal process ;

(f) the cost of legal advice and proceedings ;

(g) the encouragement of the planting and cultivation of trees and the establishment and maintenance of plantations ;

(h) expenditure in connection with the eradication or destruction of proclaimed noxious weeds and plants ;

(i) the establishment and maintenance of industrial and agricultural schools, and general assistance in the advancement of scholastic and industrial education, agriculture and industries and the improvement of stock ;

(j) the prevention or eradication of disease amongst stock ;

(k) the acquisition of land or any interest in land for any of the above purposes or for any other purpose ;

(l) the construction and maintenance of dams, furrows, watercourses, drains, sewers, culverts, and any works that may be necessary for the purpose of securing a proper water supply and the prevention of soil erosion ;

(m) the prevention, removal or abatement of any nuisance ;

(n) grants to hospitals, or in respect of hospital treatment and medical training ;

(o) contributions towards the cost of any work or service which the Council may undertake in conjunction with or under any agreement entered into between it and any Provincial or other council or any other party ;

(p) meeting expenditure not otherwise by law provided for ;

(q) any other purpose for which money may lawfully be expended by the Council.

CHAPTER VII

POWERS AND DUTIES OF COUNCILS

55. Any loss or deficiency through theft, fraud or other cause shall be reported immediately by the Chief Executive Officer or the Treasurer to the Controller and Auditor-General.

56. Such works and services as may be proposed by the General Council and approved by the Governor-General may be carried out by the said Council or by any district council to which the General Council shall with the like approval assign the carrying out of any such work or service, and, in the latter case, the said district council shall keep and furnish to the General Council proper accounts of the expenditure of the funds entrusted to it for such purpose.

57. (1) The General Council may undertake any work or service in conjunction with a Provincial or other council now or hereafter established or with any other party on such terms and in such manner as may be approved by the Governor-General.

(2) The General Council may construct and maintain works beyond its area of jurisdiction for the benefit of the Native people within such area of jurisdiction ; provided that no such work or service shall be undertaken without the written approval of the Chief Executive Officer.

58. The General Council shall in any legal proceedings in a court of law sue or be sued in the name of its Chief Executive Officer, *nomine officii*.

CHAPTER VIII

REGULATIONS

59. The Governor-General may from time to time make regulations for the administration of the affairs of the General and district councils in respect of any of the following matters :—

(i) Procedure at meetings of the General and district councils.

(ii) Payment of allowances, including transport allowances, to members of the General and district councils.

(iii) Leave of absence and other privileges of officers of the General and district councils.

(iv) The control and management of locations and commonages.

(v) The regulation of grazing rights upon commonages.

(vi) The enclosing of arable lands by occupiers.

(vii) The regulation of the number, position, and locality of huts and kraals upon commonages.

(viii) The control and management of plantations.

(ix) The control and management of agricultural institutions and farms.

(x) The provision and regulation of public outspans.

(xi) Such other matters as may from time to time be approved by the Governor-General.

60. (1) Any regulation made under this Proclamation may prescribe a penalty for any breach thereof, and may also prescribe different penalties in case of successive breaches, but no such penalty shall exceed a fine of twenty pounds or in default of payment, imprisonment for a period of three months.

(2) In imposing any penalty upon any person convicted of a breach of any regulation made under this Proclamation the court may in addition enter judgment in favour of the General Council against the offender for such an amount as it may deem to be fair compensation to the Council for any loss or expense suffered

by it in consequence of such breach, and the said judgment shall be executed in the same manner as if it had been given in a civil action in a magistrate's court.

61. Notwithstanding the repeal of the laws specified in section *three*, all regulations lawfully made under such laws and in force immediately prior to the commencement of this Proclamation shall continue in full force and effect until specifically repealed or amended or until superseded by regulations made under this Proclamation.

CHAPTER IX

GENERAL AND SUPPLEMENTARY

62. All property, movable and immovable, lawfully acquired for council purposes whether by the collection of revenue or by expenditure under the provisions of this Proclamation, or by grant, donation, or other means, shall vest in the United Transkeian Territories General Council, and immovable property shall be duly registered.

63. (1) No member of the General or of a district council may accept any salary, allowance, fee or reward for any duty or service performed by him as such member, except in accordance with such tariff as may be framed by the Governor-General, nor shall any such person become a contractor with the council of which he is a member or be interested directly or indirectly in any contract entered into with such council.

(2) In case of any contravention by any member of the provisions of sub-section (1) the seat of such member shall, *ipso facto*, be vacated and shall be filled in the manner prescribed by this Proclamation.

64. Notwithstanding the repeal of the laws specified in section *three*, the amount of any rate that would have been leviable under any such law and which has not been collected at the commencement of this Proclamation, shall be collected in accordance with the provisions of section *fifty-two* hereof.

65. In this Proclamation, unless inconsistent with the context—

" Minister " means the Minister of Native Affairs, or the Minister for the time being in charge of Native Affairs ;

" Chief Magistrate " means the Chief Magistrate of the Transkeian Territories and includes the Chief Native Commissioner appointed under section *two* of the Native Administration Act, No. 38 of 1927, for the Transkeian Territories ;

" Local Tax " means the tax referred to in sub-section (2) of section *two* of the Natives Taxation and Development Act, No. 41 of 1925, or any amendment thereof ;

" Native quitrent " means Native quitrent as defined in section *nineteen* of the Natives Taxation and Development Act, No. 41 of 1925, or any amendment thereof.

GOD SAVE THE KING.

Given under my Hand and the Great Seal of the Union of South Africa, at Underberg, this Twenty-fourth day of October, One thousand Nine hundred and Thirty-two.

CLARENDON,
Governor-General.

By Command of His Exeecllency the
Governor-General-in-Council.

E. G. JANSEN.

Schedule

Establishments : Appointment, discipline and dismissal of pensionable officers.

Education : Scholarships.

Agriculture :

    (i)   Establishment of new agricultural institutions.

    (ii) New agricultural institution buildings.

    (iii) Acquisition and disposal of farms.

    (iv) Establishment, acquisition and disposal of plantations.

Public Works : Consideration of tenders for any service, the lowest tender for which is over £100.

General : The institution of legal proceedings.

APPENDIX F

LETTERS PATENT

NATAL NATIVE TRUST

VICTORIA by the Grace of God, of the United Kingdom of Great Britain and Ireland, Queen Defender of the Faith :—To all to whom these presents shall come, greeting !

Whereas it is expedient to provide for the disposal and management of certain lands in Our Colony in Natal, which are now or may hereafter be applicable to purposes connected with the support, advantage, or well-being of the Inhabitants of Our said Colony, of African descent, hereinafter called " Natives," and it may be convenient that such lands, or some portions thereof, or some interest therein, should be vested in an Incorporated Board of Trustees in order to such disposal and management as aforesaid.

Now know ye that WE of our especial Grace, certain knowledge and mere motion, have given, granted and ordained, and by these presents for Us, Our Heirs, and Successors do give, grant, and ordain that the following persons, that is to say the Officer for the time being administering the Government of Our said Colony, and the members for the time being of Our Executive Council of Our said Colony, and such other person as may from time to time be appointed by Us, Our Heirs, or Successors by Warrant under Our or Their Sign Manual and Signet (such appointment being in all cases revocable at Our or Their pleasure) shall be one body politic and corporate in deed and in name by the name of the " Natal Native Trust," and by that name shall have perpetual succession and shall have a common seal which may by them be selected and altered at their pleasure ; and also by that name shall and may sue and be sued, plead and be impleded in all Courts whether of Law or Equity as well as in Our United Kingdom of Great Britain and Ireland as in Our Colonial possessions.

And We do hereby ordain and declare that the said Corporation may take and hold Lands within Our said Colony of Natal, or any interest in such Lands, and may grant, sell, lease or otherwise dispose of the same Lands, in such wise as they shall deem fit, for the support, advantage, or well-being of the said Natives or for purposes connected therewith.

And We do further ordain and declare that no meeting of the said Corporation shall be held unless summoned by the Officer for the time being administering the Government of Natal and that the said Officer, or some member of the Corporation appointed by him in writing under his hand shall preside at every such meeting and that no such meeting shall proceed to business unless three members of the said Corporation at the least shall be present, and that all questions raised at any such meeting shall be decided by a majority of the votes of the members present thereat, and that no rule, order, or resolution of the said Corporation shall take effect until it shall have been signed by the Officer administering the Government in token of his assent thereto.

Subject to the above provisions We do further declare and ordain that the said Corporation may at any meeting, or meetings thereof, make rules, orders, or resolutions, respecting the conduct of their business and the appointment and removal of officers to carry on the same and respecting the functions of such officers, and respecting the acceptance, management and alienation or disposal of land and other property at any time belonging to them, and respecting all other matters pertaining to the right execution of their trust.

Provided always that We do reserve to Ourselves, Our Heirs and Successors full power and authority to alter or revoke these presents or any part of them, and through one of our principal Secretaries of State to disallow and cancel any rule, order, or resolution made by the said Corporation in virtue of the powers hereinbefore conferred upon them.

In witness whereof We have caused these Our Letters to be made Patent.

Witness Ourself at Westminister the twenty-seventh day of April in the twenty-seventh year of our reign.

By warrant under the Queen's Sign Manual,

(Signed) C. ROMILLY.

APPENDIX G

DEED OF GRANT

MATTHEW NATHAN—GOVERNOR

By His Excellency Lieutenant-Colonel Sir Matthew Nathan, Royal Engineers, Knight Grand Cross of the Most Distinguished Order of Saint Michael and Saint George, Governor and Commander-in-Chief, in and over the Colony of Natal, Vice-Admiral of the same, and Supreme Chief over the Native Population.

In the Name and on behalf of His Majesty, Edward the Seventh, by the Grace of God, of the United Kingdom of Great Britain and Ireland, and of the British Dominions beyond the Sea, King, Defender of the Faith, Emperor of India :

Whereas by Royal Letters Patent bearing date the 20th day of July, 1893, constituting the office of Governor of the Colony of Natal, the said Governor is empowered in the name and on behalf of His Majesty the King to make and execute, under the public seal of the Colony, grants and dispositions of lands within the said Colony, subject to the laws in force for the time being for regulating the sale or disposal of Crown Lands :

And whereas certain lands of the Crown situated in the Province of Zululand in the Colony of Natal, hereinafter particularly described, have been selected and set apart as reserves for occupation by the Native population of the said Province, and it is expedient that the same should be granted to trustees on behalf of the said Native population :

And whereas by the Zululand Annexation Act of 1897 it is amongst other things provided that until further provision shall have been made in that behalf with the approval of His Majesty no grants or alienation of Crown lands within the Province of Zululand shall be made, nor till then shall the Natives be disturbed in the use and occupation of any lands occupied or used by them at the time of the taking effect of the said Act :

And whereas provision has been made with the approval of His Majesty for the granting of the lands so set apart as aforesaid to trustees on behalf of the Native population of the Province of Zululand, upon the trusts and for the purposes, and subject to the conditions and reservations hereinafter set forth :

Now therefore, pursuant of the powers vested in me as aforesaid and to the provision made with the approval of His Majesty, I do hereby grant, give, and transfer to the following persons, that is to say, the Governor or other officer for the time being, administering the Government of the Colony of Natal, and the members for the time being of the Executive Council of the said Colony, as trustees, under the joint name and title of the Zululand Native Trust, the following pieces of land situated in the Province of Zululand, in the Colony of Natal, that is to say :—

Reserve No. 1.   In extent 60,000 Acres, is bounded :
Northward by the Umkuzi River,
Eastward by Umkuzi River and St. Lucia Lake,
Southward by Sibicayi River and St. Lucia Lake,
Westward by Crown Lands and False Bay.
Reserve No. 2.   In extent 29,000 Acres, is bounded :
Southward by Umsunduzi River, and otherwise by Crown Lands.
Reserve No. 3.   In extent 192,000 Acres, is bounded :
Northward by Hluhluwe Game Reserve No. 2 and Hluhluwe River,
Eastward by False Bay, Inyalazi River, and Crown Land,
Southward by the Umfolozi River,
Westward by Crown Lands and Hluhluwe Game Reserve No. 2, and
surrounding the township of Somkele.
Reserve No. 4.   In extent 58,100 Acres, is bounded :
Northward by St. Lucia Game Reserve No. 3 and Umsunduzi River,
South Eastward by the Indian Ocean (Admiralty Reserve 150 ft. wide),
Southward by Crown Land, and
Westward by Umzingazi Lake, Umdibi Stream, Crown Lands and
Umsunduzi River.
Reserve No. 5.   In extent 117,000 Acres, is bounded :
Northward by Umfolozi River,
Eastward by the Imbabe and Iduzi Rivers and Crown Lands,
Southward by the Enseleni, Ukulu and Nayagata Rivers, and
Westward by Crown Lands and the Imfamanzi River.
Reserve No. 6.   In extent 12,000 Acres, is bounded :
Eastward by Umzimgazi Lake,
Westward by Insezi Lake and otherwise by Crown Lands.
Reserve No. 7A.   In extent 10,000 Acres, is bounded :
North Eastward by Inyoni River and Leper Location,
South Eastward by Crown Land,
South Westward by Lots 14, 16, 17 and 18, and
North Westward by Reserve No. 8.
Reserve No. 7B.   In extent 17,000 Acres, is bounded :
Northward by Crown Lands,
Eastward by Crown Lands, and Lots 110, 111 and 112,
South Westward by the Umhlatuzi River, and
Westward by the Amevamhlope Stream.
Reserve No. 8.   In extent 26,000 Acres, is bounded :
Northward by Lots 75 W, 78, 98 and Crown Lands,
South Eastward by Indian Ocean (Admiralty Reserve, 150 ft. wide),
Leper Location, Reserve No. 7A and Amatikulu River,
South West by Inyoni River and Lot 28, and
North Westward by Lots 31, 34, 37, 40, 41, 42, 43, 44, 45, 46, 47, 48, 49
and 50.
Reserve No. 9.   In extent 93,000 Acres, is bounded :
North Eastward by Umhlatuzi River.
South Eastward by Crown Lands and Lots 82, 83, 84, 93, 94, 95, 102,
Westward by Wagon Road to Eshowe,
South Westward by Inyezana River,
North Westward by Reserve No. 17 and Crown Lands, and surrounds
Umgoye Forest Reserve.
Reserve No. 10.   In extent 27,000 Acres, is bounded :
Northward by Crown Lands,

South Eastward by Indian Ocean (Admiralty Reserve 150 feet wide),
South Westward by Crown Lands, and
North Westward by Mzingwenya Stream, Lots 109, 150 to 164, 124, 125, 126, 127.

Reserve No. 11. In extent 182,000 Acres, is bounded :
Northward by White Umfolozi River,
Eastward by Crown Lands,
Southward by Crown Lands, and
Westward by Proviso B.

Reserve No. 12. In extent 675,000 Acres, is bounded :
Northward by the boundary of Zululand, Mhletshe Game Reserve No. 1 and Ingweni River,
Eastward by Crown Lands, Umdhletshe Game Reserve No. 1, and Hlphluwe Game Reserve No. 2,
Southward by Hluhluwe Game Reserve No. 2, Black Umfolozi River, Crown Lands, Reserve No. 20 and Hluhluwe River,
Westward by Reserve No. 20, and Hluhluwe Game Reserve No. 2, and surrounds the Town Lands of Hlabisa and Nongoma.

Reserve No. 13. In extent 34,000 Acres, is bounded :
Northward by Crown Lands,
Eastward by Mosi Swamp and otherwise by Umkuzi River.

Reserve No. 14. In extent 640,000 Acres, is bounded :
Northward by the Boundary of Zululand,
Eastward by the Indian Ocean (Admiralty Reserve 150 feet wide), and otherwise by Crown Lands.

Reserve No. 15. In extent 10,000 Acres, is bounded :
Northwestwards by the Pongolo River, and otherwise by Crown Lands.

Reserve No. 16. In extent 306,000 Acres, is bounded :
Northward by the Usuto River,
Eastward by Crown Lands,
Westward by the Zululand Boundary,
Southward by the Umkusi River, and Zululand Boundary and surrounds the Magistracies of Ingwavuma and Ubombo.

Reserve No. 17. In extent 111,000 Acres, is bounded :
Northward by the Umvuzane and Umhlatuzi Rivers and Umhlatuzi Crown Lands,
South Eastward by Reserve No. 9, and
Southward by Umkukuzi and Umlalazi Rivers and the Crown Land Farms in the Eshowe District.

Reserve No. 18. In extent 367,000 Acres, is bounded :
Northward by the boundary of Zululand and Nondweni Crown Lands,
Eastward by the boundary of Zululand and Nondweni Crown Lands,
South Eastward by Reserve No. 10,
Westward by the boundary of Zululand and surrounds the Town Lands of Nqutu.

Reserve No. 19. In extent 396,000 Acres, is bounded :
North Eastward by the boundary of Zululand and Umhlatuzi River,
Southward by Reserve No. 17, Crown Lands, Reserve No. 21 and Tugela River,
North Westward by the boundary of Zululand and Reserve No. 18 and surrounds Qudeni Crown Lands, Nkandhla Town and Nkandhla Forest Reserve.

Reserve No. 20. In extent 305,000 Acres, is bounded :
North Eastward by Reserve No. 12,

South Eastward by Crown Lands,
Southward by White Umfolozi River,
Westward by the boundary of Zululand, and surrounds the Town Lands of Mahlabatini.
Reserve No. 21.   In extent 220,000 Acres, is bounded :
North Eastward by Crown Lands,
South Eastward by Crown Lands,
North Westward by Reserve No. 19, and otherwise by Tugela River.
be the same greater or less in extent than as aforesaid : as will more fully appear from the diagrams framed by the Surveyor and hereunto annexed.

To have and to hold the same in Perpetual Trust on behalf of the Aboriginal Native inhabitants of the Province of Zululand, hereinafter referred to as the Natives of Zululand, upon the trusts and for the purposes and subject to the conditions and reservations herein contained, that is to say :

I.

The lands shall be held for occupation by the Natives of Zululand, and for their support, advantage, and well-being and for any purposes connected therewith.

II.

The trustees may grant, sell, lease, mortgage or otherwise dispose of any part of the lands hereby granted for the support, advantage or well-being of the Natives of the Province of Zululand or for any purpose connected therewith ; but no such alienation or disposal shall be made except with the previous consent of His Majesty's Secretary of State or under the authority of a special Act of Parliament.

III.

The trustees shall have all powers necessary and incidental to the proper execution of their office and rights of ownership and to regulate and control the use and occupation of the lands, and in particular to exercise authority in any of the following matters :

(a) The apportionment of land for use and occupation by Natives.
(b) The admission of Natives as residents upon the lands.
(c) The removal of Natives from the lands.
(d) The removal of Natives from one part of the lands to another.
(e) The entry and sojourn upon the lands of persons other than resident Natives.
(f) The allotment of the lands for the use and occupation of tribes; the definition or alteration of boundaries of lands so allotted.
(g) The allotment of lands for kraal sites, and for cultivation pasturage, and commonage.
(h) All matters relating to roads, by-roads, fences, watercourses, woods and streams, and the use of water, wood, clay, and stone.
(i) The preservation of health, and observance of decency.
(j) The powers, authorities, and duties of any officers appointed under the authority given by Clause 4 hereof.
(k) The duties of Chiefs, District Headmen, and kraal-heads in connection with the lands and the distribution of people therein, the allotment of kraal sites and sites for cultivation, and the removal of kraals.

IV.

No meeting of the trustees shall be held unless summoned by the Officer for the time being administering the Government of Natal, and the said Officer or such of the trustees as shall be appointed by him in writing under his hand shall preside at every such meeting.

No such meeting shall proceed to business unless three members at least shall be present, and all questions raised at any such meeting shall be decided by a majority of the votes of the members present thereat.

No rule, order or resolution of the trustees shall take effect until it shall have been signed by the Officer administering the Government in token of his assent thereto.

Subject to the above provisions the said trustees may at any meeting or meetings make rules, orders, or resolutions respecting the conduct of their business and the appointment and removal of officers to carry on the same and respecting the functions of such officers.

V.

All rights to and in respect of any streams and water rising upon or flowing over or through the lands are hereby reserved to the Colonial Government of Natal, which shall be entitled without compensation to take any such water and lead and carry the same for any public purpose, provided that such quantities be left as shall reasonably suffice for the domestic requirements of the Natives and for enabling them to use the land according to the objects of this grant.

VI.

The Government shall at all times have the right, without compensation to the trustees, to resume and take any parts of the lands hereby granted which may be required for the purpose of any road, railway, canal, watercourse, outspan or other like public purpose. Provided however that reasonable compensation shall be made for any damage caused to crops, trees, plantations, buildings or other improvements by reason of the exercise of the aforesaid powers.

VII.

The said land shall in the same manner be liable to the entry thereupon by any person by order of the Colonial Government for the purpose of removing therefrom such materials, including timber or wood, as may from time to time be required for the construction or repair of any public road, railway or watercourse running through or over the said land or for any other public purpose.

VIII.

The trustees may from time to time make regulations respecting the acceptance and management, and subject as aforesaid, the alienation or disposal of land and other property at any time belonging to them, and for the exercise of the powers and authority committed to them by these presents, and for all other matters pertaining to the right execution of their trust.

IX.

The trustees hereinbefore appointed may sue and be sued under the name of the Zululand Native Trust.

Given under my hand and the Public Seal of the Colony at Pietermaritzburg, this 6th day of April, in the Year of Our Lord One Thousand Nine Hundred and Nine.

Signed W. A. DEANE,
Minister of Agriculture.

Prepared in the Surveyor General's Office.

Signed J. L. WATSON,
Surveyor-General.

Registrar of Deeds.

APPENDIX   H

GOVERNMENT NOTICE No. 39 DATED 22nd JANUARY, 1932
It is hereby notified for general information that His Excellency the Governor-General has been pleased, in terms of section *sixteen* (1) (*h*) of the Natives Taxation and Development Act, 1925, to approve of the accompanying Regulations for the financial administration of the Native Development Account.

REGULATIONS GOVERNING THE FINANCIAL ADMINISTRATION OF THE NATIVE DEVELOPMENT ACCOUNT
(Framed under section *sixteen* (1) (*h*) of Act No. 41 of 1925)

1.   In these regulations unless inconsistent with the context—

" Account " means the Native Development Account established under section *twelve* of Act No. 41 of 1925 ;

" accounting officer " means the accounting officer of the Department of Native Affairs :

" Act " means the Natives Taxation and Development Act, 1925, and any amendments thereof ;

" Minister " means the Minister of Native Affairs or, in his absence, any Minister of State acting in that capacity ;

" officer " includes all employees appointed under the provisions of the Act.

2.   The Financial Regulations framed under section *sixty-one* of the Exchequer and Audit Act, 1911, shall, *mutatis mutandis*, govern the administration of the Account in so far as they are not inconsistent with the Act and these regulations, provided that whenever in the Financial Regulations the authority or approval of " Parliament " or " the Treasury " is prescribed as necessary for any payment or appointment it shall be sufficient that the authority of the Minister has been obtained, and provided further that any question of the applicability or otherwise, of the Financial Regulations, shall be determined by the Minister after consultation with the Treasury.

3.   Annual Estimates of Expenditure shall be submitted to the Minister in such form as may from time to time be determined by him in consultation with the Treasury.

Copies of such estimates when approved by the Minister shall be supplied to the Secretary for Finance and the Controller and Auditor-General.

4.   Estimates of revenue for each financial year shall be submitted to the Minister by the accounting officer who shall show under such heads and in such form as may be prescribed—

(*a*)   the anticipated revenue for the ensuing financial year ;

(*b*)   the original estimates of revenue for the expiring financial year ;

(*c*)   a revised estimate of the revenues that will be received during the expiring financial year ;

T

(d) the actual receipts for the preceding financial year ;

(e) the balance brought forward from the preceding financial year ;

(f) any further particulars that may be prescribed.

5. (1) The revenue of the Account shall consist of—

(a) the grant made from the Consolidated Revenue Fund in terms of section *three* of the Act ;

(b) the moneys specified in section *twelve* of the Act ;

(c) unexpired balances repaid to the Account in terms of section *seven* of the Regulations published under Government Notice No. 1507 of the 2nd September, 1927 ;

(d) interest and profits received in respect of the investment or loan of the funds of the Account ;

(e) moneys derived from any undertaking or activity financed by the Account and fees collected in respect of any such undertaking or activity or for the services of any officer or employee of the Account ;

(f) such other moneys as may by competent authority be directed to be paid to the Account.

(2) The Account shall be divided into two sections, viz. :—

A. General Account to which shall be credited the revenues derived from sources (a), (c) and (d) above, together with the proportion of general tax included in (b) and such other revenues not included in (b) as the Minister may direct.

Payments shall be made from this section of the Account for the maintenance, extension and improvement of educational facilities amongst Natives and in respect of services which the Minister shall deem to be of a national or general character.

B. Local Account to which shall be credited all revenues other than those credited to the A General Account. Payments shall be made from this section of the Account in respect of services of a local character and in allocating expenditure due consideration shall be given, in conformity with the proviso to section *thirteen* (1) of the Act to the areas within which the moneys were collected.

6. The banking account of the Account shall be with the Paymaster-General.

7. Recoveries of advances shall be paid to the credit of that section of the Account from which the advance was made.

8. All fees received by any officer in his official capacity shall be paid to that section of the Account from which such officer's salary is paid but such fees or portion thereof may be assigned to the officer by proper authority as personal remuneration.

9. Where, on account of his professional, technical or other special qualifications the services of an officer are placed temporarily at the disposal of some other government administration or of a corporation, private body or individual, to carry out in his official capacity a service of public interest, any fee, bonus or honorarium which may be payable in respect of his work shall be paid into the Account provided that in special circumstances the Minister may authorise the payment to that officer from the Account of a sum equivalent to the fee, bonus or honorarium aforesaid, or such portion thereof as may adequately meet the needs of the case. The Controller and Auditor-General shall be advised of all such payments made to officers.

10. No moneys due directly to the Account shall be written off as irrecoverable without the authority of the Minister. Statements of all revenue so written off shall be submitted to the Controller and Auditor-General.

11. The approved Estimates of Expenditure shall serve as the authority for the accounting officer to incur expenditure on any sanctioned service or establishment to the amount authorised on the estimates.

If at any time it is found necessary to incur expenditure which will occasion an excess on the whole vote, or for any purpose or service not provided for in the estimates, the authority of the Minister shall first be obtained.

12. All questions relating to the keeping of accounts, including the interpretation of instructions and authorities, classification of expenditure and excesses upon votes, sub-heads or services arising out of authorities already given, shall be determined by the Minister in consultation with the Treasury.

13. The power of limiting or suspending expenditure provided on the estimates, if in his opinion the financial situation renders such limitation or suspension desirable, shall be vested in the Minister. All such limitations or suspensions shall be notified to the Controller and Auditor-General.

14. The Minister may authorise the application of a saving upon one sub-head to meet an excess upon another sub-head of the same or a sub-head of another vote or to meet expenditure under a new sub-head of the same or another vote and the sum required shall be regarded as transferred from the one sub-head to the other, the amount available for expenditure under the former sub-head being thereafter regarded as reduced by the sum transferred.

15. The payment of grants-in-aid to institutions, boards, committees, etc., shall be subject to the rendering of such accounts and other information relative to the expenditure of the grant as the Minister in consultation with the Controller and Auditor-General may direct.

16. Notwithstanding that provision for a post may have been made on the estimates, no appointment may be made thereto until the sanction of the Minister has been specifically obtained for the expenditure involved in making such appointment.

17. The sanction of the Minister shall be required for any increase of the fixed establishment.

The expression " increase of the fixed establishment " shall be held to cover—
(1) the creation of any new post not provided for in the estimates ;
(2) the alteration of the scale of salary attached to any existing appointment by raising the minimum or the maximum or the rate of annual increment.

18. All stationery, printing, etc., which cannot conveniently be ordered from the Printing and Stationery Department and all furniture-cleansing material, etc., required by officers shall be obtained as the Minister may direct, subject to the provisions of Regulation No. 21.

19. The Minister shall as soon as may be after the 31st March in each year cause to be published in the *Gazette* statements showing the income and expenditure of the Account during the preceding year and showing also the balances at the beginning and end of that year.

20. The Minister may authorise, for purposes to which the funds of the Account may be applied, advances or loans from the funds of either section of the Account upon such terms and conditions as he may direct.

21. The provisions of the regulations set forth in Annexure G of the Financial Regulations published under Government Notice No. 535 of the 24th March, 1926, and the Government Supplies Board Regulations published under Government Notice No. 1471 dated 11th September, 1931, shall, *mutatis mutandis*, govern in so far as applicable the purchase, receipt, custody of and the accounting for stores, livestock, libraries and equipment the property of or maintained by the Account, provided that whenever by these regulations the authority of the

Treasury is required it shall be sufficient that the authority of the Minister has been obtained.

22.   If, in exceptional cases, circumstances are brought to light which afford reasonable grounds for a departure from these regulations such departure may be authorised by the Minister after consultation with the Controller and Auditor-General and the Treasury.

APPENDIX I

GOVERNMENT NOTICE No. 1453 DATED 4th NOVEMBER, 1932

By virtue of the powers conferred upon him by section *six* of the Native Service Contract Act, 1932, His Excellency the Governor-General has been pleased to make the regulations set forth hereunder.

O. PIROW,
Minister of Justice

NATIVE SERVICE CONTRACT REGULATIONS

1. In these regulations " the Act " means the Native Service Contract Act, 1932 (Act No. 24 of 1932) and any expression to which a meaning has been assigned in the Act, shall, when used in these regulations, bear the same meaning.

2. (1) The document of identification referred to in sub-section (1) of section *two* of the Act shall—

(a) if issued [otherwise than in connection with the payment of the general tax under the Natives Taxation and Development Act, 1925 (Act No. 41 of 1925)] to a male Native who is or appears to be more than eighteen years of age, be substantially in the form set forth in the First Schedule to these regulations ;

(b) if issued to any such Native when paying such tax be substantially in the form set forth in the Second Schedule to these regulations ;

(c) if issued to a male Native who is or appears to be not more than eighteen years of age, be substantially in the form set forth in the Third Schedule to these regulations.

Provided that during the period commencing on 1st July and ending on the 31st December, 1933, any receipt issued between the 31st December, 1931, and the 1st July, 1933, to any Native for the payment of the general tax imposed by the said Act No. 41 of 1925, shall be deemed to be a document of identification of such Native, if he has not been furnished upon or after the last-mentioned date, with a document of identification in the form of the First Schedule or Second Schedule to these regulations.

(2) Such documents of identification shall be issued by all receivers as defined in section *nineteen* of the aforesaid Act No. 41 of 1925.

(3) Any male Native who is or appears to be more than eighteen years of age shall, on application (in person or by representative) to a receiver referred to in sub-section (2) be furnished free of charge with a document of identification substantially in the form of the First Schedule to these regulations if he satisfies such receiver—

(a) that he has not already been furnished with a document of identification for an adult, within the calendar year in which the application is made ; and (*b*) that he requires it for the purpose of proceeding to any place which he may lawfully visit or for the purpose of entering into a service contract or labour tenant contract.

(4) A document of identification substantially in the form of the Second Schedule to these regulations shall be issued to any male Native or his representative when he pays to a receiver referred to in sub-section (2) the general tax imposed by the said Act No. 41 of 1925.

(5) Any guardian of a Native who is or appears to be more than ten and not more than eighteen years of age shall, on application (in person or by representative) to a receiver referred to in sub-section (2) be furnished free free of charge with a document of identification for the said Native juvenile, substantially in the form of the Third Schedule to these regulations, if such guardian satisfies such receiver—

(*a*) that the juvenile requires it for the purpose of proceeding to any place which he may lawfully visit or for the purpose of entering the service of an employer, and

(*b*) that no such document was previously issued to or for such juvenile within a period of three years preceding the date of the application.

(6) If any receiver referred to in sub-section (2) is satisfied that a Native juvenile as aforesaid has no guardian or that his guardian is not available, he may in his discretion issue to such juvenile, on his own application, a document of identification.

(7) A document of identification in the form of the First or Third Schedule to these regulations shall be valid for a period of three years from the date of issue or if during that period another document of identification is issued to the holder, until the date of issue of the last-mentioned document.

(8) A document of identification in the form of the Second Schedule to these regulations shall be valid until another such document is issued to the holder, but the period of its validity shall not extend beyond the year following the year of issue.

(9) Whenever a document of identification is issued to or for a person who is the holder of another document of identification, the last-mentioned document shall be surrendered to the issuing officer.

(10) Whenever a Native to whom a document of identification was issued, satisfies a receiver referred to in sub-section (2) that such document has been lost or destroyed and applies for a new document of identification within the period of validity of the lost or destroyed document, such receiver shall furnish him, on payment of a fee of one shilling with a new document of identification which shall, if the lost or destroyed document related to an adult Native, be substantially in the form of the First Schedule to these regulations.

(11) Whenever any receiver referred to in sub-section (2) is satisfied that the holder of a document of identification produced to him has lawfully acquired a domicile different from the domincile recorded thereon, such receiver shall alter such document so as to show the holder's new domicile.

3. (1) A labour tenant contract or a service contract entered into in terms of section *three* of the Act between the guardian of a Native juvenile on behalf of such juvenile, on the one hand, and the owner of the land whereon such guardian is domiciled, on the other hand, for a period in excess of one year, or a labour tenant contract or a service contract entered into in terms of sub-section (1) of section *four* of the Act, shall be in the form, as nearly as may be, of—

(*a*) the Fourth Schedule to these regulations, if the contract is a labour tenant contract under section *three* of the Act ; or

(b) the Fifth Schedule to these regulations, if the contract is a service contract under section *three* of the Act ; or

(c) the Sixth Schedule to these regulations, if the contract is a labour tenant contract under sub-section (1) of section *four* of the Act ; or

(d) the Seventh Schedule to these regulations, if the contract is a service contract under the said sub-section (1),

and such contracts shall respectively contain the particulars for which provision is made in the said Schedules.

(2) Such contract shall be signed before and attested by a competent officer, who shall previously acquaint himself with the terms of the contract, fully explain its meaning and effect to the parties thereto and satisfy himself that the parties desire to enter into the contract as recorded.

4. (1) The Minister of Native Affairs shall from time to time cause a sufficient number of documents of identification in the form of the First and Third Schedules to these regulations to be printed and kept available at every office where there is stationed a receiver referred to in sub-section (2) of section *two* and where there is likely to be any demand for such documents.

(2) The Minister of Native Affairs shall from time to time cause a sufficient number of documents in the form respectively of the Sixth and Seventh Schedules to these regulations to be printed and kept available at the office of every Native Commissioner and every additional or assistant Native Commissioner in the Transvaal and in Natal.

(3) The forms referred to in sub-section (2) shall be furnished to any person applying therefor on payment of sixpence for every such form.

(4) The Commissioner for Inland Revenue shall from time to time cause a sufficient number of documents of identification in the form of the Second Schedule to these regulations to be printed and kept available at every office where there is stationed an officer referred to in sub-section (1).

FIRST SCHEDULE

DOCUMENT OF IDENTIFICATION UNDER ACT No. 24 OF 1932.

Date Stamp.

Holder's tax or identification number..

Holder's name and surname...

Approximate age....................

Father's name..

Chief's name ....

Headman's name..

Tribe or race ....

Domicile*...

District of domicile..

Holder's signature ....

Holder's thumb or finger impression.

....
Issuing Officer.

*If the holder's domicile is in a location as defined in Act No. 24 of 1932, insert " In a location." If he is domiciled outside such a location, insert " On private land."

WARNING TO EMPLOYERS

If the holder hereof is domiciled on private land in the Transvaal or in Natal, no person may employ him during any period unless he produces his labour tenant contract with the owner of such land (as defined in Act No. 24 of 1932) or a statement signed by such owner or his agent showing in either case that the holder is not bound to render such owner service during the said period.

ENDORSEMENTS UNDER ACT No. 24 OF 1932

Statement by Owner or his Agent in terms of Section 2 (3)

I, ...declare that I am the *Agent of the** owner (as defined in Act No. 24 of 1932) of the land whereon the holder hereof is domiciled, and that he is not obliged to render *me/my principal**

any service during the period.......................................

....
Signature of Owner or his Agent.
*Delete inapplicable words.

RECORD OF LABOUR TENANT CONTRACT OR SERVICE CONTRACT UNDER SECTION 4 (1) OR 4 (2)

Name of holder's employer..

Place of residence of holder's employer...................................

Date of labour tenant or service contract..................................
Period during which holder is bound under labour tenant or service contract (to be

specified clearly with reference to particular dates)....................

....

Wage (if any) stipulated..

Date..........................

Place..........................

....
Signature and Qualification of Competent
Officer.

SECOND SCHEDULE

TAX RECEIPT UNDER ACT No. 41 OF 1925, AND DOCUMENT
OF IDENTIFICATION UNDER ACT No. 24 OF 1932

PREVIOUS YEAR'S RECEIPT.

No.............................

Date............................

Where issued...................

Holder's Tax and identification number ....

Date stamp ....

Holder's name and surname ....

Approximate age...............

Father's name..

Chief's name..

Headman's name..

Tribe or race..

Domicile* ....

District of domicile...

Annual liability still owing : Local tax £............Quitrent £..............

Crown rent £..............

Received from holder.......................for.......................

....
Receiver : Issuing Officer.

Holder's signature..
Holder's thumb or finger impression.

*If the holder's domicile is in a location as defined in Act No. 24 of 1932,
insert " In a location."   If he is domiciled outside such a location, insert " On
private land."

WARNING TO EMPLOYERS

If the holder hereof is domiciled on private land in the Transvaal or in Natal, no person may employ him during any period unless he produces his labour tenant contract with the owner of such land (as defined in Act No. 24 of 1932) or a statement signed by such owner or his agent showing in either case that the holder is not bound to render such owner service during the said period.

ENDORSEMENT UNDER ACT No. 24 OF 1932

Statement by Owner or his Agent in terms of Section 2 (3)

I, ..., declare that I am the *Agent of the** owner (as defined in Act No. 24 of 1932) of the land whereon the holder hereof is domiciled, and that he is not obliged to render *me/my principal** any service during

the period ....

....
Signature of Owner or his Agent.
*Delete inapplicable words.

RECORD OF LABOUR TENANT CONTRACT OR SERVICE CONTRACT UNDER SECTION 4 (1) OR 4 (2)

Name of holder's employer...

Place of residence of holder's employer................................

Date of labour tenant or service contract...............................
Period during which holder is bound under labour tenant or service contract (to be

specified clearly with reference to particular dates)....................

....

Wage (if any) stipulated..

Date...........................

Place..........................

....
Signature and qualification of Competent
Officer.

THIRD SCHEDULE

DOCUMENT OF IDENTIFICATION FOR A NATIVE JUVENILE UNDER ACT No. 24 OF 1932.

Name and surname of holder...

Age or approximate age of holder at date of issue hereof.....................

Name and surname of father or other guardian of holder.....................

....

Name of holder's chief...

Name of holder's headman..

Domicile of holder's father or other guardian (state whether in or outside a location

as defined in Act No. 24 of 1932) ....

....

District of domicile..
Impression of holder's thumb or finger.

Holder's signature ....
Office date stamp.

....
Issuing Officer.

WARNING TO EMPLOYERS

No person may employ the holder hereof unless he procures his father's or other guardian's permission in writing, and if the father or other guardian is domiciled outside a location, also the permission in writing of the owner (as defined in Act No. 24 of 1932) or the agent of the owner of the land whereon the father or other guardian is domiciled. For form of permission see back.

LAND OWNER'S PERMISSION TO ENTER INTO A CONTRACT OF SERVICE (GRANTED UNDER SECTION 2 (1) OF ACT No. 24 OF 1932)

I, ..., declare that I am the *agent of the** owner (as defined in Act No. 24 of 1932) of the land whereon the father or other guardian of the holder hereof is domiciled and that the holder hereof has my permission to enter into a contract of service during the period...............

....
Signature of the Owner or his Agent.

Date...........................

Place...........................

GUARDIAN'S PERMISSION TO ENTER INTO A CONTRACT OF SERVICE (GRANTED UNDER SECTION 2 (1) OF ACT NO. 24 OF 1932)

I, ..., declare that I am the *father/guardian** of the holder hereof and that he has my permission to enter into a contract of service during the period...........................

....
Father's or guardian's signature or mark.

Date...........................

Place...........................

I, ..., declare that...........
.... in my presence placed his mark under the statement set forth above after I had explained its meaning and effect to him, and that he has in fact given the permission referred to therein.

....
Signature of Witness.
*Delete inapplicable words.

FOURTH SCHEDULE

LABOUR TENANT CONTRACT BETWEEN THE EMPLOYER OF A NATIVE JUVENILE AND THE LATTER'S GUARDIAN (UNDER SECTION 3 OF ACT No. 24 OF 1932)

Labour tenant contract entered into between ....
.........................of .... (hereinafter called the employer) and............................(hereinafter called the labour tenant) in his capacity as guardian of......................[hereinafter called the servant(s)]*

Whereas the employer is the owner (as defined in Act No. 24 of 1932) of the farm..in the District of ....and whereas the labour tenant is domiciled on the said farm ; and the servant(s) *is/are a youth/girl** of.................years of age and the *son(s)/ daughter(s)/ward(s)** of the labour tenant ; now, therefore, the employer and the labour tenant [on behalf of the servant(s)] agree as follows :—

1. The employer hereby *grants permission/confirms the permission granted** to the labour tenant to occupy and cultivate portion of the above-mentioned farm indicated to him during......................as from the .... and to keep and graze the following live stock on the said farm, namely.........
....

2. *As a part of the** consideration for such permission, the labour tenant binds the servant(s) to render to the employer at...................services as ....during†.................in respect of every period of twelve months during which the permission referred to in clause 1 continues.

3. The labour tenant hereby undertakes to place the servant(s)* in the employer's service in terms of this contract and to see to it, so far as lies in his power, that the servant(s)* fulfil(s)* *his/her/their** obligations under this contract.

4. This contract shall further be subject to the following special conditions*
....
....
....
....

Signature of Employer.

....

Signature or mark of Labour Tenant.

I declare that I am a competent officer as defined in Act No. 24 of 1932 ; that I acquainted myself with the terms of the contract set forth above ; that I fully explained its meaning and effect to the parties thereto, and that they signed it in my presence, after I had satisfied myself that they desired to enter into the contract as recorded.

....

Signature and Qualification of Attesting
Officer.

Date..........................
Place........................

*Delete inapplicable words and letters.
†Specify clearly the duration of the term of service and when the services must be rendered.

FIFTH SCHEDULE

SERVICE CONTRACT BETWEEN THE EMPLOYER OF A NATIVE JUVENILE AND THE LATTER'S GUARDIAN
(Under Section 3 of Act No. 24 of 1932)

Service contract entered into between.............of................ (hereinafter called the employer) and.....................(hereinafter called the guardian) in his capacity as guardian of..............................

....

....
[hereinafter called the servant(s)].*

Whereas the employer is the owner (as defined in Act No. 24 of 1932) of the farm.......................................in the District of.....

.... ; and whereas the guardian is domiciled on the said farm, and the servant(s) *is/are a youth(s)/girl(s)** of.........years of age and the *son(s)/daughter(s)/ward(s)** of the guardian ; now therefore the employer and the guardian [on behalf of the servant(s)]* agree as follows :—

1. The employer hereby engages the services of the servant(s)* as a ......
.......for a period of......................as from................. at a wage of...............to be paid...............in arrear to the *servant(s)/guardian,** and undertakes to furnish the servant(s)* with suitable food and accommodation.

2. The guardian hereby binds the servant(s)* to render to the employer during the aforesaid period and at..............................services
as a ....
....

3. The guardian hereby undertakes to place the servant(s)* in the employer's service in terms of this contract and to see to it, so far as lies within his power, that the servant(s) fulfil(s) *his/her/their** obligations under this contract.

4. This contract shall further be subject to the following special conditions*
....
....

....
Signature of employer.

....
Signature or mark of guardian.

I declare that I am a competent officer as defined in Act No. 24 of 1932 ; that I acquainted myself with the terms of the contract set forth above ; that I fully explained its meaning and effect to the parties thereto and that they signed it in my presence, after I had satisfied myself that they desired to enter into the contract as recorded.

Date........................
Place........................

....
Signature and qualification of attesting Officer.
*Delete inapplicable words and letters.

SIXTH SCHEDULE

LABOUR TENANT CONTRACT UNDER SECTION 4 (1) OF
ACT No. 24 OF 1932

(To be executed in duplicate.)

Labour tenant contract entered into between ....

.... of ....

(hereinafter called the employer) and....................................

(hereinafter called the labour tenant).

    1. The employer (who is the owner, as defined in Act No. 24 of 1932, of the

farm...............................in the District of..................)

hereby grants permission to*.........................to occupy and cultivate

a portion of the said farm indicated to the labour tenant, during a period of......

as from the...................................and to keep and graze

during the said period the following live stock on the said farm, namely........

....

....

    2. As a consideration for such permission the labour tenant undertakes to

render service to the employer at.........................as a...........

during†...........................in respect of every period of twelve

months during which the permission referred to in clause 1 continues.

    3. This contract shall further be subject to the following special conditions‡

....

....

....

....
                        Signature of Employer.

....
               Signature or mark of labour tenant.

    I declare that I am a competent officer as defined in Act No. 24 of 1932 ; that
I acquainted myself with the terms of the contract set forth above ; that I fully
explained its meaning and effect to the parties thereto and that they signed it in
my presence after I had satisfied myself that they desired to enter into the contract
as recorded.

    The tax or identification number on the labour tenant's document of identifi-

cation is ....

Date........................

Place........................

....
           Signature and qualification of attesting
                      officer.

---

    *Insert according to the facts of the case, " the labour tenant " or the name
and relationship to the labour tenant of the member of his family or of the kraal or
household to which he belongs, to whom the permission is granted.

    †Specify clearly the duration of the term of service and when the services
must be rendered.

    ‡To be deleted if there are no special condtions.

SEVENTH SCHEDULE

SERVICE CONTRACT UNDER SECTION 4 (1) OF ACT No. 24 OF 1932.
(To be executed in duplicate.)

Service contract entered into between.................................

....

of ....

(hereinafter called the employer) and...................................

....................(hereinafter called the servant).

1.   The employer hereby engages the services of the servant and the servant

undertakes to render service to the employer as a...........................

at..............................during a period of.....................

as from the..............................at a wage of.................

2.   This contract shall further be subject to the following special conditions*

....

....

....

....
Signature of employer.

....
Signature or mark of servant.

I declare that I am a competent officer as defined in Act No. 24 of 1932 ; that I acquainted myself with the terms of the contract set forth above ; that I fully explained its meaning and effect to the parties thereto and that they signed it in my presence after I had satisfied myself that they desired to enter into the contract

recorded.   The servant's tax or identification number is.....................

Date..........................

Place.........................

....
Signature and qualification of attesting
officer.

*To be deleted if there are no special conditions.

APPENDIX J

GOVERNMENT NOTICE NO. 672 OF 1924

NATIVES (URBAN AREAS) ACT, 1923.

MODEL LOCATION REGULATIONS.

The following Model Location Regulations, which have been framed by the Department of Native Affairs for the guidance of Urban Local Authorities, are published for general information.

Department of Native Affairs,
Pretoria, 22nd April, 1924.

J. F. HERBST,
Secretary for Native Affairs.

MODEL LOCATION REGULATIONS

(Framed under section *twenty-three* (3) of the Natives (Urban Areas) Act of 1923)

1. The following regulations shall apply to such area or areas as may be defined and set apart for the purposes of a location by the urban local authority, with the approval of the Minister of Native Affairs.

2. The urban local authority shall appoint an officer who shall be known as the location superintendent. Such officer shall reside at a place approved by the urban local authority, and shall carry out such instructions as he may receive from time to time from the urban local authority in regard to the administration of the location. He shall receive all complaints, representations, or recommendations that may from time to time be made by the inhabitants of the location, and shall lay them before the urban local authority for consideration.

3. The superintendent shall, as soon as possible after the 31st March, 30th June, 30th September, and 31st December in each year, prepare a report in regard to the conditions, health, and management of the location, which shall be laid before the urban local authority. Such reports shall be available for inspection by an officer appointed under sub-section (2) of section *eleven* of the Natives (Urban Areas) Act, 1923.

4. The superintendent shall cause a copy in English and Dutch and in the Native language most commonly used in the location of all regulations, orders, or instructions relating to the control, management, and use of the location to be posted and maintained in a conspicuous place in the location for the information of residents, and any person defacing or tampering with any such notice shall be guilty of an offence.

5. The medical officer to the urban local authority shall annually prepare a report on the health and sanitary conditions of the location, which shall be laid before the urban local authority. Copies of every such report shall be forwarded to the Administrator of the Province and the Secretary for Native Affairs.

U

6. Every person over the age of eighteen years desirous of taking up his residence in the location and erecting a dwelling for that purpose shall apply to the location superintendent for a site permit. If the superintendent is satisfied that the applicant is a fit and proper person to reside in the location he shall grant a permit and point out a site upon which a dwelling shall be erected, provided that if a dwelling is not erected within a reasonable time such permit may be cancelled and withdrawn.

Every such site shall be in extent not less than 50 feet by 50 feet.

7. The urban local authority shall from time to time issue such general directions as it may see fit in regard to the method of construction and the materials to be used in the erection of dwellings or buildings or in the addition to or alteration of any dwelling already erected, provided that no dwelling shall be erected which is not sufficiently lighted and ventilated and does not provide at least 30 square feet of floor and 300 cubic feet of air space for each intended inmate over the age of ten years, and at least half of the amount for each intended inmate below that age.

8. Any person to whom a site permit has been granted shall give notice to the superintendent of the completion of any new dwelling or building, or of the alteration of any dwelling or building occupied by him, and no such building or dwelling shall be occupied or used until it has been inspected and approved by the superintendent.

9. Every person over the age of eighteen years desirous of taking up his residence in the location and of occupying a dwelling erected by the urban local authority shall apply to the location superintendent, who shall, if he is satisfied that the applicant is a fit and proper person to reside in the location, allot to him a dwelling of the class for which application is made if such is available, and shall issue to him a residential permit authorizing him to reside therein.

10. No site permit or residential permit shall be transferred, and no site or dwelling shall be sub-let, except with the written permission of the superintendent and to a person approved of by him.

11. No person other than the holder of a site permit who has erected a dwelling in the location and the holder of a residential permit together with their wives and families, being children under eighteen years of age or unmarried daughters, shall reside in the location unless he shall first have obtained a " Lodger's permit," which shall be granted by the superintendent, if he is satisfied that the applicant is a fit and proper person therefor, and that he has found suitable accommodation. For the purposes of finding such accommodation a temporary permit for six days may be granted. All permits under this section shall specify the dwelling, with the name of the occupier thereof, in which the lodger shall alone reside. Such permit shall not be transferable. Any visitor to the location desiring to remain longer than three hours shall report himself to the superintendent, who shall, on his being satisfied that the applicant is a fit and proper person, issue to him a temporary permit available for a specified period.

12. The superintendent shall keep (in a form to be prescribed by the local authority) a register of all persons to whom site permits, residential permits, or lodger's permits are issued, and such persons shall be known as registered occupiers. The register shall set out the name, race, and occupation of every registered occupier, and the name, sex, age, and occupation (if any) of each member of his family residing with him, and shall specify the site or dwelling on or in which he resides.

13. A return showing the population of the location shall be submitted by the superintendent to the urban local authority every month.

14. The superintendent shall keep a record of the names of the persons whose applications for site permits, residential permits, or lodger's permits have been refused, and the reasons for each such refusal, and shall submit a copy of such record to the urban local authority every month.

15. Any person who shall have been refused a site permit, a residential permit, or a lodger's permit by the superintendent may appeal to the local authority and finally to the magistrate, who shall ultimately decide upon every such application.

16. The superintendent shall number each dwelling and shall, for the purpose, be provided by the local authority with proper tin plates or boards bearing the number of the dwellings legibly painted thereon in large figures, one of which plates or boards bearing the number of his dwelling shall be affixed and kept so affixed by every holder of a site permit or of a residential permit on the exterior of his dwelling in some conspicuous and convenient place, pointed out to him by the superintendent.

17. Every registered occupier shall pay to the urban local authority such sums by way of rent, charges for water and sanitary, health, medical, and other services as may be fixed in a tariff to be framed from to time by the urban local authority and approved by the Administrator and by the Minister. All such sums shall be payable monthly in advance to the superintendent.

18. Any person failing or refusing to pay any sum for which he is liable under these regulations within one month from the date on which it becomes due and payable shall be guilty of an offence, and upon conviction shall be liable to a fine not exceeding £5 or in default of payment to imprisonment with or without hard labour for a period not exceeding one month, provided that no fine paid or imprisonment undergone shall have the effect of cancelling the liability or barring an action for the recovery of the amount due by such person.

19. Any person failing or refusing to pay any sum for which he is liable under these regulations within one month from the date on which it becomes due and payable may be ordered by the superintendent to remove from the location forthwith. Any person failing to comply with such order shall be guilty of an offence, and the court in addition to any penalty may make an order for the ejectment of such person from the location.

20. If any registered occupier be ejected under the preceding section or leave his site or dwelling without the permission of the superintendent and be absent for a period of two months without paying rent or abandon his site or any dwelling for the said period, the urban local authority shall have the right to dispose of any improvements or property on the site, and after deducting the amount of any rent due and any expenses shall hand the balance of the proceeds (if any) to the person so ejected or so leaving or abandoning his site or dwelling, provided that the urban local authority shall give fourteen days' notice of its intention to exercise this right by serving such notice, where possible, on the occupier and by attaching a copy thereof to the door of the dwelling.

21. Every holder of a site permit or residential permit shall keep the dwelling and buildings on his site in good condition and order. No person shall keep or cause or suffer to be kept or deposit or allow to be deposited on any site or premises any accumulation of filth, manure, dirt, refuse, garbage, or rubbish so as to be a nuisance or injurious or dangerous to health, and the holder of a site permit or residential permit shall further keep his site free from weeds or rubbish at all times, and shall, unless exempted from such provision, whitewash or disinfect to the satisfaction of the medical officer all buildings thereon inside and outside in the months of January and July in each year, and at all such other times as the medical officer or the superintendent, acting under his instructions, may require.

22.   No outhouse, shed, fence, or other structure shall be erected on any site unless the written permission of the superintendent shall first have been obtained, and such permission shall only be given if the superintendent is satisfied that the design and the materials to be used are suitable to the purpose for which the structure is intended.   All outhouses, sheds, fences, and other structures erected without permission may be removed or destroyed by order of the superintendent.

23.   It shall be the duty of the superintendent, subject to any instructions he may receive from the urban local authority, to point out from time to time a place or places where rubbish, filth, or litter of any kind may be deposited, and each holder of a site permit shall be bound to deposit at least once during each and every week all rubbish, filth, and litter from off his site at such place as shall be set apart for the purpose from time to time by the superintendent, and any person depositing any rubbish, filth, or litter of any kind except at such place or places as shall have been pointed out, or committing any nuisance within or in the neighbourhood of the location, shall be guilty of an offence.

24.   The urban local authority shall set apart a place in or near the locatio where the inhabitants may wash clothes, and the superintendent shall from time to time issue instructions regulating the use of such wash-places by the inhabitants of the location, and any inhabitant of the location found washing clothes in any other place not set apart for such purpose shall be guilty of an offence.

25.   The urban local authority shall provide a sufficient and available supply of pure water and assign and provide sufficient and suitable sanitary conveniences for the use of the inhabitants, separate and distinct for males and females ; provided that any holder of a site permit may, with the sanction of the local authority, erect a suitable and approved pail-closet in connection with his dwelling, provided that he shall conform to the general sanitary regulations in that behalf of the urban local authority, and shall pay the charge prescribed by the regulations for the removal of night-soil from such pail-closet.

26.   In the event of any person in the location suffering from any infectious or contagious disease, the registered occupier of the dwelling in which such person resides or is found, or in the case of his death or incapacity the eldest adult resident in such hut or dwelling, shall immediately report the same to the superintendent.

27.   The medical officer or his authorized assistants may at all times enter any hut or dwelling or building in the location and examine all persons therein, and any resident who shall appear to the medical officer to be suffering from or to have been exposed to the infection of any infectious disease may by order of the medical officer be removed to such place either within or beyond such location as the urban local authority may appoint for receiving such persons, and may by a like order be therein detained until such time as, in the opinion of the medical officer, he shall be free from infection.

28.   The registered occupier of any dwelling in which a birth or death occurs, or, in the case of his death or incapacity, the eldest adult resident in such dwelling, shall forthwith report the same to the superintendent.

29.   The superintendent shall keep in a form to be prescribed by the urban local authority a register showing the number and other description of the horses, mules, donkeys, horned cattle, sheep, goats, pigs, and dogs belonging to every inhabitant.   All horses, mules, donkeys, horned cattle, sheep, goats, and pigs which may be found in the location, and which have not been so registered as aforesaid, or of whose arrival no notice has been given to the superintendent, or of the rights to or ownership of which no satisfactory account shall be given to the superintendent, may be seized and taken possession of by him, and be impounded in the nearest pound, and shall thereupon be dealt with and treated as other impounded animals in the said pound.

30. The local authority shall assign a place or places in the neighbourhood of the location for the erection of kraals, enclosures, sheds, or buildings for keeping such stock as may be the property of the inhabitants of the location, and shall make such orders as may be necessary and reasonable for the proper regulation thereof ; and no person shall keep any horse, mule, donkey, horned cattle, sheep, goat, or pig within the location except with the permission of the superintendent and subject to his being satisfied in regard to the suitability and cleanliness of the accommodation provided therefor.

31. For the purposes of enabling the superintendent to keep any register required by these regulations, it shall be the duty of every inhabitant of the location to give the superintendent such information as he may require for the purpose, and every such person who, on being requested by the superintendent to do so, shall neglect or refuse without reasonable cause to give such information shall be guilty of an offence.

32. No person other than a registered occupier, his wife and family, being children under eighteen years of age or unmarried daughters, or the holder of a temporary permit, shall be in the location between the hours of 9 p.m. and sunrise unless he can show that his presence in the location is for good and sufficient reasons.

33. The superintendent may prohibit any entertainment in the location which, from its character, is in his opinion likely to create a disturbance or be a nuisance to the residents. The registered occupier of any site on which such prohibited entertainment takes place, as well as all persons taking part therein, shall be guilty of an offence.

34. Every person who shall obstruct the superintendent or other employee of the urban local authority in the execution of his duty shall be guilty of an offence and be liable on conviction to a fine not exceeding £5 sterling.

35. Any person or persons contravening any of the location regulations in respect of which a penalty is not specially provided shall, upon first conviction, be liable to a fine not exceeding two pounds sterling, and upon second or subsequent conviction to a fine not exceeding five pounds sterling.

36. Every inhabitant of the location shall have the right to appeal to the magistrate against any action of the location superintendent or other official of the local authority charged with the administration of the regulations. After due inquiry, at which the location superintendent or official of the local authority shall be entitled to be heard in support of his action, the magistrate shall be empowered to order such location superintendent or official of the local authority to grant the appellant facilities under the regulations if he is of opinion that such have been unreasonably withheld.

37. " Magistrate " shall for the purposes of these regulations include a Native commissioner or Native sub-commissioner.

ADVISORY BOARDS

1. The Advisory Board shall consist of three members elected by the registered occupiers as herein after provided and three members appointed by the urban local authority. The superintendent of the location/Native village shall be *ex officio* chairman of the board.

2. The superintendent shall in the month of December of each year summon a meeting of all the registered occupiers in the location/Native village for the purpose of nominating members of the Advisory Board for the ensuing calendar year, of which meeting public notice shall be given by posting an announcement thereof in some conspicuous place in the location/Native village for a period of not less than fourteen days.

3.   Where there is no Advisory Board in existence at the date of the promulgation of these regulations, the superintendent shall as soon as practicable issue a notice as herein before provided summoning a meeting for the nomination of members of an Advisory Board.   Such members when elected shall hold office till the 31st December following their election.

4.   No registered occupier in the location who has not paid all rent or charges due by him to the urban local authority at the date of his nomination and no person who has within twelve months preceding the date of nomination been convicted of any crime and sentenced to imprisonment without the option of a fine shall be eligible for election as a member of the board.

5.   Nominations for election as members of the board shall be submitted in writing to the returning officer, and no nomination shall be received unless supported by the signatures or marks of at least ten registered occupiers, each of whom has paid his rent up to the end of the month preceding that in which the nominations are called for.

6.   Such nominations shall be lodged with the returning officer not later than the tenth day from the date of the public notice convening a meeting for the purposes of the election, and thereupon public notification by notice posted at the office of the superintendent of the names and nominees shall be given.

7.   At a meeting on the date and hour fixed for the purpose the returning officer shall after explaining the object of such meeting announce the names of the nominees, and if no more than three qualified residents have been nominated he shall declare such nominees to be duly elected as members of the board.   In the event of more than three nominations being made the returning officer shall fix a day on which a poll shall be held not more than fourteen days after the holding of the meeting, and shall announce for what period, being not less than two hours between 8 a.m. and 10 p.m., the poll shall be open on such day.   The returning officer shall fix the hours during which the poll shall be open, having regard to the convenience of the majority of the registered occupiers of the location or Native village.

8.   The returning officer shall cause to be posted at the office of the superintendent, not less than seven days before the polling day, a notice intimating the date upon which, the place at which and the hours during which the poll shall be held.

9.   On the polling day the returning officer shall attend during the hours fixed at the place announced as the polling station and shall record the votes given for each candidate.

10.   No person other than the returning officer, his assistants, and the person at the time recording his vote shall be admitted to the polling station.

11.   No registered occupier shall be allowed to vote at any election unless he shall produce a receipt showing that his rent up to the end of the month preceding that in which the election is held has been paid.

12.   The returning officer after satisfying himself that the person desirous of recording his vote is entitled to do so shall ask him for which of the candidates nominated he wishes to vote, and shall record the votes given by any such person, being not more than the number of candidates to be elected, by placing a mark opposite the name of each candidate named by the elector on a list of names of the nominated candidates.   The returning officer shall thereupon mark such person's receipt to show that a vote has been recorded in respect thereof.

13.   As soon after the closing of the poll as practicable the returning officer shall count the votes given for each nominated candidate and shall announce the election of the three candidates who have received the greatest number of votes.

14.   In the case of a tie the question as between the candidates obtaining an equal number of votes shall be determined by the casting of lots.

15.   The members of the board shall hold office for a period of one year, but shall be eligible for reappointment.

16.   In case any member be convicted of any crime and sentenced to imprisonment without the option of a fine, or shall be convicted of any contravention of the location regulations, or shall leave the limits of the location for a period exceeding six weeks without having obtained leave of absence from the board, or shall fail to attend three consecutive meetings of the board, or shall resign or shall from illness, death, or other causes become incapable of further service, such member's seat shall, *ipso facto*, be vacated, and the returning officer shall thereupon proceed to hold a fresh election to fill the vacancy in the manner laid down in the preceding sections of these regulations, and any member thus elected to fill any vacancy shall hold office up to the date of the expiration of the term of office of the member whose place he had filled.

17.   The ordinary meeting of the board shall be held once a month on such day and at such hour as the superintendent may fix after consultation with the members of the board.   Notice of all such meetings shall be posted at the superintendent's office at least three days before the meeting.

18.   The chairman may at any time, upon being satisfied of the necessity of so doing, call a special meeting of the board ; but no business shall be transacted at any special meeting except such as the meeting may have been specially convened to consider.

19.   The chair shall be taken at the appointed hour, but if at the expiration of a quarter of an hour after the appointed time there shall not be a sufficient number of members present to form a quorum, the chairman shall declare the meeting adjourned until the date of the following meeting or such earlier date as may appear desirable.   And notice of such adjourned meeting shall be posted at the superintendent's office at least three days before the date thereof.

20.   Four members shall form a quorum.

21.   The names of members present and the proceedings of the meeting shall be recorded in a minute book to be kept by such person as the chairman shall appoint to act as secretary, and the business of the meeting or adjourned meeting shall be commenced by the reading and confirmation of the minutes of the previous meeting or day's proceedings.   Minutes when so read and confirmed shall be attested by the chairman's signature in the presence of the members.   A copy of the minutes shall after each meeting be sent by the chairman to the urban local authority.

22.   It shall be the duty of the secretary to bring to the notice of the chairman all matters which may have been reserved for consideration from a previous meeting and all notices of motion received by him, and the chairman shall place such matters before the board for discussion, but the order of business subsequent to the confirmation of the minutes shall be in his discretion.

23.   In discussing any question before the board, the speaker shall address the chair standing.

24.   If two members address the chair at the same time and neither shall give way, the chairman shall call upon the one who is in his opinion entitled to precedence.

25.   When a motion or amendment is made by a member, it must be seconded by another member, otherwise it shall be dropped, and all further debate on the subject shall be discontinued, and an entry shall be made in the minutes that such was not seconded.

26.   A motion or amendment previously to being put to the vote shall be read aloud by the secretary or chairman.

27.   A motion or amendment, made or seconded, shall not be withdrawn unless by leave of the board.

28.   Every member present who is entitled to vote shall give his vote on a division, unless he shall assign a reason judged by the chairman to be sufficient for declining to vote, but no member shall vote on any matter in which he has any pecuniary interest.

29.   " Returning officer " means the person appointed by the magistrate or Native commissioner of the district in which the urban area is situated to exercise the powers and perform the duties assigned to returning officers by these regulations

APPENDIX K

PROCLAMATION No. 168 OF 1932 : NATAL CODE OF NATIVE LAW

Whereas it is expedient to amend the Natal Code of Native Law contained in the Schedule to Natal Law No. 19 of 1891 and various amending statutes :

And whereas such Code and amendments were continued in full force and effect by section *twenty-four* of the Native Administration Act, 1927 (Act No. 38 of 1927), except in so far as amended under the provisions of that section :

And whereas provision is made in the said section *twenty-four* of the said Act for extending the operation of the said Code of Native Law and any amendment thereof to Zululand in the Province of Natal :

Now, therefore, under and by virtue of the powers vested in me by section *twenty-four* of the Native Administration Act, 1927 (Act No. 38 of 1927), I do hereby proclaim, declare and make known as follows :—

1. The said Natal Code of Native Law shall be and is hereby amended—
(a) by the substitution of the Schedule to this Proclamation for the Schedule to Law No. 19 of 1891 (Natal) ; and
(b) by the repeal of the following Natal Acts, that is to say :—
> Act No. 13 of 1894.
> Act No. 40 of 1896.
> Act No. 8 of 1897.
> Act No. 5 of 1898.
> Act No. 1 of 1901.
> Act No. 25 of 1902.
> Act No. 47 of 1903.
> Act No. 7 of 1910.

2. The operation of the said Code of Native Law as amended by this Proclamation is hereby extended to Zululand.

3. The provisions of this Proclamation shall commence and take effect from the 1st November, 1932.

GOD SAVE THE KING.

Given under my Hand and the Great Seal of the Union of South Africa, at Pretoria, this Seventeenth day of September One thousand Nine hundred and Thirty-two.

CLARENDON,
Governor-General.

By Command of His Excellency the
Governor-General-in-Council.
E. G. JANSEN.

SCHEDULE

NATAL CODE OF NATIVE LAW

INTRODUCTORY

This Code is divided into seventeen chapters which severally relate to the following subject matters :—

CHAPTER I

EXPLANATORY

1. (1) In this Code " The Act " means the Native Administration Act, No. 38 of 1927, as amended, and any expression used in the Act shall when used in this Code have the same significance except in so far as is herein otherwise expressly provided.

(2) In this Code terms connoting family relationships such as " husband," " wife " and the like in addition to their ordinary significance are applied to such relationships arising out of customary unions, and the terms " divorce," " nullity," " married " and " unmarried " have a corresponding application.

(3) In this Code :—

(a) " Affiliation " means the attachment of one or more junior houses to a senior or superior house—either the *indhlunkulu*, the *ikohlo* or the *iqadi*—for the purpose of providing against the failure of an heir in such senior or superior house, and " affiliated " has a corresponding meaning.

(b) " Chief's Deputy " replaces the term " District Headman " hitherto in use and means any person appointed by a Chief under the provisions of section *seventeen* to control any particular section of his tribe.

(c) " Chief Native Commissioner " means the Chief Native Commissioner appointed for the Province of Natal under sub-section (1) of section *two* of the Act.

(d) " Customary union " means a " customary union " as defined in the Act provided that such has been entered into in accordance with the essential requirements prescribed by this Code.

(e) " *Etula* " in so far as it is enforceable at law means the custom whereby an obligation is imposed upon a junior house to refund *lobolo* which may have been taken from a senior house to establish such junior house. The *lobolo* of the eldest daughter of such junior house is usually indicated as the source from which the liability is to be met but the custom is not recognised as extending to the handing over of the " *etula* " girl herself as a pledge of payment.

(f) " House " means the family and property, rights and status, which commence with, attach to and arise out of the customary union of any Native woman or the marriage of any Native woman.

(g) " House property " means property vested in and pertaining specially to any house in a kraal. Such property is acquired by donations or apportionment and by receipt of *lobolo* in respect of the girls of the house.

(h) " *Ikohlo* " (*ikohlwa*) is the left hand senior house of a kraal which has been divided into sections as described in section *one hundred* and with its affiliated houses forms the *ikohlo* (*ikohlwa*) section ; it is usually established with kraal property and does not, in the absence of an express declaration to the contrary, make any refund of such property.

(i) " *Indhlunkulu* " means the " great house "—the chief house in a kraal ; from it the other houses take their position and with its affiliated houses it forms the *indhlunkulu* section of the kraal.

(j) " Inmate " in relation to a " kraal " means a person usually residing therein and includes the head of a family resident in a kraal subject to the control of the kraal head.

(k) " *Iqadi* " (*inqadi*) is the right hand senior house of a kraal which has been divided into sections as described in section *one hundred* and with its affiliated houses forms the *iqadi* (*inqadi*) section ; for purposes of succession it ranks next to the *indhlunkulu* section.

(l) " Kraal " means the domestic establishment and ordinary place of residence of Natives and may consist of one or more houses and includes individual dwellings occupied by Natives on mission stations or private lands.

(m) " Kraal head " means the owner or the person having charge of a kraal.

(n) " Kraal property " means all the property in a kraal other than (i) property vesting in or pertaining specially to any particular house of that kraal and (ii) the personal property of any major inmate or of any inmate not related to or belonging to the family of the kraal head.

(o) " *Lobolo* " means cattle or other property which in consideration of an intended customary union the intended husband, his parent or guardian or other person agrees to deliver to the parent or guardian of the intended wife.

(p) " *Ngqutu Beast* " means a beast which is payable by the husband or seducer as the case may be to a woman, or the house to which she belongs, upon the entrance into a customary union or the seduction of her daughter.

(q) " Official witness " means a person appointed as such under section **sixteen** to officiate at the celebration of customary unions.

(r) " *Sisa* " means a custom whereby cattle or other livestock are deposited by their owner with some other person on the understanding that such person shall enjoy the use of them, but that the ownership shall remain with and increase accrue to the depositor.

(s) " *Ukungena* " means a union with a widow undertaken on behalf of her deceased husband by his full or half brother or other paternal male relative for the purpose (i) in the event of her having no male issue by the deceased husband of raising an heir to inherit the property or property rights attaching to the house of such widow or (ii) in the event of her having such male issue of increasing the nominal offspring of the deceased.

(t) " *Ukuvusa* " means a form of vicarious union which occurs when the heir at law or other responsible person uses property belonging to a deceased person or his own property to take a wife for the purpose of increasing or resuscitating the estate of such deceased person or to perpetuate his name and provide him with an heir.

(4) The following terms are not used elsewhere in this Code but in Native law have the meanings respectively assigned to them hereunder :—

(a) " *Insonyama* " denotes certain choice portions of a beast which under one form of the " *etula* " custom are in recognition of status handed over by an inferior house to the head of a superior house in the kraal when a beast is slaughtered by such inferior house. Observance of this custom is of evidential value in determining the status of the houses concerned but is not enforceable at law.

(b) " *Isizinda* " denotes the appointment by a kraal head of one of his sons— usually the first born son—to be the formal head of the family in his own stead after his decease. The appointment carries with it no property rights or obligations.

(c) " *Umhlubulo* " denotes certain portions of a beast which under one form of the " *etula* " custom are handed over by the head of a superior house to and are the perquisite of an inferior house in the kraal when a beast is slaughtered by such superior house. Observance of this custom is of evidential value in determining the status of the houses concerned but is not enforceable at law.

CHAPTER II

THE SUPREME CHIEF AND SUPREME CHIEF'S ORDERS

2. The Governor-General, as Supreme Chief, shall in respect of Natives in the Province of Natal exercise and enjoy all powers, authorities, functions, rights, immunities and privileges which according to the laws, customs and usages of Natives are exercised and enjoyed by any Supreme or Paramount Native Chief and which shall be deemed *inter alia* to include the following :—

(a) Power to call upon chiefs personally to render military or other service and to supply armed men or levies for the suppression of disorder or rebellion.

(b) Authority in the exercise of his functions and powers to punish disobedience of his orders or disregard of his authority by fine or imprisonment or by both fine and imprisonment.

(c) The function of Upper Guardian of all Native orphans and minors in law.

3. (1) The orders and directions of the Supreme Chief may be carried into execution by the Secretary for Native Affairs, the Chief Native Commissioner,

any Native commissioner or any other officer duly authorized by the Supreme Chief or by the Minister of Native Affairs. Any such person in carrying out such orders and directions shall be regarded as the deputy or representative of the Supreme Chief.

(2) Any order or direction of the Supreme Chief may be transmitted by telegram to the person or persons charged with the execution thereof and such telegram shall be sufficient authority for such person or persons to act upon such order or direction : provided that any such telegram shall within a period not exceeding fourteen days be confirmed by certificate under the hand of the Secretary for Native Affairs or of the Chief Native Commissioner.

(3) Any order made or direction given by the Supreme Chief shall be sufficient authority to the person or persons charged with the execution thereof and to all others, upon whom the duties thereunder or derived therefrom may successively devolve, to do all such things and to give all such instructions as are required for the effective carrying out of the order or direction.

4. The authority of administrative officers under this Code shall be deemed to include such incidental powers as may be necessary to ensure that their administration is not impede d or rendered nugatory for want of definite provision therefor.

5. (1) The Supreme Chief, the Minister of Native Affairs, the Secretary for Native Affairs, the Chief Native Commissioner, and Native commissioners may command the attendance of chiefs and Natives for any purpose of public interest, public utility, or for the purpose of carrying out the administration of any law, at any reasonable time and under reasonable circumstances, and in pursuance of any such purpose may require them to render obedience, assistance, and active co-operation in the execution of any reasonable order.

(2) Disregard or defiance of any order made under the provisions of sub-section (1) shall be deemed to be disregard or defiance of an order of the Supreme Chief and any Native guilty thereof or showing disrespect to any officer referred to in sub-section (1) shall be guilty of an offence.

(3) When any such offence as is in sub-section (2) referred to is committed under circumstances rendering prompt action necessary, any such officer as is specified in sub-section (1) may order the immediate arrest of the offender and call upon him to show cause why he should not be punished. Should he fail to furnish a satisfactory explanation such officer may summarily punish the offender by a fine not exceeding ten pounds or by imprisonment for a period not exceeding two months.

(4) Any action taken as in sub-section (3) provided by a Native commissioner shall be reported immediately to the Chief Native Commissioner who may confirm, reduce, or disallow the punishment.

(5) Any punishment imposed under the provisions of sub-section (3) shall, subject to the provisions of sub-section (4), on a certificate under the hand of the officer who imposed it, have effect and be acted upon by the Native commissioner of the district as if it were a sentence passed by him in the exercise of criminal jurisdiction duly conferred upon him under section *nine* of the Act.

(6) A Native summarily punished as in sub-section (3) provided shall not, unless the punishment be disallowed by the Chief Native Commissioner, be prosecuted in any court of law for the same offence.

6. (1) When any homicide, assault, theft or other injury to person or property has occurred and it is shown to the satisfaction of the Supreme Chief that the same was caused by Natives and if there is reason to believe that there is a combination or conspiracy among any tribe or community or body of Natives to suppress evidence relating to such offence or to conceal the identity of the perpetrator or

perpetrators thereof, or by passive or other resistence to constituted authority to encourage the repetition of such offence, it shall be lawful for the Supreme Chief to impose a fine not exceeding twenty pounds or four head of cattle upon each or any of the adult male members of such tribe, community or body.

(2) From the proceeds of any fine imposed under sub-section (1) the Minister may award to any person injured by the offence such compensation as he deems equitable and just.

7. (1) Any Native who shall participate in an assembly of armed men held without authority or who shall directly or indirectly promote or assist in any such assembly shall be guilty of an offence, whether or not such assembly leads to a breach of the peace or other offence.

(2) When any such assembly as is referred to in sub-section (1) has taken place and it is shown to the satisfaction of the Supreme Chief that there is a combination or conspiracy among any tribe or community or body of Natives or between different tribes, communities or bodies of Natives to suppress the names of those who participated in, promoted or otherwise assisted in such assembly or to conceal or shield any such person or persons from justice, it shall be lawful for the Supreme Chief to impose a fine not exceeding twenty pounds or four head of cattle upon each or any of the adult male members of any such tribe, community or body.

8. Whenever the Supreme Chief is satisfied that any Native is dangerous to the public peace, if left at large, he may by proclamation authorise the summary arrest and detention of such Native in such place and subject to such conditions as he may determine ; provided that any Native so arrested and detained may after the lapse of three months from the date of his arrest apply to the Supreme Court for his release, which shall thereupon be granted by the said Court unless such person shall then be detained under lawful warrant other than such proclamation.

9. (1) Any punishment, whether of fine or imprisonment, imposed by the Supreme Chief may be enforced under the authority of an order signed on behalf of the Supreme Chief by the Secretary for Native Affairs specifying the punishment and the Native by whom it is to be suffered ; provided that in the case of a fine imposed upon each adult male member of any tribe or community, as in sub-section (1) of section *six*, or in sub-section (2) of section *seven* provided, it shall not be necessary to specify by name each Native by whom such fine is payable.

(2) Every such order, or a copy thereof certified by the Chief Native Commissioner, shall be forwarded to the Native commissioner of the district in which such Native may be found and shall have effect and be acted upon by the Native commissioner as if it were a sentence passed by him in the exercise of criminal jurisdiction duly conferred upon him under section *nine* of the Act.

(3) The Supreme Chief may remit the whole or any part of any punishment, whether of fine or imprisonment, imposed by him.

10. (1) Neither the Supreme Court nor any other court of law shall have jurisdiction to question or pronounce upon the validity or legality of any act done, direction or order given or punishment inflicted by the Supreme Chief in the exercise of his powers, authorities, functions, rights, immunities and privileges.

(2) No interdict or other legal process shall issue for the stay of any administrative act or order of any officer acting as the representative or deputy of the Supreme Chief or requiring any such officer to answer any suit or proceedings in respect of any such act or order unless the court be satisfied that *prima facie* the act or order is without lawful authority.

CHAPTER III

TRIBAL BOUNDARIES

11. Tribal boundaries shall be as defined from time to time under paragraph (*a*) of sub-section (1) of section *five* of the Act and boundaries previously defined in terms of section *five* of Act No. 40 of 1896 (Natal) or any prior law shall unless and until changed or modified, be deemed to have been defined under the said paragraph.

12. A Native shall be deemed to be a member of the tribe of the chief within whose area of jurisdiction he resides ; provided that when the effect of the definition of any boundary is to separate a Native from his own tribe or chief, such Native may, with the approval of the Native commissioner and subject to the provisions of section *fourteen*, within two years of such definition remove to the area appointed for such tribe or chief : Should he fail to do so, he shall, after the expiry of the said period of two years, be deemed to have incorporated himself in the tribe of and to be subject in all respects to the chief within whose area of jurisdiction he has remained.

13. Any Native disregarding any tribal boundary duly defined or without authority removing from the area of any tribe to and taking up his abode in that of another shall be guilty of an offence.

14. No Native shall remove his kraal from one district to another except with the approval of the Chief Native Commissioner.

CHAPTER IV

CHIEFS AND HEADMEN

15. The powers, authorities, duties, functions, rights and privileges of chiefs and headmen are as prescribed in the Act and the regulations framed thereunder read in conjunction with this Code.

16. (1) Chiefs and headmen are responsible for the appointment of a sufficient number of official witnesses to serve the requirements of the tribes or communities under their jurisdiction as regards the celebration of customary unions, for the due compliance by the members of such tribes or communities with the regulations relating to such unions and for the due notification to the Native commissioner by the official witnesses of all such unions.

(2) A chief or headman may with the approval of the Native commissioner terminate the appointment of any official witness falling under his jurisdiction and when so directed by the Native commissioner must terminate any such appointment.

17. (1) Chiefs are responsible for the appointment of a sufficient number of chief's deputies for sections of their tribes, such appointments being subject to the approval of the Native commissioner.

(2) For the purposes of section *twelve* of the Act the term " chief " shall be deemed to include a chief's deputy.

(3) A chief may with the approval of the Native commissioner terminate the appointment of any chief's deputy in respect of any section of his tribe and when so directed by the Native commissioner must terminate any such appointment : provided that the appointment of any chief's deputy, who has been authorized under section *twelve* of the Act read in conjunction with sub-section (2) of this section to hear and determine civil claims, may not be terminated except with the approval of the Supreme Chief.

18. Chiefs and headmen have authority to require compliance by the people under their jurisdiction with their duties under Native law and may give orders

for that purpose. The enforcement of obedience to authority, of the duty of children to their parents and of the obligations of inmates of kraals towards their kraal heads shall in particular fall within the scope of their authority. In exercising their functions under this section chiefs and headmen may impose a fine not exceeding two pounds for any defiance or disregard of their orders.

19. (1) In carrying out or causing to be carried out the directions or orders of the Supreme Chief, chiefs and headmen act as his minor deputies and when so acting may impose a fine not exceeding two pounds for any act of defiance or of disobedience to a lawful order.

(2) Native commissioners in their capacity as deputies of the Supreme Chief have power to enquire into all acts of chiefs and headmen in their capacity as minor deputies of the Supreme Chief.

20. In exercising their lawful judicial functions, chiefs and headmen are entitled to the privileges of a court of law in respect of disobedience of their orders or contempt of court and may impose a fine not exceeding two pounds for any such offence.

21. A fine imposed by a chief or headman under the provisions of this Code shall for the purposes of appeal and recovery be regarded as a fine imposed in the exercise of jurisdiction under section *twenty* of the Act. Should any such fine be not paid or recovered or be paid or recovered only in part, the person in default may be brought before the Native commissioner having jurisdiction, who after due enquiry may sentence the defaulter to imprisonment for a period not exceeding one month in lieu of payment of the fine.

22. Any Native found in a chief's or headman's kraal and unable to give a satisfactory account of himself or any Native disturbing the peace within the precincts of such kraal shall be guilty of an offence and may be arrested by order of such chief or headman and charged with the offence before the Native commissioner.

23. (1) For the purposes of *general* succession as in section *one hundred and nine* defined, the heir of a deceased hereditary chief shall be the person whom the Governor-General appoints or recognises for appointment, under sub-section (7) of section *two* of the Act, as successor to the chieftainship.

(2) Before deciding whom to appoint or to recognise for appointment, under sub-section (7) of section *two* of the Act, as chief in succession to a hereditary chief, the Governor-General, should he by reason of any dispute or other circumstance deem it desirable, may cause inquiry to be made by three advisers to be appointed by him. Such advisers shall be selected by reason of their special knowledge of the language, customs and laws of the Natives and shall report to the Governor-General through the Chief Native Commissioner. They shall have all the powers conferred by law on magistrates' courts for the summoning of witnesses, their examination under oath and to compel the production of documents.

24. (1) In all cases of disputed chieftainship or succession to chieftainships, of tribal quarrels or dissatisfaction and of friction between chiefs or tribes the Chief Native Commissioner shall make enquiry personally or otherwise, as he may deem best, for the information of the Supreme Chief.

(2) In exercising his functions under sub-section (1), the Chief Native Commissioner or his deputy shall have all the powers conferred by law on magistrates' courts for the summoning of witnesses, their examination under oath and to compel the production of documents.

CHAPTER V

PERSONAL STATUS

25. Every Native is either a kraal head or a kraal inmate subject to the kraal head in all kraal matters.

26. Any Native may acquire property, but this right, in so far as females, minor sons and kraal inmates are concerned, is subject to the provisions of section *thirty-five*.

27. (1) A Native male becomes a major in law on marriage or upon entering into a customary union, or on attaining the age of twenty-one years. For the purposes of this sub-section age may in the absence of proof be determined and recorded by the Native commissioner whose decision shall be final.

(2) Subject to the provisions of section *twenty-eight* a Native female is deemed a perpetual minor in law and has no independent powers save as to her own person and as specially provided in this Code.

28. (1) Any unmarried female, widow or divorced woman, who is the owner of immovable property or who by virtue of good character, education, thrifty habits or any other good and sufficient reason is deemed fit to be emancipated, may be freed from the control of her father or guardian by order of the Native commissioner's court and vested with the full powers of a kraal head or with full rights of ownership in respect of any property she may have acquired and with full power to contract or to sue or be sued in her own name. Any such widow or divorced woman may in the discretion of the court be given control over the property of her minor children.

(2) Application by a woman for emancipation as in sub-section (1) provided shall be upon affidavit and motion to the court of the Native commissioner having jurisdiction and upon notice to the applicant's father or guardian and the court shall grant its order thereon.

29. A minor shall not be competent to enter into a contract except with the assistance or consent, express or implied, of his guardian. A contract otherwise entered into by a minor shall not be valid or binding unless shown to be for the benefit of such minor or of the kraal to which he belongs.

30. A child born of an unmarried Native woman becomes a member of the house of the mother of such woman and is subject to the kraal head. In the event of a subsequent customary union between the parents of such illegitimate child, it becomes a member of the house established by the union.

31. A child born of a married woman during the subsistence of a customary union entered into by her ranks as a child of the house of such married woman.

32. (1) (a) A child born of a widow becomes a member of the family of such widow's deceased husband.

(b) A child born of a divorced woman within ten months of her divorce becomes a member of the family of such woman's previous husband.

(c) A child born of a divorced woman after the lapse of ten months from the date of her divorce becomes a member of the family of such woman's father or guardian.

(2) Notwithstanding anything in sub-section (1) in the event of a subsequent customary union between the parents of a child born of a widow or divorced woman after the lapse of ten months from the date of her becoming a widow or of her divorce, as the case may be, such child becomes a member of the house established by the union.

Chapter VI

Kraal Heads

33. The head of a kraal is such by virtue of being either—

(a) the owner thereof ; or

(b) the guardian during the minority of the heir in accordance with the provisions of section *forty-six* ; or

(c) the guardian appointed by the Native commissioner or the Chief Native Commissioner under the circumstances described in sections *forty-seven* and *forty-eight*.

34. (1) In the case referred to under paragraph (b) of section *thirty-three*—

(a) the heir may assume control of the kraal on attaining majority in accordance with the provisions of section *twenty-seven* or otherwise at such time as the Native commissioner or the chief may determine ;

(b) the kraal head administers the general estate during the minority of the heir and also such house property as may be in the kraal for the benefit of the future kraal head and house heirs respectively and is subject to the duties and responsibilities of an ordinary kraal head.

(2) In the case referred to under paragraph (c) of section *thirty-three* the kraal head during the period of his appointment administers the general estate and also such house property as there may be in the kraal and is subject to the duties and responsibilities of an ordinary kraal head.

35. (1) A kraal head is entitled to the earnings of his minor children and to a reasonable share of the earnings of the other members of his family and of any other kraal inmates. Such earnings are to be utilized by him primarily for the maintenance and benefit of the houses providing them and for general kraal purposes.

(2) While a kraal head is allowed a wide discretion in disposing of the earnings referred to in sub-section (1) it is not permissible for him to benefit one house at the expense of another.

(3) A kraal head acting unreasonably in the exercise of his rights under this section may be restrained by the Native commissioner or the chief.

36. The kraal head is the owner of all kraal property in his kraal. He has charge, custody and control of the property attaching to the houses of his several wives and may in his discretion use the same for his personal wants and necessities, or for general kraal purposes or for the entertainment of visitors. He may use, exchange, loan or otherwise alienate or deal with such property for the benefit of or in the interests of the house to which it attaches, but should he use property attaching to one house for the benefit or on behalf of any other house in the kraal an obligation rests upon such other house to return the same or its equivalent in value.

37. It is the duty of the kraal head to keep distinct the estates of the various houses in his kraal and to settle all disputes in regard thereto.

38. The inmates of a kraal irrespective of sex or age are in respect of all kraal matters under the control of and owe obedience to the kraal head.

39. A kraal head is responsible to his chief and to the Supreme Chief for the good conduct of the inmates of his kraal and acquires rights and incurs obligations under contracts entered into by the inmates of his kraal when acting with his authority express or implied.

40. Notwithstanding anything to the contrary in any other law, a kraal head may within the precincts of his kraal summarily arrest any person defying his authority or disturbing the peace or committing or reasonably suspected of committing or attempting to commit any crime or offence against person or property.

Any person so arrested must be handed over without delay to the Native commissioner or to a police officer to be dealt with according to law.

41. A kraal head may inflict reasonable, but not excessive, corporal punishment upon the inmates of his kraal for the purpose of correction and to maintain peace and order therein.

42. The powers and privileges of a kraal head may by order of a Native commissioner's court be vested in a woman in accordance with the provisions of section *twenty-eight*.

43. (1) A kraal head may appoint some fit and proper person to act as kraal head during his absence and a person so appointed shall during the period of his appointment be in the same position as a kraal head for the purposes of this Code. In default of any such appointment. the heir, or should the heir be a minor, his guardian, shall take charge of the kraal during the absence of the kraal head.

(2) During the absence of a kraal head, a woman may, with the written authority of the Native commissioner first had and obtained, take all such steps, including the institution of legal proceedings without the assistance of her guardian, as may be necessary to protect the property of the absent kraal head or of minor inmates.

CHAPTER VII

GUARDIANSHIP

44. (1) Under Native law a father is the natural guardian of his legitimate minor offspring.

(2) The natural guardian of an illegitimate minor is the head of the house to which such minor belongs.

(3) The natural guardian of a married woman is her husband.

(4) The natural guardian of a widow is the head of the kraal to which she belongs.

(5) The natural guardian of a divorced woman is the person who would have been her guardian had she remained unmarried.

45. In the event of the natural guardian of any minor being dead or being incapacitated, whether by insanity, idiocy, imprisonment or otherwise, for a period in excess of a year the guardianship of such minor shall devolve upon the head of the kraal to which such minor belongs.

46. (1) If upon the death of a kraal head other than a chief the heir is too young to assume the position, the kraal falls under the temporary care of the eldest surviving paternal uncle or paternal grandfather of the minor heir provided that should occasion require the Native commissioner may, in the exercise of his administrative functions under this Code, appoint any other suitable person to be the guardian of the heir and to take charge of the kraal.

(2) If upon the death of a kraal head being a chief, the heir is too young to assume the position, the Chief Native Commissioner shall appoint some suitable person to be the guardian of the heir and to take charge of the kraal.

(3) Guardianship under this section terminates upon the heir assuming the control of the kraal as in section *thirty-four* provided.

47. If a kraal head be sentenced to a term of imprisonment in excess of a year or be absent from the Province for longer than a year, without providing for the management of his affairs, and there be need for the appointment of a guardian to take charge of his kraal, the Native commissioner, in consultation with the chief of the Native so imprisoned or absent, or if such kraal head is a chief the Chief Native Commissioner, may appoint a guardian who shall be responsible for the due and faithful care, custody and general administration of the kraal.

48. A kraal head or guardian charged with the custody of any person or property, against whom complaint is made of having acted foolishly or prodigally in respect of such person or property and who upon enquiry by the Native commissioner is found to be unfitted for his position may be suspended therefrom and such person or property may be placed under the guardianship of some other person by the Native commissioner, or, if such kraal head is a chief or such guardian has been appointed by the Chief Native Commissioner, by the Chief Native Commissioner.

49. Complaints under section *forty-eight* may be made by any person, male or female, who has an interest in the matter and shall be dealt with administratively.

50. (1) Any person assuming or having been appointed to the guardianship of a minor shall be responsible for the due and faithful administration of such minor's estate and may be required to furnish such security as the Native commissioner may deem necessary or advisable.

(2) Any person who is the subject of guardianship in respect of either his person or his property may bring an action against his guardian without the assistance of a *curator ad litem* unless the court otherwise directs.

51. Any guardian who institutes legal proceedings on behalf of a person or estate under his guardianship without the permission of the Native commissioner first had and obtained may be ordered by the court to bear the costs of the proceedings.

52. (1) Guardians may claim reasonable remuneration for care and diligence exercised in the management of affairs committed to their charge. In the event of a dispute such remuneration shall be fixed by the Native commissioner.

(2) When guardians have been required to maintain children at their own expense, it is usual to allow a beast for each child, but the Native commissioner may allow such additional remuneration as he may consider fair and reasonable.

53. Any person claiming as guardian the custody of a minor may make application therefor to the Native commissioner who is empowered, after due enquiry, to make such order as he may deem just and equitable.

54. Any parent or guardian may inflict reasonable, but not excessive, corporal punishment upon any child or ward under his care for the purpose of correction.

55. No person may be compelled to assume the position of guardian against his wish.

56. Destitute minors rank as wards of the Supreme Chief in his capacity as Upper Guardian.

Chapter VIII

Customary Unions and Cognate Unions

A. *Customary Unions*

57. (1) A customary union is a civil contract entered into by and between the intending partners, subject to the essential requirements of this Code, and endures until the death of the first dying unless earlier dissolved by a competent court of law.

(2) Polygamous customary unions are recognised.

(3) Notwithstanding anything in any other law, any customary union as defined in the Act entered into between Natives in Zululand either prior to the application of this Code to that Territory or thereafter until the requisite official

witnesses shall have been appointed shall be deemed to be valid and shall for all purposes be regarded as a customary union under the provisions of this Code.

(4) Nothing in this section contained shall be deemed to affect the operation of sections *thirteen, fourteen* and *fifteen* of Law No. 46 of 1887 (Natal).

58. A customary union is not prohibited between—

(*a*) a man and his wife's sister ; or

(*b*) a widow or divorced woman and her late husband's brother.

59. (1) The essentials of a customary union are—

(*a*) the consent of the father or guardian of the intended wife, which consent may not be withheld unreasonably ;

(*b*) the consent of the father or kraal head of the intended husband should such be legally necessary ;

(*c*) a declaration in public by the intended wife to the official witness at the celebration of the union that the union is with her own free will and consent.

(2) Notwithstanding anything in sub-section (1) the consent of her father or guardian is not required in respect of the entrance into a customary union of an emancipated female with the status of a kraal head, but this sub-section shall not be construed as prejudicing the claim of any person entitled to the *lobolo* payable in respect of such emancipated female by her intended husband.

(3) The consent of his father or kraal head is not required in respect of the contracting of a customary union by a Native male who has attained majority or is otherwise under the provisions of this Code capable of entering into contracts on his own behalf.

60. The Native commissioner may administratively investigate any complaint that a father, guardian or kraal head has unreasonably withheld his consent to a proposed customary union and should he, as the result of such investigation, be satisfied that no just impediment exists, he may authorise the union to proceed and may make such order regarding the payment of *lobolo* as he may deem just.

61. When a customary union has been arranged, the kraal head or the parties concerned shall report the day fixed for the celebration of such union to the chief or the chief's deputy or the headman who shall direct the official witness to attend at the time and place of the celebration.

62. The official witness shall at an early stage of the ceremony publicly ask the woman whether it is of her own free will and consent that she is about to enter into the customary union with the intended husband. Should the woman decline to announce her consent, declare her dissent or otherwise appear to be unwilling to proceed with the intended union, the official witness shall forthwith prohibit any further proceedings in connection with the ceremony, shall, if necessary, take the woman under his protection and shall forthwith report the matter to the Native commissioner.

63. At a convenient time during the ceremony the bridegroom, or his father or his kraal head, or other person who has contributed the *lobolo* in respect of the union shall publicly declare to the official witness the source or sources from which the *lobolo* was taken or obtained, in order then and there to ascertain and determine the following particulars with a view to their being subsequently recorded in the register referred to in section *sixty-four*—

(*a*) the *lobolo* payable to and actually received by the party entitled thereto ;

(*b*) the source from which the *lobolo* was obtained ;

(*c*) where liability has been incurred in respect of the *lobolo* paid, the name of the person or the house to which it is to be re-paid and the manner of re-payment ;

(*d*) where any balance of *lobolo* is still owing, the time when and the manner in which it is to be paid ;

(*e*) if no *lobolo* has been paid, the nature of the agreement by which the obligation, if any, is to be discharged ;

(*f*) if there is to be an affiliation of the wife, the name of the woman to whose house she is being affiliated and the purpose of such affiliation ;

(*g*) if the union is to be an *ukuvusa*, the name of the deceased and the purpose for which such union is being contracted.

64. A register of customary unions shall be kept in the office of the Native commissioner in the form prescribed in Annexure " A " to this Code and shall be open at all convenient times for inspection, free of charge, by any person interested in any entry therein.

65. (1) The official witness shall within one month after the celebration of any customary union witnessed by him attend at the office of the Native commissioner with the partners, together with their fathers or guardians, or their representatives where necessary, for the registration of such union ; and it shall be the duty of the official witness and of any person attending with him at the office of the Native commissioner to furnish all the information required to complete such registration in due and proper form. The partners shall be required to sign the register after the entries made therein have been explained to them.

(2) The Native commissioner may order the registration with or without the appearance of the partners or their representatives of any customary union that has not been registered.

66. The partners to a customary union shall upon due registration of the union each be furnished by the registering officer, free of charge, with a certificate of the union in the form prescribed in Annexure " B " to this Code.

67. Any payment of *lobolo* made subsequently to the registration of a customary union may be recorded in the register referred to in section *sixty-four* in the presence of the parties interested or their representatives.

68. The accuracy of any entry in a register of customary unions relating to any obligation upon a house created by or at its establishment may be impeached before the Native commissioner in the presence of the parties interested by any person having a direct interest in such entry within one year after such person becomes cognisant thereof but not thereafter.

69. Any person who makes or causes to be made, for the purpose of entry in the register of customary unions, any false statement or declaration regarding any matter relating to an obligation upon a house arising from or created by a customary union shall be deemed to be guilty of an offence.

70. Registration of a customary union in a register of customary unions shall be accepted as conclusive evidence of that union and such registration may be proved by the production of the register or of a copy of the relative entry therein certified by the officer having custody of such register.

B. *Cognate Unions.*

71. The essentials of *ukungena* are—

(*a*) that the union be contracted for one or other of the purposes specified in the definition of *ukungena* under section *one* ;

(*b*) that the union be entered into with the free consent of the woman ;

(*c*) that it be a family arrangement entered into with the approval of the family head, and, in the case of a chief, where the raising of an heir to the chieftainship is involved, with the sanction of the majority of the tribe ;

(*d*) that no *lobolo* be paid in respect of the union.

72. The offspring of an *ukungena* rank as if they were in fact children of the deceased husband.

73. An *ukungena* may at any time be dissolved by either party.

74. An *ukuvusa* is recognised as a customary union for the purposes of sections *fifty-seven* to *seventy* inclusive of this Code.

75. The effect of *ukuvusa* is to create a separate and entirely independent estate in the name of the deceased.

CHAPTER IX

DIVORCE AND ANNULMENT OF CUSTOMARY UNIONS

76. (1) An action for divorce in respect of a customary union may be maintained by either partner on any of the following grounds :—

(a) Adultery on the part of the other partner.

(b) Continued refusal on the part of the other partner to render conjugal rights.

(c) Wilful desertion on the part of the other partner.

(d) Continued gross misconduct on the part of the other partner.

(e) That the other partner is undergoing a term of imprisonment of not less than five years.

(f) That conditions are such as to render the continuous living together of the partners insupportable or dangerous.

(2) The wife of a customary union may in addition maintain a suit for divorce from her husband by reason of—

(a) gross cruelty or ill-treatment on the part of the husband ;

(b) accusations of witchcraft or other serious allegations made against her by the husband.

77. A declaration of nullity in respect of a customary union may be applied for and obtained by, or on behalf of, either partner on any of the following grounds :—

(a) insanity of the other partner at the time of the celebration of the union ;

(b) impotence or other permanent physical defect on the part of the other partner preventing consummation of the union ;

(c) the absence of any of the essentials of a customary union as set forth in section *fifty-nine ;*

(d) the fact that the woman was at the time of the celebration of the union the wife by marriage or the partner under a customary union of another man ;

provided that a declaration of nullity in respect of a customary union on the ground of the insanity of one of the partners shall not be obtainable unless the fact of such insanity was unknown to the other partner at the time of celebration of the union and unless the action be instituted within a reasonable time after the celebration of the union.

78. (1) A wife who seeks divorce shall on leaving her husband's kraal forthwith seek the protection of her father or other person, hereinafter referred to as " the protector," who would have been her guardian had she remained unmarried, which protection may not be withheld ; and upon her declaring her refusal to live with her husband and her intention to seek divorce her father or protector shall as soon as practicable attempt to reconcile the partners and should he fail to effect a reconciliation he shall accompany the wife to the court of the Native commissioner to institute proceedings for a divorce.

(2) In the case of a wife seeking divorce who has no father or protector or whose father or protector is absent or refuses to assist her, the court of the Native commissioner may upon her application or upon notification of the facts appoint a *curator ad litem* for the purposes of her case and the person so appointed shall act in accordance with sub-section (1).

(3) A husband who seeks divorce must notify his intention to the father or protector of the wife who shall as soon as practicable attempt to reconcile the partners and should he fail to effect a reconciliation the husband may proceed to the court of the Native commissioner to institute proceedings for a divorce.

79. A woman suing for divorce must be assisted in the action by her father, protector or by a *curator ad litem* appointed under sub-section (2) of section *seventy-eight*.

80. In any action for the restitution of conjugal rights or in the alternative an order of divorce, in which a claim to the return of *lobolo* is advanced by the husband, he must cite in addition to the wife her father or protector.

81. The dissolution of a customary union by divorce, except when decreed at the suit of a wife by reason of the wrongful acts, misdeeds or omissions of the husband, must be accompanied by the return of a least one beast or its equivalent by the father or protector of the woman to the husband.

82. Upon the dissolution of any customary union the children are regarded as belonging to the father, but the court may make such orders as to their custody and maintenance as may be just and expedient.

83. When granting any decree of divorce the court shall give clear and explicit orders and directions as to the matters following :—

   (a) that the woman shall be under the guardianship of her father or protector and that she reside at such guardian's kraal or at such other place as the court may direct ;

   (b) the custody of the young children of the union, and any necessary provision for their maintenance ;

   (c) the number of cattle, if any, to be returned by the woman's father or guardian to the husband.

84. In decreeing the nullity of any customary union, the court shall order the return of the *lobolo*, together with the actual increase of the cattle, and shall make such order as to the refund of the actual expenses, including the *ngqutu* beast, incurred in connection with the union, as it may deem just.

CHAPTER X

LOBOLO

85. (1) In the absence of any agreement to the contrary, the *lobolo* in respect of a customary union is payable on the day of the celebration of such union. Any cattle delivered before that day shall be regarded as " sisa " cattle and any increase or decrease of such cattle prior to the day of celebration shall be to the profit or loss, as the case may be, of the person by whom or on whose behalf delivery was effected.

(2) Should any of the *lobolo* cattle die within fourteen days of the celebration of the union or of delivery, whichever be the later date, such cattle shall, if their death be duly reported, be replaced by the person by whom or on whose behalf delivery was effected.

86. *Lobolo* shall consist of fair average cattle or their equivalent in other stock or property and for the purposes of any dispute the value of each head of *lobolo* cattle shall be regarded as five pounds ; provided that the Supreme Chief may by proclamation vary this assessment from time to time.

87. (1) The *lobolo* for a girl or woman who is a ward is determined according to the rank or position of her father or guardian and is determined by agreement, but shall not be in excess of the scale prescribed in the following table :—

For a woman who is the daughter of		Maximum number of cattle as *lobolo*.
(*a*)	A chief	.. No limit.
(*b*)	The son, brother or uncle or a chief	15 head.
(*c*)	A headman, chief's deputy or official witness	15 head.
(*d*)	Any other Native	10 head.

(2) In any case of doubt the *lobolo* must not exceed ten head of cattle or their equivalent.

(3) The *lobolo* payable in respect of a divorced woman or widow upon her entering into a customary union shall in case of dispute be determined by the Native commissioner but shall not exceed five head of cattle or their equivalent in the case of a divorced woman if by reason of the misdeeds of her former husband no cattle were returned upon the divorce.

(4) The *lobolo* agreed upon and the manner of payment shall be entered in the register of customary unions.

88. Any person receiving *lobolo* in excess of the scale prescribed in section *eighty-seven* shall be guilty of an offence.

89. When a widow enters into a customary union, the *lobolo* in respect of the union is payable to the house to which she belonged in the kraal of her deceased husband.

90. The person to whom *lobolo* is delivered, or in case of his death the heir of the house receiving the *lobolo*, is bound, by the receipt thereof, should just occasion require, to protect and give asylum to the woman in respect of whom such *lobolo* was delivered.

91. (1) Younger sons are usually assisted by the kraal head in paying the *lobolo* for their first wife and younger brothers are usually assisted by the eldest brother or heir to their house with the approval of the kraal head.

(2) The rendering of such assistance as is referred to in sub-section (1) is not enforceable at law but where it can be shown that a younger son or brother has consistently contributed towards the support of his house under an agreement that he would be provided with *lobolo* or a portion thereof for a wife, the refusal or failure of the kraal head, eldest brother or heir, as the case may be, to implement such agreement will entitle such younger son or brother to recover a reasonable portion of the earnings so contributed by him.

92. (1) Assistance rendered by a kraal head from kraal property to any son in obtaining a wife by contributing the whole or portion of the *lobolo* is a gift and creates no liability to the *indhlunkulu* unless it be clearly stipulated to the contrary at the time of the celebration of the union.

(2) Where house property is used for the purpose indicated in sub-section (1) an obligation rests upon the house established by the union to make a refund.

(3) Where kraal property is used for *lobolo* by a kraal head for the purpose of establishing a house in his kraal, no liability rests upon the house so established for the return of such property unless it be clearly stipulated to the contrary at the time of the celebration of the union.

(4) Where house property is used for the purpose indicated in sub-section (3) an obligation rests upon the house so established to make a refund.

(5) Any such stipulation as is referred to in sub-section (1) or sub-section (3) may be recorded in the register of customary unions.

(6) Any liability arising under the circumstances referred to in this section shall, in the absence of any express agreement to the contrary, be liquidated from the *lobolos* of the daughters of the house established by the relative customary union and the heir of such house continues to be liable until the debt is discharged.

93. (1) Claims for the recovery of *lobolo* shall be recognised in Natal and Zululand, provided, however, that such recognition shall not extend to any claim arising out of a customary union contracted in Natal proper prior to the third day of November, 1909.

(2) Any agreement made for the payment of *lobolo* in respect of the daughter of a chief's deputy being within the scale prescribed by section *eighty-seven* and entered into prior to the application of this Code to Zululand, shall, notwithstanding anything in the Native Code of 1878, be regarded as valid and binding and any payments made thereunder shall not be disturbed.

94. (1) Should a woman die within twelve months of her having entered into a customary union without having surviving issue of the union, a portion of the *lobolo* not exceeding one half of the number of cattle delivered in respect of the union may, in the discretion of the Native Commissioner, be recovered. Should there be surviving issue of the union no *lobolo* shall be recoverable.

(2) Claims under sub-section (1) shall not be retrospective in Zululand.

95. (1) No claim to payments known variously as *vulamlomo, ubikibiki, ihlawulo, mnyobo, iqaqamazinye, izikwehlela* and the like in respect of any proposed customary union shall be recognised and where such payments have been made the Native commissioner may direct that they be included as part of the *lobolo* or that they be refunded to the party or parties making them.

(2) Such payments as are referred to in sub-section (1) may, if the proposed union does not take place, be recovered by the party making them.

96. (1) Upon a woman entering into a customary union for the first time, the *ngqutu* beast may, in addition to *lobolo*, be claimed, unless it has already been paid by the husband in respect of the woman's seduction or unless the woman has previously been seduced by some person other than the husband.

(2) The *ngqutu* beast is payable to the woman's mother, if alive, and, together with its increase, becomes her property, to be dealt with by her for the benefit of her house or as she may deem fit, and may not be attached except for her personal debts.

(3) If the woman's mother is divorced at the suit of her husband or through no fault on the part of her husband wilfully deserts or abandons his kraal, her right in and to the *ngqutu* beast ceases and determines and it becomes the property of the house to which she belonged.

(4) If the woman's mother be not alive the *ngqutu* beast is payable to the house to which she belonged and together with its increase becomes the property of that house.

(5) The *ngqutu* beast is not regarded as *lobolo* for the purposes of section *eighty-seven* and is not recoverable upon dissolution by death or divorce of the customary union in respect of which it was paid.

CHAPTER XI

THE KRAAL FAMILY SYSTEM

97. (1) (a) Whenever a customary union is contracted by a kraal head a house, which, subject to the provisions of paragraphs (b) and (c), is either a senior or an affiliated house, is established for the wife of the union.

(b) Except as provided in paragraph (c), there are not more than two senior houses in a kraal, to one or other of which the remaining houses are affiliated either by the automatic operation of the essential principle governing affiliation, namely, that a junior house becomes affiliated to the senior house which provides the *lobolo* for the wife of such junior house, or by public declaration by the kraal head at the time of the celebration of the union.

(*c*) In the kraals of chiefs and others of rank, influence or wealth there may be three senior houses, to one or other of which the remaining houses in the kraal are affiliated, as indicated under paragraph (*b*).

(2) A kraal may in addition to the houses of the kraal head's various wives contain those of relatives of the kraal head and also foreign houses on sufferance. A poor relation married or single may have his house and property in the kraal. A destitute Native may, for services rendered to the kraal, receive in return the use of a certain number of cattle and the right to occupy a house in the kraal. The house of any such Native would occupy an inferior position in the kraal.

(3) In the absence of affiliation, the various houses in a kraal are distinct from and independent of each other and each may acquire its own property and property rights.

98. With Natives other than hereditary chiefs the first wife is the chief wife and her house is the *indhlunkulu*.

99. (1) As regards wives taken by a commoner subsequent to the first their status and that of their houses depend upon whether or not any formal pronounce-ment or declaration of status is made by the kraal head at the time of the celebra-tion of the customary union.

(2) If no such formal pronouncement is made, the second wife ranks next to the chief wife and her house becomes a senior house ranking next to the *indhlu-nkulu*, houses established by subsequent customary unions becoming affiliated to the *indhlunkulu* or the other senior house as indicated in paragraph (*b*) of sub-section (1) of section *ninety-seven*.

100. ·(1) A formal pronouncement or declaration of status at the time of the celebration of a customary union is made in pursuance of the intention of the kraal head to divide his kraal into sections, of which there may be four, though in actual practice, except in the case of chiefs and others of rank, influence or wealth, there are seldom more than two.

These sections are :—
A. The *indhlunkulu* section—composed of the *indhlunkulu* with its affiliated houses.
B. The *ikohlo* section—composed of the *ikohlo* with its affiliated houses.
C. The *iqadi* section—composed of the *iqadi* with its affiliated houses.
D. An inferior section—composed of the houses of poor relations and strangers which are usually placed in an inferior position in the kraal.

(2) The children of any woman whose status has been formally pronounced or declared as indicated in sub-section (1) shall not be affected in their status or rights by the subsequent divorce or death of such woman.

101. (1) When the kraal head takes a second wife and upon the celebration of such customary union makes a formal pronouncement or declaration as to her status and that of her house, such usually takes the form of declaring her the chief *kohlo* wife and establishing the *ikohlo*.

(2) The houses established by customary unions contracted by the kraal head subsequent to establishment of the *ikohlo* are usually affiliated either to the *indhlunkulu* or the *ikohlo*, in accordance with the essential principle governing affiliation or by public declaration by the kraal head at the time of celebration of the union.

102. A kraal head upon taking his third or any subsequent wife may declare the establishment of the *iqadi* with the woman as chief *qadi* wife and in this event houses established by subsequent customary unions contracted by the kraal head must be affiliated to either the *indhlunkulu*, the *ikohlo* or the *iqadi* in accordance with the essential principle governing affiliation or by public declaration by the kraal head at the time of celebration of the union.

103. (1) An affiliated junior house is identified and grouped with the senior house to which it is affiliated, but affiliation of itself does not affect the property and property rights of the affiliated house.

(2) An affiliated house *etulas* to the senior house to which it is affiliated.

104. (1) The status of the wives of a hereditary chief in charge of a tribe is not declared until after the assumption by the chief of his chief wife who is usually taken later in life than the first and second wives.

(2) The *lobolo* of the chief wife of a hereditary chief is usually contributed wholly or in part by the tribe and her status is publicly announced.

(3) (a) A chief is required, upon the assumption of his chief wife, to report to the Chief Native Commissioner or to the Native commissioner of the district the names of his various wives and the status of each.

(b) A chief is required promptly to report to the Chief Native Commissioner or to the Native commissioner of the district the birth of the first-born son of his chief wife, and, in the event of such son predeceasing him, his death.

(c) Any report made under paragraph (a) must be recorded and attested by the officer to whom it is made and must be subscribed to by the chief or his duly authorized representative in the presence of at least two witnesses. Any such report must be treated as strictly confidential but if made to a Native commissioner must be transmitted by him to the Chief Native Commissioner.

(4) In the event of a hereditary chief who is the husband of several wives dying without having taken his chief wife, it is the duty of the elders of the tribe to assemble and confer status upon the widows, appointing the chief wife and determining the *ikohlo*, the *iqadi* and junior houses or in other customary and lawful manner fixing the rank of each house.

105. (1) A kraal head may at any time, subject to any regulations regarding the erection of kraals or buildings, separate and divide the various sections of his kraal into sub-kraals.

(2) Any such separation or division as is in sub-section (1) referred to in no way impairs the control, direction, rights or authority of the kraal head, who during his lifetime is the responsible head and sole authority equally in his kraal or in the sub-kraals created by such separation or division.

106. (1) Any major inmate of a kraal may, after notifying the kraal head and the chief, leave the kraal, and, subject to any regulations regarding removals and the erection of kraals or buildings, establish his own separate and independent kraal in the same or any other district or may attach himself to and become an inmate of some other kraal.

(2) A disinherited male may establish his own kraal or with the approval of the head of such kraal attach himself to and become an inmate of some kraal other than that of the kraal head who disinherited him.

107. When a girl enters into a customary union her father may give her goods or cattle and such become the property of and belong to the house established by such union.

Chapter XII

Inheritance and Succession

108. (1) Kraal property and personal property may be devised by will.

(2) House property may not be devised by will and upon the death of the kraal head any such property must devolve and be administered under Native law.

109. Subject to the provisions of sections *twenty-three* and *one hundred and seventeen*, under Native law succession, which may be either *general*, that is succession to the status and position of kraal head and to such kraal property as

has not been devised by will, or *special* that is succession to house property, follows the rule of primogeniture and devolves upon and through males only.

110. Subject to the provisions of section *twenty-three* upon the death of a kraal head, whose kraal has been divided into sections as in section *one hundred* described, the heir to his position as head of the main kraal, to the kraal property, if such has not been devised by will and otherwise falls in terms of section *twenty-three* of the Act and the regulations framed thereunder to be administered under Native law, and to the property of the *indhlunkulu* shall be determined in accordance with the following table :—

(a) The eldest son of the *indhlunkulu* or if he be dead such eldest son's senior male descendant.

(b) Failing such eldest son or any male descendant through him, the second son of the *indhlunkulu*, or if he be dead his senior male descendant and so on through the sons of the *indhlunkulu* and their male descendants in due order of seniority.

(c) If there be no son or male descendant of any son of the *indhlunkulu* the eldest son of the house first affiliated to the *indhlunkulu* or his senior male descendant and so on through the sons of such first affiliated house and their male descendants in due order of seniority.

(d) If there be no son or male descendant of any son of the house first affiliated to the *indhlunkulu* the eldest son of the house second affiliated to the *indhlunkulu* or his senior male descendant and so on through the sons of such house and their male descendants in due order of seniority and through the various affiliated houses in the order of their affiliation.

(e) If there be no heir in the *indhlunkulu* or in any house affiliated thereto, recourse will be had to the *iqadi* for a general heir and thereafter to the affiliated *qadi* houses in order of their affiliation to the *iqadi*. If there be no heir in any *qadi* house, recourse will be had to the *ikohlo* with subsequent recourse to the affiliated *kohlo* houses in the order of their affiliation.

(f) If there be no heir in the *iqadi* or *ikohlo* sections of the kraal, the father of the deceased, or if he be dead, the kraal head's eldest brother of the same house or his senior male descendant and so on through the brothers of that house and their male descendants in order of seniority.

(g) If there be no brother of the deceased of the same house or male descendant of any such brother, the deceased's eldest brother of the allied or affiliated house of higher rank or next rank as the case may be or his senior male descendant and so on through the brothers of such allied or affiliated house and their male descendants in order of seniority and thereafter through the brothers of the remaining houses in order of rank and their male descendants.

(h) If there be no brother of the deceased or male descendant of any brother of any house, the paternal grandfather and failing such the foregoing principles shall in like manner be applied until the male lines of next-of-kin, both collaterals and ascendants, are exhausted.

111. Upon the death of a kraal head whose kraal has not been divided into sections as in section *one hundred* described, the heir to his position as such, to the kraal property, if such has not been devised by will and otherwise falls in terms of section *twenty-three* of the Act and the regulations framed thereunder to be administered under Native law, and to the property of the *indhlunkulu* is determined in accordance with the principles laid down in section *one hundred and ten* save that in such a case there is no *iqadi* or *ikohlo* and the senior houses rank according to priority of their establishment with the result that if there be no heir in the

indhlunkulu or in any house affiliated thereto, recourse is had to the next senior house and its affiliated houses in the order of their affiliation and so on.

112. (1) Upon the death of a kraal head the property, rights and claims of the various houses remain with the respective heirs thereof.

(2) Succession to the property rights and claims of any house other than the *indhlunkulu* is governed by the principles laid down in sections *one hundred and ten* and *one hundred and eleven* save that in determining the heir the particular house concerned is first excussed and thereafter the allied and affiliated houses (if any) in order of rank or affiliation before recourse is had to the *indhlunkulu* heir.

(3) When the sections of a kraal have been separated into sub-kraals as in section *one hundred and five* provided, the heirs of the various houses upon the death of the kraal head become the kraal heads of the respective sub-kraals.

113. Succession to personal property, whenever in terms of section *twenty-three* of the Act and the regulations framed thereunder such property must devolve according to Native law, is governed by the principles laid down in sections *one hundred and ten* and *one hundred and eleven* save that in determining the heir the immediate family of the deceased is first excussed, then the house to which the deceased belonged and thereafter the allied or affiliated houses (if any) in order of rank or affiliation before recourse is had to the *indhlunkulu* heir.

114. In the event of there being no male heir, any property, whether kraal, house or personal property, which must in terms of section *twenty-three* of the Act and the regulations framed thereunder, devolve according to Native law, reverts to the Supreme Chief and the females of the kraal or family fall under the guardianship of the Supreme Chief or of such person, being a Native, as he may appoint.

115. Notwithstanding anything in sections *one hundred and ten, one hundred and eleven* and *one hundred and twelve* a congenital idiot cannot rank as an heir. The support of such a person is a charge upon the house to which he belongs.

116. An heir succeeding to property, whether kraal, house or personal, becomes liable for debts in respect thereof only to the extent of the assets to which he succeeds.

117. Notwithstanding anything in any other law, when a woman, who has been emancipated under the provisions of section *twenty-eight* and who has not contracted a marriage or a customary union subsequent to such emancipation, dies intestate or partly intestate and without issue other than daughters or illegitimate sons, so much of the property in her estate as she has not disposed of by will shall be divided equally among such children.

118. (1) (a) A son may be disinherited by his father on application to the chief by reason of the fact that he refuses to be controlled by his father or has by gross misconduct disgraced the family or refuses to make reasonable contribution towards the maintenance of the family, or for other good and sufficient cause.

(b) Such application shall form the subject of an enquiry by the chief, with due notice to the son, and an appeal shall lie from the decision of the chief to the Native commissioner, whose decision shall be final.

(c) Where the applicant is a chief, the application shall be made to the Supreme Chief who shall deal with the application as he may deem fit.

(2) A son who is disinherited becomes absolutely without status, voice or claim in regard to the family or property of his house or father's kraal.

Chapter XIII

Medicine Men and Herbalists

119. Native medicine men and herbalists are known as *izinyanga zokwelapa* (those skilled in healing) and *izinyanga zemiti* (herbalists) respectively and may practise for gain if duly licensed as such but not otherwise.

120. (1) A Native commissioner may in his discretion issue to any Native a licence to practise as a medicine man or herbalist when such issue is by way of renewal of a licence previously held by such person and application therefor is made within three months after the date of expiry of the previous licence.

(2) Save as provided in sub-section (1) no licence to practise as a medicine man or herbalist may, in terms of sub-section (2) of section *ninety-eight* of the Medical, Dental and Pharmacy Act, No. 13 of 1928, be issued except on the order of the Minister of Public Health.

121. The fee payable for a licence to practise as a medicine man or herbalist is three pounds and the holder of any such licence may practise as both a medicine man and a herbalist or as one or the other throughout the Province of Natal for a period of one year from the date of its issue.

122. (1) A duly licensed medicine man or herbalist may upon being consulted claim a retaining fee (*ulugxa*). Should a cure result a further fee is claimable but should the treatment be ineffective nothing more than the *ulugxa* may be demanded.

(2) No claim in respect of services rendered by a medicine man or herbalist shall be recognised in a court of law unless proof of the issue of a licence to such person be adduced.

(3) No unlicensed medicine man or herbalist may claim any fee or reward in respect of services rendered by him.

123. Gross or culpable blunders or negligence entailing bad results renders a medicine man or herbalist liable to a civil action for damages apart from any criminal charge which may be laid against him.

124. Any Native who practises as a medicine man or herbalist in contravention of the provisions of section *one hundred and nineteen* shall be guilty of an offence.

125. (1) Natives licensed as medicine men or herbalists may not assume the European title of " doctor " or " chemist " or any other designation mentioned in paragraph (*b*) of section *thirty-seven* of the Medical, Dental and Pharmacy Act, No. 13 of 1928, and may not offer or hire their services to or prescribe for or perform any operation upon a person other than a Native.

(2) Natives licensed as medicine men or herbalists may prescribe, deal in and sell Native medicines only.

(3) Any Native contravening the provisions of sub-section (1) or sub-section (2) shall be guilty of an offence which, in addition to any other penalty to which he may be liable, shall involve cancellation of his licence.

126. No intoxicating liquor of any kind may be obtained by a Native under a prescription or direction of a Native medicine man or herbalist, except with the written approval of a magistrate or Native commissioner. Any contravention of this section shall constitute an offence.

127. A Native woman may without a licence practise as a midwife for women of her own race and may make such reasonable charges for her services as may be agreed upon or as are recognised as customary.

128. The fees and earnings of a medicine woman or midwife belong to her house and she may institute action for the recovery thereof only with the assistance of her husband or guardian.

129. (1) Any Native who for gain practises as a diviner (known to the Natives as *inyanga yoku bula, isanusi* or *isangoma*) or as a rain doctor or lightning doctor, or professes a knowledge of witchcraft, or of the use of spells or charms, or advises any person to bewitch or injure persons or property, or supplies any person with the pretended means of witchcraft, shall be guilty of an offence.

(2) Any person charged under sub-section (1) may be convicted of obtaining money by false pretences.

(3) Should a licensed medicine man or herbalist be convicted of a contravention of sub-section (1) his licence shall be cancelled.

(4) The court may order the confiscation and destruction of putative spells, charms or supernatural agencies found in the possession of any person convicted of a contravention of sub-section (1).

<hr>

CHAPTER XIV

ACTIONABLE WRONGS

130. Except as is expressly in this chapter otherwise provided, a wrongful act committed against any Native founds an action on the part of such Native for damages against the transgressor and in instituting such action the plaintiff need not be assisted by his kraal head, father or guardian unless he is minor.

131. In an action for damages for slander or other injury, it is not essential for the plaintiff to claim any specific sum, the court being left to assess the amount thereof.

132. (1) Defamation of character is an actionable wrong.

(2) Every malicious statement alleging evil conduct on the part of any person constitutes defamation : provided that should any person cast an aspersion upon the character of another in the course of a heated quarrel, and within a short period thereafter publicly withdraw and publicly apologise for the same, no claim in damages will lie : provided, further, that no action for defamation will lie if the words used were addressed to any person in authority, with reference to the plaintiff or complainant, in good faith, and not with express malice.

(3) In an action for damages for defamation of character the allegations complained of shall substantially be embodied in the summons or statement of claim but the words need not necessarily include a translation.

133. Any unmarried girl whose chastity has been publicly denied, scoffed at, or impeached by any person, is entitled to damages for the slander.

134. The destruction of crops by cattle or other stock will found an action for damages against the owner or person having the custody and control of such stock, unless such damage has been caused by the contributory negligence of the owner of the crops.

135. When by reason of negligence on the part of any person in starting or failing properly to control a grass fire loss is sustained by any other person, an action for damages lies against the person responsible for such fire.

136. Trespass on cultivated land does not found an action for damages unless the trespass is accompanied by special damage.

137. (1) The seduction of an unmarried female gives rise to an action against the seducer in damages for the *ngqutu* beast. In addition to such beast a further beast may be awarded as damages in respect of each and every child which such woman bears to the seducer ; provided that should such child or children be born during the subsistence of an engagement no claim to damages shall be recognised unless the marriage does not take place ; provided further that should the seducer marry the woman, payments other than the *ngqutu* beast made in respect of her seduction shall be regarded as forming part of the *lobolo*.

(2) Any person having illicit intercourse with a divorced woman or widow as the result of which a child is born shall be liable in damages to her father or guardian, such damages not to exceed one beast in respect of each child so born. In the event of a subsequent customary union between the parties, any payment of damages shall be regarded as forming part of the *lobolo*.

(3) Any claim for damages in respect of the seduction of or illicit intercourse with a girl or woman is extinguished by the death of such girl or woman unless her death is due to child-birth consequent upon such seduction or illicit intercourse.

138. Any Native committing adultery with a woman living with her husband shall, irrespective of any criminal penalty, be liable in damages to the husband ; provided that no action for damages shall lie in the case of connivance on the part of the husband or if at the time of the adultery the woman and her husband were not living together as man and wife.

139. Any Native suing his wife under a customary union for divorce on the grounds of her adultery may, when the other party to the adultery is known, simultaneously and in the same action sue such party for damages.

140. Any person abducting the wife, child, or ward of another or inducing the wife, child, or ward of another to leave her kraal without the consent of her husband, father or guardian, shall be liable in damages to such female's husband, kraal head or guardian, as the case may be : provided that no action will lie if the absence is only in connection with the betrothal visit of a girl to the kraal of a proposed future husband.

141. (1) A guardian is liable in respect of delicts committed by his ward while in residence at the same kraal as himself.

(2) Notwithstanding anything in section *twenty-seven* or in any other provision of this Code.—

(a) a father is liable in respect of delicts committed by his children while in residence at the same kraal as himself ;

(b) a kraal head is liable in respect of delicts committed by any unmarried inmate of his kraal while in residence at the kraal.

(3) Legal proceedings arising out of any delict such as is referred to in subsection (1) or in sub-section (2) may be instituted against either the person committing the delict or such person jointly with his father, guardian or kraal head as the case may be.

142. No inmate of a kraal may sue the kraal head for damages by reason of a delict of the kraal head, but he may apply to the Native commissioner to be removed from the control of the kraal head or may apply for protection in respect of his individual property or for such other relief as may be necessary.

143. The illegal or wrongful acts of a chief, headman, chief's deputy or other Native official render him liable in damages to the aggrieved party who may sue upon such claim in the court of the Native commissioner having jurisdiction, but not in the court of any Native chief.

CHAPTER XV

CIVIL PROCEDURE AND MISCELLANEOUS PROVISIONS

144. (1) The jurisdiction and procedure of any court administering Native law shall be as prescribed in the Act and the regulations framed thereunder.

(2) Nothing in this Code shall be deemed in any way to affect or impair the operation of section *eleven* of the Act.

(3) Where Native law is applied in any such matter as is referred to in section *eleven* of the Act, the court may take cognisance of any relevant Native custom which is not opposed to the principles of public policy or natural justice, whether or not such custom is defined and dealt with under this Code ; provided that where such custom is so defined and dealt with the provisions of this Code shall prevail.

W

145. Native good manners and respect to authority require the observance of the following rules :—

(a) Every Native, on entering a court or into the presence of a chief or officer, should salute the superior officer present with uplifted right hand and uncovered head, and likewise on leaving he should salute in a similar manner.

(b) Persons bringing sticks or weapons into court, or into the immediate presence of chiefs or superior officers, are deemed guilty of unbecoming behaviour and may be punished for contempt.

(c) Inferiors always salute first, and the superior acknowledges the salute.

(d) While a judge or officer of the Government or chief is speaking no one may interrupt, but on conclusion of such speech any person, by invitation or permission, may shortly give an opinion on any point at issue. No such opinion may be given or remarks made after judgment has been finally pronounced.

(e) Upon judgment being given the parties salute the court and retire.

146. (1) Native females are not to be deemed or treated in any way as property or chattels, notwithstanding any property rights which may be connected with or arise out of customary unions entered into by them.

(2) The mere indication of a woman or girl as the source from which, through her *lobolo*, a debt or obligation is to be met shall not invalidate a contract based purely on Native law and custom, but this shall not apply to any other contract.

147. (1) Delivery is given and taken at the place of the party who sells, barters or is to deliver the property, unless a special stipulation to the contrary is made.

(2) Constructive delivery is recognised under Native law,

148. When property has been stolen and delivered by the thief to an innocent purchaser for value, the true owner is entitled to vindicate his property against the possessor.

149. (1) Cattle or things sold by one Native to another Native are understood to be sold for cash, unless there is a special contract for credit.

(2) Where the sale has been for cash the seller upon failure of the buyer to pay may, at any time within one month from delivery, claim the return of the property sold from any person then in possession, irrespective of any rights such persons may have. After one month the seller has merely a right of action for the price.

(3) In the absence of any special agreement to the contrary, cattle or other stock sold or bartered are taken as guaranteed to be free from latent disease, and articles sold or bartered are taken to be guaranteed to be free from latent flaw or defect.

150. (1) In the absence of any agreement to the contrary, a cow in calf is reckoned as one beast.

(2) Claims for increase of cattle and other stock shall not be allowed, except in the following cases :—

(a) where it is proved that the defendant has agreed to allow increase, or admitted his liability to account for same ;

(b) where there has been a deposit or placing of cattle, or other stock, as in cases of *sisa* ;

(c) where guardians have used for their own purposes the cattle or other stock of their wards ;

(d) where, after actual or constructive delivery of breeding cattle or other stock, such have been allowed to remain with the defendant ; in such cases claims in respect of progeny living at the date of the action will be allowed.

(3) In claims arising out of *sisa*, the party to whom the cattle were given under *sisa* must satisfactorily account for the original number and all increase, when called upon to do so ; he may not set off any deaths, unless he has proof that he notified the deaths to the owner of the cattle or otherwise duly accounted for the same. The person with whom *sisa* cattle are placed is entitled only to the use thereof. It is customary, however, for the owner of the cattle occasionally to donate a beast from the increase to the other party, but no claim at law can be made for this without proof of a specific contract so to donate.

151. (1) Notwithstanding anything in Act No. 41 of 1908, Natal, loans as between Native and Native shall be recoverable in any competent court.

(2) Interest is unknown in Native law and parties claiming interest as having accrued upon any debt or claim will have to prove a distinct contract to pay the same.

(3) No claim for interest may in any case amount to more than the principal sum in respect of which interest is claimed.

(4) When execution upon a judgment debt fails to satisfy that debt, the balance of such debt shall, till paid, bear interest at the rate of *six per cent per annum* upon the value thereof.

152. (1) No Native may avail himself of or be brought under the operation of any insolvency law or regulation, to the prejudice of claims against him by any other Native, unless he is a trader as defined under the Insolvency Act No. 32 of 1916 or any amendment thereof.

(2) Save as otherwise in this Code provided, prescription is unknown in Native law and no claim arising out of Native law shall be affected by the operation of any law of limitation or prescription of action.

153. (1) Sums due from or paid by the Government to chiefs and headmen by way of salary, bonus or stipend are privileged and may not be attached for debt by the process of any court.

(2) Any such salary, bonus or stipend as is referred to in sub-section (1) may be stopped, suspended or reduced for a stated period by the Supreme Chief as a disciplinary measure in the event of wrongful behaviour on the part of a chief or headman.

154. Native dwellings, commonly called huts, are deemed to be movable property.

CHAPTER XVI

OFFENCES

A. Offences against Public Order, Authority, Decency and Morals

155. Any person who disregards or defies the authority or any order of the Supreme Chief shall be guilty of an offence.

156. Any chief who summons an armed assembly of his tribe or who classes or causes to be classed the men of his tribe into companies or regiments without the permission of the Supreme Chief first had and obtained shall be guilty of an offence.

157. Any chief who is required by the Supreme Chief either directly or by a deputy or messenger of the Supreme Chief to do or refrain from doing any public act or acts, and who acts in defiance of or neglects promptly to obey such order, shall be guilty of an offence.

158. Any person who spreads any false report of a nature calculated to cause disquiet or anxiety, or affecting the Government and its acts, shall be guilty of an offence.

159. Whenever more than five persons are assembled together, from whose conduct a breach of the peace may be apprehended, the kraal head or other person in authority, may command them to disperse and upon their refusal so to do each and all of them shall be guilty of an offence.

160. (1) Any person who defies the authority of a kraal head, or enters a kraal when permission to do so has been refused, or remains in or about any kraal after being requested to withdraw, shall be guilty of an offence.

(2) Any person found concealed in or watching in or about the precincts of any kraal between sunset and sunrise and not being able to give a good account of himself shall be guilty of an offence.

161. (1) Any person, not being a member of the police, or not otherwise authorised thereto, who carries assegais, axes, knobkerries or other dangerous weapons to any feast, dance, or other gathering, shall be guilty of an offence, and, in addition to any other punishment to which he may be liable, the weapons carried by him shall be confiscated.

(2) Punishment may be inflicted for any such offence as is referred to in subsection (1) irrespective of any liability on the part of the person so offending to prosecution for taking part in any faction fight or riot.

162. (1) The following acts constitute offences :—

(*a*) the seduction of an unmarried girl ;

(*b*) the abduction of an unmarried girl ;

(*c*) enticing any female from the control or custody of her father, husband or guardian, or attempting to have illicit intercourse with any female ;

(*d*) adultery in respect of both males and females ;

(*e*) knowingly harbouring without just or reasonable cause the wife, daughter or ward of another after demand has been made for her return.

(2) No voluntary and *bona fide* temporary visit of any girl to the kraal of her lover with a view to betrothal constitutes an offence on the part of such lover.

(3) Intercourse arising out of *ukungena* is neither adulterous nor illicit.

163. (1) Any Native female who leads an immoral life, or is found elsewhere than at her kraal and is unable to give a good account of herself, may be arrested and brought before the Native commissioner, and upon her failure satisfactorily to explain her way of living or to give a good or valid reason for her absence from her kraal, the Native commissioner may order that she return to and remain at her kraal, the kraal head of which shall be bound to provide for and maintain her.

(2) Any female who neglects to obey or leaves her kraal in defiance of an order under sub-section (1) shall be guilty of an offence.

B. *Offences against the regulations regarding Customary and Cognate Unions.*

164. Any kraal head or guardian of any party to a customary union who celebrates or permits the celebration of such a union save in the presence of an official witness, or who celebrates or permits the celebration of such union after the official witness has stopped or directed the suspension of such celebration, shall be guilty of an offence.

165. Any kraal head or other person who coerces or attempts to coerce any girl or woman to enter into a union against her will shall be guilty of an offence.

166. Any misconduct or breach of duty on the part of an official witness in contravention of any provision of this Code constitutes an offence, and in addition to any other punishment to which he may be liable such official witness may be summarily dismissed from his office by the Native commissioner.

C. *Miscellaneous Offences.*

167. Any Native who disregards or fails to comply with any duty, obligation, direction or prohibition imposed upon him by this Code shall be guilty of an offence.

168. Any person who by natural duty is responsible for due provision of the necessaries of life for any other person and fails or neglects to provide those necessaries shall be guilty of an offence.

169. (1) Any Native who carries an assegai, sword-stick (*intyumentyu*) battle axe, stick shod with iron, or any other dangerous weapon shall, unless he is engaged upon some public duty or is a member of the police, or has been authorised in writing by a Native commissioner so to do, or is engaged in hunting or in *bona fide* night travelling outside an urban area, shall be guilty of an offence and upon conviction, in addition to any other penalty to which he may be liable, the weapon or weapons may be confiscated by the court.

(2) The written authority of a Native commissioner for the purposes of sub-section (1) may be granted in respect of a particular area or for the whole Province, or may be limited to a specified period or to a particular service, duty or employment.

170. (1) A kraal head shall report immediately to his chief or headman the occurrence of any serious crime or the death of any person under suspicious circumstances at or near his kraal ; and the chief or headman shall, on receiving such report, transmit the same without delay to the Native commissioner or nearest police officer.

(2) A kraal head, chief or headman who neglects or fails to comply with his duty under sub-section (1) shall be guilty of an offence.

171. Any Native who, knowing or having good reason to suspect the presence of a contagious or infectious disease among cattle under his control, fails to give proper warning of such disease to his neighbours and others interested, or who, having bought or acquired diseased cattle, drives them into or through any location or other place used by others for the grazing of cattle shall, irrespective of his civil liability for any damage or loss so caused, be guilty of an offence.

CHAPTER XVII

GENERAL PENALTY

172. In the absence of any specific penalty for any offence under this Code, the court convicting any person of such offence may impose upon him a fine not exceeding ten pounds or in default of payment imprisonment for a period not exceeding three months.

ANNEXURE A.

(FORM OF REGISTER UNDER SECTION *SIXTY-FOUR*)

REGISTER OF CUSTOMARY UNIONS CONTRACTED UNDER THE PROVISIONS OF THE CODE OF NATIVE LAW

1. No........................   2. District.................
3. Date of registration ....
4. Name and surname of husband.................................
   ....
5. Name of husband's father..
6. Chief ....
7. Name and surname of wife.....................................
   ....
8. Name of wife's father..
9. Condition. If divorced, name of former husband.................
   ....
10. Rank of wife's father ....
11. His chief ....
12. No. and rank of wife in her husband's kraal.......................
    ....
13. If affiliated, name of house to which she is affiliated and object of such affiliation ....
    ....
14. If an *ukuvusa* union, the name of the deceased and purpose for which union contracted ....
    ....
15. Number of *lobolo* cattle actually paid over (or their equivalent) on the date of the registration of the union..............................
    ....
16. Balance of *lobolo* due and conditions as to payment.................
    ....
    ....
17. Source from which *lobolo* obtained ....
18. If a liability incurred in securing such *lobolo*, manner of repayment and to whom due ....
    ....
19. Signature of official witness ....
20. Signature of woman's father or guardian..........................
21. Signatures of partners :
    (*a*)...................   (*b*).........................
    ....
                                   Native Commissioner.
    Record of subsequent *lobolo* payments :
    ....
    ....
    ....

ANNEXURE B.

(CERTIFICATE UNDER SECTION *SIXTY-SIX*)

CERTIFICATE OF CUSTOMARY UNION

This is to certify that a customary union between........................

....

and .... the

daughter of..was   registered

at the office of the Native Commissioner for the District of...................

on...

....
Native Commissioner.

(Reference to folio in Register of
  Customary Unions.)

....

Office of the Native Commissioner.

Place........................

Date........................

APPENDIX L

GOVERNMENT NOTICE No. 2256 DATED 21st DECEMBER, 1928

CHIEFS' CRIMINAL JURISDICTION

It is hereby notified for general information that the Minister of Native Affairs has, under the authority vested in him by sub-section (4) of section *twenty* of the Native Administration Act, 1927 (No. 38 of 1927), made the following regulations in connection with the exercise of criminal jurisdiction by Native chiefs.

REGULATIONS MADE BY THE MINISTER OF NATIVE AFFAIRS UNDER THE AUTHORITY OF SECTION *TWENTY* (4) OF ACT No. 38 OF 1927

1. If a convicted person shall fail or neglect to pay the penalty imposed upon him by the judgment of a Native chief in terms of section *twenty* of the Act, such judgment shall be executed as if it were a judgment of a Native chief in a civil claim heard before him under the provisions of section *twelve* of the Act.

2. Any fine or portion of a fine recovered from a convicted person shall be paid to the tribal funds administered by the chief who imposed the penalty, and shall be accounted for by him in accordance with the customs of the tribe unless the Minister shall in special cases or areas otherwise direct.

3. Any Native desiring to appeal against the judgment of a chief shall within seven days of the date of such judgment, in person, notify the chief and the magistrate of the district of his intention so to appeal. Upon receiving such notification aforesaid, the magistrate shall fix a day for the hearing of the said appeal, and shall take such steps as may be necessary to secure the attendance of the necessary witnesses, both for the prosecution and for the defence, before his court in the same manner as if they were witnesses in a criminal trial in the court of such magistrate.

4. The public prosecutor in the court of such magistrate shall be charged with the prosecution of such accused person before the magistrate, and the trial shall be conducted in a manner similar to the trial of an accused person in a criminal case before such magistrate.

5. If on the day appointed for the trial the appellant shall fail to appear, the court may in its discretion either postpone the hearing or dismiss the appeal.

APPENDIX M

**GOVERNMENT NOTICE No. 2255 OF 1928, AS AMENDED
BY GOVERNMENT NOTICE No. 1312 OF 1931**

CHIEFS' CIVIL COURTS

REGULATIONS MADE BY THE MINISTER OF NATIVE AFFAIRS IN
TERMS OF SECTION *TWELVE* OF ACT No. 38 OF 1927

1. The procedure in connection with the trial of civil disputes between Natives before a chief under section *twelve* of Act No. 38 of 1927, and the execution of the judgments of the said chief, shall be in accordance with the recognized customs and laws of the tribe to which such chief has been appointed or in respect of which he has been recognized.

2. Where the judgment debtor or any person acting on his behalf or at his instigation resists with force, or by a show of force, the seizure of any property about to be seized by any messenger of a chief in the lawful execution of a judgment of the said chief and the messenger shall be of opinion that seizure of such property cannot be effected without a breach of the peace, he shall immediately report the circumstances to the judgment creditor, who, if he so desire, may apply to the Native Commissioner of the area in which such property is for process in aid which process, if granted, shall be executed as if it were a process of the court of the said Native Commissioner.

The same procedure shall *mutatis mutandis* apply in regard to the execution of a chief's judgment where the property to be attached is in an area outside the jurisdiction of the said chief.

3. The Native Commissioner to whom such application is made shall be and is hereby empowered to grant such process upon being satisfied that the judgment debtor, or in his absence the person in charge of such property, has been notified by the judgment creditor of his intention to make such application and of the day upon which such application would be made and that the judgment of the chief has remained unsatisfied.

4. The Native Commissioner granting such process shall make such order in regard to costs as he may deem fit.

5. Any party desiring to appeal against any judgment or order of a Chief's Court shall notify such Chief or his representative of his intention and lodge his appeal in person with the Native Commissioner within thirty days from the date of the pronouncement of the Chief's judgment or order, provided that for good cause shown the Native Commissioner may extend the period.

6. The Native Commissioner with whom such appeal is lodged shall record the information of the appellant in regard to his claim before the chief and the judgment thereon and shall thereupon fix a day for the hearing of the appeal and notify the appellant and the respondent accordingly.

7. The Chief on receiving any notice of appeal shall immediately report to the Native Commissioner particulars of the claim lodged with him, the reply of the judgment debtor, if any, and his judgment or order thereupon, and the reasons therefor which shall be recorded by such Native Commissioner.

8. Upon the day fixed for the appearance of the parties the Native Commissioner shall hear and determine the case as if it were a case of first instance in such court, and the successful party may take out the process of the Court of such Native Commissioner for the execution of the judgment or order.

9. The following special provisions shall apply in respect of Chiefs' Civil Courts in Natal :—

(i) All judgments of a Chief's Court shall be entered, together with the names of the parties and particulars of claim, in a register to be kept by the Clerk of the Native Commissioner's Court for the purpose. Such entries shall be made as soon as possible but in any case not later than fourteen days after judgment is given, and no judgment shall be enforced unless and until it is so registered.

(ii) The Native Commissioner may require the attendance of the parties to the case as well as that of the Chief or his deputy, when the judgment is being registered, and the fact of their attendance shall also be recorded.

(iii) Entries referring to a judgment may be corrected or added to in the presence and with the consent of the Chief or his deputy and of the parties to the case.

(iv) The duty of notifying the Native Commissioner of any judgment delivered in a Chief's Court shall be upon the Chief, who shall attend at the Native Commissioner's Office in person or by deputy for this purpose.

(v) The following fees shall be payable in connection with any proceedings in a Chief's Civil Court, and shall be recoverable against the party adjudged to pay the costs :—

	s.	d.
To Chief for hearing and judgment (to be paid by Plaintiff in advance).	10	0
To Chief for registering judgment	2	6
To Chief for attending and giving reasons in terms of regulation No. 7	2	6
To Chief for necessary travelling	2	0
To Messenger—inclusive fee per day or portion thereof	2	0

APPENDIX N

GOVERNMENT NOTICE No. 2253 OF 1928 AS AMENDED BY GOVERNMENT NOTICES Nos. 1313 OF 1931 AND 1078 OF 1932

COURTS OF NATIVE COMMISSIONERS IN CIVIL PROCEEDINGS

REGULATIONS

It is hereby notified for general information that His Excellency the Governor-General has been pleased, in terms of sub-section (4) of section *ten* of the Native Administration Act, No. 38 of 1927, to make the following regulations in respect of Courts of Native Commissioners elsewhere than in the Transkeian Territories.

Courts.

1. The proceedings shall be conducted in open court subject to such exceptions as are hereinafter provided.

2. The court may, in the interests of good order, public health, public morals, or generally in the interests of justice, direct, in its discretion, that a trial shall be held in camera, or in some other place than the court-room.

3. All oral evidence shall be given after the witness has been duly sworn or admonished to speak the truth. Provided that if a witness deemed by the court to be material to the issue is unable to attend the court, for good cause shown, the evidence of such witness may be recorded at such time and place as may seem to the court most convenient or by means of interrogatories or before a Commissioner for which purpose the provisions of sections *forty-nine* and *fifty* of Act No. 32 of 1917 or any amendments thereof shall apply.

4. All pleadings and claims preferred in open court and all evidence heard by a court shall be fully recorded and the record of every case shall contain all documents admitted as pleadings or evidence and any judgment or order given by the court.

5. The records and proceedings of the court shall be accessible to the public under supervision of the clerk, at convenient times and upon prepayment of the fees prescribed in Table A of the Second Annexure hereto.

6. After the expiration of a period of thirty years from the date of judgment, the Minister may order such records and proceedings to be removed to a central place for custody.

7. A civil record-book substantially in the form prescribed in the First Annexure hereto shall be kept in the office of the clerk of the court and it shall be open to inspection by the public at convenient times without charge.

Assessors.

8. A Native assessor shall, before taking his seat in court as such, take an oath substantially in the form prescribed in the Third Annexure hereto.

9. The fees and travelling allowances of Native assessors shall be paid by the Crown, in accordance with the scale prescribed in Table C of the Second Annexure hereto.

Clerk of the Court.

10. Each Native commissioner shall assign the duties of clerk of the court to a member of his staff, who shall exercise the functions, assigned to him in terms of these regulations.

11. The clerk of the court shall—

(a) sign all process of court ;

(b) write out and prepare, upon the request of any party any process of court or notice of appeal, or any other document upon prepayment of the fees prescribed in Table A of the Second Annexure hereto, which shall be paid by means of revenue stamps affixed to such process ;

(c) upon payment of the fees prescribed in Table A of the Second Annexure hereto, furnish copies of records to any person entitled thereto or such copies may be made free of charge by such person under the supervision of the clerk.

A refusal by the clerk of the court to do any act which he is empowered by these regulations to do shall be subject to review by the court.

12. All acts required to be done by the clerk of the court may be done by the Native commissioner.

13. The Clerk shall keep a cash book and promptly record therein particulars of payments into and out of Court.

Messenger of Court.

14. The Minister may appoint for every court of Native commissioner a messenger of the court upon such terms and conditions as he may determine.

15. The messenger may, with the prior approval of the Native commissioner, appoint deputy-messengers, for whose actions as such he shall be responsible.

16. It shall be competent for the Native commissioner to appoint an acting messenger for a specified period or occasion.

17. Whenever process of the court in a civil case is to be served and executed and no messenger or deputy-messenger has been appointed at the place where the court is held, a member of any police force shall, subject to the rules, be as qualified to serve and execute all such process and all other documents in such a case as if he had been duly appointed deputy-messenger. The fees payable in respect of or in connection with any such service to a messenger shall in any such case be chargeable, but shall be paid into the Consolidated Revenue Fund.

18. The messenger shall receive and lodge in the gaol all persons arrested by any order, writ or judgment of the court, or committed to his custody by the court.

19. All process delivered to the messenger shall be served and executed by him forthwith and thereafter he shall record his return on such process, which shall immediately be lodged with the Clerk of the Court and such return shall be *prima facie* evidence of the matters therein stated.

20. In any case in which the messenger is unable to pay over any moneys to the persons entitled thereto, he shall deposit the same with the clerk of the court within seven days from the receipt thereof.

21. The messenger shall maintain the following records substantially in the form prescribed in the First Annexure hereto :—

(a) a register of all process served.

(b) a register of all process executed.

22. It shall be competent for any Native commissioner to suspend a messenger from his office for good cause. Such suspension shall be reported forthwith to the Minister, who shall direct the further action to be taken.

APPENDIX N 349

23. No messenger may during the tenure of his office either practise as an attorney or law agent or be in the employ of such : Nor shall he carry on the business of a labour agent or runner of a labour agent.

24. (a) A party to a suit or application may appear in person to conduct his case or may be represented by his guardian or, in the discretion of the Court, by a relative authorized by the party.

(b) The authority of any person appearing for a party may be challenged by the other party within forty-eight hours after he has notice that such person is so appearing ; and thereupon such person may not, without the leave of the Court, so appear further until he shall satisfy the Court that he has authority so to appear and the Court may adjourn the hearing of the suit or application to enable him to do so.

25. (1) The process of the Court for commencing an action shall be by way of summons calling upon the defendant to appear to answer the claim of the plaintiff. Such summons, which shall be substantially in the form prescribed in the First Annexure hereto, shall be issued by the clerk of the Court and shall call upon the defendant to appear, with his witnesses, before the Court at a stated place and on a date not less than seven days after service of the summons if the distance between the place of service and the Court-house is not more than fifteen miles and not less than ten days if the place of service is beyond that distance.

(2) All process of the Court shall be dated on the day on which it is issued and shall be signed by the officer issuing it.

(3) (a) Service of summons may be effected by the plaintiff himself by delivery in the presence of a witness to the defendant personally, or to some adult member of the kraal or dwelling at which the defendant resides, provided that in the event of a non-personal service the Court may, at any stage of the proceedings require personal service to be made in such manner as it may direct. If the plaintiff so requests summons shall be served in the manner prescribed for the service of summons in Magistrates' Courts by the Messenger upon payment to the Clerk of the Court of the fees prescribed in Table B of the Second Annexure hereto.

(b) No costs and charges shall be recoverable in respect of the service of summons by plantiff in terms of paragraph (a).

(4) All process of the Court which is required to be served outside the area of jurisdiction of the Court shall, when endorsed by the Native Commissioner of the area or, where there is no Native Commissioner, by the Magistrate of the district in which it is to be served (and every Native commissioner or Magistrate as the case may be is hereby required on production to him of such process to endorse the same) be served—

(a) by the Messenger of the Native Commissioner's Court for the area in which it is to be served upon payment by the party causing the process to be issued of the fees prescribed in Table B of the Second Annexure hereto ; or

(b) if no Native Commissioner's Court has jurisdiction for the area in which it is to be served then by the Messenger of the Magistrate's Court of the district upon payment of the fees prescribed for the service of such process issued out of a Magistrate's Court.

26. On the day fixed for the appearance of the parties, they shall be called upon and—

(a) if they both appear, the court shall, before hearing evidence, explain the summons to the defendant and call upon him to answer the claim therein and to prefer any counterclaim he may have which the plaintiff shall be called upon to admit or deny. Whereupon the court shall proceed with the hearing of the cause summarily and without further pleadings ;

(b) if the claimant or applicant or his representative appears and the defendant or respondent is in default, the court, if it is satisfied from evidence on oath that the summons was duly served on the defendant or respondent personally, or upon some adult member of the kraal or dwelling at which the defendant or respondent resides, may enter judgment or make an order in favour of the claimant consistent with such evidence as may be adduced, together with an order for costs ; or the court may adjourn the hearing as it may deem fit ; or

(c) if the defendant or respondent or his representative should appear and the claimant or applicant be in default, the court may postpone the hearing or may dismiss the summons and may award to the defendant or respondent costs in accordance with tariff rates set forth in the Second Annexure hereto.

27. The court may at any stage of the proceedings postpone the hearing or amend any claim, application, or counterclaim or reply which is vague, embarrassing or inconsistent with the evidence adduced or for other reason appearing to the court to be sufficient, provided that the interests of justice are not prejudiced thereby.

28. The court may in any action—

(a) give judgment for the plaintiff ; or

(b) give judgment for the defendant ; or

(c) give absolution from the instance if it appears to the court that the evidence does not justify the court in giving judgment for either party, and

(d) make such order as to costs as may be just.

29. Any plaintiff or applicant whether in convention or reconvention may at any stage of the proceedings withdraw his claim or application, but the party so withdrawing shall be ordered to pay such costs as the court may direct, provided, however, that such withdrawal shall not be a defence to any subsequent action when the costs of the preceding action have been paid.

30. (1) The Court may rescind or vary any judgment granted by it in the absence of the party against whom the judgment was given.

(2) The court may rescind or vary any judgment granted by it which was void *ab origine* or was obtained by fraud or by mistake common to the parties.

(3) The court may correct patent errors in any judgment in respect of which no appeal is pending.

(4) The court may rescind or vary any judgment in respect of which no appeal lies.

(5) Any judgment of the court may, on the application of any person affected thereby who was not a party to the action or matter, made within seven days after he has obtained knowledge of such judgment, be rescinded or varied by the court.

31. No appeal shall lie from the decision of a court in civil proceedings if, before the hearing thereof is commenced, the parties notify such court that an agreement has been come to between them that the decision of the said court shall be final. Such agreement shall be noted by the court and shall in all respects be binding upon the parties.

Witnesses.

32. The Clerk of the Court shall at the request of any party issue a subpoena substantially in the form prescribed in the First Annexure hereto, calling upon the witness or witnesses named therein to appear before the Court at a fixed time and date. Such subpoena may be served by such party personally in the manner prescribed by sub-section (3) of section *twenty-five* for the service of summons or at the request of the party concerned and upon prepayment of the necessary witness allowances and Messenger's fees, by the Messenger. There shall be tendered

to each witness at the time of service of a subpoena witness allowances in accordance with the tariff obtaining in Magistrate's Courts.

33. (a) If any person, being duly subpoenaed to give evidence or to produce any books, papers or thing in his possession or under his control, which the party requiring his attendance desires to show in evidence, fails, without lawful excuse, to attend or, unless duly excused, fails to remain in attendance throughout the trial, the court may, upon being satisfied upon oath or by the return of the messenger that such person has been duly subpoenaed, and that his reasonable expenses have been paid or offered to him, impose upon the said person a fine, not exceeding twenty-five pounds, for his default, and in default of payment to imprisonment for a period not exceeding one month, whether or not such person is otherwise subject to the jurisdiction of the Court.

(b) If any person so subpoenaed shall fail to appear or, unless duly excused, to remain in attendance throughout the trial, the court may also, upon being satisfied as aforesaid and in case no lawful excuse for such failure shall seem to the court to exist, issue a warrant for his apprehension in order that he may be brought up to give his evidence and to be otherwise dealt with according to law, whether or not such person is otherwise subject to the jurisdiction of the court.

(c) The court may, on cause shown, remit the whole or any part of any fine or imprisonment which it may have imposed under this section.

(d) The court may order the costs of any postponement or adjournment occasioned by the default of a witness or any portion of such costs to be paid out of any fine imposed upon such witness.

34. (1) Whenever any person appearing either in obedience to a summons or subpoena as herein before provided or by virtue of a warrant, or being present and being verbally required by the court to give evidence, refuses to be sworn or, having been sworn, refuses to answer such questions as are put to him, or refuses or fails to produce any document or thing which he is required to produce, without offering any just or lawful excuse for such refusal or failure, the court may adjourn the proceedings for any period not exceeding eight days and may, in the meantime, by warrant commit the person so refusing or failing, to a gaol, unless he sooner consents to do what is required of him. If such person upon being brought up at the adjourned hearing again refuses to do what is required of him, the court if it sees fit, may again adjourn the proceedings and commit him for a like period and so on again until such person consents to do what is required of him.

(2) Notwithstanding the committal of any person under sub-section (1), the court may conclude or otherwise dispose of any case or matter wherein such person was required as a witness, but such court shall thereupon order the release of such person.

Execution.

35. At any time after judgment has been given the judgment creditor may demand from the judgment debtor satisfaction of the judgment and if the judgment debtor shall fail to comply forthwith with the demand, the judgment creditor may apply to the clerk of the court for the issue of process in execution. Thereupon the court shall issue such process and the provisions of Chapter VIII of the Magistrates' Courts Act, 1917 (Act No. 32 of 1917) and any amendment thereof and the relative orders together with the prescribed forms [with the exception of section *fifty-eight* and the orders relating thereto, and subject to the substitution of the word " ten " for the word " three " in sub-section (1) of section *fifty-two* and the substitution of the word " three " for the word " one " in paragraph (c) of section *fifty-six*] shall apply *mutatis mutandis* in connection with such process.

36. If any property taken in execution is claimed by any person other than the execution debtor, such claimant shall lodge with the messenger of the court

a statement of the grounds upon which it is claimed that such property is not executable in the suit in question. Thereupon the messenger shall forthwith inform the execution creditor of such claim, and transmit to him such statement or a copy thereof. If the execution creditor does not within seven days of the receipt of such information and statement admit such claim, such claimant may within ten days of the last day allowed for such admission take out an interpleader summons substantially in the form prescribed in the First Annexure hereto, from the court of the district in which the property has been attached, calling upon such creditor to show cause why such property shall not be declared to be unexecutable for the said judgment.

37. Upon the issue of such interpleader summons any action which may have been brought in any court whatsoever in respect of such property shall be stayed and the court in which such action has been brought or any judge or judicial officer thereof may, on proof of the issue of such summons, order the party bringing such action to pay the costs of all the proceedings in such action after the issue of the aforesaid summons, and such action shall abide the result of the proceedings taken upon such summons.

38. Upon the day appointed for the hearing of the claim set forth in such interpleader summons, the court shall summarily and without pleadings adjudicate thereon and may make all such orders as to additional expenses of execution occasioned by the claim as may be just.

39. Any person who—

(1) obstructs a messenger in the execution of his duty or in any way, whether by escape or otherwise, prevents him from carrying out his duty ;

(2) being aware that goods are under arrest, interdict, or attachment by the court, makes away with or disposes of those goods in any manner not authorized by law or knowingly permits those goods, if in his possession or under his control, to be made away with or disposed of in any such manner ;

(3) being a judgment debtor and being required by a messenger to point out property to satisfy any warrant issued in execution of judgment against such person, either—

(a) falsely declares to that messenger that he possesses no property or not sufficient property to satisfy the warrant ; or

(b) although owning such property neglects or refuses to point out the same ; or

(4) being a judgment debtor refuses or neglects to comply with any requirement of a messenger in regard to the delivery of documents in his possession or under his control relating to the title of the immovable property under execution,

shall be guilty of an offence and liable upon conviction to a fine not exceeding fifty pounds, or, in default of payment, to imprisonment for a period not exceeding three months or to such imprisonment without the option of a fine.

Civil Imprisonment.

40. (1) Subject to the provisions of sub-sections (2) and (3), whenever judgment has been given in favour of a judgment creditor upon a claim arising out of a transaction in which the judgment debtor by means of wilful misrepresentations induced the judgment creditor or his predecessor in title to grant any credit, and such judgment has remained unsatisfied during a period of seven clear days, the judgment creditor may take out a summons either in the court wherein the original judgment was given or in the court of any district wherein the judgment debtor resides to appear to show cause why a decree of civil imprisonment should not be made against him.

(2) Notwithstanding the provisions of sub-section (1), the provisions of sections *thirty-five* and *forty* of the regulations published under Government Notice No. 2253 of 1928 shall in the form in which they were before the promulgation of the present amendments be applicable in connection with any judgment based wholly upon a liability which was in existence before such promulgation : Provided that a judgment debtor shall not be ordered to pay the cost of any proceedings instituted by his judgment creditor with a view to effecting the civil imprisonment of such debtor because of his failure to satisfy such judgment.

(3) Any order made before the promulgation of the present amendments for the payment by a judgment debtor of any costs of proceedings instituted by his judgment creditor with a view to effecting his civil imprisonment shall be void in so far as the payment ordered has not already been made.

41. (1) A summons for civil imprisonment shall be served by the delivery by the Messenger of a copy thereof to the respondent personally, unless the Court shall, for good cause shown, give leave for such summons to be served in some other specified manner : provided that in the event of non-personal service the Messenger shall state in his return the reason for such non-personal service and the cause, so far as ascertainable by him, of the respondent's absence, and the Court may confirm such service on being satisfied that the summons would, in the ordinary course, have reached the hands of the respondent.

(2) The court may, upon the return of the summons and whether the judgment debtor appears or not, make a decree of civil imprisonment against such debtor for a period not exceeding three months and upon such conditions as to the court may seem fit and issue a warrant for his arrest and detention in any gaol named in such warrant.

42. The provisions of the Magistrates' Courts Act, 1917 (Act No. 32 of 1917), and any amendment thereof and the rules framed thereunder in respect of the maintenance and discharge of civil debtors shall apply *mutatis mutandis* to the maintenance and discharge of civil debtors committed to gaol under the provisions of the preceding section.

Costs and Fees.

43. (1) The stamps, fees, costs and charges in connection with any proceedings in a court, including all fees or charges of court or of the clerk of court, the messenger, or of legal practitioners, shall be payable in accordance with the scales prescribed in the Second Annexure hereto.

(2) Taxation by the clerk of the court shall be subject to review free of charge by the Native commissioner.

Forms.

44. The forms contained in the First Annexure hereto may, where applicable, be used with such variations as circumstances may require ; but non-compliance with this rule shall not in itself invalidate the proceedings.

General.

45. All process of the court for service or execution and all documents or copies to be filed of record shall be on foolscap paper.

46. Whenever any practitioner has, in the opinion of any Native commissioner, been guilty of misconduct, or dishonourable practice, he shall report the fact to the Incorporated Law Society concerned.

Interpretation.

47. In these regulations, unless inconsistent with the context—

" Act " means Act No. 38 of 1927 ;

" claimant " means the plaintiff or applicant for any order as provided in these regulations ;

" clerk " means " clerk of the court " as provided for in these regulations ;

x

" court " means a court of Native commissioner ;

" judgment " includes a sentence, decree, rule or order of a court ;

" messenger " means " messenger of the court " as provided for in section *fourteen* of these regulations, and includes a deputy or acting messenger or a member of the Police acting in that capacity ;

" officers of the court " shall include the Native commissioner, the clerk of the court and the messengers of court ;

" party " means any person who is a party to any proceedings or his representative as provided in these regulations ;

" process " means any summons, subpoena, writ, warrant, notice, interdict or the like.

FIRST ANNEXURE.

FORM No. 1.

Civil Record-book of the.........................*Native Commissioner's Court held at*...........................

Number of Case.	Plaintiff.	Defendant.	Date of Statement of Claim.	Date of Hearing.	Judgment or Order.	Subsequent Proceedings or Remarks.

FORM No. 2.

SUMMONS.

In the Court of the Native Commissioner at...........................
To A B,

of..................................

You are hereby required to appear before this court at..............on the

...........day of................19....at the hour of........o'clock in

the forenoon, together with your witnesses, if you have any, to answer the claim of

C X D, of...

as follows* ....

....

....

....
Clerk of the Court.

Place.........................

Date.........................

*Set out clearly and concisely the nature of the claim so that the Defendant will know what case he has to meet.

FORM No. 3.

SUBPOENA.

In the Court of the Native Commissioner at...........................
To A B,

of..................................

You are hereby required to attend personally before the court at...........

on the..............day of..............19....at ....o'clock in the

forenoon as a witness in the case of...................*versus*.............

and to produce...

....

And take notice that if you disregard this order you may be arrested and punished for contempt of court.

....
Clerk of the Court.

Place.........................

Date.........................

FORM No. 4.

INTERPLEADER SUMMONS.

In the Court of the Native Commissioner at..............................

To A B,

of...................................

Summon......................(describing the execution creditor), of

...................., that he appear before this Court, holden at........

on the...............day of.................19...., at..........o'clock in the forenoon, with his witnesses, if he have any, to have it determined and declared

whether movable property, to wit.......................................

attached on the.................day of....................19.... by the messenger of this court by virtue of a warrant of execution issued by this court on

the...............day of.................19.... in the action in which you,

the said...................(describing the execution creditor) obtained judg-

ment against...(describing the

execution debtor) and which said property is claimed by.....................
(describing the claimant) as being his property, and not liable to execution, be or

be not his property and be or be not so liable. And serve upon the said........

............a copy of this summons, and return you on the said day of........

............19....what you have done on this summons.

....
Clerk of the Court.

Place.........................

Date.........................

FORM No. 5.

MESSENGER'S REGISTER OF PROCESS.

Number of Case.	Names of Parties.		Nature of Process.	Date of Receipt of Process.	Date sent out for Service.	By whom served and Date.	Fees, Travelling and Service.
	(a) Plaintiff.	(b) Defendant.					

FORM No. 6.

MESSENGER'S WARRANT BOOK.

Number of Case.	Names of Parties.		Date of Writ.	Property or Amount to be Recovered and Costs.	Date of Execution.	Property or Amount recovered.	Manner and Date of Disposal.
	Plaintiff.	Defendant.					

SECOND ANNEXURE.

TABLE A.

Fees of Office to be paid by means of Revenue Stamps affixed to the Process.

1.	Summons	£0	5	0
2.	Summons—interpleader	0	5	0
3.	Summons—civil imprisonment	0	2	6
4.	Subpoena	0	1	0
5.	Interrogatories	0	5	0
6.	Bill of costs	0	1	0
7.	Any warrant of execution	0	2	6
8.	Security for restitution	0	5	0
9.	Security Bond other than security for restitution	0	2	6
10.	Any document not otherwise provided for ..	0	2	0
11.	Notice of Appeal	0	7	6
12.	Request for a copy of a record to be made by Clerk of the Court—			
	(*a*) For the first 100 words or portion thereof		1	0
	(*b*) For each additional 100 words or portion thereof		0	6
	(*c*) In the case of appeals to the Native Appeal Court provided a request therefor is made to the Clerk of the Court within 7 days of the notice of the appeal, a uniform charge for each 100 words or portion thereof		0	3
13.	Request to inspect record if the number and year is not given. For every year to be searched		0	6

The fees for items numbered 1 to 10 shall be reduced by one-half where the process or other document is prepared by the party or his agent.

TABLE B.

Messenger of the Court's Fees.
NATIVE MESSENGER.

	£	s.	d.
Service of summons or subpoena, each person ..	£0	2	6
Execution of any process	0	2	6
Inventory and copy	0	1	0
Inventory, extra copies for additional judgment debtors. Each such	0	0	6

Driving stock. Actual cost not exceeding 2d. per mile for each
ten head of stock.

Herding stock. Actual reasonable cost.

Moneys collected or the proceeds of sale in execution of movables
or the value of such movables where the warrant of execution is withdrawn or the debtor's estate is sequestrated,
1 per cent.

Execution of immovable property. The fees prescribed in Table
B of the Second Annexure to Proclamation No. 145 of 1923,
or any amendment thereof.

	£	s.	d.
Travelling allowance, per mile	0	0	4

EUROPEAN MESSENGER.
The fees prescribed for the time being for magistrates' courts.

TABLE C.

ASSESSORS.

	£	s.	d.
Detention at court for each day or portion of a day during which a trial lasts	£0	10	0
Travelling allowance. For each 36 miles or portion thereof of the combined journey necessarily travelled by the shortest route to the court from the usual place of residence and return thereto	0	10	0

TABLE D.

Fees payable to Attorney.

		£	s.	d.
1.	Instructions to sue or defend	0	5	0
2.	Demand	0	5	0
3.	Any summons	0	5	0
4.	Subpoena (not more than one for each four witnesses called)	0	2	6
5.	Subpoena—each copy for service	0	1	0
6.	Interrogatories	0	5	0
7.	Any warrant	0	5	0
8.	Every notice given to opposite party	0	2	6
9.	Attending court (applying for costs on notice of discontinuance)	0	5	0
10.	Attending court when action in list for trial but adjourned	0	5	0
11.	Attending court on trial of defended action (this amount may in the discretion of the court be increased to £2 2s.). First hearing	1	1	0
12.	Attending court to hear reserved judgment ..	0	5	0

13. Attending court to make any motion (this amount may in
    the discretion of the court be increased to £1 1s.) .. o 10 6
14. Attending court on application decree civil imprisonment o 10 o
15. Bill of costs ; notice and taxation and service ; attending
    taxation .. .. o 5 o
16. Notice of application for review of taxation and service o 3 o
17. Attending on review of taxation .. .. .. o 5 o
18. Agreement not to appeal .. .. o 5 o

TABLE E.

Fees for Counsel.

The same as for attorneys and additional thereto.

THIRD ANNEXURE.

NATIVE ASSESSOR.

I, A B, do swear that I will truly and faithfully assist the court as an assessor and will to the best of my ability and without fear, favour or affection for any one, give my honest opinion upon any matter referred to me by the court.

APPENDIX O

GOVERNMENT NOTICE No. 2254 DATED 21st DECEMBER, 1928

NATIVE APPEAL COURTS : RULES

It is hereby notified for general information that His Excellency the Governor-General has been pleased, in terms of sub-section (5) of section *thirteen* of Act No. 38 of 1927, to make the following rules for Native Appeal Courts :—

1.   The Minister shall appoint officers to perform the duties of Registrars of the Native Appeal Courts : provided that the President of any such court may in case of necessity appoint any person to act temporarily as such registrar.

2.   A refusal by the Registrar of the Native Appeal Court to do any act which he is required or empowered by these rules to do shall be subject to review by the President of the Native Appeal Court on application either *ex parte* or on notice, as the circumstances may require.

3.   (1) Upon a request in writing by any party to any civil proceedings in a Court of Native Commissioner within seven days after judgment and before noting appeal and upon payment by such party of a fee of ten shillings, the officer who delivered such judgment shall, within seven days, deliver to the Clerk of such Court a written judgment showing—

(*a*) the facts the Court found to be proved ; and

(*b*) the reasons for the judgment of the Court.

(2)   Such written judgment shall become part of the record.

4.   Where an appeal to the Native Appeal Court has been noted, the Court of Native Commissioner from which the appeal is brought may, upon application, direct that execution of its judgment shall be suspended pending the decision upon the appeal, upon such terms, if any, as the Court of Native Commissioner may determine as to security for the due performance of any judgment which may be given upon the appeal.

5.   A party to any civil proceedings in a Court of Native Commissioner shall not lose the right to appeal through satisfying or offering to satisfy the judgment in respect of which he appeals, or any part thereof, or by accepting any benefit from such judgment, or from any rule or order in such proceedings.

6.   An appeal from any judgment of a Court of Native Commissioner shall be noted within twenty-one days after the date of such judgment, but the Court of Appeal may in any case extend such period upon just cause being shown.

7.   (1) A respondent may abandon the whole or any part of a judgment appealed against by the delivery to the clerk of the court wherein such judgment was given, of a notice to him setting forth the extent of such abandonment.   Such clerk shall immediately advise the appellant of the terms of such notice.

(2)   The clerk of the court shall duly record on the record and in the civil record book the terms of the notice of abandonment and the judgment of the court

as altered by him in terms of such notice of abandonment shall thereupon become the judgment of the court.

(3) Where the party so abandoning was the plaintiff or applicant, judgment in respect of the part abandoned shall be entered for the defendant or respondent with costs.

(4) Where the party so abandoning was the defendant or respondent, judgment in respect of the part abandoned shall be entered for the plaintiff or applicant in terms of the claim in the summons or application.

8. (1) An appeal from any judgment of a Court of Native Commissioner shall be noted by the delivery, to the clerk of such court, of a notice complying with the requirements of rule 10.

(2) The respondent to any such appeal may, within seven days after service upon him, of the notice of appeal in terms of rule 9, in like manner note a cross-appeal.

(3) The party noting an appeal or cross-appeal shall give security to the satisfaction of the Clerk of the Court in the sum of £5 for the payment of the costs of the other party.

9. (1) After the noting of an appeal or cross-appeal a copy of the notice of appeal or cross-appeal shall forthwith be served upon the other party. Such copy may be served, free of charge, by the party who noted the appeal or cross-appeal, in person, by delivery to the other party personally in the presence of a witness; or at the request of the party noting the appeal or cross-appeal, such copy shall be served by the messenger of the court concerned, upon prepayment by such party, of the messenger's fees for service.

(2) If such service is effected by the party who noted the appeal or cross-appeal, in person, as aforesaid, such party shall forthwith notify the clerk of the court with whom the appeal or cross-appeal was noted, of the time, place and manner of such service, and such service shall have no force or effect until the clerk of the court has been so notified.

10. A notice of appeal or of cross-appeal shall state—

(a) whether the whole or part only of the judgment or order is appealed against, and if part only, then what part; and

(b) the grounds of appeal clearly and specifically: provided, however, that where the appellant was not represented by a legal practitioner during the proceedings in the Native Commissioner's Court against whose judgment the appeal is brought, it shall suffice to note an appeal against the judgment as a whole without specifying in detail the grounds of appeal.

11. The noting of an appeal or cross-appeal and the date thereof shall be recorded by the clerk of the Native Commissioner's Court in the "Remarks" column of the Civil Record Book.

12. (1) Upon the delivery of a notice of appeal the officer who delivered the judgment against which the appeal is brought shall within seven days deliver to the clerk of his court a statement in writing showing (as far as may be necessary, having regard to any written judgment already delivered by him)—

(a) the facts he found to be proved;

(b) the grounds upon which he arrived at any finding of fact specified in the notice of appeal as appealed against; and

(c) his reasons for any ruling of law or for the admission or rejection of any evidence so specified as appealed against.

(2) Such statement shall become part of the record.

(3) The provisions of this rule shall also, *mutatis mutandis*, apply to a cross-appeal.

13. The party noting an appeal or cross-appeal, shall, subject to the provisions of rule No. 20 hereof, prosecute such appeal at the next session of the Native Appeal Court and in default of such prosecution the appeal or cross-appeal shall lapse provided that the Court of Appeal may permit such appeal or cross-appeal to be prosecuted at any subsequent session of such court.

14. Within seven days of receiving notice of appeal the Clerk of the Native Commissioner's Court shall transmit to the Registrar of the Native Appeal Court concerned the record in the action duly certified by the officer who tried such action.

15. The appellant shall prepay the cost of double registered postage by means of postage stamps which shall be attached to the record and duly cancelled.

16. Upon an appeal being noted the Clerk of the Native Commissioner's Court shall—

(1) immediately notify the Registrar of the Native Appeal Court, apart from compliance with the requirements of rule 14 hereof ;

(2) inquire from the appellant and respondent whether either wishes a copy of the record supplied to him at the prescribed fee ;

(3) inform the Registrar of the Native Appeal Court of the result of his inquiry ;

(4) require the appellant or his legal adviser to state at what place and in what manner, whether by formal process of court or by written notice from the Clerk of the Native Commissioner's Court, he will accept notice of hearing. The respondent or his legal adviser shall likewise be asked if he will accept notice of hearing from the Clerk of the Native Commissioner's Court without formal process of court. In the event of no informal notice of hearing being arranged the appellant shall be required to deposit with the Clerk of the Native Commissioner's Court such sum of money as is sufficient to cover the costs of service of formal notice.

17. Where the appellant, unrepresented by a legal practitioner, withdraws the noting of an appeal, the Clerk of the Native Commissioner's Court shall immediately inform the respondent or his legal representative and the Registrar of the Native Appeal Court.

18. (a) Upon publication in the *Gazette* of any notice under sub-section (6) of section *thirteen* of Act No. 38 of 1927 the clerk of each Native Commissioner's Court affected thereby shall immediately—

(1) post a copy of the notice on the court notice board ;

(2) issue the notice of hearing referred to in rule No. 16 hereof.

(b) A like notice shall be issued at the time of all subsequent noting of appeals for hearing at such session.

(c) The Clerk of the Native Commissioner's Court shall transmit to the Registrar of the Native Appeal Court a signed copy of each notice of hearing issued under this rule.

19. Written particulars of any objection or exception or of any application in connection with an appeal shall be filed in triplicate with the Registrar of the Native Appeal Court (or, in his absence, with the Clerk of the Native Commissioner's Court at the centre where the session of the Native Appeal Court is to be held) not less than one clear day prior to the commencement of such session.

20. Save by special leave of the President of a Native Appeal Court, no appeal noted less than twenty-eight days before the commencement of a session of such court, shall be heard during such session.

21. In any case in a Native Appeal Court a party may appear on his own behalf or be represented by his guardian or by a duly authorized relative or by a legal practitioner.

22. In the hearing of an appeal the parties shall be limited to the grounds stated in the notice of appeal, except where the appellant is not represented by a legal practitioner and was not so represented in the Native Commissioner's Court from which such appeal is brought.

23. The Native Appeal Court may reserve judgment, and the court may deliver the same either at a later stage of the session during which the appeal is heard, or at any later date and at some other place fixed by the president of such court.

24. (1) The Registrar of the Native Appeal Court shall cause the judgment of the Native Appeal Court to be entered upon the original record. Such judgment shall be signed by the president and the other members of the court and such original record shall thereupon be returned to the Court of Native Commissioner from which the appeal was made.

(2) The judgment of the Native Appeal Court shall be recorded by the Clerk of the Native Commissioner's Court appealed from in the " Remarks " column of the Civil Record Book and such judgment may be enforced as if it had been given in such last mentioned court.

25. Upon publication in the *Gazette* of any notice under sub-section (6) of section *thirteen* of Act No. 38 of 1927 the Registrar of the Native Appeal Court shall arrange, through the Native commissioners concerned, for the attendance of such Native assessors as may be required during the session of such court.

26. Native assessors attending any session of the Native Appeal Court shall be paid allowances as prescribed for assessors by the Regulations for Courts of Native Commissioners.

27. The costs incurred by the attendance of Native assessors at the Native Appeal Court shall be a charge against the public funds.

28. The fees which may be charged by attorneys and advocates, as between party and party are the fees laid down in Tables B and C respectively of the Schedule to these rules.

29. Taxation by the Registrar of the Native Appeal Court shall be subject to review, free of charge, by the president of the court.

30. Where any provision of these rules has not been fully complied with, the Native Appeal Court may on application order compliance therewith within a stated time.

SCHEDULE

TABLE " A."

Fees of office to be paid by means of revenue stamps affixed to the process :—

		£	s	d
1. Security bond		£0	2	0
2. Bill of costs		0	2	0
The fee for items Nos. 1 and 2 shall be reduced by half if drawn up by the party or his agent.				
3. Taxation of bill of costs		0	2	0

TABLE " B."

	£	s	d
1. For copying the record for every 100 words or part thereof	0	0	6
2. For conducting case in court to include all charges of Attorney in Appeal Court	2	2	0
provided that the court may in its discretion increase the fee to an amount not exceeding	4	4	0

3. For all other local attorney's charges according as the
Clerk of the Court may consider reasonable, if not
specially decided by him 1 1 0

TABLE " C."

Fees to counsel :
    The same as for attorneys and additional thereto.

APPENDIX P

PART II OF SUCCESSION REGULATIONS PUBLISHED UNDER GOVERNMENT NOTICE No. 2257 OF 1928 AS AMENDED BY GOVERNMENT NOTICE No. 946 OF 1932

PART II.

(Applicable in respect of the Cape Province, excluding the Transkeian Territories)

1. Succession in terms of sub-section (2) of section *twenty-three* of the Native Administration Act, 1927 (No. 38 of 1927), shall be regulated, subject to the following provisions, in terms of the annexed Table of Succession.

Male descent in the said table shall mean descent through males only.

When the deceased Native quitrent allotment holder was a female, it shall be recognised that she herself constituted a principal house. In such case paragraphs 1, 2 and 9 of the table only shall apply.

2. (a) If, within a period of not less than six months after the death of the deceased, the Native Commissioner of the district in which the land is situate has, after due inquiry, been unable to determine which male person, if any, is entitled to succeed to such land in accordance with these regulations he shall, by notice posted at the court-house of the district, and at or on the land in question, call upon any person claiming to be entitled to succeed to such land in terms of the Table of Succession, to lodge his claim thereto with such Native Commissioner within three months from the date of such notice.

(b) If, after the lapse of a period of not less than two years from the death of the deceased, the Native Commissioner of the district in which such land is situate is satisfied upon reasonable grounds that the male person entitled to succeed thereto in accordance with these regulations has either absconded from the district or is absent therefrom and his whereabouts is unknown, such Native Commissioner shall, by notice posted at the courthouse of the district, and at or on the land in question, call upon such person to lodge his claim thereto with the said Native Commissioner within three months from the date of such notice.

(c) If, within the period prescribed in sub-sections (a) and (b) hereof, no such claim or claims be lodged, or if any be lodged, and, after due inquiry, be disallowed by the Native Commissioner, the Chief Native Commissioner may authorize the transfer of the land to the person next entitled thereto in accordance with the order of precedence laid down in the Table of Succession.

3. (a) When the holder of any land dies leaving surviving him any widow or partner who was at all times the sole person with whom he had contracted either a marriage or a customary union or who, if not such sole person, was partner of the principal house, such widow or surviving partner shall, until her re-marriage or entrance into another customary union, be entitled, during her residence at the kraal of her late husband, or partner, or at such kraal as may be approved by her late husband's or partner's relatives, to the use and occupation of such land, subject

to the obligations imposed by the conditions of title ; and during such use and occupation such land shall remain registered in the name of the deceased.

(b)   Any widow or surviving partner entitled under the provisions of this section to the use and occupation of land shall be held to have forfeited her rights to such land if, within three months of the personal service upon her of a written notice signed by the Native Commissioner of the district in which such land is situated, calling upon her to notify her aceeptance of such rights, she has failed to notify such acceptance.

4.   (1) Should the heir under the Table of Succession, at the date when he becomes entitled to succeed to the land registered in the name of the deceased, be already in possession of land in a location held in individual tenure, he shall be required by the Native Commissioner to elect within three months after the death of the deceased or after the termination of any usufructuary rights enjoyed by any widow or surviving partner of the deceased under the provisions of section *three*, as the case may be, whether he will remain in possession of the land at the time held by him or take possession of the land to which he has become entitled to succeed; and the Chief Native Commissioner shall authorize the transfer of the land which the heir does not select to the person next entitled to succeed to the deceased in accordance with the Table of Succession, who shall not be in possession of land in a location held in individual tenure and who shall not be ineligible to hold such land.

(2)   The provisions of section *two* shall apply, *mutatis mutandis*, to succession in accordance with this section, provided that the date from which the periods of six months and two years therein specified shall be reckoned shall be the date of election by the heir and not the date of the death of the deceased.

5.   It shall be lawful for any person entitled to succeed to land under the provisions of these regulations to renounce his right to such land which shall thereupon devolve upon the person next entitled thereto under these regulations, provided that, whenever the person entitled to succeed to such land is a minor, such renunciation shall be made by the guardian of such minor and shall be effective only subject to the following conditions :—

(i)   that evidence on oath or by way of solemn declaration has been given to the Native Commissioner of the district in which the land is situated in support of the renunciation and that such further information relative to the renunciation as the Native Commissioner may require has been furnished ; and

(ii)   that the Native Commissioner is satisfied that it would be in the interests of the minor that the renunciation should be accepted ; and

(iii)   that the approval of the Chief Native Commissioner has been obtained.

6.   Whenever, under the provisions of these regulations, land shall have reverted to the Crown, the Governor-General may in his discretion authorize its transfer to a female member of the family of the deceased or any descendant of any such female or may cause such land to be sold and the proceeds thereof to be divided amongst the female members of the family of the deceased or their descendants.

7.   (1) If any Native shall desire to disinherit the person entitled to succeed to his land under these regulations by reason of gross misconduct or incapacity to deal with or manage the land or insanity or for any other just cause the Native Commissioner of the district in which such land is situated, on the application of such Native, shall summon before him the person whom it is proposed to disinherit, and, in the presence of such person or in his absence in case he should neglect, refuse or be unable by reason of insanity to appear at the time and place mentioned in the summons, shall inquire into all the circumstances and may

declare such person disinherited. Subject to the provisions of sub-section (2), any person so disinherited shall not be entitled to succeed to such land which shall upon the death of the holder thereof devolve upon the person next entitled thereto under the provisions of these regulations.

(2) At any subsequent time prior to the death of the holder the Native Commissioner, upon representations to him, either by the holder or by the person disinherited may re-open the inquiry and in the event of his being satisfied that the grounds for such disherison no longer exist may rescind such disherison.

(3) A record shall be kept of all proceedings under sub-sections (1) and (2) of this section and it shall be competent for any person interested in any declaration of disherision or the rescission thereof to appeal to the Chief Native Commissioner against any decision of a Native Commissioner within a period of fourteen days from the date of such declaration or rescission. The decision of the Chief Native Commissioner shall be final.

SCHEDULE

TABLE OF SUCCESSION

1. The deceased's eldest son of the principal house or, if he be dead, such eldest son's senior male descendant, according to Native custom.

2. If there be no male descendant of the deceased's eldest son, the deceased's next son of the principal house or his senior male descendant, and so on through the deceased's sons or their senior male descendants respectively and through the deceased's several houses in their order according to Native custom.

3. If there be no son or male descendant of any son of the deceased, the father of the deceased.

4. If the father of the deceased be dead, the deceased's eldest brother of the same house or his senior male descendant, and so on through the brothers of that house or their senior male descendants respectively according to Native custom

5. If there be no brother of the deceased of the same house or male descendant of any such brother, the deceased's eldest brother of the allied house of higher rank or next rank as the case may be or his senior male descendant and so on through the brothers of such allied house and their senior male descendants respectively according to Native custom, and thereafter through the brothers of the remaining houses in order of rank according to Native custom and their senior male descendants respectively.

6. If there be no brother of the deceased or male descendant of any brother of any house, the deceased's eldest paternal uncle in the same house as the deceased's father or such paternal uncle's senior male descendant and so on through the paternal uncles of that house and their senior male descendants respectively according to Native custom.

7. If there be no paternal uncle of the deceased or male descendant of any paternal uncle of the house to which deceased's father belonged, the deceased's eldest paternal uncle of the allied house of higher rank or next rank as the case may be according to Native custom or his senior male descendant and so on through the deceased's paternal uncles of such allied house and their senior male descendants respectively, and thereafter through the deceased's paternal uncles of the remaining houses in order of rank according to Native custom or their senior male descendants respectively.

8. If there be no paternal uncle of the deceased or any male descendant of any such uncle of any house, the paternal grandfather of the deceased.

9. If there be no heir competent and willing to accept transfer of the land under the provisions of this Table of Succession the land shall revert to the Crown.

APPENDIX Q

GOVERNMENT NOTICE No. 1664 DATED 20th SEPTEMBER, 1929

It is hereby notified for general information that His Exccllency the Governor-General has been pleascd, under the powers vested in him by sub-section (10) of section *twenty-three* of the Native Administration Act, 1927 (Act No. 38 of 1927), to make the accompanying regulations for the administration and distribution of Native estates.

REGULATIONS FRAMED UNDER THE PROVISIONS OF SUB-SECTION (10) OF SECTION *TWENTY-THREE* OF THE NATIVE ADMINISTRATION ACT, 1927, FOR THE ADMINISTRATION AND DISTRIBUTION OF NATIVE ESTATES.

1. In these regulations, unless inconsistent with the context—
" the Act " means the Native Administration Act, 1927, as amended by the Native Administration Act, 1927, Amendment Act, 1929 ;
" estate " means the estate of a deceased Native ;
" Native Commissioner " in respect of any District for which no Native Commissioner has been appointed means the Magistrate of that District.

2. If a Native dies leaving no valid will, so much of his property as does not fall within the purview of sub-section (1) or sub-section (2) of section *twenty-three* of the Act shall be distributed in the manner following :—

(a) If the deceased was at the time of his death the holder of letters of exemption issued under the provisions of Natal Law No. 28 of 1865, the property shall devolve as if he had been a European.

(b) If the deceased had during his lifetime contracted a marriage in community of property or under antenuptial contract, the property shall devolve as if he had been a European.

(c) When any deceased Native resident at the time of his death in an urban or industrial area is not survived by any wife, partner, or child under a marriage or customary union and was at the time of his death living with any woman as his putative wife under such conditions as in the opinion of the Minister to render the application of Native law and custom to the devolution of his property inequitable or inappropriate, such property shall devolve as if the deceased and such putative wife had been married.

(d) If the deceased does not fall under any of the classes described in paragraphs (a), (b), and (c), the property shall be distributed according to Native law and custom.

3. (1) All the property in any estate falling within the purview of paragraphs (a), (b), and (c) of section *two* of these regulations shall be administered under the

supervision of the Native Commissioner of the District in which the deceased ordinarily resided and such Native Commissioner shall give such directions in regard to the distribution thereof as shall seem to him fit and shall take all steps necessary to ensure that the provisions of the Act and of these regulations are complied with.

(2) Whenever it shall appear to the Native Commissioner of the District in which any deceased Native ordinarily resided or, in the case of immovable property, to the Native Commissioner of the District where such property is situate, that it is necessary, in connection with the distribution of any property in the estate of such Native falling within the purview of sub-section (1) or sub-section (2) of section *twenty-three* of the Act or of paragraph (d) of section *two* of these regulations, that an inquiry should be instituted to determine the person or persons entitled to such property, such Native Commissioner may call before him any person who may be able to furnish information in regard to the proper distribution of such property and after hearing such persons as he may consider necessary shall give such directions in regard to the distribution thereof as shall seem to him fit to ensure that the provisions of the Act and of these regulations are complied with.

(3) Where any dispute or question has arisen concerning the administration or distribution of any such property as is referred to in sub-section (2), such Native Commissioner shall summon before him all the parties concerned and such witnesses as he may consider necessary. He may impose an oath or solemn declaration upon any person whom he deems it necessary to examine and shall summarily and without pleadings hear and determine the issue.

(4) A Native Commissioner in declaring his finding in regard to any dispute or question referred to in sub-section (3) may make such award as to costs of the proceedings as may seem to him fit and costs so awarded, which shall be assessed according to the tariff prescribed in the rules for courts of Native Commissioner, may be recovered in the same manner as costs arising out of any civil proceedings in a Native Commissioner's or Magistrate's Court.

(5) An appeal from the finding of a Native Commissioner in regard to any dispute or question referred to in sub-section (3) shall lie to the appropriate Native Appeal Court and the procedure in any such appeal shall be the same as that laid down in respect of appeals in civil proceedings from courts of Native Commissioner.

4. (1) For the administration and distribution of any property in the estate of a deceased Native referred to in section *two* of the regulations the appointment of an executor shall not be necessary. Provided that whenever the Native Commissioner of the District in which the deceased Native ordinarily resided considers it desirable he may issue a certificate to any person whom he may deem suitable, appointing him to represent the estate and to assume responsibility for the payment of debts, the collection of assets and the general administration and distribution of the property. Such certificate shall be issued in any case where it becomes necessary to pass transfer to any person of immovable property, not being land in a location held under quitrent conditions, registered in the name of the deceased.

(2) A person to whom a certificate has been issued under sub-section (1) shall have full power and authority to represent the estate in relation to such property including power on behalf of the estate and subject to the approval of the Native Commissioner to pass and to receive transfer of immovable property.

(3) The Native Commissioner may require any person to whom a certificate has been issued under sub-section (1) to furnish such security for the due and proper administration of such property as he may deem necessary and to render a just, true and exact account of his administration within such period and at such intervals as the Native Commissioner may prescribe.

(4) Any person failing within the period prescribed to render any account which may be required of him under sub-section (3) or any person who under the provisions of that sub-section renders other than a just, true and exact account shall be guilty of an offence.

(5) The Native Commissioner may at any time revoke a certificate issued by him to any person under sub-section (1)

5. (1) Whenever a Native has died leaving a valid will which disposes of any portion of his estate and there is in such estate any such property as is referred to in sub-section (1) or sub-section (2) of section *twenty-three* of the Act, the Native Commissioner shall furnish the executor in the estate with all such information regarding such property, its value and the realization thereof or any portion thereof as may be necessary.

(2) In the administration of any such estate as is referred to in sub-section (1) the claims of any creditors shall be satisfied from the portion of the estate administered under the Administration of Estates Act, 1913 (Act No. 24 of 1913), in terms of sub-section (9) of section *twenty-three* of the Act. Should such portion be insufficient to meet such claims the executor in the estate shall notify the Native Commissioner concerned who shall, in consultation with the executor, cause to be realised so much of the property falling within the purview of the said sub-section (1) or sub-section (2) as is *executable* in respect of the deceased's liabilities and as is necessary to meet the balance of such claims. The executor shall thereupon proceed to liquidate the claims and submit his account to the Master in due course.

6. (1) Notwithstanding anything in section *three* of these regulations, if a Native in the employ of any person dies without leaving such a will as is referred in sub-section (9) of section *twenty-three* of the Act the Native Commissioner of the District in which such Native was immediately prior to his death employed, may collect and realise any asset in and may enforce any claim belonging to the estate of such Native.

(2) Such Native Commissioner may from any moneys collected or realised by him under sub-section (1) pay any preferent claims requiring immediate liquidation against the estate of such Native and if such Native was domiciled in a District other than the one wherein he was employed such Native Commissioner shall render a true account of all assets collected by him under sub-section (1) and of any moneys expended by him under this sub-section to the Native Commissioner in whose District such Native was domiciled.

7. (1) A Native Commissioner, in exercising his functions under the Act or these regulations, may take all such steps as he may consider necessary to safeguard and preserve the inheritance or interests of minors and may deposit the cash inheritance of any minor in the Guardian's Fund, furnishing at the same time to the Master particulars as to the deceased parent, the date of birth of the minor and the name and address of the guardian.

(2) Nothing in these regulations shall be deemed to limit or restrict the exercise by the Supreme Chief of his functions as the upper guardian of Native orphans and minors in the Provinces of Natal, Transvaal and Orange Free State.

8. (1) Whenever any Native who is the parent of a minor child entitled to claim from that Native any inheritance from the estate of that Native's deceased spouse, being an estate which has been administered under the supervision and control of a Native Commissioner under the provisions of these regulations, wishes to marry again that Native shall (whether the marriage be by special licence or after publication of banns) obtain a certificate under the hand of such Native Commissioner to the effect that arrangements have been made to his satisfaction for the preservation and protection of the inheritance of such minor.

(2) Such certificate shall be delivered to the marriage officer or minister of religion before whom the marriage is intended to be solemnised.

(3) Any such Native who marries again without obtaining such a certificate as is required under sub-section (1) and any marriage officer or minister of religion who solemnises any such marriage unless there has first been delivered to him the certificate required by this section in respect of the parties shall be guilty of an offence.

9. Whenever it shall appear to the Master of the Supreme Court in the administration of an estate under sub-section (9) of section *twenty-three* of the Act, that no executor has been appointed, or that the executor testamentary is either unable or unwilling to act, he may, subject to the provisions of section *thirty-four* of the Administration of Estates Act, 1913, appoint and require the Native Commissioner of the District in which the deceased ordinarily resided, to act in his official capacity as executor dative in the estate, but such Native Commissioner shall not be required to find security for the administration of the estate.

10. The Master of the Supreme Court to whom the death of any person has been reported may call upon the Native Commissioner of the area in which the deceased died or was ordinarily resident to certify whether or not such deceased person was a Native as defined under the Act.

11. Part I of the regulations published under Government Notice No. 2257 dated the 21st December, 1928, is hereby repealed.

APPENDIX R

NATIVE EDUCATION : STATISTICS OF SCHOOLS, PUPILS AND AMOUNTS EXPENDED FROM THE NATIVE DEVELOPMENT ACCOUNT

Year	No. of Schools	No. of Pupils	Amount of Tax Collected	Amount paid from Development A/c. From Tax	From Treasury	Total Subsidy	Grant per Pupil
			£	£	£	£	£
			CAPE PROVINCE.				
1926-27	1,604	117,880	83,457	59,600	240,000	299,600	2.54
1927-28	1,638	122,261	85,802	63,324	240,000	303,324	2.48
1928-29	1,668	122,571	88,916	79,067	240,000	319,067	2.61
1929-30	1,726	131,915	90,841	91,155	240,000	331,155	2.51
1930-31	1,738	137,804	92,718	102,687	240,000	342,687	2.41
1931-32	1,730	143,361	82,472	106,000	240,000	346,000	2.42
			NATAL PROVINCE.				
1926-27	553	37,921	64,455	22,561	49,000	71,561	2.10
1927-28	566	37,820	61,161	30,428	49,000	79,428	2.10
1928-29	628	41,222	62,224	42,963	49,000	91,963	2.23
1929-30	698	47,425	65,051	54,108	49,000	103,108	2.17
1930-31	703	48,525	65,182	61,018	49,000	110,018	2.26
1931-32	667	46,381	56,034	63,000	49,000	112,000	2.45
			TRANSVAAL PROVINCE.				
1926-27	394	43,176	56,113	15,450	46,000	61,450	1.42
1927-28	467	47,632	63,913	24,998	46,000	70,998	1.49
1928-29	498	57,742	64,799	32,884	46,000	78,884	1.37
1929-30	588	67,254	67,145	46,051	46,000	92,051	1.37
1930-31	594	72,801	69,419	53,078	46,000	99,078	1.37
1931-32	592	73,579	67,143	57,638	46,000	103,638	1.37
			ORANGE FREE STATE PROVINCE.				
1926-27	194	17,701	20,507	13,313	5,000	18,313	1.03
1927-28	176	17,726	22,070	14,927	5,000	19,927	1.12
1928-29	192	19,305	21,323	25,405	5,000	30,405	1.57
1929-30	203	22,333	22,267	31,006	5,000	36,006	1.61
1930-31	216	24,638	21,338	34,223	5,000	39,223	1.55
1931-32	211	26,302	21,449	35,500	5,000	40,500	1.54
			UNION.				
1926-27	2,745	216,678	224,532	110,924	340,000	450,924	2.08
1927-28	2,847	225,439	232,946	133,677	340,000	473,677	2.10
1928-29	2,986	240,840	237,262	180,319	340,000	520,319	2.12
1929-30	3,215	268,927	245,304	222,320	340,000	562,320	2.09
1930-31	3,251	283,768	248,657	251,006	340,000	591,006	2.08
1931-32	3,200	289,623	227,098	262,965	340,000	602,138	2.08

ceval quichon   marlaguette quichon   jon quichon   billy quichon   camille quichon   david quichon   isaac quichon

enriquetta quichon   dominique quichon   marie-ange quichon   tristan quichon   anna quichon   zachary quichon   iris quichon

babakar quichon   olive quichon   florence quichon   édith quichon   carole quichon   mica quichon   hermès quichon

ge quichon   noémie quichon   henri quichon   sacha quichon   gwendoline quichon   marthe quichon   bertrand quichon

he quichon   vladimir quichon   gloria quichon   rabiatou quichon   shirine quichon   casimir quichon   pierre-émilien quichon

© 2004, l'école des loisirs, Paris
Loi numéro 49 956 du 16 juillet 1949 sur les publications
destinées à la jeunesse : septembre 2004
Dépôt légal : septembre 2004
Imprimé en France par Jean Lamour à Maxéville

anaïs vaugelade

MAMAN QUICHON SE FÂCHE

l'école des loisirs

Un soir où personne n'avait envie d'aller
se coucher (et pourtant il était très tard,
pour des petits Quichon), Maman Quichon
annonça : « Je vais me fâcher. »

Mais personne n'y fit attention.

Alors Maman Quichon dit :
« Je vais me transformer en pierre. »

Là-dessus, elle se transforma en pierre.
Et personne n'y fit attention.

C'est Annabella Quichon qui s'inquiéta
la première : « Maman, hé, Maman ! » dit-elle.
Mais Maman Quichon ne répondit pas.

Ensuite, Virgile Quichon et Léa Quichon
lui firent quelques petites chatouilles.
Mais Maman Quichon ne répondit pas.

BOÏNG.

Alors les soixante-treize enfants Quichon
décidèrent de lui donner tous ensemble
un très gentil bisou.

Mais Maman Quichon ne répondit pas.
« Qu'est-ce qu'on va faire ? »
se lamentèrent les enfants Quichon ;
déjà les plus jeunes commençaient à pleurer.
« Maman, Maman, arrête d'être une pierre »,
suppliait la petite Florence Quichon.

Et soudain, Maman Quichon s'étira, soupira,
sourit et dit :

« Allez, ça suffit ! Et maintenant, tout le monde au lit ! »

Les soixante-treize enfants Quichon
se jetèrent sous les couvertures.

« Maman, promets que tu ne te transformeras
plus jamais en pierre », demanda
la petite Florence Quichon.
« D'accord, je le promets », répondit
Maman Quichon ; et, pour leur souhaiter
bonne nuit, elle fit un gros, gros bisou
à ses soixante-treize enfants chéris.

léa quichon   virgile quichon   nachid quichon   cléo quichon   gaëtan quichon   philippe quichon   sylvie quichon

elsa quichon   claude quichon   annabella quichon   fatoumata quichon   cyril quichon   lucette quichon   stéphanie quichon   patrick

baboussia quichon   guersihom quichon   raphaëlle quichon   marvin quichon   yoko quichon   guillaume quichon   rita quichon

jean-françois quichon   viviane quichon   stella quichon   diane quichon   paolo quichon   chaïm quichon   mickey q

pervenche quichon   louisiane quichon   kenbougoue quichon   gary quichon   buster quichon   sébastien quichon   théodora quichon   ruché qu

American Lives

James Beckwourth

Rick Burke

Heinemann Library
Chicago, Illinois

Designed by Sarah Figlio
Photo research by Kathy Creech
Printed and Bound in the United States by
Lake Book Manufacturing, Inc.

08 07 06 05 04
10 9 8 7 6 5 4 3 2 1

Library of Congress
Cataloging-in-Publication Data
Burke, Rick, 1957-
  James Beckwourth / by Rick Burke.
      v. cm. -- (American lives)
Includes bibliographical references (p.) and index.
Contents: Blackfeet battle -- Childhood -- Missouri -- St. Louis -- Mountain man -- The Crow -- The Seminole wars -- The Cheyenne -- California and war -- Beckwourth Pass -- The book -- Growing old -- Remembering James.
  ISBN 1-4034-4191-X -- ISBN 1-4034-4204-5 (pbk.)
 1. Beckwourth, James Pierson, 1798-1866--Juvenile literature. 2.African American pioneers--West (U.S.)--Biography--Juvenile literature.
3. African American trappers--West (U.S.)--Biography--Juvenile literature. 4. Pioneers--West (U.S.)--Biography--Juvenile literature.
5. Trappers--West (U.S.)--Biography--Juvenile literature. 6. West (U.S.)--Biography--Juvenile literature. 7. Frontier and pioneer life--West (U.S.)--Juvenile literature. [1. Beckwourth, James Pierson, 1798-1866. 2. Pioneers. 3. African Americans--Biography.] I. Title. II. American lives (Heinemann Library (Firm))
  F592.B393B87 2003
  978'.02'092--dc21

2003004970

Acknowledgments
The author and publishers are grateful to the following for permission to reproduce copyright material: Title page, pp. 4, 6, 8, 13T, 16, 20, 22, 23, 25, 27, 29 Hulton Archive/Getty Images; p. 5 Cincinnati Historical Society, negative B-95-001; pp. 7, 9, 10, 13B Bettmann/Corbis; p. 11 The Granger Collection, New York; p. 12 Stapleton Collection/Corbis; pp. 14, 15, 24 Reproduced from the Biographical Memoir of Daniel Boone, The First Settler of Kentucky: Interspersed With Incidents in the Early Annals of the Country, Timothy Flint, 1836; p. 17 Corbis; p. 18 David Muench/Corbis; p. 19 Mead Art Museum, Amherst College, Museum Purchase Acc. No.: AC P.1939.7; p. 21 University of Kentucky Archives; p. 26 Reproduced from Kentucke and the Adventures of Col. Daniel Boone, John Filson, 1784; p. 28 Raymond Gehman/Corbis

Cover photograph by Hulton Archive/Getty Images

The publisher would like to thank Michelle Rimsa for her comments in the preparation of this book.

Every effort has been made to contact copyright holders of any material reproduced in this book. Any omissions will be rectified in subsequent printings if notice is given to the publisher.

Some words are shown in bold, **like this.** You can find out what they mean by looking in the glossary.

For more information on the image of James Beckwourth that appears on the cover of this book, turn to page 29.

Contents

Blackfeet Battle

James Beckwourth saw 500 Blackfeet warriors charging on horseback toward him and his small group of trappers, women, and children. James and the trappers sent the women and children to a forest of willow trees for safety. The men stayed and fired their rifles at the Blackfeet, trying to keep the warriors away. For six miles (10 kilometers), the trappers battled the Blackfeet. However, the Blackfeet kept coming.

James had to think quickly and use his skills many times during his life as a **frontiersman**.

James found himself in the middle of the fight. As arrows and bullets flew past them, the trappers made it to the willow forest, where the women and children already were. They were not safe, though. The trappers were running out of bullets. James and a man named Calhoun charged through the Blackfeet group to get help. James found another group of trappers and brought them back to the fight. James's actions saved the women and children. This was just one of the many dangerous adventures in James Beckwourth's life.

Childhood

James Beckwourth was born on April 26, 1798, in Fredericksburg, Virginia. James's father was Jennings Beckwourth. Not much is known about James's mother. Some people believe she was a slave owned by Jennings. By Virginia law, this made James a slave, too. But Jennings never treated James as a slave. He loved his son.

Slaves were used to pick cotton and help **harvest** crops.

Military Man

Jennings Beckwourth fought in the **Revolutionary War** *(1775–1783) against Britain. Jennings was a major in George Washington's army. The United States became an independent country when it won the war.*

The Life of James Beckwourth

1798	1812	1824	1828
Born on April 26, in Fredericksburg, Virginia	*Became a* **blacksmith's apprentice**	*Became a trapper*	*Captured by the Crow tribe*

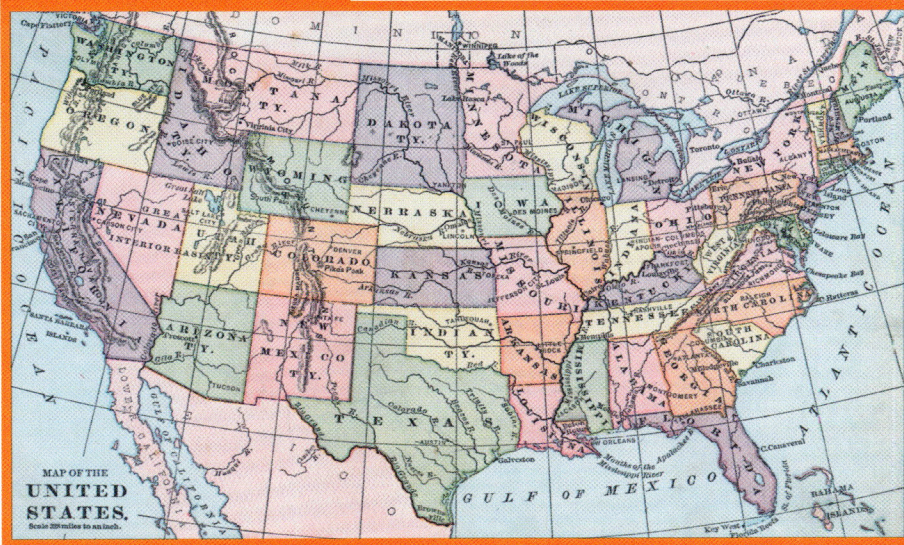

MAP OF THE
UNITED
STATES.
Scale 288 miles to an inch.

This map shows the boundaries of the states and territories in the early 1800s.

When James was young, his father moved the family to Missouri. Jennings bought over 1,000 acres of land between the Mississippi and Missouri Rivers. The land, which was called the Point, was near the present-day city of St. Louis. Jennings loved to hunt, and he passed down that love to his son James.

James's Mother

James's mother's name is unknown. When slaves were born, their names and birth dates were not always written down.

1842	1850	1854	1867?
Established a trading post at Pueblo, Colorado	*Found Beckwourth Pass*	*Told the story of his life for a book*	*Died in Montana*

7

Missouri

James's family was just one of many families that moved to Missouri. The families built homes and farms on land that Native Americans had used. The Native American tribes of the Osage, Fox, and Sauk used that land to hunt and trap animals. The tribes were unhappy that settlers were moving in. They wanted the land back. Sometimes warriors of the tribes attacked the families to scare others from moving to Missouri and taking more land.

As more settlers moved west, Native Americans were pushed out. Their villages were either destroyed or packed up and moved to another part of the country.

Log cabins were common in the 1800s. People would gather materials from the land and create a new home for their families.

When James was about nine years old, he rode his horse to the home of a friend. When James got there, he found the dead bodies of his friend's family. A Native American **raiding** party had attacked them. James rode back to the Point as fast as he could to warn his own family. James's father gathered a group of men and hunted down the raiders. If it had not been for James's quick action, his family might have been the next to be killed.

St. Louis

James was sent away to school to learn to read and write. In 1812, James became an **apprentice** to a **blacksmith** named George Casner. James did not like being a blacksmith. He wanted to hunt in the woods.

Being a blacksmith is hard work. Blacksmiths heat iron and steel and hammer them into shape. They make tools such as hammers, nails, axes, and knives.

AM I NOT A MAN AND A BROTHER?

People who were slaves had no rights. They were often treated as if they were not human beings.

James and Casner did not get along very well. One day, they got into an argument. James and Casner began to fight, and James ran away. Unfortunately, James was still considered to be a slave. A slave could be **punished** for hitting a free man. James's father went to court to have James freed from slavery before he could be punished. Once James was a free man, he never went back to work for Casner.

Mountain Man

James Beckwourth's life changed when he saw an announcement in a newspaper. A man named William Ashley owned the Rocky Mountain Fur Company. He needed men who would go into the Rocky Mountains and trap animals for their fur. Beckwourth saw Ashley's ad and moved west to become a trapper.

Beaverskin hats were very popular in Europe. Trappers were paid high prices for the furs they sold.

Cold Work

Trappers worked during the winter, when the fur of the animal was thicker. Trappers who worked in the mountains were also called mountain men.

Mountain men had to wear a lot of clothing to keep them warm and hide from animals.

Beckwourth loved being a trapper. He was able to hunt and explore. Beckwourth met and worked with mountain men who were well known in the west. Their names were Jim Bridger, Jedediah Smith, Jim Clyman, and Edward Rose. In the summer of 1825, Beckwourth and the others from the Rocky Mountain Fur Company met with other trappers at Henry's Fork on the Green River. It was the first Mountain Man **Rendezvous.** There, the men traded their furs, had contests to show their skills, and told stories.

The Crow

In 1828, Beckwourth went on a trapping trip with Jim Bridger. One day, the two were working together, but Beckwourth walked down the side of a stream to set traps. He walked right into the middle of a Crow **war party.** Beckwourth's fellow trappers had started a **rumor** that Beckwourth was actually a Crow, and the Native Americans had heard it. They captured Beckwourth and took him back to their village. A chief named Big Bowl thought Beckwourth was the son that he had not seen in many years. Beckwourth became a member of the Crow tribe.

Jim Bridger was a great beaver trapper, fur trader, and guide to the West.

Crow Names

James had at least ten Crow names. Some of them were Morning Star, Enemy of Horses, Bloody Arm, and Medicine Calf.

After he had lived with the Crow for several years, the tribe made Beckwourth their war chief. Beckwourth led the Crow on many **raids** to fight other tribes and steal their horses. A Crow warrior showed his bravery by going on raids to steal horses from other tribes. Beckwourth would sometimes steal horses from the fur companies and then sell the same horses back to the companies.

Fights between Native Americans and settlers often left people hurt or dead. Crow chief Arapooash died during battle against the Blackfeet in 1834.

The Seminole Wars

After six years, Beckwourth left the Crow people and went back to St. Louis. Beckwourth only spent a few months in the city before he needed new adventures. He traveled to the swamps of Florida to fight in the Seminole Wars. U.S. President Andrew Jackson wanted the Seminoles to leave so white farmers could have the land. The Seminole fought against the U.S. Army to keep their land.

Native American chiefs were captured by U.S. soldiers during the Seminole Wars.

The Trail of Tears

Congress and President Jackson wanted the Native Americans's land to give to white people. From 1838–1839, the Cherokee tribe was forced to walk to land in Oklahoma that had been set aside for them. Many people died on the way. Their journey is known as the Trail of Tears.

Beckwourth became a **messenger** for the U.S. Army. He was at the Battle of Okeechobee, which was the last major battle of the Second Seminole War. Once the war was over, Beckwourth was ready for a change. He missed the cold air and the adventures of the West, so he headed back there.

The Battle of Okeechobee happened on December 25, 1837. The Second Seminole War was the longest and most expensive war against the Native Americans in United States history.

The Cheyenne

After the Seminole Wars, Andrew Sublette and Louis Vasquez, owners of a fur company, hired Beckwourth to trade with Native American tribes along the Santa Fe Trail. The tribes included the Cheyenne, Arapaho, and Sioux, all of whom were enemies of the Crow tribe. On his first trip to meet the Cheyenne, Beckwourth told the tribe that he ran away from the Crow because he killed a chief. Beckwourth told the Cheyenne that if he was going to die, he wanted to be killed by the great Cheyenne people.

Santa Fe Trail

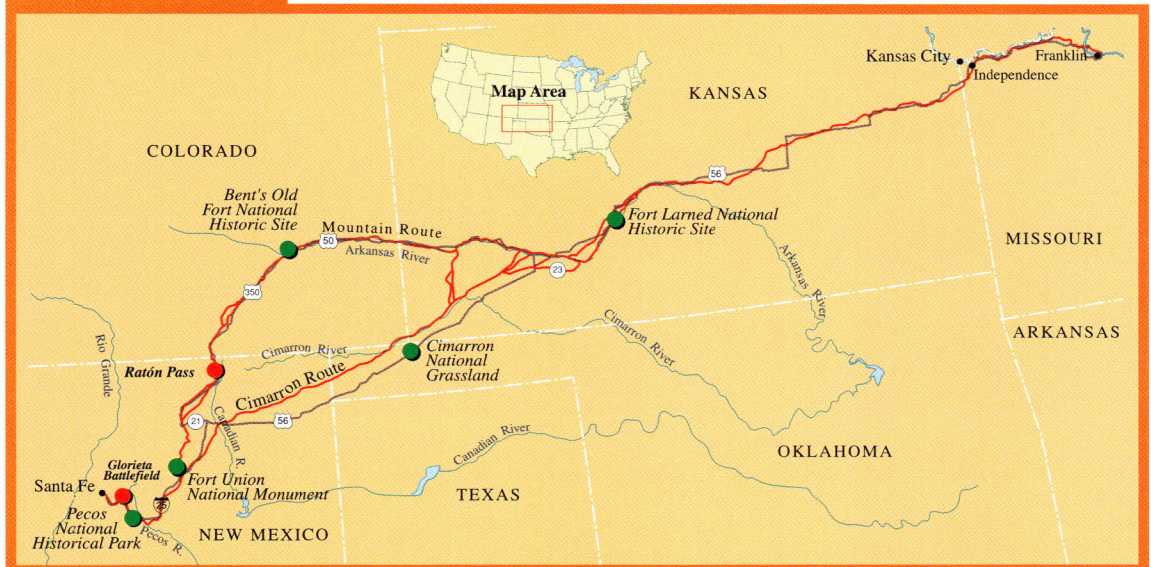

The Santa Fe Trail was a kind of highway that connected Missouri with Santa Fe, New Mexico.

Fur traders came to Pueblo, Colorado, in the 1840s.
When the California gold rush began in the 1850s,
many people started coming to the Pueblo area to live.

An **interpreter** named William Bent told
James that the Cheyenne would make James
into "sausage meat." But Bent was wrong.
The Cheyenne thought James was brave, and
they traded furs with him. James made a lot
of money for Sublette and Vasquez. James
then moved to Colorado to start his own
trading post. About twenty other trappers
and their families followed him. James named
his post Pueblo. Soon, James got bored with
Pueblo and wanted another adventure. He
found it by moving to California.

California and War

Beckwourth arrived in California in 1844. At that time, California belonged to Mexico. Some Americans living in California wanted the land to be free from Mexico. These people were called Los Osos, which means "The Bears." Beckwourth fought with them against the Mexicans at the Battle of Cahuenga. Soon after, the United States went to war with Mexico. Beckwourth helped the Americans by stealing 2,000 Mexican horses and driving them out of California.

There were many battles between the United States and Mexico over the land we now call California.

Beckwourth was again hired by the U.S. Army to be a **messenger** during the war. His job was to carry messages between Santa Fe, New Mexico, and Fort Leavenworth, Kansas. The trip was about 700 miles (1,127 kilometers), and it took Beckwourth nearly three weeks to travel by horse. Beckwourth carried important messages that helped the United States win the war. California became a state on September 9, 1850. New Mexico became a state on January 6, 1912.

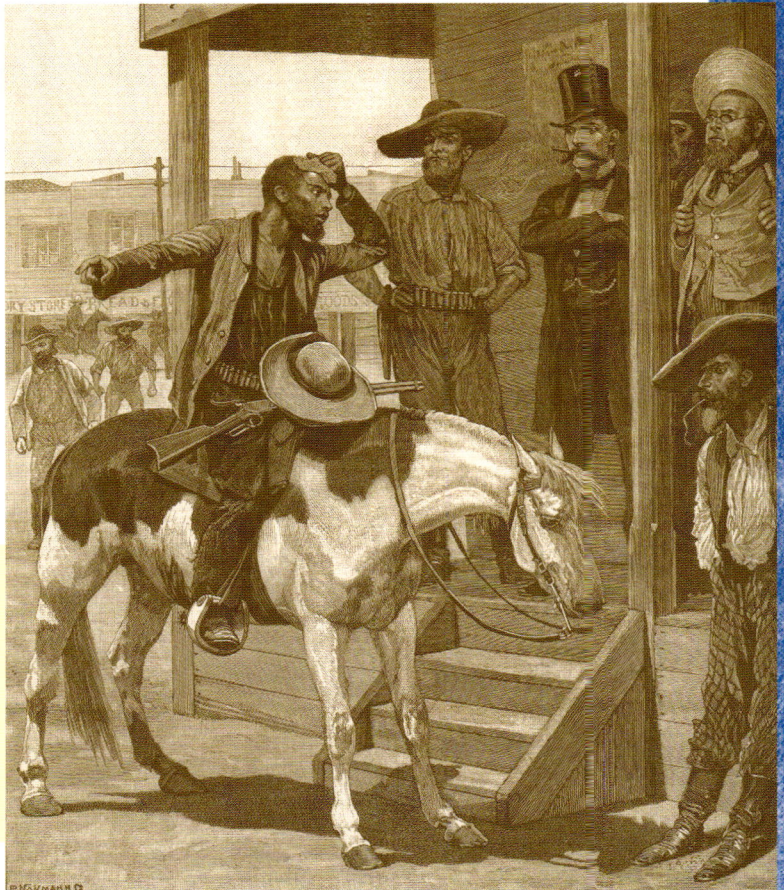

Messengers were very important for getting news to people far away.

Beckwourth Pass

Gold was discovered at Sutter's Mill in California in 1848. People soon came there from all over the world, hoping to find gold and get rich. In 1850, Beckwourth climbed a high peak in the Sierra Nevada Mountains. He discovered an easier way through the mountains to the American Valley for people making the journey west to California.

Sutter's Mill was a popular place to search for gold. Many people traveled a long distance to California. When they arrived, they were able to get supplies there.

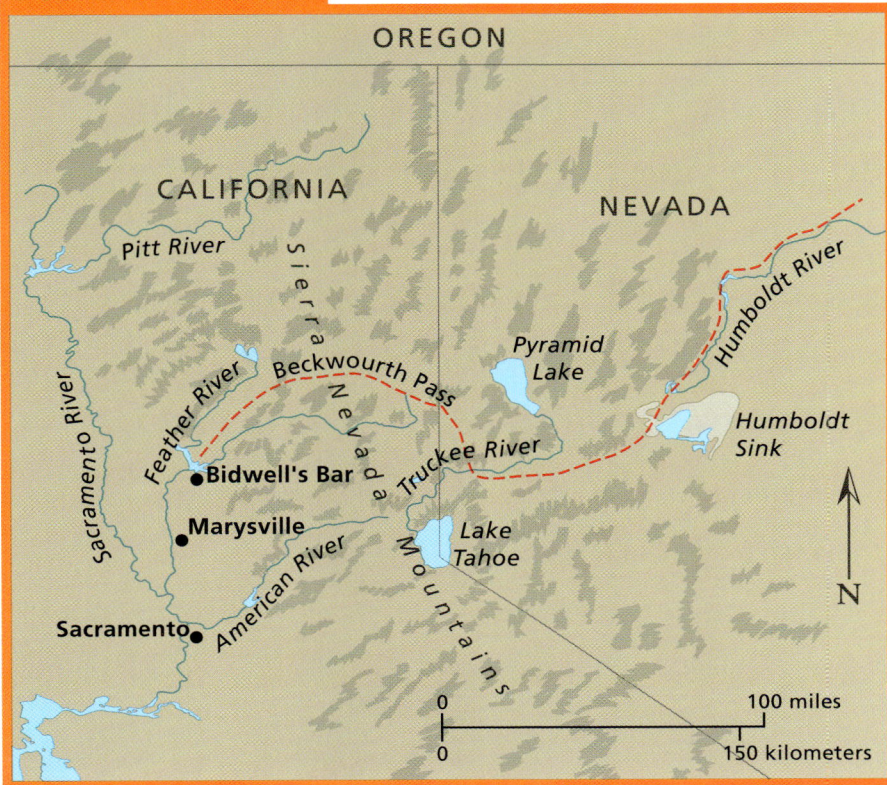

Beckwourth Pass

Today, travelers can follow portions of Beckwourth's Pass by car and on foot.

The pass through the mountains was named Beckwourth Pass. By 1855, almost 10,000 wagons a year traveled through Beckwourth Pass. Beckwourth built a trading post and ranch on the California side of the pass. He sold supplies to travelers as they arrived in California. Some families arrived in California without food or money. Beckwourth gave them food from his store so the children would not starve. People who stopped at Beckwourth's ranch always heard good stories, too.

The Book

In 1854, Beckwourth wanted the story of his life to be told in a book. He told his stories of his adventures to Thomas D. Bonner. Bonner was a justice of the peace, which was like being a judge. Bonner's book was called *The Life and Adventures of James P. Beckwourth, Mountaineer, Scout, and Pioneer, and Chief of the Crow Nation of Indians.*

THE

LIFE AND ADVENTURES

OF

JAMES P. BECKWOURTH,

MOUNTAINEER, SCOUT, AND PIONEER,

AND

CHIEF OF THE CROW NATION OF INDIANS.

With Illustrations.

WRITTEN FROM HIS OWN DICTATION,

BY T. D. BONNER.

NEW YORK:
HARPER & BROTHERS, PUBLISHERS,
FRANKLIN SQUARE.
1856.

James Beckwourths's book was published in 1856. It is still available in bookstores and libraries today.

The book made Beckwourth famous throughout the United States and in some countries of Europe. Readers loved the adventures told in the book. Some people traveled to the Beckwourth Ranch just to see the brave man from the stories.

In 1972, Delmont Oswald published this version of the book. He checked the facts of Beckwourth's stories, and found many to be true.

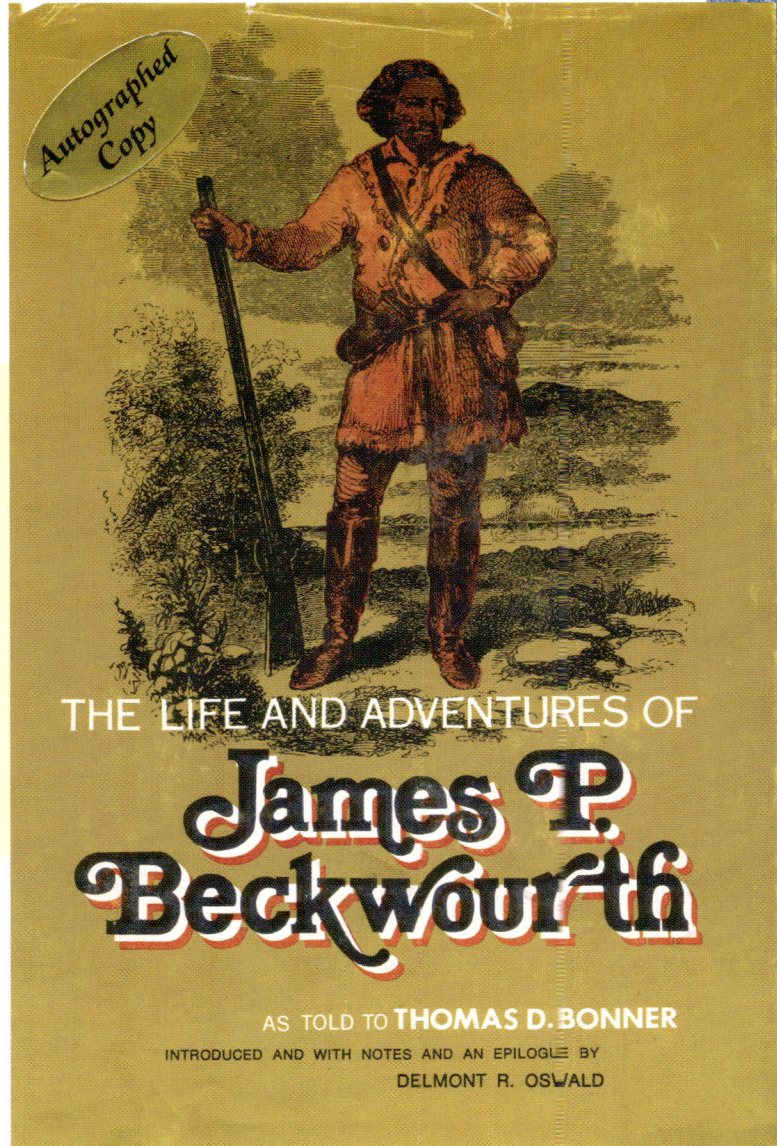

Autographed Copy

THE LIFE AND ADVENTURES OF James P. Beckwourth

AS TOLD TO **THOMAS D. BONNER**
INTRODUCED AND WITH NOTES AND AN EPILOGUE BY
DELMONT R. OSWALD

Growing Old

In 1858, Beckwourth left California. Stories say he lost the Beckwourth Ranch after betting on a race. He wandered across the West before taking over another trading post just north of present-day Denver, Colorado. The West that Beckwourth knew was changing. Railroads now crossed the United States. The trains brought more and more people who took the lands of the Native American tribes living there.

Workers celebrated after completing the Transcontinental Railroad on May 10, 1869. The railroad linked Nebraska and California.

For the Crow, war was a big part of their lives. A person who could not fight well was looked down upon. Beckwourth knew how to make the Crow stay peaceful.

Many tribes decided to fight back. They attacked the army and the new settlers. Some leaders in the army thought the Crows would soon be going to war. Colonel Henry Carrington asked Beckwourth to ride to Montana and convince the Crows to stay peaceful. Beckwourth happily took the job. It had been years since he had been in a Crow village. Unfortunately, Beckwourth was old and sick when he made his journey. He died in Montana.

Remembering Beckwourth

James Beckwourth saw some of the most important events in the early history of the United States. He told the story of those events to the people of the country. Some people who study history say Beckwourth lied when he told his stories, but others say that Beckwourth was almost always right, although he did confuse names and dates.

Beckwourth was known as a good story teller, but he was also called a "**gaudy** liar" by many.

Of the trappers making a living in the Rocky Mountains, none was as well known as James Beckwourth.

Beckwourth was born a slave, but he was able to gain his freedom. He used his freedom to have adventures that other people can only dream about. Beckwourth helped the United States to grow by showing people the way westward. James Beckwourth was a **blacksmith,** mountain man, **scout,** pioneer, war chief, and most of all, an American.

Glossary

apprentice person who is learning a trade or art by experience under a skilled worker

blacksmith person who makes things out of iron by heating and hammering it

Congress part of U.S. government that makes the laws

frontiersman person who explores unsettled areas, particularly in the United States

gaudy showy

harvest gather a crop

interpreter person who explains what someone is saying in another language

messenger person who delivers a message

punish make someone suffer for doing something wrong

raid attack

rendezvous planned meeting

Revolutionary War war from 1775 to 1783 in which the American colonists won freedom from Great Britain

rumor story that is being told but has not been proven to be true

scout person who searches for information

war party group of Native Americans that goes out together, prepared to do battle

More Books to Read

Bonner, T.D. *Life and Adventures of James P. Beckwourth*. Murrieta, Calif.: Classic Textbooks, 1999.

Kamma, Anne. *If You Were a Pioneer on the Prairie*. New York: Scholastic, 2003.

McCall, Edith. *Adventures of Taking Wagons Over the Mountains*. Royal Fireworks Publishing Company, 2001.

Morely, Jacqueline. *You Wouldn't Want to Be an American Pioneer!* New York: Scholastic, 2002.

Places to Visit

James P. Beckwourth Outdoor Education Center
2444 Washington Street, Suite B
Denver, CO 80205
Visitor Information: (303) 831-0564

Plumas County Museum
500 Jackson St.
Quincy, CA 95971
Visitor Information: (530) 283-6320

Beckwourth Frontier Days
Marysville, CA
Visitor Information: (530) 749-3901

Index